Transition and Growth in Post-Communist Countries

Transition and Growth in Post-Communist Countries

The Ten-year Experience

Edited by

Lucjan T. Orlowski

Professor of Economics, Sacred Heart University, Fairfield, CT, USA

Edward Elgar

Cheltenham, UK • Northampton, MA, USA

Published by
Edward Elgar Publishing Limited
Glensanda House
Montpellier Parade
Cheltenham
Glos GL50 1UA
UK

Edward Elgar Publishing, Inc.
136 West Street
Suite 202
Northampton
Massachusetts 01060
USA

A catalog record for this book is available from the British Library

M/C

Library of Congress Cataloging in Publication Data
Orlowski, Lucjan T.
    Transition and growth in post-communist countries : the ten-year experience / Lucjan Orlowski.
    Includes bibliographical references and index.
    1. Europe, Eastern—Economic policy—1989– 2. Europe, Eastern—Economic conditions—1989– 3. Post-communism—Europe, Eastern. 4. Public welfare—Europe, Eastern. 5. Former Soviet republics—Economic policy. 6. Former Soviet republics—Economic conditions. 7. Post-communism—Former Soviet republics. 8. Public welfare—Former Soviet republics. I. Title.

HC244 .O655 2001
338.947—dc21

00–050291

ISBN 1 84064 556 3
Printed and bound in Great Britain by MPG Books Ltd, Bodmin, Cornwall

Contents

Figures

Tables

Contributors

Nicholas Barr   Professor, Department of Economics, London School of Economics and Political Science, London, UK.

Lajos Bokros   Director, Financial Advisory Services, Europe and Central Asia Region of the World Bank. Former Finance Minister of Hungary.

Andrzej Bratkowski   Senior Researcher, CASE, Warsaw, Poland.

Marek Dąbrowski   Professor of Economics. Deputy Chairman, CASE. Former Deputy Minister of Finance, Poland.

Mikhail Dmitriev   Scholar in Residence, Carnegie Moscow Center of Carnegie Endowment for International Peace, Moscow, Russia.

Stanley Fischer   Professor of Economics. First Deputy Managing Director, International Monetary Fund, Washington, DC, USA.

Stanisława Golinowska   Professor of Economics, CASE, Warsaw, Poland.

Stanisław Gomulka   Professor, Department of Economics, London School of Economics and Political Science, London, UK.

Daniel Gros   Deputy Director, Senior Research Fellow and Economic Policy Department Head, Centre for European Policy Studies (CEPS), Brussels, Belgium.

David Lipton   Managing Director, Moore Capital Strategy Group, Washington DC, USA. Former member, Carnegie Endowment for International Peace. Former Under Secretary for International Affairs, US Treasury.

Lucjan T. Orlowski   Professor and Chairman, Department of Economics and Finance, Sacred Heart University, Fairfield, CT, USA.

Jacek Rostowski   Professor, Department of Economics, Central European University, Budapest, Hungary.

Michal Rutkowski   Head, Social Protection Group – Europe and Central Asia Region, World Bank, Washington, DC, USA.

Ratna Sahay   Advisor, Research Department, International Monetary Fund, Washington, DC, USA.

Winfried Schmähl   Professor, Center for Social Policy, Bremen University, Germany.

Marc Suhrcke   United Nations Children's Fund (UNICEF), Innocenti Research Centre, Florence, Italy and EBRD, London, UK.

Andrew M. Warner   Research Fellow at Center for International Development at Harvard University, Cambridge, MA, USA.

Stanisław Wellisz   Professor, Department of Economics, Columbia University, New York, USA.

Discussion panel members

Leszek Balcerowicz   Governor, The National Bank of Poland. Professor of Economics. Former chairman, Council of the Center for Social and Economic Research (CASE). Formerly Poland's Deputy Prime Minister and Minister of Finance.

Daniel Daianu   Professor, Academy of Economic Studies in Bucharest, Romania. Former Finance Minister of Romania. Former Chief Economist, National Bank of Romania.

Vaclav Klaus   Professor of Economics. President, Chamber of Deputies of the Czech Parliament. Former Prime Minister and Minister of Finance of the Czech Republic.

Jacques de Larosiere   International banker, advisor to Paribas. Former President, EBRD. Former Governor, Bank of France. Former Managing Director, IMF.

Gramoz Pashko   Professor of Economics at Tirana University, Albania. Chief Economic Advisor to the Prime Minister of Albania. Former Deputy Prime Minister and Minister of the Economy. Former Deputy at the Parliament.

Jeffrey D. Sachs   Gallen L. Stone Professor of International Trade and Director of the Center for International Development at Harvard University, Cambridge, MA, USA.

Abbreviations

AEA	American Economic Association
ALMPs	active labour market policies
ASEAN	Association of Southeast Asian Nations
BSLF	banking sector liquidity fund
CA	current account
CASE	Center for Social and Economic Research (Poland)
CBRF	Central Bank of the Russian Federation
CEE	Central and Eastern Europe/European
CEPR	Centre for Economic Policy Research (London)
CIS	Commonwealth of Independent States
CMEA	Council for Mutual Economic Assistance (former)
CPI	consumer price index
CZK	Czech koruna
DB	defined benefit
DC	defined contribution
EBRD	European Bank for Reconstruction and Development
ECB	European Central Bank
EMS	European Monetary System
EMU	European Monetary Union
ERM	Exchange Rate Mechanism
ESCB	European System of Central Banks
EU	European Union
FDI	foreign direct investment
FF	fully funded (pension)
FSU	former Soviet Union
FYR	former Yugoslav Republic
GDP	gross domestic product
GDR	German Democratic Republic (former)
GNP	gross national product
HUF	Hungarian forint
ICRG	International Country Risk Guide
IFIs	international financial institutions
IMF	International Monetary Fund
IPOs	initial public offerings

LI   liberalization index
NBER   National Bureau of Economic Research
NBH   National Bank of Hungary
NBP   National Bank of Poland
NCB   national central bank
NDC   notional defined contributions
NFL   net foreign liabilites
NIS   Newly Independent States
NPV   net present value
OECD   Organization for Economic Cooperation and Development
OFSU   other FSU countries
PAYG   pay-as-you-go
PLN   Polish zloty
PPP   purchasing power parity
R&D   research and development
SDR   Special Drawing Rights
SEC   Securities and Exchange Commission
SME   small and medium-sized enterprise
TEs   transition economies
TFA   technology frontier area
TFP   total factor productivity
TI   Transparency International
UK   United Kingdom
UNDP   United Nations Development Programme
USA   United States of America
USD   United States dollar

Preface

The transition from central planning to a market economy in Central and Eastern Europe has been a monumental task of unprecedented magnitude in world economic history. Establishing the foundations of a pluralistic democratic society and a competitive market-based economy has been a complex amalgam of political decentralization, radical programmes of macroeconomic stability, and long-term changes in the legal and institutional framework of business. Firms and individuals have gradually gained well-deserved independence from government bureaucracies that suppressed their creativity for many decades under communism. But the new economic freedom has emerged primarily in those countries whose governments have enacted major political reforms and have successfully established foundations of a modern democratic society. The unequivocally reformed economic systems have dramatically improved the competitiveness and creativity of businesses, labour productivity and the standard of living in these countries.

The tenth anniversary of the collapse of the Berlin Wall and the subsequent enactment of major programmes of economic liberalization, privatization and stabilization in Central and Eastern Europe provides a special opportunity for the key architects of these programmes to reflect on their achievements and to identify some unfinished tasks. Some of the top leaders of the economic transformation of former Soviet-dominated countries gathered on 15–16 October 1999 in Warsaw at the conference 'Ten Years After: Transition and Growth in Post-Communist Countries', organized by the Center for Social and Economic Research (CASE). The conference was aimed at reviewing the ten-year record of political and economic transition. This volume, with the exception of the three chapters in Part II, is a compilation of the scholarly papers and political reflections presented at that conference. The three studies have been written especially for this volume, although they comprise the key statements presented by the authors at the Warsaw conference.

Part I of the volume focuses on various factors determining economic growth in transition countries. Almost without exception, the authors agree that the countries whose authorities have manifested a strong commitment to reform, supported by decisive actions toward liberalization, privatization and macroeconomic stability, have clearly outperformed the non-reformers. The reforming countries that have recently demonstrated fast-track economic growth have improved the living standards of their societies dramatically.

Part II examines various aspects of global integration of the emerging financial markets in transition economies. By reviewing various responses to international financial crisis, the authors suggest divergent, intrinsically conflicting approaches to the integration of the monetary systems in transition countries with the European Union's common currency area.

Despite the unquestionable success of the ongoing transition, its terminal point still remains out of sight. There is still a myriad of tasks that need to be addressed and resolved in the future. They generally pertain to the existing structural deficiencies in these economies, the elimination of which will entail high social costs. For this reason, a reconstruction of social safety nets is becoming a focal point of transition. Therefore, Part III of the volume examines various aspects of social safety-net reforms, and particularly pension reforms in transition countries along with their economic and social implications.

In a somewhat unconventional vein, the book's concluding part features a discussion panel of prominent policy makers who have been instrumental in designing the course of the economic transition.

Although the methodological approach of the volume is based on policy evaluation from a historical perspective and on policy recommendations, the analysis is supported by concrete empirical evidence. I, therefore, hope that both policy makers and the general public will learn from the presented studies of the first-decade experience and will draw conclusions for a more coherent future path of transition.

I am grateful for the opportunity to work with the outstanding group of prominent contributors whom I thank for their input and collaboration. I wish to acknowledge the efforts of the organizers of the Warsaw conference, particularly Ewa Balcerowicz, Barbara Błaszczyk, Marek Dąbrowski and Jarosław Neneman.

I am immensely grateful to my wife Halina B. Orlowski for her sensible conceptual advice and extensive editorial assistance. I further thank my research assistant Georg Grassmück for his logistical and technical help. Without their dedicated support, this volume would not have been successfully completed.

Lucjan T. Orlowski
Fairfield, 25 April 2000

PART I

Uneven Reforms – Unbalanced Growth

1. The transition economies after ten years

Stanley Fischer and Ratna Sahay[1]

INTRODUCTION

Economic performance among the transition economies (TEs) of Central and Eastern Europe (CEE) and the former Soviet Union (FSU) has differed widely in the ten years since the start of the Polish economic reform programme. The countries that have done best are those who have pursued their reform agendas most consistently; they are also those who seemed from the start most committed to reform.[2] By and large, they are also the countries closest to Western Europe, and those who had spent the least time under communist rule.

Figure 1.1 presents charts of output levels in transition time for the 25 TEs studied in this chapter.[3] Output declined in all countries in the initial years of transition. However, the more successful have been growing since the mid-1990s, and several are well on their way towards joining the European Union (EU). Although they still confront many reform tasks, they have graduated from the ranks of TEs. Output in the least successful countries continued to decline virtually every year, and most of them still face many of the challenges of transition.

In this chapter we first summarize the macroeconomic performance of TEs. We then try to account for the widely differing outcomes in the 25 countries. We start by reviewing the initial conditions confronting these economies, and the reform strategy that was proposed a decade ago, as well as some of the associated controversies. We then provide an analysis of the determinants of economic growth, which is consistent with the conventional view that both macroeconomic stabilization and structural reforms are necessary for growth.

However, the contrast between the more and less successful transitions, the latter largely in the FSU, raises many questions about both the details of the transition strategy and the political factors that determine the choice of economic policies. In the concluding sections we take up some of those questions, and touch on the broader political economy issues that dominate the prospects for TEs.

MACROECONOMIC PERFORMANCE

Output Growth

A decade ago it was generally expected that output would fall at the start of the reform process, as a result of both macroeconomic stabilization and the reallocation of resources from unproductive sectors to sectors that would be profitable at world prices. As stabilization took hold, and the new sectors began to grow while the old sectors declined, aggregate output would start growing; output was then expected to grow more rapidly than in the advanced economies, and some closing of income gaps or even eventual convergence would take place.

As Figure 1.1 shows, output did fall in all 25 countries at the start of the transition process, although the extent to which output collapsed far exceeded expectations. By the time output had bottomed out, it had fallen by more than 40 per cent on average. By 1998, output had begun to grow in more than 20 of the 25 economies, though growth was glacial in some of them.

The quality of output data, especially in the early stages of transition, is an important issue. Output as well as rates of growth for TEs were likely to be understated in the official data – on account of both the emergence of the non-state sector, which in the early days of transition was typically not fully included in the statistical net, and also because of the development of the untaxed economy. Despite these concerns regarding the data, we believe that the statistical evidence sheds some light on the initial transition years. Attempts have been made in recent years to estimate the non-recorded sector. In comparing our data with the most comprehensive but still incomplete data set such as Johnson et al.'s (1997), we find that while the relative magnitudes of decline could differ across countries, the qualitative conclusions regarding broad groupings of countries, as described here, remain unchanged.[4]

It is useful to group the 25 economies into three categories: the CEE countries; the Baltics; and the other FSU countries (OFSU).[5] The Baltics and OFSU are together referred to as FSU countries. Sometimes a distinction is made between the 'early reformers' in CEE, countries that implemented comprehensive stabilization and structural reform packages early in the transition period, and those, which started late, the 'late reformers'. Late reformers in CEE are Albania, Bulgaria, FYR Macedonia and Romania, while the rest of the CEE countries are early reformers.

Figure 1.2 shows output patterns for the three categories in both calendar and transition time.[6] The average output declines in CEE at 28 per cent were much smaller than those in the Baltics (43 per cent) and the OFSU (54 per cent). The country-level data are shown in Table 1.1. However, the Baltics seemed to have suffered similar output losses as those in the late reformers of CEE.

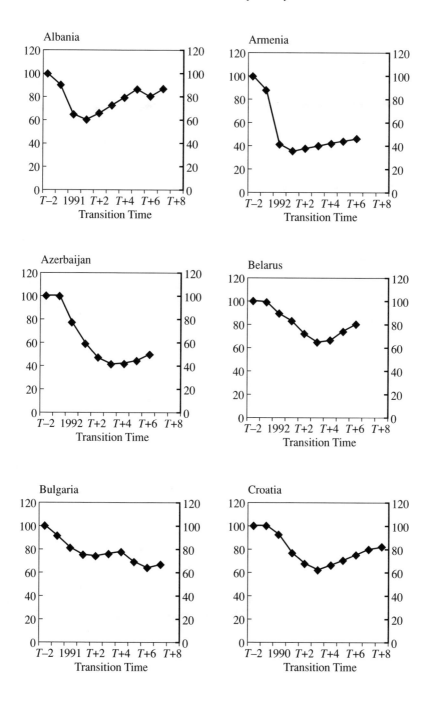

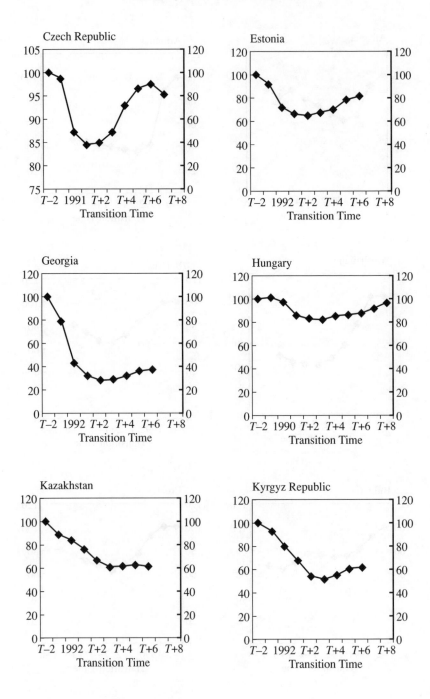

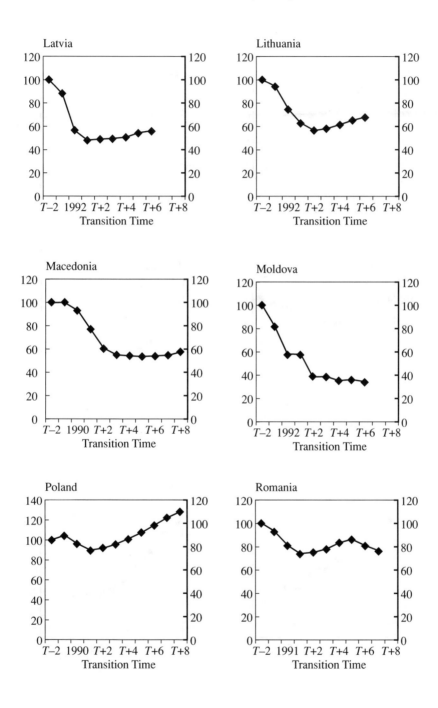

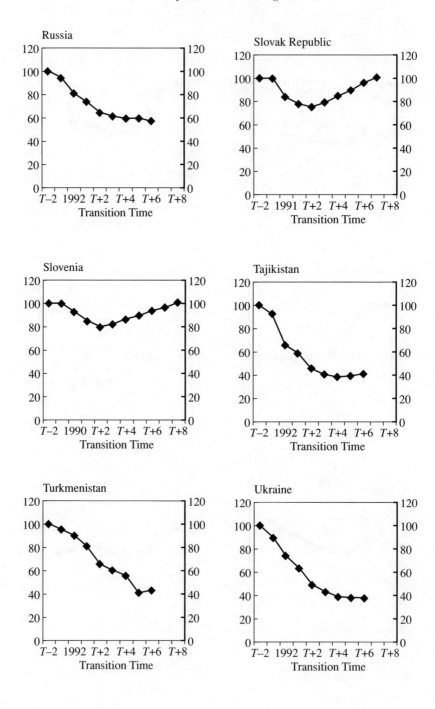

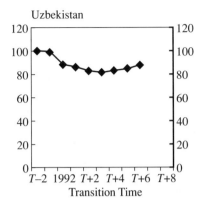

Uzbekistan

Note: Transition time is defined as the year in which the communist regime collapsed, a rough measure of the date at which the country began to move towards a market economy.

Source: IMF.

Figure 1.1   GDP index in transition time (T − 2 = 100)

Typically, output had bottomed out by 1992 in CEE, by 1994 in the Baltics, and by 1995 in OFSU.

The pick-up in growth rates since the output troughs has been impressive in many countries (Table 1.1). Cumulatively, the recoveries in Albania, Poland, the Slovak Republic, Croatia, Georgia and Armenia, in that order, have been the highest, ranging from 43 per cent to nearly 30 per cent, as of 1998. Average growth rates in FSU countries have been higher than in CEE. This result is consistent with catch-up, given that per capita incomes are lower and the fall in output had been greater in the OFSU countries, but of course not all OFSU countries have yet returned to growth or seem to be catching up.

Despite the beginnings of growth in most countries, the data show very few countries as having surpassed their pre-transition year output levels. Relative to 1989 or the pre-transition year, only Poland, the Slovak Republic and Slovenia had higher measured output levels in 1998. However, if the benchmark test date is six years after transition began (to take account of the later start in the FSU), Poland was the only country that had a higher level of output compared to its pre-transition year. On average, by either measure, by 1998 or six years after transition began, the CEE countries had recovered at least 90 per cent of their measured output relative to the pre-transition year, while the corresponding figures for the Baltics and OFSU were 70 and 60 per cent, respectively.[7]

Although measured GDP is the single most useful summary statistic of economic performance, its weaknesses need to be borne in mind. In the first instance, the data are likely to be inaccurate as discussed earlier. But even if the

Real GDP index (1989 = 100)

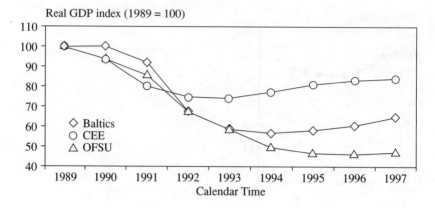

Real GDP index ($T - 3 = 100$)

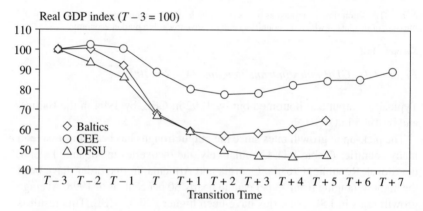

Real GDP index ($S - 4 = 100$)

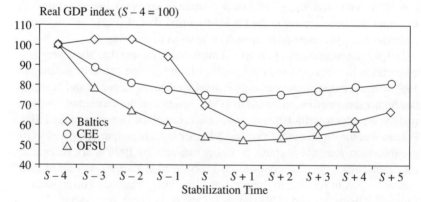

Source: IMF.

Figure 1.2   Output profile in transition economies

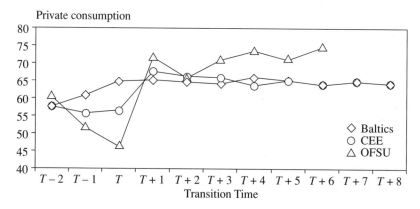

Private consumption

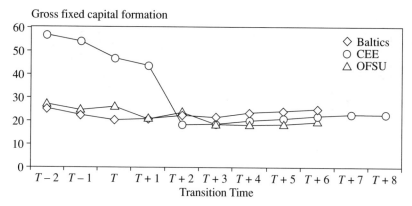

Gross fixed capital formation

Source: IMF.

Figure 1.3   *Private consumption and investment in transition economies (per cent of GDP)*

data were accurate, they would suffer from well-known problems as a welfare indicator: analytically, the calculation of real output is likely to depend heavily on the base prices when relative prices change significantly as they have in the transition process; the quality of the same consumption basket is likely to have improved after liberalization; income distribution has changed radically in many TEs; and the share of consumption in output has generally increased.

Bearing in mind the unreliability of consumption and investment data in TEs, Figure 1.3 suggests that private consumption rose sharply and fixed investment declined as shares of GDP, around the time transition began.[8] The higher consumption levels relative to GDP suggest that welfare levels declined on average less than implied by the behaviour of output.[9]

Table 1.1 Transition economies: output performance, 1989–1998

Country	Cumulative output decline to lowest level (1989 = 100)[1]	Year in which output was lowest[1]	Cumulative output growth since lowest level[2]	Simple average of output growth since lowest level	Year in which output was highest[1]	Ratio of output in 98 to output in TT − 1[1]	Ratio of output in TT+6 to output in TT − 1
Albania	39.9	1992	43.0	6.3	1989	0.96	0.88
Armenia	65.1	1993	29.7	5.4	1989	0.53	0.53
Azerbaijan	63.1	1995	17.8	5.4	1989	0.50	0.50
Belarus	36.9	1995	24.0	7.0	1989	0.81	0.81
Bulgaria	36.8	1997	4.0	4.0	1989	0.72	0.70
Croatia	37.7	1993	30.8	3.1	1989	0.82	0.75
Czech Republic	15.4	1992	12.8	2.0	1989	0.97	0.99
Estonia	36.4	1994	25.7	4.3	1989	0.89	0.89
Georgia	74.6	1994	30.6	6.7	1989	0.48	0.48
Hungary	18.1	1993	16.3	3.0	1989	0.95	0.87
Kazakhstan	40.0	1998	0.0	na	1989	0.69	0.69
Kyrgyz Republic	50.4	1995	20.1	4.6	1989	0.66	0.66
Latvia	52.8	1993	17.0	3.0	1989	0.64	0.64
Lithuania	40.8	1994	19.8	4.5	1990	0.71	0.71
Macedonia, FYR	46.6	1995	7.4	2.5	1989	0.57	0.54
Moldova	66.3	1998	0.0	na	1989	0.42	0.42
Poland	13.6	1991	42.6	5.2	1998	1.23	1.10
Romania	26.7	1992	3.4	0.7	1989	0.82	0.87

Russia	45.1	1998	0.0	na	1989	0.61	0.61
Slovak Republic	24.7	1993	32.9	5.7	1998	1.00	0.96
Slovenia	20.4	1992	25.4	3.8	1989	1.00	0.93
Tajikistan	74.0	1996	7.1	3.7	1989	0.45	0.45
Turkmenistan	59.5	1997	4.5	4.5	1989	0.45	0.45
Ukraine	63.8	1997	0.8	0.8	1989	0.42	0.42
Uzbekistan	14.4	1995	7.0	2.3	1990	0.88	0.88
Memorandum items[3]						
All transition	41.8	1993	17.0	4.0	1989	0.7	0.7
All CEE	28.0	1992	21.9	3.6	1989	0.9	0.9
CEE: early reformers	21.6	1993	26.8	3.8	1989	0.9	1.0
CEE: late reformers	37.5	1992	14.5	3.4	1989	0.7	0.8
Baltics	43.3	1994	20.8	3.9	1989	0.7	0.7
Other FSU	54.4	1995	11.8	4.5	1989	0.6	0.6

Notes:

1. Output decline from 1989 to the year in which output was the lowest. For countries in which output has not begun to grow, 1998 is taken as the year of minimum output. Output is real GDP measured on an annual average basis.

2. Lowest level refers to the lowest output level reached during 1989–98.

3. CEE: early reformers refer to Croatia, the Czech Republic, Hungary, Poland, the Slovak Republic and Slovenia. CEE: late reformers refer to Albania, Bulgaria, Macedonia, FYR and Romania. Baltics refer to Estonia, Latvia and Lithuania. Other former Soviet Union refer to Armenia, Azerbaijan, Belarus, Georgia, Kazakhstan, the Kyrgyz Republic, Moldova, Russia,Tajikistan, Turkmenistan, Ukraine and Uzbekistan. Simple average for values and mode for years.

Sources: International Monetary Fund, International Financial Statistics, World Economic Outlook; IMF Staff estimates.

Inflation and Stabilization

Most countries entered the transition process with a monetary overhang and the need for price liberalization. Inflation was either already present or a major threat. Starting with Poland in 1990, stabilization packages had been put in place by 1995 in all of the countries except Turkmenistan. Depending on the extent of the monetary overhang and the delay in starting a stabilization programme, the 12-month pre-stabilization inflation rates varied widely: from the hyperinflationary 57,000 per cent per annum in Georgia to 26 per cent in Hungary (Table 1.2).

By 1998, inflation rates had been brought down to single digits in most countries (see last column of Table 1.2), with deflation occurring in at least three countries. On average, the CEE countries have lower inflation rates than those in the FSU. This average, however, distorts the clear successes of most FSU countries because of the high rates of inflation in Russia and Belarus in 1998.[10] The early reformers in CEE (listed in Table 1.2) have been more successful than the late reformers. The countries with a currency board – Bulgaria, Estonia and Lithuania – have had the most impressive inflation performance.

Inflation stabilization is one of the major successes of the transition process. At the time that prices were freed, reigning in inflation had been a leading concern. Price jumps could easily have led to an inflationary spiral, triggered ever-rising wage demands, and resulted in the dollarization of the economies.[11] Keeping these concerns in mind, several checks were introduced in the stabilization programmes to contain inflation: tight monetary and credit policies, wage control policies, monetary reforms and non-inflationary sources of financing the budget deficits.[12] Figure 1.4 shows how inflation was brought under control very soon after stabilization programmes were implemented. Unlike in Latin America, wage indexation did not set in and highly dollarized countries became de-dollarized as inflation fell (a good example is Poland).[13]

The choice of exchange rate regime was an important part of the initial stabilization strategy. Countries in CEE and the Baltics chose a mix of fixed (Croatia, the Czech Republic, Estonia, Hungary, Poland and Slovakia) and flexible (Albania, Bulgaria, FYR Macedonia, Latvia, Lithuania, Romania and Slovenia) regime while all OFSU countries are on record as having chosen a flexible regime at the start of their programmes (Table 1.2). There were several reasons for adopting a flexible regime in OFSU: the concern that real shocks would occur during the transition period, the view that the peg could not be maintained for long as the starting credibility of OFSU countries was low, the lack of foreign exchange reserves to back a peg, and simply the inability to assess the rate at which the local currency should be pegged.[14]

Although many FSU countries announced their regimes as flexible, the exchange rate was generally de facto pegged to the dollar or the Deutsche mark soon after starting the stabilization programmes (see note 4 in Table 1.2). Several countries undertook monetary reforms and introduced new currencies. Lithuania in April 1994 and Bulgaria in July 1997 instituted currency boards. Latvia pegged to the Special Drawing Rights (SDR) in February 1994. Russia and Ukraine announced narrow exchange rate corridors in 1995. With most exchange rates either explicitly or implicitly fixed, inflation rates began to decline rapidly, steadily reaching relatively low levels by 1998.[15]

Today, all but four countries have formally adopted a flexible regime. There are several reasons why many countries moved from pegs to more flexible regimes. Some allowed more flexibility when the peg came under pressure, sometimes to appreciate. Poland took a pre-emptive decision to exit gradually from the dollar peg by adopting a basket peg in May 1991, followed by a crawling peg in October 1991, and finally introducing a flexible regime (very wide band) in May 1995. Even from an international perspective, the Polish case is viewed today as one of the few successful exits from a peg. The koruna was floated following the Czech exchange market crisis in 1995. Following the Czech crisis, the Slovak Republic also exited successfully from a peg. De facto pegging by several countries in the FSU that have flexible regimes today could also be considered a success since it helped bring inflation down rapidly but did not require a formal exit from the peg when more flexibility was needed. The dangers of not exiting into a more flexible arrangement in time in the context of unsustainable fiscal policies and high capital mobility are exemplified by the Russian case.

At the time of transition, fiscal balances had also deteriorated sharply.[16] As Figure 1.4 shows, in OFSU the average fiscal deficit worsened to more than 15 per cent of GDP in 1992, in CEE it worsened to 4–5 per cent, while in the Baltics the fiscal balance went from a surplus of more than 5 per cent to near zero. As stabilization programmes were implemented, the fiscal balance improved sharply in the OFSU, worsened moderately in CEE, and slightly in the Baltics. However, throughout the post-1992 period, the average deficits for both the Baltics and CEE remained lower by 2–4 percentage points than in the OFSU countries. By 1997, the Baltics had registered surpluses once again, while the average deficits for CEE and OFSU were about 4 and 5 per cent, respectively.

For TEs, fiscal deficits in the initial years were almost inevitable. While it was clear that hard budget constraints would need to be imposed on state enterprises (Kornai, 1986), the scope for raising revenues in the short run was limited. Traditional tax systems and the institutional set-up for collecting revenues had collapsed. Consequently, revenues declined sharply.[17] (Figure 1.5.) On the other hand, demands on expenditures were high, as investments in

Table 1.2   Transition economies: stabilization programmes and inflation performance, 1989–1998

Country	Stabilization programme date	Pre-programme inflation[1]	Exchange regime adopted[2]	Maximum annual inflation	Year in which inflation was highest	Year in which inflation fell below 50%	Exchange regime today[2]	Inflation in 1998
Albania	August 1992	293	Flexible	237	1992	1993	Flexible	8.7
Armenia	December 1994	1,885	Flexible/Fixed[4]	10,896	1993	1995	Flexible	–1.2
Azerbaijan	January 1995	1,651	Flexible/Fixed[4]	1,787	1994	1996	Flexible	–7.6
Belarus	November 1994[3]	2,180	Flexible/Fixed[4]	1,997	1993	1996	Flexible	181.7
Bulgaria	February 1991[3]	245	Flexible	579	1997	1998	Fixed[5]	1.0
Croatia	October 1993	1,903	Fixed	2,585	1989	1994	Flexible	5.3
Czech Republic	January 1991	46	Fixed	52	1991	1992	Flexible	6.8
Estonia	June 1992	1,086	Fixed[5]	947	1992	1993	Fixed[5]	4.5
Georgia	September 1994	56,476	Flexible/Fixed[4]	7,486	1993	1996	Flexible	10.6
Hungary	March 1990	26	Fixed	35	1990	na	Flexible	10.6
Kazakhstan	January 1994	2,315	Flexible/Fixed[4]	2,961	1992	1996	Flexible	1.9
Kyrgyz Republic	May 1993	934	Flexible/Fixed[4]	958	1992	1993	Flexible	18.3
Latvia	June 1992	818	Flexible/Fixed[6]	1,162	1992	1993	Fixed	2.8
Lithuania	June 1992	709	Flexible/Fixed[5]	1,162	1992	1994	Fixed[5]	2.4
Macedonia, FYR	January 1994	248	Fixed	1,780	1992	1995	Flexible	–2.4
Moldova	September 1993	1,090	Flexible	2,198	1992	1995	Flexible	18.2
Poland	January 1990	1,096	Fixed	640	1989	1992	Flexible	8.5
Romania	October 1993[3]	314	Flexible	295	1993	1995	Flexible	40.6
Russia	April 1995[3]	218	Flexible/Fixed[6]	2,510	1992	1996	Flexible	84.4
Slovak Republic	January 1991	46	Fixed	58	1991	1990	Flexible	5.6
Slovenia	February 1992	288	Flexible	247	1991	1993	Flexible	7.5
Tajikistan	February 1995[3]	73	Flexible	7,344	1993	1994	Flexible	2.7

Turkmenistan	Not started	20	Not applicable	9,743	1993	1997	Flexible	19.8
Ukraine	November 1994	645	Flexible/Fixed[5]	10155	1993	1990	Flexible	20.0
Uzbekistan	November 1994	1,555	Flexible	1,281	1994	1996	Flexible	26.1
Memorandum items[7]								
All transition		820		2,764	1992	1996		19.1
All CEE		450		651	1991	1993		9.2
CEE: early reformers		567		603	1991	1992		7.4
CEE: late reformers		275		723	1992	1995		12.0
Baltics		871		1,091	1992	1993		3.2
Other FSU		1,142		4,943	1993	1996		31.2

Notes:

1. Pre-programme inflation is inflation in the twelve months previous to the month of the stabilization programme. For Turkmenistan, the figure is for the latest year available (1998). All other inflation is calculated from December to December.
2. Fixed regimes are those that have a currency board, pegged (explicitly or implicitly) at a fixed rate or have a narrow crawling band. Flexible regimes include those that are free or managed floating.
3. The date of the first stabilization attempt.
4. Since 1995, these countries adopted a de facto peg to the US dollar for one to two years.
5. Currency board. Lithuania adopted a currency board in April 1994 and Bulgaria adopted one in July 1997.
6. The Latvian currency was pegged to the SDR in February 1994; Russia announced an exchange rate corridor in July 1995. Both countries had flexible exchange rate regimes prior to these dates.
7. CEE: early reformers refer to Croatia, the Czech Republic, Hungary, Poland, the Slovak Republic and Slovenia. CEE: late reformers refer to Albania, Bulgaria, Macedonia, FYR and Romania. Baltics refer to Estonia, Latvia and Lithuania. Other former Soviet Union refer to Armenia, Azerbaijan, Belarus, Georgia, Kazakhstan, the Kyrgyz Republic, Moldova, Russia, Tajikistan, Turkmenistan, Ukraine and Uzbekistan. Simple average for values and mode for years.

Source: International Monetary Fund, International Financial Statistics, World Economic Outlook; IMF Staff estimates.

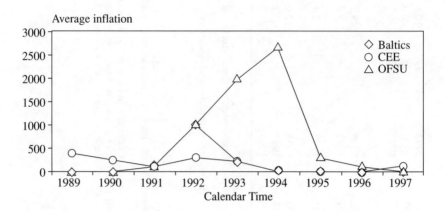

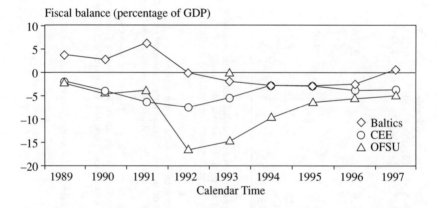

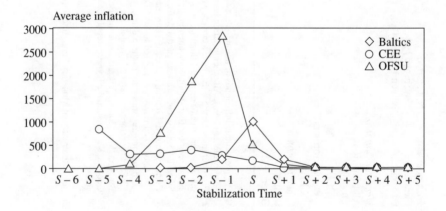

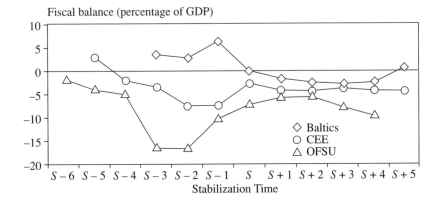

Fiscal balance (percentage of GDP)

Source: IMF.

Figure 1.4   Inflation and fiscal profile in transition economies

reforms undertaken by the state could not be postponed. Also, despite the financing constraints, spending on human capital (education and health) were not cut, at least as a share of GDP (Figure 1.5). Since public debt was generally low and GDP growth potential was high, a relatively long period of sustained fiscal deficits was consistent with successful stabilization.

However, a closer look at country-level data shows that the stabilization process was not sustained in countries that had persistent fiscal deficits *and* slow structural reforms; this is most evident in the case of Russia but it applies also to OFSU countries such as Belarus, Tajikistan and Uzbekistan.[18] Further, while the sharp fiscal contraction during the initial years of stabilization in OFSU looks impressive at the macroeconomic level, the revenue declines were very sharp, and underlying cuts were often not well targeted or planned in several countries.[19] In most OFSU countries, the cuts seemed to have been involuntary as they occurred because of tight financing constraints.[20] The sudden decline in expenditures in OFSU from an average of 45 per cent of GDP in 1992 to 29 per cent in 1995 came at a cost. The cuts were often last minute or arbitrarily shifted off budget or simply led to the non-payment of bills. The problem of budgetary arrears, significant in some countries, has posed major threats to stability and budget discipline in both the public and private sectors.

In sum, the performance of TEs in bringing inflation down from very high levels has been impressive virtually across the board. On the fiscal front, even though the balances for the transition countries have generally improved since transition began, there is no clear relationship between the fiscal balance and GDP growth.

Total revenue/GDP (per cent)

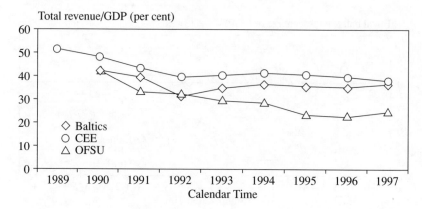

Education expenditures/GDP (per cent)

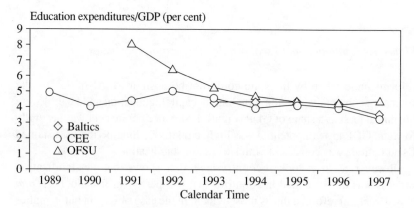

Health expenditures/GDP (per cent)

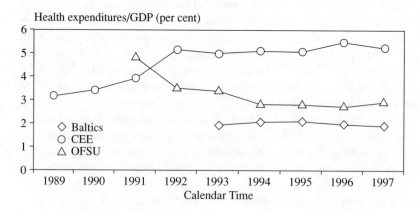

Source: IMF.

Figure 1.5   Fiscal revenue and selected expenditure in transition economies

ACCOUNTING FOR OUTPUT PERFORMANCE

Initial Conditions

Despite the similarities in their economic systems and typically very high rates of human capital development, the economic characteristics of the 25 countries varied widely at the start of the transition process (Table 1.3). The OFSU countries were less familiar with market-based institutions than the Baltics and the CEE countries, having had 20–30 years more of communist rule. Natural resources were more abundant in some OFSU, especially Azerbaijan, Kazakhstan, Russia and Turkmenistan, than in CEE and the Baltics. Per capita incomes varied quite widely: on average, the CEE countries were better off than those in the FSU, and among the latter the Baltics had higher per capita incomes. In a similar vein, the countries that had lower per capita incomes were also more agrarian. Dependence on intra-regional trade was highest in the Baltics, followed by OFSU and CEE, respectively. Looking forward, the Baltics and CEE were geographically better placed than the OFSU to reorientate their trade towards the industrialized countries.

In general, macroeconomic imbalances were worse in the FSU countries than in the CEE countries. Czechoslovakia started with the best macroeconomic conditions, with Hungary also in a relatively good position. Bulgaria, Croatia, Hungary and Poland had inherited large external debts, while others had accumulated virtually no debt. Following the break-up of the Soviet Union, Russia assumed all the Soviet era foreign debt (which was still relatively modest), thereby freeing other FSU countries from past external obligations.

It is interesting to explore the extent to which initial conditions alone account for subsequent performance in the context of simple cross-section regression. We considered seven variables that could represent initial conditions: the share of agriculture in GDP, natural resource endowment index, years under communism, secondary school enrolment ratio, trade dependency, an index of overindustrialization, and distance of the capital from Düsseldorf.[21] Of the seven variables considered, only two – the number of years under communism, and the rate of secondary school enrolment, which serves as an index of economic development at the time of transition – can explain much of the cumulative growth performance among TEs. We find that,

$$CG_{T+6} = -57.2 + 1.1\ SSE - 1.1\ YUC \qquad (1.1)$$
$$\phantom{CG_{T+6} = }(-2.11)\ \ (2.96)\ \ \ \ \ (-4.51)$$

Adjusted R-squared = 0.460, Number of observations = 25, where $T + 6$ is the 6th transition year for each country, CG is cumulative growth of GDP from T to $T + 6$, SSE is the secondary school enrolment ratio (Table 1.3), and the *t*-

Table 1.3 Countries in transition: initial conditions, 1989–1991

Country	PPP adjusted GDP per capita[1] (1989)	Share of CMEA trade in 1990 GDP[2]	Share of agriculture[3]	Natural resource endowment[4]	Distance from Düsseldorf (km)	Years under communism	Foreign debt in pre-transition year (% of GDP)	Secondary school enrolment in pre-transition year (share of school-age population)
Albania	629	102	26	0	1494	45	36.9	0.78
Armenia	2,453	21	11	0	3143	74	0.0	na
Azerbaijan	2466	33	22	2	3270	75	0.0	0.90
Belarus	6,667	45	22	0	1435	75	0.1	0.92
Bulgaria	5,740	15	11	0	1574	43	50.6	0.75
Croatia	6,919	6	10	0	913	44	74.7	0.85
Czech Republic	8,207	10	7	0	559	43	12.2	0.91
Estonia	6,475	27	20	0	1449	51	0.0	1.00
Georgia	2,203	19	22	1	3069	70	0.0	0.89
Hungary	6,081	10	14	0	1002	41	64.0	0.75
Kazakhstan	4,133	18	29	2	5180	75	0.0	0.96
Kyrgyz Republic	2,770	21	33	0	1293	75	0.0	0.99
Latvia	5,204	31	19	0	1293	51	0.0	0.89
Lithuania	3,603	34	27	0	1299	51	0.2	0.88
Macedonia	3,720	6	12	0	1522	44	0.0	0.57
Moldova	3,562	25	32	0	1673	52	0.0	0.77
Poland	5,687	17	13	1	995	42	63.4	0.82
Romania	3,535	3	14	1	1637	43	2.9	0.92
Russia	5,627	18	15	2	2088	74	12.1	0.91
Slovak Republic	6,969	10	7	0	824	43	6.8	0.96
Slovenia	11,525	5	5	0	815	44	0.0	0.90
Tajikistan	1,778	22	27	0	4938	75	8.6	1.01

Turkmenistan	3,308	34	29	2	4254	75	0.0	na
Ukraine	4,658	25	21	1	1664	75	0.0	0.91
Uzbekistan	2,577	24	31	1	4788	75	0.0	0.98
Memorandum items[5]								
All transition	4,660	23	19	1	2087	58	13.3	0.88
All CEE	5,901	18	12	0	1134	43	31.1	0.82
CEE:								
early reformers	7,565	9	9	0	851	43	36.8	0.87
CEE:								
late reformers	3,406	32	16	0	1557	44	22.6	0.76
Baltics	5,094	31	22	0	1347	51	0.1	0.93
Other FSU	3,517	25	25	1	3066	73	1.7	0.92

Notes:
1. Calculated by dividing PPP adjusted GDP by total population.
2. Share of intra-FSU trade in 1990.
3. Share of agriculture in 1989 according to DDGT.
4. Natural resource endowment according to DDGT (1997); 0 = poor, 1 = moderate, 2 = rich.
5. CEE: early reformers refer to Croatia, the Czech Republic, Hungary, Poland, the Slovak Republic and Slovenia. CEE: late reformers refer to Albania, Bulgaria, Macedonia, FYR and Romania. Baltics refer to Estonia, Latvia and Lithuania. Other former Soviet Union refer to Armenia, Azerbaijan, Belarus, Georgia, Kazakhstan, the Kyrgyz Republic, Moldova, Russia, Tajikistan, Turkmenistan, Ukraine and Uzbekistan. Simple average for values.

Sources: World Development Indicator; World Economic Outlook; de Melo et al. (DDGT) (1997); and Krajnyák and Zettelmeyer (1997).

statistics are reported in parentheses. Thus, *YUC*, years under communism, which indicate how far removed the countries were from a market economy, and the school enrolment ratio explain nearly 50 per cent of the growth performance.[22]

Transition Strategies

Within a short time, a consensus – based in part on Poland's approach (Lipton and Sachs, 1990a) – began to emerge among mainstream economists on the main lines of the recommended transition strategy. Figure 1.6, published in 1991, summarizes that consensus. Looking back, we are struck particularly by the fact that the list included elements that are now thought to have been overlooked at the initial stages, for instance, legal reforms. The length of time that was then envisaged for both institutional reform and the restructuring of large-scale enterprises is also noteworthy. Finally, note also that the schedule in Figure 1.6 envisages more gradual trade reform than actually occurred.

Several points of controversy emerged within the overall strategy, particularly over so-called 'shock therapy', and oversequencing. Rapid policy action was possible in some areas of reform – price and trade liberalization, and inflation stabilization, and perhaps small-scale privatization – but in others it was clear that reform would take a long time. The controversies over shock treatment related mainly to macroeconomic stabilization and the pace at which privatization could be attempted, and, to a lesser extent, over the pace of trade liberalization; for some reason there was less controversy over the pace of price liberalization. On sequencing, the argument was that some reforms were preconditions for others – for instance, that privatization would fail unless the right legal framework or financial system or both were in place, or that price decontrol should not take place until macroeconomic stabilization could be assured.

The shock therapy and sequencing debates were therefore closely related. There is little question that some sequencing of reforms, along the lines shown in Figure 1.6, would have been better in an ideal world in which it was known *ex ante* that the reforms were certain to be implemented, than an attempt to move on all fronts simultaneously. That is not to say, however, that the economics of the optimal pace of reform is well established, for example, on price and trade liberalization, or on the right sequencing of privatization and the development of the financial system.

Those who advocated moving rapidly where possible based their arguments not only on the economics – that the cumulative output loss would be smaller if actions were taken quickly – but also especially on political economy grounds. Here Balcerowicz's notion of 'extraordinary politics' carried particular weight: the argument was that following the collapse of the old system, there was a window in which the consensus for reform was stronger than it would ever be again, and that was the time to move. Political economy arguments were also

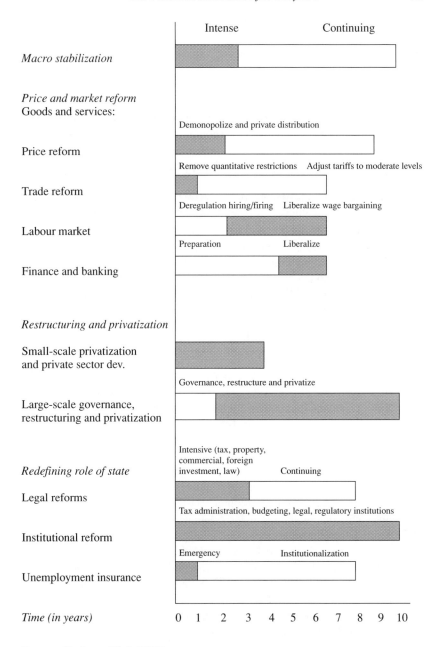

Source: Fischer and Gelb (1991)

Figure 1.6   Phasing of reform

prominent in decisions on Russian reform, both the initial price decontrol and privatization (see Boycko et al., 1993). Veterans of attempted stabilization and reforms in developing countries tended to take a robust view of the sequencing debate – that the best should not be allowed to become the enemy of the good, and that no reform that looked politically feasible should be slowed merely on sequencing grounds.

The liveliest debates on privatization focused mainly on the speed with which it should occur and the form it should take (for example, mass privatization versus direct sales). Within each country, there was generally a discussion of whether foreigners should be allowed to buy shares. The big bang arguments that were made then can be found in Lipton and Sachs (1990b), Balcerowicz (1994) and Blanchard et al. (1992). The main arguments centred on the need to separate the firms quickly from the state, to stop asset stripping, and to avoid newly formed vested interest groups from blocking privatization later on. Those favouring a more gradual approach were Newbery (1991), who was concerned about inefficiencies arising from monopolies, Dewatripont and Roland (1995), who believed that rapid privatization might be politically too costly, and Aghion and Blanchard (1994), who were worried about a rapid increase in unemployment.

Aid and Capital Flows

It was taken for granted by most proponents of reform that external financial assistance would be needed at the early stages to encourage reform and help sustain the reformers. External technical assistance would also be necessary in light of the lack of experience in the running of a market economy and its institutions of control. Despite much talk of a Marshall Plan, financial assistance on a massive scale simply did not materialize. The tasks of external financial and technical assistance were assigned largely to the international financial institutions (IFIs), whose number was augmented by the creation of the European Bank for Reconstruction and Development (EBRD). Advice from well-known academics and bilateral technical and financial assistance, including from the EU, played a prominent part as well.

A recent paper by Garibaldi et al. (1999) analyses the volume and composition of capital flows in the 25 TEs and attempts to account for the nature of inflows in different countries. They find that on average capital inflows (on a per capita net basis) to the transition region in the 1990s were at similar levels to those in Latin America and more advanced Asian economies, and much higher than in other developing countries.

However, aggregate numbers for the region conceal the fact that the distribution of inflows across countries has been highly uneven. The CEE and the Baltic countries have received far more capital inflows per capita than the OFSU countries did (Figure 1.7a). Annual data on capital inflows (Figure 1.7b) and foreign direct investment (FDI) for the four sub-groups (Russia was considered separately) clearly reveals the success of CEE and the Baltics, particularly the latter, in systematically attracting inflows over time.[23] While no data are available for Russia prior to 1994, its situation stands out (Figure 1.7b): Russia is the only country that on a net basis exported capital throughout the transition period.

The composition of inflows, on the other hand, shows some similarities across countries (Figure 1.8). Long-term inflows have been significantly higher than short-term inflows. In addition, there was a large recourse to exceptional financing (defined as debt forgiveness, restructuring, official aid) at the beginning of the transition period and a subsequent reorientation of capital flows towards FDI and other private flows. This validates the notion that provided reforms were implemented, official assistance could speedily be replaced by private sector inflows.

Taking stock, large external assistance that was expected to finance the reform process did not materialize. Instead, technical assistance combined with limited new official aid was given. Over time, private flows began to trickle in but became significant only in a limited set of countries in CEE and the Baltics, those that seemed to have the best records in the speed with which reforms were implemented.

Implementation of Reforms

Many authors (Åslund et al., 1996; Sachs, 1996a; Stiglitz, 1999; Linn, 1999; Wyplosz, 1999; EBRD Transition Report, 1999) have recently sought to summarize the extent of policy change since the start of the transition process. In presenting inflation outcomes and fiscal data in Figure 1.4, we have summarized progress in macroeconomic stabilization. To measure the extent of structural reforms, we rely on information provided by the EBRD and computed as indices by de Melo et al. (1996). These indices are presented in Table 1.4 and graphed in Figure 1.9.[24] Three indices are monitored over time: the LIP which measures the extent of privatization and financial sector reforms, the LIE which measures the extent of the market-orientated reforms of the external sector, and the LII which captures the degree of internal liberalization of prices and market, including the extent to which competition exists in the economy. LI, the overall liberalization index, is computed as a weighted average of the three: LIP is given the highest weight (40 per cent), while the other two are weighted equally. The highest value that any of these LI measures can take is unity; a value of one indicates the levels in matured market economies. We also present the CLI index (for each year it is the sum of LIs to that point, starting in 1989), which is a variable reflecting both the speed and the level of reforms to date.

Cumulative capital flows (net): 1992–97[1] (USD per capita)

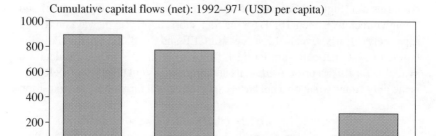

Annual capital flows (net) (USD per capita) CEE: 1991–97

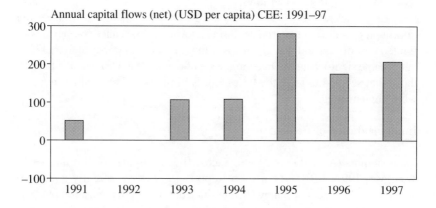

Annual capital flows (net) (USD per capita) BAL: 1992–97

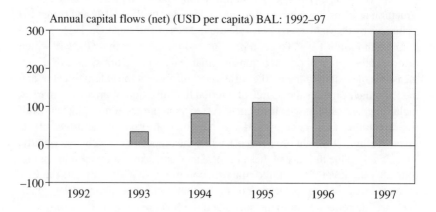

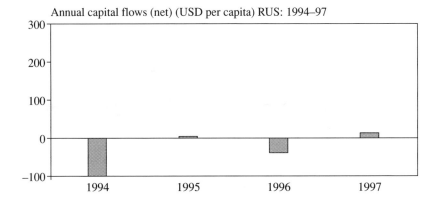

Annual capital flows (net) (USD per capita) RUS: 1994–97

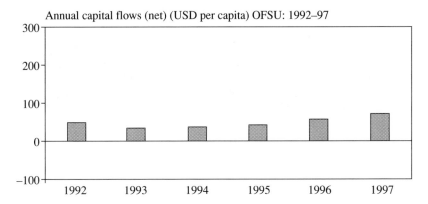

Annual capital flows (net) (USD per capita) OFSU: 1992–97

Notes:
For Russia, the period covered is 1994–97.
CEE denotes Central and Eastern European countries, BAL denotes the Baltic countries, RUS denotes Russia, and OFSU denotes the remaining countries of the former Soviet Union.

Source: Garibaldi et al. (1999).

Figure 1.7   Capital flows in transition economies

The indices presented in Table 1.4 and Figure 1.9 confirm that, almost by definition, the early reformers of CEE score highest in terms of the extent and speed of reforms, CLI; the early reformers of CEE are followed by the Baltics, the later reformers of CEE, and then the OFSU. Comparing two sub-periods, 1989–94 and 1995–97, for the LI index, it is noteworthy that the Baltics caught up with the early reformers in CEE by the second sub-period, despite the late start. Comparing the performance across the LIP, LIE and LII indexes, fewer

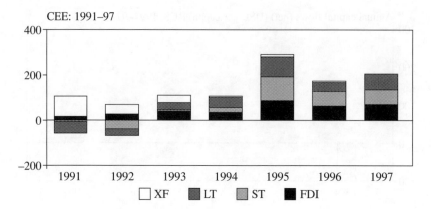

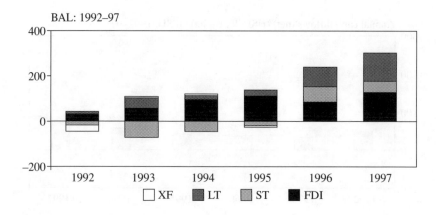

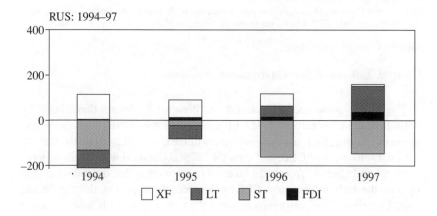

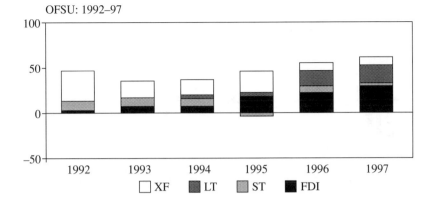

OFSU: 1992–97

Legend: ☐ XF ▨ LT ▨ ST ■ FDI

Note: CEE denotes Central and Eastern European countries, BAL denotes the Baltic countries, RUS denotes Russia, and OFSU denotes the remaining countries of the former Soviet Union. Also, XF is exceptional financing, LT is long-term flows, ST is short-term flows, and FDI is foreign direct investment.

Source: Garibaldi et al. (1999).

Figure 1.8   Composition of capital flows (USD per capita)

LIP reforms seemed to have occurred. However, in absolute terms, both LIE and LII had reached 80 per cent of the levels of matured market economies by the second sub-period. In addition, it is striking to see that LIE in both the early reformers of CEE as well as the Baltics had reached industrial country levels by 1995–97.

The averages over sub-periods conceals the extent of progress in the initial years (Figure 1.9). Looking at annual data, we find that as early as in 1992–93, all CEE countries, including the late reformers had liberalized the internal and external sectors (measured by LII and LIE) by 90 per cent. While the Baltics had also reached these levels by 1993, they had done so even faster, given that liberalization had begun only in 1991–92. The OFSU had reached only 60 per cent by 1993. As can be expected, given the time-consuming nature of the process, the progress in LIP has been slower for all sub-groups, with OFSU being the slowest.

Despite the relative lagging of the privatization sub-index, the speed with which the private sector has grown since the start of transition is also impressive. Comparing the private sector's share of GDP across the various sub-groups, the Baltics lead with 62 per cent in private hands during 1995–97 (Table 1.4). For the same period, the Baltics are followed by the early reformers of CEE (59 per cent), the late reformers of CEE (49 per cent), and the OFSU (40 per cent), respectively.

Table 1.4 Structural indicators in transition economies

	Year	Cumulative lib index (CLI)	Lib index (LI=LIP+LIE+LII)	Private sector conditions index (LIP)	External lib index (LIE)	Internal lib index (LII)	Private sector share of GDP (PSDCSD)	Unemployment rate
Albania	1989–94	0.8	0.4	0.2	0.5	0.5	26.0	15.5
	1995–97	3.8	0.8	0.5	0.9	0.9	67.5	13.5
Armenia	1989–94	0.6	0.2	0.2	0.2	0.3	30.1	4.9
	1995–97	2.7	0.7	0.5	0.9	0.7	47.5	8.9
Azerbaijan	1989–94	0.4	0.2	0.1	0.1	0.3	14.0	10.0
	1995–97	2.0	0.5	0.3	0.5	0.7	25.0	12.2
Belarus	1989–94	0.4	0.2	0.2	0.2	0.2	11.1	1.0
	1995–97	1.9	0.4	0.2	0.4	0.7	15.0	3.1
Bulgaria	1989–94	1.4	0.5	0.2	0.7	0.6	22.5	8.8
	1995–97	4.1	0.6	0.5	0.8	0.6	37.5	12.1
Croatia	1989–94	2.5	0.7	0.5	0.7	0.8	27.6	12.5
	1995–97	6.1	0.9	0.7	1.0	0.9	49.5	16.1
Czech Republic	1989–94	1.5	0.6	0.6	0.6	0.6	31.9	2.5
	1995–97	5.5	0.9	0.9	1.0	0.9	72.5	3.5
Estonia	1989–94	1.2	0.5	0.4	0.5	0.6	32.4	5.4
	1995–97	4.8	0.9	0.9	1.0	0.9	65.0	10.0
Georgia	1989–94	0.6	0.2	0.2	0.2	0.3	17.9	na
	1995–97	2.5	0.6	0.5	0.6	0.7	40.0	na
Hungary	1989–94	2.6	0.7	0.5	0.8	0.8	38.4	8.5
	1995–97	6.5	0.9	0.9	1.0	0.9	65.0	11.4
Kazakhstan	1989–94	0.5	0.2	0.2	0.2	0.3	11.5	0.5
	1995–97	2.6	0.7	0.5	0.9	0.8	32.5	3.1
Kyrgyz Republic	1989–94	0.6	0.3	0.3	0.3	0.3	18.5	na
	1995–97	3.4	0.8	0.7	1.0	0.8	45.0	na
Latvia	1989–94	1.0	0.4	0.3	0.4	0.6	32.8	4.5
	1995–97	4.1	0.9	0.7	1.0	0.9	61.0	6.9
Lithuania	1989–94	1.1	0.5	0.4	0.4	0.6	30.6	2.0
	1995–97	4.5	0.9	0.8	1.0	0.8	60.0	6.4
Macedonia	1989–94	2.4	0.7	0.5	0.8	0.8	22.9	na
	1995–97	5.9	0.8	0.7	0.9	0.9	45.0	34.0
Moldova	1989–94	0.6	0.3	0.2	0.3	0.3	14.8	8.4
	1995–97	3.0	0.7	0.5	0.8	0.8	35.0	13.1

Poland	1989–94	2.4	0.7	0.6	0.8	0.7	40.7	12.8
	1995–97	6.2	0.9	0.8	1.0	0.9	59.0	13.0
Romania	1989–94	0.9	0.4	0.3	0.4	0.4	26.6	6.0
	1995–97	3.6	0.7	0.6	0.8	0.8	47.5	8.4
Russia	1989–94	0.7	0.3	0.3	0.3	0.4	28.1	2.1
	1995–97	3.4	0.7	0.6	1.0	0.7	59.0	9.2
Slovak Republic	1989–94	1.5	0.6	0.6	0.6	0.6	31.3	7.1
	1995–97	5.2	0.9	0.8	0.9	0.9	64.5	13.1
Slovenia	1989–94	2.6	0.7	0.5	0.8	0.8	20.2	9.7
	1995–97	6.2	0.9	0.7	1.0	0.9	42.5	14.1
Tajikistan	1989–94	0.4	0.2	0.2	0.0	0.3	11.9	0.6
	1995–97	1.7	0.4	0.3	0.3	0.6	17.5	2.5
Turkmenistan	1989–94	0.3	0.1	0.1	0.1	0.2	12.1	na
	1995–97	1.1	0.3	0.2	0.2	0.4	17.5	na
Ukraine	1989–94	0.3	0.1	0.1	0.1	0.2	21.3	0.4
	1995–97	1.9	0.5	0.4	0.6	0.7	39.3	1.1
Uzbekistan	1989–94	0.4	0.2	0.2	0.1	0.2	14.6	0.3
	1995–97	2.2	0.5	0.5	0.5	0.6	35.0	0.4
Memorandum items[*]								
All transition	1989–94	1.1	0.4	0.3	0.4	0.5	22.7	5.9
	1995–97	3.8	0.7	0.6	0.8	0.8	45.8	9.8
All CEE	1989–94	1.9	0.6	0.5	0.7	0.7	28.6	9.3
	1995–97	5.3	0.8	0.7	0.9	0.9	55.1	13.9
CEE: early reformers	1989–94	2.2	0.7	0.6	0.7	0.7	31.7	8.8
	1995–97	5.9	0.9	0.8	1.0	0.9	58.8	11.8
CEE: late reformers	1989–94	1.4	0.5	0.3	0.6	0.5	23.9	10.1
	1995–97	4.3	0.7	0.5	0.9	0.7	49.4	17.0
Baltics	1989–94	1.1	0.5	0.4	0.5	0.6	32.0	4.0
	1995–97	4.5	0.9	0.8	1.0	0.9	62.0	7.8
Other former Soviet Union	1989–94	0.6	0.3	0.2	0.2	0.3	20.1	3.1
	1995–97	2.8	0.6	0.5	0.7	0.7	39.6	6.0

Note: CEE: early reformers refer to Croatia, the Czech Republic, Hungary, Poland, the Slovak Republic and Slovenia. CEE: later reformers refer to Albania, Bulgaria, Macedonia, FYR and Romania. Baltics refer to Estonia, Latvia and Lithuania. Other former Soviet Union refer to Armenia, Azerbaijan, Belarus, Georgia, Kazakhstan, the Kyrgyz Republic, Moldova, Russia, Tajikistan, Turkmenistan, Ukraine and Uzbekistan. Simple average for values.

Sources: International Monetary Fund; de Melo et al. (DDGT) (1997).

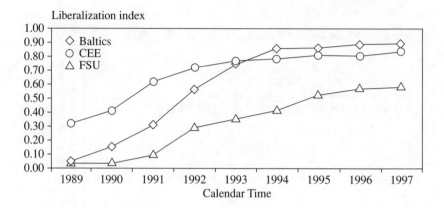

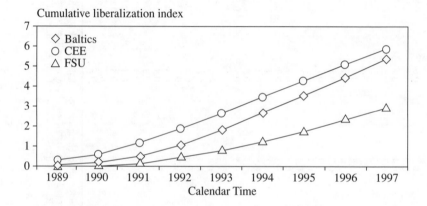

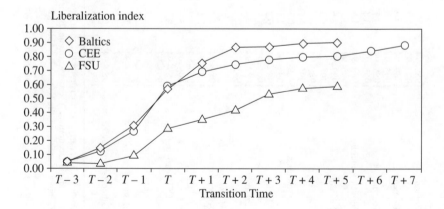

Cumulative liberalization index

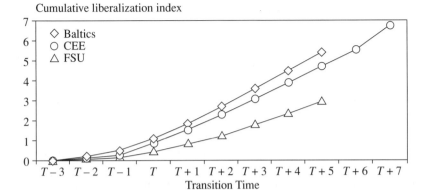

Source: De Melo et al. (1996).

Figure 1.9   Structural reforms profile in transition economies

Explaining Growth Performance

Returning briefly to Figure 1.2, it can be seen that the maximum annual output decline occurred in the year that transition began, and that output had fallen substantially before stabilization began (see last panel). It is also interesting that while the recovery of OFSU is much slower than the other two groups in transition time, it is very similar in stabilization time: output begins to grow within two years after stabilization began. This suggests that the large output losses at the start of transition are likely to have been more associated with the transition process, due to disorganization as modelled by Blanchard (1996), and Blanchard and Kremer (1997), or due to adverse initial conditions as implied by de Melo et al. (1997) and Berg et al. (1999), and not due to tight stabilization policies.[25]

There has been substantial previous work that analyses the relative contributions of stabilization and structural reforms to growth.[26] In an attempt to be more specific, we now turn to regression results presented in those studies. In virtually all papers that attempt to explain growth performance, the common set of explanatory variables is initial conditions, structural reforms and macroeconomic policy variables. While the importance of the explanatory variables within each sub-group differs across the studies, the results generally confirm that growth is more rapid when macroeconomic stabilization is undertaken early and the greater the extent of structural reforms.

Rather than attempt to survey the empirical evidence, we draw on the results presented in Berg et al. (1999) henceforth referred to as BBSZ. We do this for three reasons: first, most of the growth models tested in previous papers are nested in the specifications; second, dynamic effects of the explanatory variables are introduced; and, third, differential effects of the independent variables on public and private sector output are allowed for. Using several specifications and a general-to-specific econometric approach, BBSZ decompose the relative contributions to growth of initial conditions, structural reforms and macroeconomic variables.

BBSZ find that the decline in output in the initial years is distinctly attributable to adverse initial conditions and, to a lesser extent, to macroeconomic imbalances (fiscal deficit and inflation). Importantly, this paper finds no evidence that progress in structural reforms even in the initial years contributed to the output decline. When the differential impact of reforms on the state and private sectors is considered, a substantial negative effect on the state sector is found after two years; however, this is more than offset by the positive impact on the private sector. Finally, the driving force behind the recovery was found to be the impact of structural reforms, and to some extent, the positive impact of tight macroeconomic policies. Unlike in previous studies (Heybey and Murrell, 1999 and Wolf, 1999), which find that the speed of reforms does not matter, BBSZ find that countries that reform faster, recover faster. The latter is consistent with the findings of Åslund et al. (1996).

BBSZ also find that the larger initial output decline in FSU is mainly explained by slower structural reforms and much less due to more adverse initial conditions.[27] Similarly, the slower growth performance in OFSU in the later years of transition is overwhelmingly due to slower structural reforms. It is noteworthy that Poland and the Baltics had among the worst initial conditions (Table 1.1) but have managed to perform well because of good macroeconomic and structural reform policies. In sum, adverse starting conditions can and were overcome by countries that adopted anti-inflationary policies and faster structural reforms.

The results obtained in these studies are illustrated by the following three regressions, run with panel data updated until 1998 (data in other studies, including BBSZ's study end in 1996 or before).[28] The three regression results are:

$$\text{Annual growth} = -7.51\ WD - 1.67\ INF - 0.16\ FIS + 10.38\ LI \qquad (1.2)$$
$$(-3.41) \qquad (-4.46) \qquad (-2.21) \qquad (3.10)$$
Adjusted R-squared $= 0.428$, Number of observations $= 164$;

$$\text{Annual growth} = -9.02\ WD - 1.06\ INF - 0.11\ FIS + 2.01\ EBSM + 5.98\ EBLIB$$
$$(1.3)$$
$$(-4.17) \quad (-2.66) \quad (-1.59) \quad (2.79) \quad (3.35)$$
Adjusted R-squared $= 0.484$, Number of observations $= 164$;

$$\text{Annual growth} = -6.53\,WD - 1.68\,INF - 0.11\,FIS + 11.85\,PS \qquad (1.4)$$
$$(-2.97) \quad\ (-4.55) \quad\ (-1.52) \qquad (3.15)$$
$$\text{Adjusted } R\text{-squared} = 0.443, \text{ Number of observations} = 164;$$

where: Annual growth = annual growth of GDP, WD = war dummy, INF = natural log of inflation, FIS = fiscal balance (a surplus is a positive number) in per cent of GDP, LI = liberalization index as computed by de Melo et al. (1996), $EBSM$ = EBRD small-scale privatization index, $EBLIB$ = EBRD price liberalization index, and PS = share of private sector in GDP as compiled by BBSZ. The starting year for each country was taken to be the transition year (see note 3), and thus differed among countries. All explanatory variables were lagged one period. The t-statistics are in parentheses.

The three regressions contain two types of explanatory variables (excluding the control for wars which is consistently a significant 'initial conditions' variable). They were the macroeconomic policy variables (inflation and fiscal balance) and structural reform variables captured by the liberalization index in equation (1.2), by the EBRD indices in equation (1.3), and by the share of the private sector in equation (1.4). The macroeconomic policy variables were the same in all three regressions, while the structural reform variables differed according to the source used.[29]

All three results confirm that anti-inflation policies and structural reform policies were beneficial to growth. Moreover, equation (1.4) shows that of the various structural and institutional variables (see note 28) compiled by the EBRD, price liberalization and small-scale privatization contributed more to growth than large-scale privatization and other variables. The results on the fiscal balance are less clear-cut. Fiscal balance is not significant in equations (1.3) and (1.4), while it is in equation (1.2) and can be interpreted as saying that deficits help growth provided inflation is under control. However, we do not wish to dwell on the fiscal variable for reasons explained earlier that relate to measurement problems. This general message from the regressions is consistent with those found in earlier studies.

TAKING STOCK

The experience accumulated in the past decade, whether viewed informally or with the help of data, charts and regressions, provides support for the view that the most successful TEs are those that have both stabilized and undertaken comprehensive reforms, and that more and faster reform is better than less and slower reform.

In this section we touch briefly on several critical questions raised by the transition experiences of the 25 countries studied in this chapter: the special cases of Belarus and Uzbekistan; the role of privatization; governance, the role of institutions, and corruption; the role of external assistance; the case of Russia; and importantly, in light of the strong confirmation of the basic paradigm for successful transition, what determines how rapidly a country adopts the needed reforms.[30]

Uzbekistan and Belarus

The output records of Uzbekistan and Belarus, seen in Figure 1.1, present a challenge to the standard transition paradigm. Both had relatively low output declines in the initial years of transition and saw a revival as early as 1995, despite the fact that their stabilization and reform process is proceeding slowly (Tables 1.2 and 1.4). In both cases, it is clear that the transition process has hardly begun.

The case of Uzbekistan is studied by Zettelmeyer (1999), who uses the methodology in BBSZ (1999) to unravel the Uzbek growth puzzle. Zettelmeyer finds that initial output declines were low because of favourable initial conditions, the factor that tends to dominate the growth process in the initial years. These favourable conditions were a low degree of industrialization, importance of cotton production, and near self-sufficiency in energy. Apart from the positive contribution of the small-scale services sector that was common across all countries, the revival came about by combining rigid state control with subsidies that were largely financed by cotton exports, and by developing the energy sector for domestic purposes. These two factors, cotton exports and self-sufficiency in energy, mitigated the external financing constraints faced by other Asian FSU countries at similar levels of development. It should also be noted that the growth rate in Uzbekistan since the recovery has averaged only 2.3 per cent per annum, about half the OFSU average (Table 1.1).

While we are not aware of any published study on why the Belarus output decline was smaller, the main explanation for its growth performance is its close trade ties with Russia.[31] Throughout the transition period, Belarus continued to export consumer goods to Russia, which helped preserve its industrial production. However, since the Russian crisis in August 1998, Belarus's economy has undergone a severe shock with output levelling off or even falling in 1999 and inflation rising to nearly 350 per cent (12-month rate) by July 1999. Belarus, like Uzbekistan, has attempted to insulate itself by following a protective and active industrial policy. It has also been investing in housing projects to help stimulate domestic demand and generate employment.

As is becoming evident in both countries, these policies are not likely to be enough to sustain growth, and it appears they will both need to undertake the reforms that were implemented years ago in the more successful transition countries. In the meantime, it is reasonable to predict that they will grow more slowly than those that have undertaken more extensive reforms will.

Privatization

The statistical evidence presented in this chapter highlights the importance of privatization as a key element in the reform process (see regression presented earlier). Nellis (1999), Stiglitz (1999) and Frydman et al. (1999) provide thought-provoking assessments of the record on privatization. Given the inherently time-consuming nature of the process, privatization did proceed at a fairly rapid pace in most countries (Table 1.4), whether by privatizing state-owned firms or by the emergence of the new sector. Some countries chose the mass privatization route (such as Czechoslovakia and Russia) with the use of vouchers, while others chose to and were able to sell enterprises (Hungary and Poland).

Several conclusions have emerged. At a general level, the imposition of hard budget constraints on enterprises, whether public or private, appears to be an important determinant for successful privatization. Country experiences indicate that insider privatization, whether worker controlled (as in the former Yugoslavia) or manager controlled (as in Russia), does not seem to have led to self-induced restructuring, as expected (Frydman and Rapaczynski, 1994; Frydman et al., 1999). Small-scale privatization, whether by vouchers or by sale to insiders was generally successful.[32] Productivity in private enterprises is higher than in state enterprises, even after controlling for the fact that the better enterprises were likely to be privatized first; and privatized firms appear to have performed better than state enterprises across all samples. Survey data in Estonia show that new firms were more productive than privatized state firms were. Also, experience from Slovenia and the Czech Republic indicates that foreign-owned firms performed better than domestic privatized firms did. While restructuring before privatization seemed to have met with some success in Poland, this was not true in Romania.

This suggests that the strategy implied in Figure 1.6, of starting with rapid small-scale privatization and taking longer over the privatization of large enterprises, would have been successful, provided that the larger companies were sold. For instance, the slower more individualized (by firm) Hungarian approach appears now to have been more successful than the more rapid Czech voucher scheme. Drawing some of the lessons of recent experience, countries that still have to privatize are proceeding very deliberately, with the assistance of foreign financial advisors at every step in the process as in Uzbekistan and Romania (Nellis, 1999).

Governance

It is commonplace to say that a market economy requires an institutional infrastructure of laws, regulations, accounting procedures, markets, and the institutions to enforce them, including a judiciary. The need for legal reform, the creation of financial markets, the creation of a central bank and effective fiscal system, and other aspects of modern government, were widely recognized from the start of the transition process. Considerable amounts of technical assistance in these areas were provided both by the IFIs and also bilaterally to all the TEs. Indeed, there has been some success in reducing corruption via limiting opportunities for rent-seeking by reducing excessive and complex regulations, such as licensing requirements and various tax exemptions, as well as by engaging in civil service reforms. The outcomes have, none the less, differed a great deal, with corruption and governance problems apparently endemic in some countries, and far less prevalent in others.

There can be little doubt that the absence of a predictable legal framework has hindered growth, most visibly by reducing the flow of foreign investment, but no less importantly by reducing domestic investment and encouraging capital flight. The cure for these problems lies mainly in domestic politics, but external assistance to encourage transparency and strengthen institutions, and the conditioning of future assistance on progress in these areas, can contribute. We should also hope that the same process that undermined support for the communist system – that people saw that the market system worked better – will produce an effective political backlash against corruption, as people understand that corruption is not only immoral and illegal, but also holds back economic growth. That is more likely to happen in more democratic and open political systems.

The Role of External Assistance

Although we do not include variables representing the extent of foreign aid in the regressions, Figures 1.7 and 1.8 are consistent with the view that foreign assistance at the early stages helped sustain reforms, but that foreign assistance on its own was not enough. The critical question is how to ensure that external assistance supports reform: the international financial institutions use conditionality for that purpose, but the familiar finding that programmes work best when they are owned by the country means that conditionality is not enough. The question of whether more massive assistance to the TEs, especially in the FSU, would have driven reform ahead more rapidly remains on the table but cannot be answered definitively: the Marshall Plan analogy is suggestive, but the absorptive capacity of Western Europe after the Second World War was surely much greater than that of the TEs in the early 1990s. The transfer problem, the question of whether resources could have been transferred to the transition countries on a larger scale without creating the Dutch disease, also deserves consideration.

Figures 1.7 and 1.8 also show that growth was facilitated by foreign private financing but only in those countries that had successful stabilizations and reforms. A virtuous circle was created for the fast reformers.

Russia

The Russian transition experience stands out as unique. Given the size and power of Russia, that was inevitable. The key question is why, despite a promising start in 1992, rapid privatization in 1994–95, and stabilization in 1995, the subsequent reform process has been slow and halting. The structural reform indices in Table 1.4 show that Russia has lagged in the implementation of structural reforms. The answer surely lies in large part in the failure to drive ahead with reforms following the presidential election of 1996, an election in which powerful vested interests, some of them created by the loans for shares scheme, strengthened their hold on political as well as economic power, in the process deepening corruption. Russia, like many countries, seems to have suffered from the curse of oil – from the availability of a ready source of wealth, available without much productive effort, a prize to be fought over, rather than an investment to develop and foster.[33]

The failure of Russia to solve its fiscal problems, combined with easy access to external capital, particularly in 1997, and the continuing capital flight, led to an excessively large fiscal deficit and significant short-term debt (the stock of which, however, was not large relative to GDP). When the external environment became unhealthy, with oil prices falling and the cost and availability of foreign financing worsening, and in the context of a weak banking system and an excessively inflexible exchange rate, a financial collapse could not be prevented. If reforms had been vigorously pursued from 1996, the collapse could have been avoided.

The question now is when, rather than whether, the political system will reach the conclusion that the reform effort has to be renewed. The improvement of governance will have to be a large part of this effort. It is encouraging that despite the collapse of 1998 the Russian government has not turned inward, and has continued to seek to maintain its economic and financial relations with the rest of the industrialized world.

What Determines the Extent of Reform?

The main theme of this chapter is that the policies to ensure growth are well known. That immediately raises the next question: what determines the extent to which a country embraces transition and reform comes to the fore? This is clear from the discussion of Russia. It is clear also from another aspect of the regressions presented in this chapter – that as a statistical matter, initial conditions go far in accounting for the performance of output, but that the behaviour of output can also be accounted for by the extent of stabilization and reform. That suggests that the extent of reform has been strongly correlated with the initial conditions – that the reformers are those closer to Western

Europe, with a shorter period under communism, and more advanced economically when they fell under Soviet control or when the transition process began. That is a large part of the story, but not the whole story, for instance because there are both fast and slow reformers in CEE.

For many countries, the prospect of joining the European Union has been a powerful spur to reform. The absence of that prospect for the OFSU countries except perhaps eventually Ukraine must be among the factors retarding reform.

The benefits of a successful transition process must be clear by now. The challenge for supporters of reform in those countries in which it is lagging, and for those who would support them from the outside, is to find a set of incentives that would sustain a reform coalition.

NOTES

1. We thank Marek Belka, Lajos Bokros and David Lipton for insightful comments. This study was also presented at the AEA meetings in Boston, January 2000 – it has benefited from comments by Andy Berg, Mark De Broeck, Prakash Loungani, Johannes Mueller, Miguel Savastano, Jerry Schiff, Carlos Végh and Jeromin Zettelmeyer. We thank Haiyan Shi and Manzoor Gill for excellent research assistance and Cindy Galang for administrative assistance. The views expressed in this chapter are those of the authors and not necessarily those of the International Monetary Fund.
2. In mitigating the output decline, Uzbekistan is an exception, a country that has done relatively little reforming. Belarus is another country where the pattern of output is not very different from that of more successful reformers, but reform has been, at best, slow.
3. Transition time, T, is defined as the year in which the communist regime collapsed, a rough measure of the date at which the country began to move towards a market economy. See Figure 1.1 for country-specific years in which transition began. Note that the GDP index is normalized to 100 in the year $T - 2$ for all countries in Figure 1.1.
4. Research on this question suggests much larger underestimation in FSU than in CEE countries (Johnson et al., 1997; De Broeck and Koen, 1999; and others). But even under the most optimistic scenario, output fell by significantly more in the FSU than in CEE. Attempts are being made to adjust the official data, including retrospectively, to reduce these biases in TEs. Official statistics in Russia, Kazakhstan and Lithuania already include these revisions.
5. The ten CEE countries discussed in this chapter are: Albania, Bulgaria, Croatia, the Czech Republic, Hungary, FYR Macedonia, Poland, Romania, the Slovak Republic and Slovenia. The Baltics are: Estonia, Latvia and Lithuania. The OFSU are: Armenia, Azerbaijan, Belarus, Georgia, Kazakhstan, the Kyrgyz Republic, Moldova, Russia, Tajikistan, Turkmenistan, Ukraine and Uzbekistan.
6. The output measure shown in Figure 1.2 for each group is a simple (that is, unweighted) average of the output levels in each country, with 100 as the base-year level.
7. The choice of the transition year is also not free from controversy. As Lajos Bokros and Vaclav Klaus have pointed out (in this volume), by defining it as the year in which the communist regimes fell, one does not take into account that countries may have been at different stages of their business cycle. This is a valid point. In the case of Hungary, the problem of defining the transition year is somewhat different as slow reforms were introduced over a long period. We chose 1990 as the starting date because reforms accelerated during that year.
8. Private consumption and gross fixed capital formation are measured in nominal terms as a share of GDP because investment and GDP deflators are either non-existent or highly unreliable.

9. The big changes in consumption demand seen in Figure 1.3 can be explained by the adjustment of consumption towards equilibrium levels following the end of central planning. See Calvo et al, (1996) and Denizer and Wolf (1998) for discussions of suppressed consumption and forced saving during the transition.

10. Excluding Russia and Belarus, the average annual inflation for OFSU in 1998 was only 10.9 per cent.

11. Dollarization would have limited the monetary authorities' ability to conduct monetary policy and reduced the base for inflation tax.

12. In fact, Treasury bills were introduced in many countries very early in the reform process.

13. See Sahay and Végh (1996a) for evidence on dollarization in TEs.

14. See Zettelmeyer and Citrin (1995).

15. Fischer et al. (1996a, 1997) show that stabilization tended to be more successful in countries with fixed exchange rate regimes, a result that was consistent with experience in other developing countries. Loungani and Sheets (1997) present evidence on the relationship between the degree of independence of central banks and inflation outcomes in TEs. For a discussion of the relative merits of a fixed exchange rate system over a flexible regime at the start of the transition process, see Sachs (1996b), and Sahay and Végh (1996b).

16. Given the high inflation it is natural to assume that the high deficits at the start are mainly nominal rather than operational: however, given the generally low levels of domestic government debt at the time, nominal and operational deficits were similar. There are none the less many problems with the measurement of fiscal deficits in TEs. The most common are that they may be defined differently across countries (for example, central versus general government, including or excluding extra-budgetary items) or that the definition within one country may have changed over time. In general, deficits in the fast reformers may look worse than they actually are as compared to other countries simply because accounting practices are better in fast reformers.

17. In OFSU, revenue declined by more than 11 per cent of GDP between 1991 and 1995. Some reasons for the revenue decline are higher output losses in traditional tax bases (such as profits of state enterprises, industrial production, state trading companies) and revenue-losing tax reforms.

18. The 12-month inflation rates as of July 1999 for Belarus, Tajikistan and Uzbekistan were 343, 38 and 27 per cent, respectively.

19. Subsidies in targeted sectors continued, a proliferation of exemptions mushroomed, tax collection weakened, and the full revenue potential of the energy sector was not realized. In the mid-1990s, for example, production subsidies in Kazakhstan, Russia, Ukraine and Uzbekistan still amounted to about 11–13 per cent of GDP (Cheasty and Davis, 1996).

20. Both external private financing and revenues from privatization sales were disappointingly low. By some estimates, nine FSU countries, on average, could have generated 13 per cent of GDP from privatization proceeds annually between 1989 and 1995 (Cheasty and Davis, 1996). In fact, only about one per cent was collected for financing the fiscal deficit, either because more than anticipated shares were distributed freely or because the privatization process itself did not pick up speed.

21. The idea is to test whether physical location matters. The distance is a crude measure of how far is the country in question from the centre of Europe (similar to the one in Warner's chapter but not from the coast).

22. Using another set of initial condition variables, de Melo et al. (1997) find that initial macroeconomic imbalances had a strong influence on growth and inflation in the short run.

23. The case of Russia was so different from all other countries that for analytical purposes, it was considered as a group of one by Garibaldi et al. (1999).

24. These have been updated by Berg et al. (1999) for 1996–97.

25. Concerns regarding a credit crunch were voiced at the time (see Calvo and Frenkel, 1991 and Calvo and Coricelli, 1992). However, supply-side factors seemed to dominate the *ex-post* analysis.

26. These include de Melo et al. (1996), Fischer et al. (1996a, 1996b, 1997), Sachs (1996a), Selowsky and Martin (1997), Åslund et al. (1996), Hernández-Catá (1997), Havrylyshyn et al. (1998), Wolf (1999), Heybey and Murrell (1999) and Berg et al. (1999).

27. Using a qualitatively different approach, this is supported by the findings of De Broeck and Koen (1999). They account for the contribution of total factor productivity (TFP) and factor input in explaining the output performance in the 15 FSU countries. The paper finds that, in addition to the negative effects of a rise in unemployment and decline in capital investment, a decline in TFP also contributed to the sharp decline in output in the initial years. In fact, TFP growth has a distinct V-shaped pattern, turning positive from 1995–96 when GDP growth generally resumed.
28. The starting year for the annual data was the start of the transition year for each country, while the ending year was 1998. The sample was therefore an unbalanced panel.
29. In equation (1.3), all eight EBRD variables were initially used but only two were found to be significant and are reported. The eight EBRD variables are: large-scale privatization index; small-scale privatization index; enterprise restructuring index; price liberalization index; trade and foreign exchange index; competition policy index; banking reform index; and securities markets index.
30. We omit the much-discussed contrast between the transition strategies and outcomes in China and the FSU. On this, see Sachs and Wing Thye Woo (1994), with whom we fundamentally agree.
31. We are grateful to Tom Wolf for his insights on Belarus.
32. Even in Russia, Barberis et al. (1996) show positive restructuring returns to the privatization of small shops.
33. See also Fischer (1992), Boycko et al. (1993), Åslund (1996), Boone and Fedorov (1997) and Brainard (1998) for an evolving discussion on Russia's economic problems.

REFERENCES

Aghion, Philippe and Olivier Jean Blanchard (1994), 'On the speed of transition in Central Europe', in Stanley Fischer and Julio J. Rotemberg (eds), *NBER Macroeconomic Annual 1994*, Cambridge, MA: MIT Press, pp. 283–320.

Åslund, Anders (1996), 'Reform vs. "rent-seeking" in Russia's economic transformation', *Transition*, **2** (2), 12–16.

Åslund, Anders, Peter Boone and Simon Johnson (1996), 'How to stabilize: lessons from post-communist countries', *Brookings Papers on Economic Activity*, **1**, 217–313.

Balcerowicz, Leszek (1994), 'Fallacies and other lessons', *Economic Policy*, **9** (19), supplement, December, 17–50.

Barberis, Nicolas, Maxim Boycko, Andrei Shleifer and Natalia Tsukanova (1996), 'How does privatization work? Evidence from Russian shops', *Journal of Political Economy*, **104** (4), 764–90.

Berg, Andrew, Eduardo Borensztein, Ratna Sahay and Jeromin Zettelmeyer (1999), 'The evolution of output in transition economies', IMF Working Paper 99/73, Washington, DC: International Monetary Fund.

Blanchard, Olivier (1996), 'Assessment of the economic transition in Central and Eastern Europe – theoretical aspects of transition', *American Economic Review*, **86** (2), 117–22.

Blanchard, Olivier and Michael Kremer (1997), 'Disorganization', *Quarterly Journal of Economics*, **112** (4), November, 1091–126.

Blanchard, Olivier, Rudiger Dornbusch, Paul Krugman, Richard Layard and Lawrence Summers (1992), *Reform in Eastern Europe*, Cambridge, MA: MIT Press.

Boone, Peter and Boris Fedorov (1997), 'The ups and downs of Russian economic reforms', in Wing Thye Woo, Stephen Parket and Jeffrey Sachs (eds), *The Economies in Transition: Comparing Asia and Eastern Europe*, Cambridge, MA: MIT Press, pp. 1–33.

Boycko, Maxim, Andrei Shleifer and Robert Vishny (1993), 'Privatizing Russia', *Brookings Papers on Economic Activity*, **2**, 139–92.

Brainard, Elizabeth (1998), 'Winners and losers in Russia's economic transition', *American Economic Review*, **88** (5), 1094–116.

Calvo, Guillermo and Fabrizio Coricelli (1992), 'Output collapse in Eastern Europe: the role of credit', IMF Working Paper 92/64, Washington, DC: International Monetary Fund.

Calvo, Guillermo and Jacob Frenkel (1991), 'From centrally-planned to market economies: the road from CPE to PCPE', IMF Working Paper 91/17, Washington, DC: International Monetary Fund.

Calvo, Guillermo, Ratna Sahay and Carlos Végh (1996), 'Capital flows in Central and Eastern Europe: evidence and policy options', in Guillermo Calvo, Morris Goldstein and Eduard Hochreiter (eds), *Private Capital Flows to Emerging Markets after the Mexican Crisis*, Washington, DC: Institute of International Economics, pp. 57–90.

Cheasty, Adrienne and Jeffrey M. Davis (1996), 'Fiscal transition in countries of the former Soviet Union: an interim assessment', *Moct–Most: Economic Policy in Transitional Economies*, **6** (3), 7–34.

De Broeck, Mark and Vincent Koen (1999), 'The great contractions in Russia, the Baltics, and the other countries of the former Soviet Union: a view from the supply side', mimeo.

de Melo, Martha, Cevdet Denizer and Alan Gelb (1996), 'From plan to market: patterns of transition', *World Bank Economic Review*, **10** (3), 379–424.

de Melo, Martha, Cevdet Denizer, Alan Gelb and Stoyan Tenev (1997), 'Circumstance and choice: the role of initial conditions and policies in transition economies', Policy Research Working Paper No. 1866, Washington, DC: World Bank.

Denizer, Cevdet and Holger Wolf (1998), 'Aggregate saving in the transition: a cross country study', mimeo, Washington, DC: World Bank.

Dewatripont, Mathias and Gerard Roland (1995), 'The design of reform packages under uncertainty', *American Economic Review*, **85** (5), 1207–23.

EBRD (1999), Transition Report, London, UK.

Fischer, Stanley (1992), 'Stabilization and economic reform in Russia', *Brookings Papers on Economic Activity*, **1**, 77–126.

Fischer, Stanley, and Alan Gelb (1991), 'Issues in socialist economy reform', *Journal of Economic Perspectives*, **5** (4), 91–105.

Fischer, Stanley, Ratna Sahay and Carlos Végh (1996a), 'Stabilization and growth in transition economies: the early experience', *Journal of Economic Perspectives*, **10**, (2), 45–66.

Fischer, Stanley, Ratna Sahay and Carlos Végh (1996b), 'Economies in transition: the beginnings of growth', *American Economic Association Papers and Proceedings*, **86** (2), 229–33.

Fischer, Stanley, Ratna Sahay and Carlos Végh (1997), 'From transition to market: evidence and growth prospects', in S. Zecchini (ed.), *Lessons from the Economic Transition*, Dordrecht: Kluwer Academic Publishers, pp. 79–101.

Frydman, Roman, Cheryl Gray, Marek Hessel and Andrzej Rapaczynski (1999), 'When does privatization work? The impact of private ownership on corporate performance in the transition economies', *Quarterly Journal of Economics*, **114** (4), 1153–91.

Frydman, Roman, and Andrzej Rapaczynski (1994), *Privatization in Eastern Europe: Is the State Withering Away?*, Budapest, Hungary: Central European University Press.

Garibaldi, Pietro, Nada Mora, Ratna Sahay and Jeromin Zettelmeyer (1999), 'What moves capital to transition economies?', mimeo, Washington, DC: International Monetary Fund.

Havrylysyhyn, Oleh, Ivailo Izvorski and Ron van Rooden (1998), 'Recovery and growth in transition economies 1990–97: a stylized regression analysis', IMF Working Paper 98/141, Washington, DC: International Monetary Fund.

Hernández-Catá, Ernesto (1997), 'Liberalization and the behaviour of output during the transition from plan to market', IMF Working Paper 97/53, Washington, DC: International Monetary Fund.

Heybey, Berta and Peter Murrell (1999), 'The relationship between economic growth and the speed of liberalization during transition', *Journal of Policy Reform*, **3** (2), 121–37.

Johnson, Simon, Daniel Kaufmann and Andrei Shleifer (1997), 'The unofficial economy in transition', *Brookings Papers on Economic Activity*, **2**, 159–239.

Krajnyák, Kornélia and Jeromin Zettelmeyer (1997), 'Competitiveness in transition economies: what scope for real appreciation?', IMF Working Paper 97/149, Washington, DC: International Monetary Fund.

Kornai, Janos (1986), 'The soft budget constraint', *Kyklos*, **30** (1), 3–30.

Linn, Johannes F. (1999), 'Ten years of transition in Central Europe and the former Soviet Union – the good news and the not-so-good news', Paper presented at the Dubrovnik Conference on 10 Years of Transition, September.

Lipton, David and Jeffrey Sachs (1990a), 'Creating a market economy in Eastern Europe: the case of Poland', *Brookings Papers on Economic Activity*, **1**, 75–147.

Lipton, David and Jeffrey Sachs (1990b), 'Privatization in Eastern Europe: the case of Poland', *Brookings Papers on Economic Activity*, **2**, 293–341.

Loungani, Prakash and Nathan Sheets (1997), 'Central bank independence, inflation and growth in transition economies', *Journal of Money, Credit and Banking*, **29** (3), August, 381–99.

Nellis, John (1999), 'Time to rethink privatization in transition economies?', International Finance Corporation Discussion Paper No. 38, Washington, DC: World Bank.

Newbery, David M. (1991), 'Sequencing the transition', CEPR Discussion Paper Series No. 75.

Sachs, Jeffrey (1996a), 'The transition at mid decade', *American Economic Review*, **86** (2), 128–33.

Sachs, Jeffrey (1996b), 'Economic transition and the exchange-rate regime – exchange-rate regimes and macroeconomic stability', *AEA Papers and Proceedings*, **86** (2), May.

Sachs, Jeffrey and Wing Thye Woo (1994), 'Structural factors in the economic reforms of China, Eastern Europe, and the former Soviet Union', *Economic Policy: A European Forum*, **9** (18), April, 101–45.

Sahay, Ratna and Carlos Végh (1996a), 'Dollarization in transition economies: evidence and policy implications', in Paul Mizen and Eric J. Pentecost (eds), *The Macroeconomics of International Currencies: Theory, Policy, Evidence*, Cheltenham, UK and Brookfield, USA: Edward Elgar, pp. 193–224.

Sahay, Ratna and Carlos Végh (1996b), 'Inflation and stabilization in transition economies: an analytical interpretation of the evidence', *Journal of Policy Reform*, **1** (1), 75–198.

Selowsky, Marcelo and Ricardo Martin (1997), 'The transition from socialism: policy performance and output growth in the transition economies', AEA *Papers and Proceedings*, **87** (2), 350–53.

Stiglitz, Joseph E. (1999), 'Whither reform?', Paper prepared for the Annual Bank Conference on Development Economics, 28–30 April, Washington, DC: World Bank.

Wolf, Holger C. (1999), 'Transition strategies: choices and outcomes', Princeton Studies in International Finance, No. 85, June, Princeton University, Department of Economics.

Wyplosz, Charles (1999), 'Ten years of transformation: macroeconomic lessons', Paper prepared for the Annual Bank Conference on Development Economics, 28–30 April, Washington, DC: World Bank.

Zettelmeyer, Jeromin (1999), 'The Uzbek growth puzzle', IMF Staff Papers **46** (3), Washington, DC: International Monetary Fund, pp. 274–92.

Zettelmeyer, Jeromin and Daniel Citrin (1995), 'Stabilization: fixed versus flexible exchange rates', in Daniel Citrin and Ashok Lahiri (eds), *Policy Experiences and Issues in the Baltics, Russia and Other Countries of the Former Soviet Union*, IMF Occasional Paper No. 133, December, pp. 93–102.

2. Comments on Fischer and Sahay

Lajos Bokros

The basic question I asked myself when reading Fischer and Sahay was whether output growth is a reliable indicator of economic performance. Apart from the usual shortcomings of income statistics, which I do not intend to discuss here, the real issue is whether the ranking of transition economies (TEs) according to their output relative to the pre-transition level has any reliable explanatory power at all. I do not think it is the case. There are so many factors behind growth patterns and they are so different for individual countries that one can hardly use this ranking for drawing a meaningful conclusion.

Fischer and Sahay highlight the problem of Uzbekistan and Belarus as countries showing a relatively small decline in output while being the archetype of no reforms. I think that these countries – and maybe even some others, such as Turkmenistan – should not be compared with the rest of the group at all. The basic reason for this is that we want to compare the countries that have maintained central planning with TEs that have abandoned central planning.

My definition of central planning is that a significant share of financial – and maybe even physical – resources is allocated by direct government decision and not by market forces without any consideration for profit and loss. This government intervention could be concealed and its consequences even further exacerbated by a highly distortive set of economic regulations, such as individualized and prohibitive taxation, multiple exchange rates, directed lending and so on. In such an environment, which is usually supported by autocratic political mechanisms, a good part of national income is actually lost in enterprises that do not produce any marketable output. For example, in Uzbekistan I visited a huge factory producing aircraft body frames that were sold to no one. The output of such a firm is accounted for as value added to national income as if it were value creation while what actually happens is quite the opposite – it is a value destruction that should be subtracted from GDP. Therefore, notwithstanding the methodological issues, I believe that GDP figures of centrally planned economies cannot and should not be compared with those of TEs that have abandoned central planning.

A different problem arises when we compare the rate of output recovery of truly reform-orientated countries. Fischer and Sahay clearly indicate that there is a cyclical pattern of development in most countries of Central and Eastern Europe. This pattern, however, did not start with the fall of the Berlin Wall. One could easily observe it well before the political changes of the late 1980s began. In this respect, selecting a specific date as a basis of comparison might be quite arbitrary and even misleading. Take the example of Poland and Hungary. Poland was at the bottom of its economic cycle when the first democratically elected government took power. After a decade of martial law, the country was an economic pariah: there was stagnation and decline partially due to the country's default on its external debt. Poland started to recover from an extremely low base. Hungary, in turn, was almost at the high end of its economic cycle. In 1986, the last congress of the communist party declared a policy of 'renewed dynamization' fuelled by another wave of excessive foreign borrowing. Unlike Poland, Hungary did not ask for any rescheduling or forgiveness of foreign debt, despite having reached higher levels of per capita foreign debt than Poland did. Hungary's growth was clearly illusive and unsustainable, nevertheless, in 1989, the country was almost at the peak of its output. To surpass it after a decade of deep restructuring is more difficult than elsewhere.

In addition, Hungary had abandoned central planning as early as 1968. As a consequence of this and other well-known substantive reforms introduced throughout the 1980s, there was no need for any shock therapy to restore macrofinancial equilibrium. It is regrettable that the first democratically elected Hungarian government misinterpreted the situation and felt that there was no need for any fiscal adjustment at all. This was wrong. The country clearly did not need shock therapy – a one-time sharp adjustment of prices and exchange rate to eliminate excess demand and monetary overhang. It needed a more traditional, almost classical type of fiscal adjustment. Government overspending, especially on the generous and poorly targeted social transfers, should have been cut back very substantially. Unfortunately, the favourable political momentum created by the political changes had been lost and it was not recaptured until the mid-1990s. Nevertheless, with respect to corporate restructuring and enterprise reform Hungary was on a par with or maybe doing even better than Poland. This is why Hungary was able to restart growth so quickly following the adoption of the austerity package in 1995 and it has been able to maintain a high, sustainable growth rate ever since.

A comparison of countries such as Croatia and Slovakia with the star reformers creates another set of problems. These countries – and some others, such as the Czech Republic – did show high growth rates even in the first half of the 1990s, following a very short period of decline at the beginning of transition. These countries all claimed to have achieved a very high level of private sector participation and efficiency gains as a result. The reality, however, proved to be very different. Growth was largely fuelled by new investments channelled to enterprises that were either halfway or nominally privatized and clearly non-restructured, relying heavily on foreign borrowing rather than on foreign direct investment (FDI). Sooner or later, it proved to be unsustainable. In Croatia, the reconstruction boom after the war provided an additional impetus. This strategy was successful for a while but it was not a sign of success. Sometimes economic stagnation and a transitional upsurge in unemployment is a more promising sign of success, particularly if it results from deep corporate restructuring. The Czech stagnation could well be taken as such a good sign if the restructuring is accelerated and supported by a rapidly improved legal framework and proper incentives to FDI. Slovakia has just started this process while the most painful part of the restructuring is yet to take place in Croatia.

There are many more distinct patterns of development, which will determine the different growth paths followed by individual countries. We can easily foresee future cases where temporary stagnation or even decline will be an encouraging sign for a country's ability to recapture sustainable growth following a quick restructuring. In other cases, prolonged decline may just be a sign of half-baked reforms with more or less adequate macro policies without meaningful supply-side adjustment. And still in others, a temporary high growth could be an alarming prelude to a future crash. One decade is simply too short a time horizon to make any meaningful judgement of past performance, not to speak of future development potential and growth opportunities. Growth – especially in the short run – does not tell us much without analysing the underlying fundamentals. I firmly believe that we should completely abandon using output recovery rates as a measure of success in transition because they do not have any meaningful explanatory power.

After a decade of painful transition we all know more or less which countries are the best performers. Poland and Hungary, along with Estonia and perhaps Slovenia, are clearly the ones which have been able to transform in the deepest and most comprehensive way. We also know that the key to success has been a consistent macroeconomic stabilization coupled with deep corporate restructuring, and a real privatization bringing in efficient governance stemming mostly from FDI. Small and medium-sized enterprise development, fast liberalization, and legal and banking reform provide other indispensable ingredients to the optimal, if not ideal, policy mix. After 25 years, it is fair to assume that the intensity and scope of reforms are closely correlated with sustained growth and with the countries' abilities to close the income gap with the EU. But in the short run, output growth is not an indicator of success and failure at all.

ICEEC PA7 P23
L16 P24

3. Ten years after: what is special about transition countries?

Daniel Gros and Marc Suhrcke

INTRODUCTION

Much attention has been devoted to transition countries. There is even a special international financial institution, the European Bank for Reconstruction and Development (EBRD), charged to look after the particular problems of countries in transition. Ten years after the start of reforms it is time to ask whether the former centrally planned economies are distinguishable among other countries and whether their special treatment is still justified.

A number of existing studies analyse transition economies (TEs) in terms of their prospects of catching up with the developed market economies. Some studies estimate the time required by TEs to catch up with the Western European level of development using a growth regression approach (Barbone and Zalduendo, 1996). Others assess the 'distance' of the Central and Eastern European (CEE) countries from Western market economies in terms of macroeconomic indicators such as inflation, budget deficit and so on (Fischer et al., 1997 and 1998; Fischer and Sahay, Chapter 1 in this volume). Krkoska (1999) analyses the macroeconomic fluctuations in TEs relative to those in Western European economies. The EBRD assesses regularly the progress of reform in each of the CEE countries and provides a quantitative evaluation in a number of important areas (for example, enterprise reform, market liberalization, and financial and legal institutions).

However, the existing literature treats much richer Western European (OECD) countries as a benchmark model for TEs. It implicitly assumes that all the characteristics that distinguish Europe's TEs are related to their past centrally planned economic systems. This is unlikely to be the case, because many of the indicators differentiating transition countries from the developed OECD countries are perceived as related to the development level of an economy. In other words, one should ask whether the communist heritage along with its central planning system is still the reason why post-communist economies differ from countries with a comparable income per capita, even after ten years.

The starting point for any post-transition 'Rip Van Winkle' would be to analyse the characteristic traits[1] of centrally planned economies that might have left a mark on economic structures because they could not be changed quickly:

1. A marked preference for industry, especially heavy industry, and a neglect of services.
2. A very high rate of investment, both in physical and human capital.
3. No need for a financial system to allocate savings to investment (done according to plan, usually without assigning a time value).
4. No need for the legal and institutional framework underpinning a market economy.

This list leaves out many other characteristics that distinguish a centrally planned from a market economy, for example the control over prices, fixed exchange rates and artificial trade patterns to name a few. However, these elements could be, and indeed have been changed almost immediately and are unlikely to distinguish an economy in transition today, ten years later.

The proposed method of analysis starts from the observation that most of the TE characteristics are in general related to the level of development or the income per capita.[2] For example, the demand for services tends to increase with income. Richer countries, therefore, generally have a larger service sector. More developed economies also have a much denser infrastructure than poorer countries do. The same can be said of the financial systems, which are generally much more developed in richer countries. Finally, the legal system tends to be underdeveloped in poorer countries, and the public sector tends to work less efficiently. The main reason for this simply might be that the administration of the highly complex framework developed in the rich capitalist part of the world relies on a public sector with a strong human capital base. However, it has also been argued that weak enforcement of property rights impedes growth (Dabla-Norris and Freeman, 1999). But which way the causation runs does not really matter in this context.

The results presented here strongly confirm the general observation that most of the elements that might distinguish an economy in transition are related to the level of economic development. GDP per capita, whether measured in purchasing power parity (PPP) or in a common currency (USD) terms, can alone explain between 40 and 70 per cent of the variance of the indicators of the legacy of transition in simple cross-section regressions. This suggests a simple research strategy. Former centrally planned economies are perceived to be different if they are systematically outliers in regressions that link indicators such as the importance of industry, energy use and so on to GDP per capita.

The subsequent sections briefly describe the indicators and data sources used, followed by the results and conclusions.

DATA AND METHODOLOGY

The data were taken from the World Bank Development Indicators database, which contains income per capita and a number of structural indicators for 148 countries. In this sample the transition countries mostly fall under the classification 'Middle income developing countries'.

Using these data we have run regressions of the following general form:

$$Indicator_i = \alpha + \beta \, GNPpc_i + \chi \, (GNPpc_i)^2 + \phi \, CEE + \gamma \, FSU + \eta \, ASEAN + \varepsilon_I$$
(3.1)

where i is the country-subscript, *Indicator* is the respective variable that is perceived to be related to per capita income *GNPpc*. *CEE*, *FSU* (former Soviet Union) and *ASEAN* (Association of Southeast Asian Nations) are the country dummies described above, and 'ε' is the error term. Unless the coefficient of the per capita GNP square term is significant at the 10 per cent level, it is dropped from the equation.

Most regressions have been run on two transformations of the raw data: first, using the natural logarithm of all variables and, second, using standardized values, that is, by subtracting the mean and then dividing by the standard deviation. As both sets of results were very similar, only the results using logarithms are reported in Table 3.1. Income per capita can be measured and compared in current USD or in PPP terms. The results are based on GNP per capita in PPP, as this measure is commonly used in cross-section comparisons. The results are similar using GNP in USD terms. This is not surprising since there is a close correlation between these two measures of development. In a regression of one on the other, the coefficient of determination R^2 is over 96 per cent and the transition countries do not constitute outliers. This is the first indication that their economies are not fundamentally different from the rest of the sample.

Three dummy variables are used throughout. Two of them are applied to CEE and FSU transition countries, respectively. *CEE* includes all the ten countries that are negotiating membership with the EU (Bulgaria, the Czech Republic, Estonia, Hungary, Latvia, Lithuania, Poland, Romania, the Slovak Republic and Slovenia) and Croatia. *FSU* includes all Commonwealth of Independent States (CIS) members, and Macedonia is added to this group.

Table 3.1   Regression results

	GNPpcPPP	GNPpc^2	CEE	FSU	ASEAN	R^2	Obs
Industry male employment 97	2.09**	–0.10**	0.55****	0.81****	–0.17*	0.68	131
	(2.6)	(–2.1)	(6.7)	(11.4)	(–1.8)		
Industry female employment 97	4.42****	–0.23****	0.87****	1.25****	0.36****	0.69	130
	(5.2)	(–4.6)	(8.3)	(11.2)	(3.1)		
Industry value added % of	1.40****	–0.08****	0.05	0.06	0.19**	0.23	120
GDP 97	(2.9)	(–2.8)	(0.7)	(0.6)	(2.5)		
Manufacturing value added %	1.24**	–0.06**	0.31****	0.38*	0.50****	0.33	110
of GDP 97	(2.4)	(–2.0)	(3.7)	(1.8)	(6.5)		
Commercial energy use pc kg	0.80****		0.67****	0.78****	–0.03	0.77	109
of oil equiv. 96	(19.0)	–	(6.7)	(3.2)	(–0.2)		
Commercial energy use pc kg	–1.75****	0.15****	0.84****	0.87****	0.04	0.80	109
of oil equiv. 96	(–2.7)	(4.0)	(7.2)	(3.6)	(0.4)		
Paved roadnet (% of all roads)[a]	1.2****		1.7****	1.52****	0.42	0.78	117
	(13.0)	–	(3.7)	(8.6)	(0.9)		
Railnet (km per surface area)[a]	0.70****		1.42****	1.07****	–0.99****	0.72	116
	(11.2)	–	(13.1)	(5.1)	(–2.8)		
Gross secondary enrolment 96	0.57****		0.48****	0.91****	0.11	0.76	119
	(14.5)	–	(7.6)	(9.4)	(0.6)		
Gross tertiary enrolment 96	1.03****		0.68****	1.49****	0.12	0.80	130
	(24.3)	–	(4.1)	(9.0)	(0.5)		
M2 % GDP 97	0.42****		–0.27**	–0.94****	0.28*	0.55	125
	(10.5)	–	(–2.3)	(–6.8)	(1.8)		
Credit to private sector % of	0.73****		–0.44***	–0.92****	0.67****	0.62	126
GDP 97	(13.4)	–	(–2.6)	(–3.8)	(2.8)		
Interest rate spread lending –	–0.37****		0.04	0.76****	–0.63****	0.43	95
deposit 97	(–6.8)	–	(0.3)	(3.6)	(–3.1)		
Corruption index (higher	0.38****		–0.08	–0.25	–0.14	0.63	80
value = less corrupt) 98	(10.8)	–	(–1.0)	(–1.47)	(–1.2)		
Euromoney country risk index	0.38****		0.78*	–0.29****	0.2**	0.77	129
97	(21.4)	–	(1.9)	(–3.3)	(2.2)		
Institutional Investor country	0.49****		–0.07	–0.51****	0.33****	0.80	108
risk index 97	(18.4)	–	(–1.1)	(–3.2)	(4.3)		
ICRG country risk index 97	0.12****		–0.02	–0.03**	0.05**	0.58	103
	(10.3)	–	(–0.4)	(–2.2)	(2.5)		
Economic freedom index	–0.16****		0.06	0.18****	–0.02	0.62	123
(higher value = freer) 99	(–11.5)	–	(1.2)	(5.2)	(–0.2)		

Notes: All variables are in logarithms. All standard errors are corrected heteroskedasticity consistent. The symbols: *, **, ***, **** indicate coefficients that are significant at the 10%, 5%, 1% and 0.1% levels, respectively. (a) Additional explanatory variable: population density; pc stands for per capita.

Source: Authors' own calculations.

The use of two different dummies was motivated by the fact that the first group started the transition somewhat earlier and has been widely recognized as having made more progress.

As a control group, the third dummy variable was added for ASEAN countries, which have been also widely perceived as relying heavily on industrial expansion during their development process.[3]

The EBRD transition indicators were not used here for the reason that they are available only for transition countries, thus are not useful for scrutinizing differences between transition countries and other countries with a similar level of development.

RESULTS

Industrial Structure

Given the preference of central planners for industry, a question is whether industry still prevails over services in today's post-communist economies in relation to their level of income. According to the 'Chenery hypothesis' (Chenery and Syrquin, 1975), sectoral growth within an economy is linked to its level of income per capita.[4] One would expect that the share of industry initially increases as a country grows richer, because the workforce typically shifts out of agriculture into the secondary sector. At high levels of income, when mainly services expand, further increases in income should not lead to higher employment in industry, and the relationship between income and employment in industry should resemble an inverted J-curve. Therefore, the square of income per capita was added to the explanatory variables in the examined regressions.

The relative importance of industry in an economy can be measured either by the share of industrial employment in total employment or by the share of industry's value added in GDP. Both indicators are used here.

Industry share in employment
The evidence on industry share in employment is strong, but only up to 1997 since the most recent available data are for the period 1990–97. Unfortunately, the most recent data available for the CEE countries are for 1994, which is still only five years after the start of transition. As Table 3.1 shows, there is a very strong correlation between GNP per capita and the share of industry in employment in the non-linear regression described above, but the transition countries clearly do not fit this line. The dummy variables for both groups of transition countries are positive and highly significant. The point estimates (between 0.5 and 1.2) indicate that the share of industry in employment in transition countries is between one and a half and more than twice as large as one would expect given their income level.

Industry share in GDP
Interestingly, the results are quite different with respect to the share of industry's value added in GDP. As illustrated in Table 3.1, the dummy variables for the

two groups of transition countries turn out to be insignificant. It is interesting to note that the dummy for ASEAN is significant, which is not the case for the industry share in employment.[5]

The results on services are not reported because they represent, as one would expect, a mirror image of those for industry: the employment share of services is clearly lower than expected for CEE countries, though not as low as for the FSU countries. As for the shares in value added, neither dummy is significant.

The difference in the results for industry shares in employment and in GDP suggests that most TEs still have a problem with structural adjustment. The number of workers in industry is still much higher than one would expect, but their productivity is relatively low, therefore the share of industry in GDP is about normal.

The legacy of the preference of central planners for *heavy* industry is more difficult to measure since it is problematical to define heavy industry precisely and since consistent cross-country data on composition of industrial output are limited. However, heavy industry in general is more energy intensive, thus its importance can be measured indirectly by the energy intensity of the economy.[6] The best indicator available in this respect is the commercial energy use, which eliminates the household consumption of energy that is more susceptible to climate. The square of income per capita is added again to the explanatory variables for the reasons outlined above. At high levels of income, that is, when only services expand, a further increase in income does not necessitate more energy consumption, hence the total relationship between income and commercial energy use resembles an inverted J-curve. The square term is highly significant, but the size and significance of the dummies for transition countries are not affected by this addition (see Table 3.1).

Here the results are unequivocal: in both groups of transition countries commercial energy usage is much higher than expected. Both dummy variables are highly significant and the magnitude of the point estimate (about 0.8–0.9) indicates that TEs consume almost twice as much energy per unit of GDP as one would expect. Could the higher use of energy be due to the large industrial sector? This does not seem to be the case. The size and the significance of the dummies for the transition countries do not change if the share of industry in value added is included. As one would expect, the share of industry in employment is not significant in predicting commercial energy use. However, it is only in this respect that the transition countries are overindustrialized (see Table 3.2).

Capital Investment

Central planners generated very high rates of investment, both in physical and in human capital.

Table 3.2   Robustness test for commercial energy use

	GNPpcPPP	GNPpc^2	Indu VA	Indu empl. (male)	CEE	FSU	ASEAN	R^2
Commercial energy use pc kg of oil equiv. 96	−2.36**** (−3.5)	0.43**** (4.6)	0.48**** (3.0)	–	0.36**** (6.0)	0.34**** (3.2)	−0.03 (−0.7)	0.81
Commercial energy use pc kg of oil equiv. 96	−1.85**** (−2.6)	0.36**** (3.9)	–	0.04 (0.3)	0.34**** (6.2)	0.36**** (3.2)	0.02 (0.5)	0.79

Note: See notes to Table 3.1.

Investment in physical capital

As a result of high investment in physical capital by central planners, TEs have inherited a vast infrastructure that depreciates very slowly, for example, roads and rail networks. The quality of the road network (proxied by the proportion of all roads that are paved[7]) and the density of the rail network (per surface area) are both closely related to income. But the countries in transition clearly constitute outliers in the sense that the dummy variables are highly significant and their point estimates suggest that they have a rail network that is at least twice as extensive as one would expect (see Table 3.1).

Investment in human capital

Human capital (measured by school enrolment rates) ranks among the most robust determinants of economic growth (Levine and Renelt, 1992). Strong investment in human capital emphasized in the past by central planners has continued. The dummies for the transition countries in regressions with gross secondary and tertiary enrolment ratios are highly significant. Their point estimates suggest that, given their income levels, countries in transition have enrolment ratios that are substantially higher than suggested by their development level.[8]

In all the cases involving the investment in infrastructure and in human capital, the dummies for ASEAN countries are not significant, suggesting that neither area of investment is particularly strong in these economies.

Financial System

Under central planning, there was no need for a financial system to allocate savings to investment. Everything was done by the plan, largely without assigning a value to time. The size of the financial sector is captured by two indicators: the ratio of M2 to GDP (a proxy measure of the size of the banking system) and the ratio of private sector credit to GDP (a proxy measure of the financing available for investment in the private sector).[9]

As shown in Table 3.1, the low M2/GDP ratio confirms the impression that transition countries are characterized by less-developed financial systems. The dummy variables for both groups are negative and significant at conventional levels. However, the size of the point estimate differs considerably. For the CEE countries, the M2/GDP ratio is about 30 per cent lower than one would expect given their level of development, whereas for the FSU the degree of monetization is less than half of what would be predicted on the basis of already low income per capita. However, it should be noted that the 1997 data used in this analysis do not incorporate the effects of the 1998 crisis in Russia.

The second indicator, credit to the private sector as a percentage of GDP, might be more relevant to measure the size of the financial sector of transition countries as it does not include financing of the government. It confirms that financial systems of the FSU countries are less developed than those of other countries with similar income levels. In this case again, the dummy for the CEE is much smaller than that for the FSU.[10]

The *efficiency* of the financial system can be assessed by the spread between lending and deposit rates. Again, the evidence is strong. In the FSU countries, this spread is significantly higher than one would expect, whereas the dummy variable for CEE is not significant.

Legal and Institutional Framework

The central planning system did not require a legal and institutional framework underpinning the market economy. Are countries in transition still different because they have not yet been able to create the institutional framework for a market economy?[11] To answer this question we evaluate the quality of this framework by looking at the scope of corruption and at various country risk indicators.

It is often argued that many countries in transition face a particularly serious corruption problem, which in turn inhibits foreign direct investment and growth. However, this is not confirmed by the data. It is difficult to measure how widespread and serious the corruption is. The only quantitative measure of corruption currently available is based on a systematic survey by Transparency International (TI). The TI corruption perception index ranks countries in terms of the degree to which corruption is perceived to exist among public officials and politicians. The latest (1999) index is available for 99 countries.

As the regression results reveal, corruption is tightly related to income. Differences in GDP per capita alone explain 60 per cent of the variability in the corruption index. However, in this relationship the transition countries do not constitute outliers. This suggests that corruption is not a problem that is *specifically* worse for transition countries.

The quality of the institutional framework can also be evaluated on the basis of various country risk indicators. Several financial and other specialized institutions provide indicators of country risk. These indicators provide a measure of risk faced by foreign investors, for example the risk of the local government interference with an expropriation, or the lack of local partners' compliance with contract. Table 3.1 presents the regression results using the indices provided by Institutional Investor, Euromoney, the International Country Risk Guide (ICRG) and the Heritage Foundation. Based on the regression of the institutional investor index, there is a strong correlation between country risk and income per capita, but a clear distinction between the two groups of transition countries emerges. The dummy for the CEE is negative and insignificant. However, it is negative and highly significant for the FSU. The regressions of the indices provided by two other institutions (Euromoney and Political Risk Services) yield similar results. The dummy for the FSU countries is always negative and significant at the one per cent level, whereas the dummy for CEE is either not significant, or marginally significant, but positive. The dummy for the ASEAN control group is always positive and significant.

The regression of the 'index of economic freedom' compiled by the Heritage Foundation yields similar results. This index attempts to measure the degree to which market forces are free to act on their own. It is again closely related to income per capita. However, the estimates obtained for the FSU countries are statistically different from what one would expect, given their low level of income. This is not the case for the CEE countries.

The most interesting aspect of these results using indicators of the quality of the institutional framework is the difference between the Central European countries, which are almost exclusively made up of EU candidates, and the FSU. For CEE countries, this aspect of transition is considered to be over, as most of them have established an institutional framework similar to the one in other market economies with comparable income levels.

CONCLUDING REMARKS

The implicitly asked question behind our analysis was: would it be possible for an economist without any access to time-series data to distinguish the former centrally planned economies among the more than 130 countries in the world? The answer seems to be yes. Even after ten years, most countries in transition are still characterized by a much higher share of employment in industry and a higher energy use than expected on the basis of their income per capita. They also have a much more extensive physical infrastructure and have a higher proportion of their population in secondary and tertiary education. However, considering indicators that measure the extent to which the institutional framework of a market economy has been put into place delivers more differentiated results. The financial and institutional framework for a market economy clearly is much weaker than one would expect for the FSU countries, whereas this is not the case for CEE. For most of the latter (that is, the ten candidates for EU membership minus Bulgaria and Romania) there is even some evidence that their framework is stronger than one would expect given their still relatively low level of income per capita. In this sense the transition is over in Central Europe. For these countries, ten years were enough to upgrade the economic software, even if the hardware is still recognizably from a different era. However, it is difficult to see why these countries should still be treated differently from other developing countries with a similar income per capita (for example, Turkey or Brazil), for example by being served by a special development bank, the EBRD. The countries in the CIS (and some from the Balkans) are clearly in a different category. They still have problems with the transition towards credible market-based institutions and financial systems. Will they need another decade to catch up?

NOTES

1. For a list of the variables used, see Appendix 3A.
2. See also Easterly (1999).
3. The *ASEAN* dummy comprises: Indonesia, Laos, Malaysia, Myanmar, the Philippines, Singapore, Thailand and Vietnam.
4. For an earlier application of this approach to Eastern Europe, but with a different focus from ours, see Döhrn and Heilemann (1991).
5. Somewhat surprisingly the results concerning the share of manufacturing in value added were different: the dummy variables for both groups of transition countries are large and highly significant. Unfortunately, no employment data are available for manufacturing.
6. It is well documented that the Soviet model of industrialization, as it had been adopted by all former CMEA countries, led to excessive energy intensity (Gray, 1995).
7. For similar evidence on the cross-country relationship between road infrastructure and income, see Querioz and Gautman (1992) and Ingram and Liu (1997). For the rail–income relationship, see also Canning (1999).
8. Besides education, health constitutes an important element of human capital. As several authors have shown (for example, Pritchett and Summers, 1996; Suhrcke, 1999) it is also closely related to per capita income across countries. Running the same regressions as above, but for various health input and output measures, reveals a very similar pattern as for the education variables: both the *CEE* and the *FSU* dummies suggest a significantly better level of health, mainly due to significantly more resources devoted to the health sector.
9. The importance of the financial sector for economic growth has been demonstrated by Levine (1997). For a similar approach to ours, see EBRD (1998).
10. Qualitatively similar results obtain for indicators measuring capital market development, such as the stock market capitalization as a share in GDP, where the point estimate of the dummy coefficients is even larger.
11. The role of the institutional framework in determining development prospects has increasingly attracted attention within the framework of the economic growth literature (Knack and Keefer, 1995).

REFERENCES

Barbone, Luca and Juan Zalduendo (1996), 'EU accession and economic growth: the challenge for Central and Eastern European countries', Policy Research Working Paper No. 1721, Washington, DC: World Bank.

Canning, David (1999), 'Infrastructure's contribution to aggregate output', Policy Research Working Paper No. 2246, Washington, DC: World Bank.

Central Intelligence Agency (1998), *The World Factbook 1998*, Washington, DC.

Chenery, Hollis B. and Moshe Syrquin (1975), *Patterns of Development 1950–1970*, Oxford: Oxford University Press.

Dabla-Norris, Era and Scott Freeman (1999), 'The enforcement of property rights and underdevelopment', IMF Working Paper, WP/99/127, Washington, DC: IMF.

Döhrn, Roland and Ullrich Heilemann (1991), 'Sectoral change in Eastern Europe: the Chenery hypothesis reconsidered', RWI Paper No. 25, Essen, Germany: Rheinisch–Westfälisches Institut für Wirtschaftsforschung.

Easterly, William (1999), 'Life during growth: international evidence on quality of life and per capita income', Policy Research Working Paper No. 2110, Washington, DC: World Bank.

EBRD (1998), Transition Report, London, UK.

Fischer, Stanley, Ratna Sahay and Carlos A. Végh (1997), 'From transition to market: evidence and growth prospects', in Salvatore Zecchini (ed.), *Lessons from the Economic Transition: Central and Eastern Europe in the 1990s*, Dordrecht, The Netherlands: Kluwer, pp. 79–101.

Fischer, Stanley, Ratna Sahay and Carlos A. Végh (1998), 'How far is Eastern Europe from Brussels?', IMF Working Paper WP/98/53, Washington, DC: IMF.

Gray, David A. (1995), 'Reforming the energy sector in transition economies: selected experiences and lessons', World Bank Discussion Paper No. 296, Washington, DC: World Bank.

Ingram, Gregory K. and Zhi Liu (1997), 'Motorization and road provision in countries and cities', Policy Research Working Paper No. 1842, Washington, DC: World Bank.

International Road Federation (1998), *World Road Statistics 1998*, Geneva.

Johnson, Bryan T., Kim R. Holmes and Melanie Kirkpatrick (eds) (1999), *1999 Index of Economic Freedom*, Washington, DC: The Heritage Foundation and The Wall Street Journal.

Knack, Steven and Philip E. Keefer (1995), 'Institutions and economic performance: cross-country tests using alternative institutional measures', *Economics and Politics*, **7** (3), 207–27.

Krkoska, Libor (1999), 'A neoclassical growth model applied to transition in Central Europe', *Journal of Comparative Economics*, **27** (2), 259–80.

Levine, Ross (1997), 'Financial development and economic growth: views and agenda', *Journal of Economic Literature*, **35** (4), 688–726.

Levine, Ross and David Renelt (1992), 'A sensitivity analysis of cross-country growth regressions', *American Economic Review*, **82** (4), 924–63.

Pritchett, Lant and Lawrence H. Summers (1996), 'Wealthier is healthier', *Journal of Human Resources*, **31** (4), 841–68.

Querioz, Christina and Steven Gautman (1992), 'Road infrastructure and economic development: some diagnostic indicators', Policy Research Working Paper No. 921, Washington, DC: World Bank.

Suhrcke, Marc (1999), 'Economic growth in the transition economies of Central and Eastern Europe', PhD thesis, University of Hamburg.

Transparency International (1999), TI Corruption Perception Index at www.transparency.de.

World Bank (1999), World Development Indicators, Washington DC.

Uneven reforms – unbalanced growth

APPENDIX 3A   LIST OF VARIABLES

World Bank Data

Male employment in industry as share in male labour force, 1990–97
Female employment in industry as share in female labour force, 1990–97
Industry value added as share in GDP, 1997
Manufacturing value added as share in GDP, 1997
Commercial energy use pc kg of oil equivalent, 1996
Gross secondary school enrolment 1996
Gross tertiary school enrolment 1996

Infrastructure

Paved roadnet (km of paved roads per km^2 of country size) 1996 (International
Road Federation, 1998)
Railnet (km of rail per km^2 of country size) 1996 (CIA, 1998)

Financial Sector (based on International Financial Statistics from the IMF)

M2 as a share in GDP, 1997
Credit to private sector as share of GDP, 1997
Interest rate spread: the rate charged by banks on loans to prime customers
minus the interest rate paid on deposits, 1997

Institutional Framework for Market Economy

Corruption Index 1998 (Transparency International 1999)
Euromoney country credit-worthiness rating, September 1997 (World Bank,
1999)
Institutional Investor credit rating, September 1997 (World Bank, 1999)
Composite International Country Risk Guide (ICRG) rating, December 1997
(World Bank, 1999)
Index of Economic Freedom 1999 (Johnson et al., 1999)

4. What are the chances of catching up with the European Union?

Andrew M. Warner[1]

INTRODUCTION AND SUMMARY

Whether transition economies eventually catch up to European income levels probably depends both on the economic policies they follow as well as possible natural obstacles to high incomes. In this chapter I examine the following two questions. Based on the best-available evidence as of the end of 1999, is the transition region currently on a path to convergence with the economies of the European Union (EU)? Second, is there evidence that the process is influenced by geographic obstacles to development that we observe in the rest of the world?

What does convergence mean in this context? At one level, it is simply the question of whether transition countries or regions are growing faster than the EU region. The answer for the entire transition region as a whole is no. Surprisingly, the data show that the answer even for the Central European sub-region is now no, although it was yes a few years ago. But the answer for particular countries is yes. I show evidence for this in the first part of this chapter (particularly Table 4.5).

Transition has led to a U-shaped pattern of GDP over time in many countries. Furthermore, in some countries output is still declining. How should we think of convergence in this context? Obviously, convergence did not happen during the downswing of the U and is not now happening in countries with declining output. This is a trivial statement that should not need further analysis.

What is more interesting is whether there are the glimmerings of convergence in the upswing of the U for those countries that have recovered. I look at whether the growth rates in the recovery phase are high enough to achieve convergence in the first sense of the word, and the answer is yes. But I also look for evidence of convergence in a stricter sense. Specifically, is there evidence that the group of countries in the recovery phase have embarked on a growth path where the poorer of this group are growing faster than the richer of this group? In other words, is there evidence that the relatively poor transition economies (TEs) such as Armenia are now growing faster than the relatively richer countries such as the Czech Republic and Hungary, after controlling for other variables? If so, we may be able to say that the group is converging within itself in addition to converging towards Europe. I show evidence on this in the regressions in Table 4.17. But the important point is that this result only emerges from the data after taking into account that the TEs have different long-run output levels.

When speaking about convergence, it is helpful to ask: convergence to what level? Do we really believe that all the TEs will converge on the same income levels if they adopt equally pro-market and pro-growth reforms? Or is it more correct to think that some other limiting factors will play a role eventually, driving a wedge between the transition group?

To answer this question, there is obviously no evidence from the future of transition countries so I bring in international evidence. The international evidence from countries that have not been under communism for extended periods is that tropical, remote and mountainous countries have significantly lower GDP per capita than countries without these characteristics. One may wish to debate whether these characteristics will be as highly correlated with growth in the future as they have been in the past, but there is no denying the fact that such countries have lower incomes now. For example, the list of landlocked countries today that have not been under Soviet central planning would include Jordan, Lesotho, Bolivia, Burkina Faso, Zimbabwe, Malawi, Mali, Central African Republic, Rwanda, Zambia, Uganda and Burundi. All of these have rather low incomes. Maybe these countries are poor for other reasons, but the fact that all of them are relatively poor makes this difficult to sustain. Switzerland, Luxembourg and some other smaller states in Europe are the only cases of relatively rich landlocked states.

Why should geography and climate affect economic growth and income? Perhaps the reason most relevant for TEs is that it makes export-led growth more difficult to achieve, because of transport costs. It frustrates one path to higher incomes that has been shown to work in other developing countries. Some would argue further that export-led growth is the only viable path for low-income developing countries. We should also expect great distances to impede technology transfer, and thus frustrate one of the growth channels emphasized by other authors such as Gomulka (1970, 1990 and Chapter 5, in this volume). Exporting probably facilitates technology transfer and vice versa.

Here I assume that the long-run income gaps between TEs and Europe will replicate the currently observed income gaps between geographically poor and geographically rich countries. This may be too pessimistic. New technologies may diminish the geographic penalties we have observed in the past. Nevertheless, I use this assumption to see what it implies for the transition countries.

The results suggest that geographical considerations do not help explain which countries have been successful during the first ten years of transition, but they do help explain the recent growth of countries that have achieved a recovery. In other words, geographic penalties did not play a role in earlier years but they have appeared more recently.

It should not be surprising that growth since the start of the transition is not strongly related to geographical attributes. The chaos of the transition in early years, the macroeconomic crisis, and the collapse of the state enterprises sector are not closely linked to geography. Ukraine has a relatively favourable geography in terms of distance to major markets and sea-lanes and yet has suffered one of the most severe output declines. In contrast, the output declines in remote Uzbekistan and Kazakhstan have been smaller than in Ukraine. In addition, reform effort is not strongly related to geography and yet it is one of the strongest determinants of growth performance. Remote Kyrgyz Republic is one of the more determined reform countries while less-remote Ukraine and Belarus are poor reformers.

If geography plays a role, it appears to play a role instead in the recovery phase of transition. I look at countries that have achieved positive growth for at least the three most recent years, and measure growth since the year in which output was lowest. This sample excludes countries such as Russia and Ukraine that have never achieved sustained positive growth, and Romania where output has declined recently.

Growth of this sample of countries in the recovery phase appears negatively correlated with their starting income and positively correlated with their geographic potential. Thus there is some evidence for catch-up within the transition group. But there is also evidence that countries are converging not to similar income levels, but to different income levels or 'income ceilings' defined by their geographical attributes.

To put this last point more concretely, Estonia is now rather poor (approximately 27 per cent of the EU level) and yet it is favourably situated in geographic terms (based on geography considerations, it could achieve 100 per cent of the EU average). Therefore Estonia is a long way from its geographically defined potential (the gap between actual and potential income under this definition is –73). On the other hand Tajikistan is now about 5 per cent of the EU average but because it is so remote its geographic-based potential is only 13 per cent of the EU average. Therefore its income gap is only about –8.

The regression result (Table 4.17 and Figure 4.2) is that recent growth is explained by the actual gap with Europe (the 27 and 5) and the income ceiling (the 100 and 13). But it is also explained more simply by the difference between these two (the –73 and –5 figures). In words, the regression result says that Tajikistan has only achieved 2.25 growth recently because it is already rather close to its long-term potential, while Estonia has achieved a much faster growth because it is still far from its long-term potential. There is evidence that TEs are converging to different long-run income levels.

My feeling is that these results overstate the long-run geographic penalties, but any adjustment I could make would be arbitrary so I leave the results as they stand. One reason for thinking there is some exaggeration is that three countries have actually 'surpassed' their long-run potential – Kazakhstan, Uzbekistan and the Kyrgyz Republic (although by only a small amount). Another cautionary note is the case of the Kyrgyz Republic. It has fairly high scores on the reform index and has been growing fairly rapidly in recent years. It is an exception to the general rule that recent growth is related to the gap between actual and potential income (see Figure 4.2 for confirmation).

The rest of this chapter contains a more detailed explanation of these results. The suggestions about the negative impacts of geographic limits are tentative, and should not be taken to deny the importance of voluntary actions. If further confirmation is needed about the positive effect of market-orientated reform on growth, note Figure 4.1, or Fischer and Sahay (Chapter 1 in this volume). But over longer horizons, international evidence suggests that both voluntary actions and natural limits will together determine the economic future of the transition countries.

RECENT FACTS ON CONVERGENCE OF TRANSITION COUNTRIES

In Table 4.1, I start with the historical evidence that suggests that the Central European ex-socialist countries do not face deep structural barriers to convergence with the West. Poland in 1955 had a per capita income higher than Greece, and about 70 per cent of the Spanish level. Hungary had virtually the same per capita income as Greece in 1935 and 1955. Czechoslovakia's income was 82 per cent of Austria's in 1935.

The wide economic gap that emerged during 40 years of Soviet-style socialism hardly needs further confirmation, but note from Table 4.1 that the economic distance between East and West Europe is still quite large. At the end of 1998 Poland's per capita GDP was 40 per cent of the Spanish level and 50 per cent of the Greek level. Hungary now is 55 per cent of Greece, and the Czech Republic now is 47 per cent of Austria. Even the richest of the Central European countries fell far behind during the socialist years. Six years of strong growth has closed the gap between Poland and Spain from 34 to 41 per cent. But Poland is the country with the greatest success so far. The other two large Central European countries have made only modest progress in convergence.

Table 4.2 shows similar data for all of the TEs and Europe, not just Central Europe. The table reports real GDP per person, adjusted for differences in international purchasing power. Europe is defined as the 15 EU countries minus

Luxembourg (hereafter EU-14), which has unusually high income due to special tax and banking legislation. By the end of 1998, the EU-14 average was 20,152 USD. At the end of 1998, the richest of the Central European countries was Slovenia, at 62 per cent of this level. The Czech Republic was at 52 per cent, and then there was a large drop-off. Hungary was 36 per cent, Poland was 33 per cent. The Baltic countries, Bulgaria and Belarus were between 20 and 30 per cent. Russia and Romania were 20 per cent. Kazakhstan was 16 per cent, Georgia 10 per cent, Turkmenistan 7 per cent and Tajikistan, the poorest, 4.5 per cent.

Table 4.1   Historical levels of GDP in Central and Western Europe (1990 dollars per capita)

	1935	1955	1970	1992	1998
Poland	1,597	2,788	4,428	5,038	6,774
Spain	2,792	3,995	7,291	14,767	16,412
Ratio: Poland/Spain	*0.57*	*0.7*	*0.61*	*0.34*	*0.41*
Hungary	2,471	2,480	5,028	6,636	7,450
Greece	2,526	2,560	6,327	12,607	13,504
Ratio: Hungary/Greece	*0.98*	*0.97*	*0.79*	*0.53*	*0.55*
Czechoslovakia (Czech Rep.)	2,410	3,922	6,460	10,220	10,820
Austria	2,926	5,087	9,813	21,029	22,896
Ratio: Czech/Austria	*0.82*	*0.77*	*0.66*	*0.49*	*0.47*

Sources: Maddison, 1996, and author's estimates.

For comparisons across all of the TEs, there is no practical alternative than to use these official figures.[2] Nevertheless, it is worth seeing how the numbers would change if we used alternative estimates. The two main sources of bias in the official numbers are the underrecording of new economic activities and the use of prices from earlier periods which place too high a weight to older, established industries. Suppose we revised the GDP numbers upward to account for hidden economic activity. Table 4.3 shows adjustments to the income gap with Europe based on the estimated share of the unofficial economy. The share of the unofficial economy in GDP is taken from Table 1 of Johnson et al. (1997, p. 183), who in turn rely on previous work by Gray (1995), Freund and Wallich (1995) and Kaufmann and Kaliberda (1996). It should be noted that, if anything, the adjustments in Table 4.3 probably *underestimate* the true income gap because Europe is assumed to have zero unofficial activity. Despite this, the gaps remain large.

Table 4.2   GDP per capita in the EU and the TEs, 1998

	GDP per capita (USD)	EU-14 average (%)
Austria	22,896	114
Belgium	23,689	118
Denmark	23,192	115
Finland	20,216	100
France	22,530	112
Germany	22,152	110
Greece	13,504	67
Ireland	19,928	99
Italy	20,502	102
Netherlands	22,160	110
Portugal	14,540	72
Spain	16,412	81
Sweden	19,560	97
United Kingdom	20,850	103
EU-14 average	20,152	100
Albania	2,420	12
Armenia	2,403	12
Azerbaijan	1,707	8
Belarus	5,285	26
Bulgaria	4,176	20
Croatia	4,663	23
Czech Republic	10,678	52
Estonia	5,484	27
Georgia	2,113	10
Hungary	7,434	36
Kazakhstan	3,227	16
Kyrgyz Republic	2,206	11
Latvia	4,163	20
Lithuania	5,000	24
Macedonia	3,060	15
Moldova, Republic of	1,334	6
Poland	6,716	33
Romania	3,975	19
Russian Federation	4,058	20
Slovak Republic	8,274	40

Table 4.2   continued

	GDP per capita (USD)	EU-14 average (%)
Slovenia	13,173	64
Tajikistan	941	5
Turkmenistan	1,514	7
Ukraine	2,153	10
Uzbekistan	2,522	12

Sources: GDP data are adjusted for purchasing power parity in the World Development Reports of the World Bank. 1996 GDP estimates are combined with real growth rates from national sources and IMF data to generate consistent GDP data across time and countries.

Table 4.3   Estimates of GDP per capita after adjusting for the unofficial economy, 1998

	Adjusted GDP per capita (USD)*	EU-14 average (%)
Albania	–	–
Armenia	–	–
Azerbaijan	4,333	21
Belarus	6,549	32
Bulgaria	6,546	32
Croatia	–	–
Czech Republic	12,039	58
Estonia	6,218	30
Georgia	5,649	27
Hungary	10,470	51
Kazakhstan	4,911	24
Kyrgyz Republic	–	–
Latvia	6,434	31
Lithuania	6,377	31
Macedonia	–	–
Moldova, Republic of	2,074	10
Poland	7,685	37
Romania	4,914	24
Russian Federation	6,948	34
Slovak Republic	9,689	47
Slovenia	–	–

Table 4.3   continued

	Adjusted GDP per capita (USD)*	EU-14 average (%)
Tajikistan	–	–
Turkmenistan	–	–
Ukraine	4,213	20
Uzbekistan	2,698	13

Notes:
* Adjustment is based on the relation: GDP(true) * (1-black) = GDP(measured), where 'black' is the per cent of the true economy in the black market.
The following countries have no reliable estimates of the unofficial economy: Albania, Armenia, Croatia, the Kyrgyz Republic, Macedonia, Slovenia, Tajikistan and Turkmenistan.

Source: Johnson et al. (1997, Table 1, p. 183), who in turn rely on previous work by Gray (1995), Freund and Wallich (1995) and Kauffman and Kaliberda (1996).

The adjusted estimates in Table 4.3 suggest that the Czech Republic would be 59 per cent of the EU-14 average, Hungary 52 per cent, Russia 33 per cent and Kazakhstan 24 per cent. In one of the largest changes, Azerbaijan's income gap with Europe would change from 8 to 21 per cent. Nevertheless, while the adjustments do occasionally close the estimated income gaps significantly, they do not change the basic fact that the income gaps between East and West remain quite large.

The previous tables showed that the income gaps are fairly large, even after adjusting for unofficial activity. The next tables show that, according to the most recently recorded growth rates, the gaps are not closing rapidly, and are even growing in some cases.

Table 4.4 contains the most recently recorded growth rates, the average for the last three years (1996–98) and the most recent year with comprehensive data (1998), both for the EU and the TEs. The table shows that Europe is growing at about 2.5 per cent per year. At the latest count, 12 of the 29 TEs are not even converging, with growth that falls short of this rate. Some TEs continue to decline, notably Turkmenistan at negative 12 per cent. Thirteen of the 29 TEs have grown more rapidly than the European average over this period.

If we focus on average growth of all the TEs and all the EU-14 countries, Table 4.4 shows that in 1998 average growth in the TEs was 2.6 per cent. Over the three-year period 1996–98 it was 2.1 per cent. Over the same two periods the EU grew at 3.2 per cent (1998) and 2.8 per cent (1996–98). Does this mean that the entire transition region has been falling behind Europe?

These figures treat all countries equally, no matter how large or small, and are thus potentially misleading indicators of regional averages. However, the

Table 4.4   Growth of GDP per capita , TEs and EU economies

	1996–1998	1998 (most recent year)
Albania	1.9	7.0
Armenia	5.7	7.6
Azerbaijan	4.8	9.2
Belarus	7.5	8.3
Bulgaria	−4.4	4.4
Croatia	5.1	2.1
Czech Republic	0.7	−2.2
Estonia	7.5	5.1
Georgia	9.3	3.9
Hungary	3.9	5.4
Kazakhstan	0.2	−2.3
Kyrgyz Republic	6.3	1.8
Latvia	6.2	5.4
Lithuania	6.2	5.6
Macedonia	1.0	2.2
Moldova, Republic of	−5.1	−8.6
Poland	5.9	4.8
Romania	−3.3	−7.0
Russian Federation	−2.1	−4.3
Slovak Republic	5.7	4.3
Slovenia	4.0	4.0
Tajikistan	−0.4	4.0
Turkmenistan	−11.9	3.3
Ukraine	−4.4	−1.1
Uzbekistan	1.0	1.9
Austria	2.4	3.2
Belgium	2.3	2.8
Denmark	2.5	2.4
Finland	4.5	4.7
France	1.9	2.7
Germany	2.0	2.7
Greece	2.6	3.3
Ireland	8.4	8.7
Italy	1.3	1.5
Luxembourg	0.9	1.1
Netherlands	2.9	3.1
Portugal	3.8	3.9
Spain	3.2	3.7
Sweden	1.7	2.6
United Kingdom	2.2	1.2

Source: As in Table 4.2.

Uneven reforms – unbalanced growth

same conclusion of no overall convergence emerges if we combine the countries
and look at larger regional economic blocs. Table 4.5 shows GDP per capita and
annual growth rates for four regional blocs: former Soviet Union (FSU);
European TEs; the EU; and three Southern European countries.[3]

Table 4.5   Regional GDP and growth

	European TEs	FSU region	EU-15	Southern European 3*
GDP per capita				
1989	6,475	6,440	–	–
1990	6,101	6,214	–	–
1991	5,415	5,769	–	–
1992	5,245	4,680	18,642	13,781
1993	5,300	4,164	18,463	13,569
1994	5,516	3,608	18,944	13,829
1995	5,835	3,450	19,334	14,177
1996	6,053	3,351	19,642	14,529
1997	6,190	3,401	20,134	15,029
1998	6,302	3,330	20,643	15,582
Growth				
1989				
1990	–5.8	–3.5	–	–
1991	–11.2	–7.2	–	–
1992	–3.1	–18.9	–	–
1993	1.0	–11.0	–1.0	–1.5
1994	4.1	–13.4	2.6	1.9
1995	5.8	–4.4	2.1	2.5
1996	3.7	–2.9	1.6	2.5
1997	2.3	1.5	2.5	3.4
1998	1.8	–2.1	2.5	3.7

Note: * See note 3 for definitions.

Source: As in Table 4.2.

Table 4.5 confirms that the entire region has not been converging in recent
years. Indeed, during the first ten years of transition, regional convergence has
only ever occurred in the Central European countries and even then for only
three years – 1994, 1995 and 1996. In 1997 and 1998 this region actually fell
further behind Europe. The FSU region has yet to record a single year with a

faster growth rate than Europe. Therefore the recent data show some slowing-down in the rate of convergence; some of the gains of mid-decade were reversed in 1997 and 1998.

Turning to individual countries, Table 4.6 shows that Poland's share of regional GDP has risen dramatically, at the expense of Russia and the FSU countries. All observers are aware of these trends, but not perhaps of the exact numbers. In 1991 it would have taken five Polands to equal Russia's GDP. By 1998 it would take only two. In 1991 Poland was a little smaller than Ukraine; now it is more than twice the size.

Table 4.6   Share of each country in total output of TEs

	1991	1998
Albania	0.3	0.5
Armenia	0.7	0.5
Azerbaijan	1.2	0.8
Belarus	3.0	3.3
Bulgaria	1.9	2.1
Croatia	0.9	1.3
Czech Republic	4.5	6.7
Estonia	0.4	0.5
Georgia	1.0	0.7
Hungary	3.0	4.6
Kazakhstan	3.5	3.3
Kyrgyz Republic	0.7	0.6
Latvia	0.7	0.6
Lithuania	1.1	1.1
Macedonia	0.4	0.4
Moldova, Republic of	0.7	0.4
Poland	8.1	15.8
Romania	4.3	5.4
Russian Federation	45.6	36.2
Slovak Republic	1.7	2.7
Slovenia	1.0	1.6
Tajikistan	0.6	0.3
Turkmenistan	0.6	0.4
Ukraine	11.5	6.6
Uzbekistan	3.0	3.6

Source: Author's calculations.

Table 4.7 compares recent growth rates in each of the TEs with the European average. The calculations are based on 1996–98 as well as the most recently available (1998) average growth rates. For those countries with faster growth than the European average we show the number of years required to close to within 75 per cent of future European income levels, *based on the currently observed growth rates of each country and of Europe as a whole*. For example, if Armenia continues to grow at 5.7 per cent per annum and Europe continues to grow at 2.4 per cent, then it will take Armenia 57 years to close its income gap from the current level of 12 per cent to the target level of 75 per cent. This calculation is of course not performed for those countries with growth rates below Europe because they are not on a path to convergence.

Table 4.7   Number of years to close to within 75 per cent of EU-14 income (based on 1996–98 and 1998 growth rates)

	Current gap (1998)	Growth (96–98)	Growth of EU-14 (96–98)	Years to close to 75% (96–98 growth rates)	Growth (1998)	Growth of EU-14 (1998)	Years to close to 75% (1998 growth rates)
Albania	12	1.9	2.4	–	7.0	2.5	42
Armenia	12	5.7	2.4	57	7.6	2.5	37
Azerbaijan	8	4.8	2.4	93	9.2	2.5	33
Belarus	26	7.5	2.4	21	8.3	2.5	19
Bulgaria	20	–4.4	2.4	–	4.4	2.5	71
Croatia	23	5.1	2.4	44	2.1	2.5	–
Czech Republic	52	0.7	2.4	–	–2.2	2.5	–
Estonia	27	7.5	2.4	20	5.1	2.5	40
Georgia	10	9.3	2.4	29	3.9	2.5	141
Hungary	36	3.9	2.4	48	5.4	2.5	26
Kazakhstan	16	0.2	2.4	–	–2.3	2.5	–
Kyrgyz Republic	11	6.3	2.4	49	1.8	2.5	–
Latvia	20	6.2	2.4	34	5.4	2.5	46
Lithuania	24	6.2	2.4	29	5.6	2.5	37
Macedonia	15	1.0	2.4	–	2.2	2.5	–
Moldova, Rep. of	6	–5.1	2.4	–	–8.6	2.5	–
Poland	33	5.9	2.4	24	4.8	2.5	36
Romania	19	–3.3	2.4	–	–7.0	2.5	–
Russian Federation	20	–2.1	2.4	–	–4.3	2.5	–
Slovak Republic	40	5.7	2.4	19	4.3	2.5	36
Slovenia	64	4.0	2.4	10	4.0	2.5	11
Tajikistan	5	–0.4	2.4	–	4.0	2.5	190
Turkmenistan	7	–11.9	2.4	–	3.3	2.5	290
Ukraine	10	–4.4	2.4	–	–1.1	2.5	–
Uzbekistan	12	1.0	2.4	–	1.9	2.5	–

Source: Author's estimates.

Of the 25 TEs, 13 were on a path to convergence according to 1996–98 growth. A slightly higher number, 15, were on a path to convergence according to 1998 growth rates. In either case, we can say that slightly more than one-half of TEs are converging. This evidence can be reconciled with the earlier evidence that *regions* are not converging by noting that several larger economies are not converging, such as Russia, the Czech Republic, Romania and Ukraine.

At current growth rates, convergence to even a modest goal such as 75 per cent of average European income will be a matter of decades. At the top of the list, Slovenia is already close to this goal and might pull it off in as little as ten years (Table 4.7). But even other well-known success stories such as Poland will require 24 years, and that is only if it can maintain growth at 5.7 per cent per annum. Azerbaijan, growing at 4.8 per cent per annum, is 93 years away.

If growth rates were accelerating, there would be grounds for more optimism about these convergence times, but we have seen that for the region as a whole, growth is not accelerating (Table 4.5). Nevertheless, there are some isolated countries, which show some evidence of acceleration in growth. If Azerbaijan can continue to grow at its 1998 rate of 9.2 per cent, its convergence time would be cut from 93 years to 33 years (Table 4.7).

In general, these convergence times are a function of two things, current income levels and the difference in growth relative to Europe. It is worth noting, however, that small differences in growth rates can make a big difference. Table 4.8 shows a matrix of convergence times based on various starting points and growth rates. By reading from left to right across the columns, note that the difference between a 3 and a 5 per cent growth rate can be huge. At 3 per cent growth, convergence is a matter of centuries; at 5 per cent growth it is at least only a matter of decades. If convergence with the West is a serious goal, 3 per cent growth is simply not sufficient.

Table 4.8 *Years required to reach 75 per cent of EU income (assumed EU growth = 2.5)*

GDP (% of EU-14)	Growth rate (%)							
	3	4	5	6	7	8	9	10
5	542	181	108	77	60	49	42	36
10	403	134	81	58	45	37	31	27
20	264	88	53	38	29	24	20	18
30	183	61	37	26	20	17	14	12
40	126	42	25	18	14	11	10	8
60	45	15	9	6	5	4	3	3

Source: Author's estimates.

To summarize, the evidence above from the first decade of transition is that convergence has happened for a few countries and time periods, but not generally for larger regions and not at rates that will make for a rapid return to European standards of living. The real question continues to be whether the transition region can grow rapidly enough to close the gap in a significant way. Mechanically, if countries can achieve a growth rate of 7 per cent per annum, that is consistent with doubling the income levels every decade, which is about the range of growth that countries need for the historical legacy of 40 or 70 lost years to be overcome. The good news is that many countries in the world, countries that are at similar income levels, are indeed achieving growth rates consistently of 7 per cent and even higher per annum.

The problem is that transition countries could get used to a fairly comfortable pace. Europe is growing at 2 or 3 per cent per annum. Growth of 4 per cent per annum is not bad, it is the beginning of what is needed, but it is hardly what is really necessary to overcome the historical legacy of Soviet socialism in a serious way.

TESTING FOR CONVERGENCE

This chapter now turns to regression results to answer the following questions about convergence. Is there evidence based on the first ten years of experience that TEs *can* converge to European income levels? By now it is clear that whether countries *will* converge to European income levels depends in part on the economic actions they take, since a lot of research has shown that growth is related to the extent of economic reforms. I intend to test for and estimate the impact of reform on convergence in two senses. First, reform may simply permit TEs to grow faster than the European average. Testing for this involves seeing whether the reform indicators enter growth regressions significantly. Second, reform may enable TEs to embark on a more general growth path where the poorer of the reforming transition countries grow faster than the relatively richer TEs. Testing for this involves seeing whether after controlling for reform, growth rates are inversely related to starting income levels.

As mentioned previously, a number of studies have pointed out the positive association between reform and growth among TEs, and we shall present new results in this regard only in the sense that we use a longer sample (through the end of 1998, see Figure 4.1, below). Nevertheless, the positive relation between reform and growth, and the positive relation between reform and other indicators of human welfare, is worth repeating because it is sometimes ignored in otherwise valuable studies. A recent report of the United Nations Development Programme (UNDP, 1999), puts much of the responsibility on the economic reform strategy: too much too fast in introducing capitalism, when gradual and sequential steps were needed. The results, says the report, were economic collapse coupled with social disaster, such as rising mortality and sharp declines in life expectancy, especially of middle-aged men caught in the economic turmoil.

As useful as the UNDP report is in drawing our attention to the deep social and health crisis gripping Russia and many of its neighbours, it is deeply flawed in its economic and historical analysis. It charges that overly rapid economic reforms are to blame for the region's crisis, while failing to note that it is precisely the countries that made the fastest transition to capitalism – Poland, Slovenia, Estonia and Hungary at the very top of the list – that are the greatest successes.

While it is important not to forget the positive relation between reform and growth, this result can lend itself to an optimistic assessment, which is not obviously correct. Although some reforming TEs may now be growing at rates far above the European average, this does not prove that they will eventually obtain parity with European income levels even if they continue on the reform path. They may eventually run up against geographic obstacles to full income convergence such as remoteness from markets, geographic barriers to trans-portation, or climate. Some of the current international evidence suggests that the remote transition countries of Central Asia may never achieve full parity with Europe.

For this reason, I shall also try to test the impact of these natural features on the rate of convergence and on the long-run income levels of transition countries. I suspect that the correct answer to the convergence question involves a role for both economic reform and geography.

Before turning to the regression results, I describe briefly the data on reform and geography.

DATA

Reform Variables

There are a number of sources for reform indicators in TEs. De Melo et al. (1996) provide indicators based on discussions with World Bank country economists. The European Bank for Reconstruction and Development presents annual indicators in the various issues of the 'Transition Reports'.[4] The Heritage Foundation provides indicators for ten aspects of 'economic freedom', for a large number of countries, including the transition countries.[5] The *Central European Economic Review* published measures of reform for the years 1995–97, based on the advice of a panel of experts,[6] and Freedom House publishes measures of political freedom.[7] Several authors have examined these rankings and have concluded that experts generally agree on the extent of reform in various countries.[8] We rely on this judgement and therefore concentrate on the first two sources for our measures of reform.

At least two further papers merge the first two of these indicators together to form a continuous reform indicator for each country. These papers are Berg et al. (1999) and Havrylyshin et al. (1998). I follow their merging procedure.[9]

The merging runs as follows. De Melo, Denizer, and Gelb (hereafter DDG) have three indicators: an internal liberalization indicator (LII), which measures liberalization of domestic prices and pro-competition policy; an external liberalization indicator (LIE), which measures trade liberalization and removal of foreign exchange restrictions; and a private sector conditions indicator (LIP), which measures privatization and banking reform. The EBRD has seven indicators: large-scale privatization, small-scale privatization, enterprise restructuring, banking reform, price liberalization, competition policy, and trade and foreign exchange system. The DDG indicators are available roughly from 1989 through 1995, and the EBRD indicators have been available since 1994.

Since the two sets of indicators overlap for two years (1994–95) one can estimate panel regressions that estimate the link between the DDG indicators and the EBRD indicators. This is done by pairing the LII index with the large-scale privatization index, small scale privatization, enterprise restructuring, and banking reform index; the LIE index with the trade and foreign exchange indicators; and the LIP index with the price liberalization, and competition policy indicators. Then the estimated coefficients from these regressions can be used along with the EBRD indicators to extend the three DDG indicators forward in time. I took an average of the three for an overall reform variable.

Table 4.9 shows the reform indexes for each transition country at the start of the transition in the early 1990s. The range of the index is 0 (no reform) to 1 (maximum reform). Since countries started the transition in different years, I have attempted to measure the reform index in the first year in which the dominant policy choice for that country was first followed. Usually this is the first full year after independence or the first full year after holding elections. In one case, Georgia, it is the first full year after the fighting in the civil war subsided, a new constitution was passed and a president was elected under the new constitution.

The reason for measuring reform as early as possible in the transition is that I shall use this variable for regressions of reform on growth and I want to guarantee as much as possible that the reform indicator is measured prior to growth, so as to avoid causality from growth to reform. These reform indexes typically do not change dramatically over time so that these initial values are fair proxies for the reform stance over the full period. This is less true for two countries, Bulgaria and Romania, which changed policies in the 1990s. For Bulgaria I decided that the 1993 value was more representative of the overall

Table 4.9   Reform indexes at the start of transition (1 = maximum reform)

	Year in which main policy path was first implemented	Reason for choosing that year	Reform index in that year	Reform index in 1992
Albania	1993	Democrats won elections in 1992	0.70	0.66
Armenia	1992	Year after independence	0.39	0.39
Azerbaijan	1992	Year after independence	0.25	0.25
Belarus	1992	Year after Minsk accords dissolved the Soviet Union	0.20	0.20
Bulgaria	1993	Elections in October 1991, but elected government lost power one year later 1993 policy decisions set the precedent for the next five years	0.66	0.86
Croatia	1992	Year after secession from Yugoslavia	0.72	0.72
Czech Republic	1991	Year after June 1990 elections in which Civic Union and Public Against Violence won elections	0.79	0.86
Estonia	1992	Year after independence	0.64	0.64
Georgia	1996	Year after Shevardnadze won elections under new constitution ending civil war	0.61	0.32
Hungary	1991	Year after free elections	0.74	0.78
Kazakhstan	1992	Year after presidential election	0.35	0.35
Kyrgyz Republic	1993	Year after Akayev started to implement reform programme	0.60	0.33
Latvia	1992	Year after independence	0.51	0.51
Lithuania	1993	Year after 1992 free elections ended political and constitutional deadlock	0.78	0.55
Macedonia	1992	Independence declared in January 1992	0.68	0.68
Moldova, Rep. of	1992	Year reforms implemented after December 1991 elections	0.38	0.38
Poland	1990	Year of reforms under Mazowiecki government	0.72	0.82
Romania	1991	Year after anti-Ceauşescu communists consolidated power	0.36	0.45
Russian Federation	1992	Year after failed 1991 coup	0.49	0.49
Slovak Republic	1991	Year after June 1990 elections in which Civic Union and Public Against Violence won elections	0.79	0.86
Slovenia	1992	Year after secession from Yugoslavia	0.78	0.78
Tajikistan	1992	Year after independence	0.20	0.20
Turkmenistan	1992	Year after independence	0.13	0.13
Ukraine	1992	Year after independence	0.23	0.23
Uzbekistan	1992	Year after independence	0.26	0.26

Source: Reform index is taken from data in Havrylyshyn et al. (1998), who in turn rely on de Melo et al. (1996) for the years 1990–93 and the indicators in the EBRD's transition reports thereafter.

policy stance rather than the 1992 value. For comparative purposes, I also show in Table 4.9 what the value of the reform index would be if we instead adopted a common rule and measured each country's policy stance in the same year (1992).

Geography Variables

In order to estimate a 'geographic penalty' for each country I use regression estimates based on worldwide data from Warner (1999). (See Appendix Table 4A.1.) These regressions estimated the extent to which the log of GDP per capita in 1990 was affected by a number of geographic and climate variables. From a larger list of variables, I found that three helped explain lower income levels: tropical climate, distance of the centre of the country to a major navigable river or coastline, and mountainous terrain. Since the transition countries have not been market economies for years they were assumed to have been driven by different economic laws and thus were not included in this estimation.

For each of the TEs I measured the same geographical variables. I then multiplied these by the estimated regression coefficients and did the same for the 14 EU countries. This provided me with a 'predicted' income gap for each of the TEs *vis-à-vis* the EU. I normalized the data so that a value of 100 would mean no geographic penalty *vis-à-vis* Europe, and a value below 100 would indicate an increasingly large gap. In other words, a country with 100 can achieve 100 per cent of Europe's income; a country with 50 can achieve 50 per cent of Europe's income.

The regression results using worldwide data are reproduced in Table 4.10. There are three columns corresponding to regressions with three dependent variables: output density (real output per land area) population density and output per person.

Table 4.11 shows the values of the geographic variables for the TEs and the EU. Column 1 has the distance measure, and column 2 has the mountainous terrain measure (standard deviation of elevation measured at each one-degree box in the country). None of the TEs are in tropical regions so that variable is not shown (it would be the same for all countries in this table and therefore would not distinguish transition countries from the EU countries). In the final two columns I show the estimated long-run income gaps due to geographic penalties. Column 3 uses only distance, column 4 uses distance and mountainous terrain. I mostly use the indicator in column 3 in the rest of this chapter. Table 4.12 shows the actual and potential output measures side by side and the difference between the two, the variable that will be called 'GDP gap' later on.

Table 4.10   Regressions of output density, population density and GDP per capita on geographic variables and urbanization (cross–country data)

	(1) Log output density	(2) Log population density	(3) Log GDP pc in 1990
Land area tropical (%)	−1.71	−0.7	−1.32
	$(3.15)^{**}$	(1.71)	$(4.87)^{**}$
Distance from river/coast (km)	−1.47	−0.42	−1.31
	$(2.64)^{**}$	(1.1)	$(4.74)^{**}$
Rough terrain (%)	−0.35	−0.15	−0.05
	$(2.33)^{*}$	(1.47)	(0.72)
Land area urban (%)	3.98	2.23	1.8
	$(3.70)^{**}$	$(2.58)^{*}$	$(3.36)^{**}$
Constant	13.8	4.61	8.46
	$(15.61)^{**}$	$(7.78)^{**}$	$(19.20)^{**}$
Observations	93	131	93
R–squared	0.35	0.11	0.47

Notes:
Absolute value of *t*-statistics in parentheses.
* significant at 5% level; ** significant at 1% level.
Output density is real GDP in 1990 PPP dollars divided by land area. Regressions show impact of three kinds of geographical attributes (tropics, distance and mountainous terrain) on output density and output per capita, but not on population density (after controlling for presense of large cities). The regression estimates in column 3 were used to calculate the geography indicators for the transition countries.

Source: Warner (1999, Table 4).

Table 4.11   Geography indicators

	(1) Average distance from the centre of the country to a major river or coast*	(2) Indicator for mountainous terrain	(3) Geography indicator based on column 1	(4) Geography indicator based on columns 1 and 2
Albania	0	448	100	96
Armenia	407	492	59	56
Azerbaijan	680	733	41	38
Belarus	76	28	90	100
Bulgaria	0	408	100	96
Croatia	0	278	100	98

Table 4.11   continued

	(1) Average distance from the centre of the country to a major river or coast*	(2) Indicator for mountainous terrain	(3) Geography indicator based on column 1	(4) Geography indicator based on columns 1 and 2
Czech Republic	112	166	86	86
Estonia	0	35	100	109
Georgia	180	756	79	73
Hungary	60	71	92	97
Kazakhstan	2495	440	4	4
Kyrgyz Republic	1961	897	8	7
Latvia	0	52	100	107
Lithuania	0	46	100	107
Macedonia	200	373	77	74
Moldova, Republic of	31	53	96	102
Poland	0	129	100	102
Romania	0	375	100	96
Russian Federation	1215	191	39	41
Slovak Republic	118	278	86	84
Slovenia	0	284	100	97
Tajikistan	1571	1525	13	12
Turkmenistan	1345	224	17	17
Ukraine	0	145	100	101
Uzbekistan	1768	539	10	9
Yugoslavia	0	na	100	na
Austria	98	622	88	82
Belgium	26	72	98	105
Denmark	0	23	100	111
Finland	0	99	100	104
France	5	251	98	100
Germany	33	91	95	98
Greece	0	338	100	97
Ireland	0	78	100	105
Italy	5	462	99	94
Netherlands	10	15	99	117
Portugal	0	250	100	98
Spain	87	397	91	88
Sweden	0	257	100	98
United Kingdom	0	126	100	104

Notes:
*   In principle, the distance = 0 if a country has a major coast/river. However, if the regional data is available for detailed assessment, the distances of a country region to a coast/river are averaged. The geography indicators in columns 3 and 4 should be interpreted as an estimate of the long-run potential output shortfall relative to the EU that the country can expect given its geographical endowments. A value of 100 or above means no significant geographic penalties. A value of 77 means that the country can achieve 77% of the EU income level.

Source: Warner (1999).

Table 4.12   Output: actual and long-run potential (% of EU-14 level)

	(1) Actual	(2) Potential (based on geographical endowments)	(3) Difference
Kazakhstan	16	4	12
Kyrgyz Republic	11	8	3
Uzbekistan	12	10	2
Tajikistan	5	13	–8
Turkmenistan	7	17	–10
Russian Federation	20	39	–19
Azerbaijan	8	41	–33
Czech Republic	52	86	–35
Slovenia	64	100	–36
Slovak Republic	40	86	–46
Armenia	12	59	–47
Hungary	36	92	–56
Macedonia	15	77	–62
Belarus	26	90	–65
Poland	33	100	–67
Georgia	10	79	–69
Estonia	27	100	–73
Lithuania	24	100	–76
Croatia	23	100	–77
Bulgaria	20	100	–80
Latvia	20	100	–80
Romania	19	100	–81
Albania	12	100	–88
Moldova, Republic of	6	96	–90
Ukraine	10	100	–90

Source: Author.

These data provide two possible ways to estimate geographic penalties for transition countries. To provide a comparison with another measure, which is not regression based, I also consider a third: the distance of the capital of each country from one of four major ports (shown as '*airdist*' in the data appendix in Table 4A.1). Together, these three comprise the geography variables.

EMPIRICAL STRATEGY

The logical scheme I shall follow in the regression estimation is the following. I first test the impact of three factors on the initial reform stance: market memory measured by years under socialism, distance from information measured by the geography variables, and religion measured by a dummy variable that takes the value of 1 if the country was predominantly Orthodox or Muslim, and 0 otherwise. In practice this variable essentially separates the countries of Central Europe which had some Calvinist influence from those which historically were under Slavic or Ottoman rule. Some have suggested that this cultural divide alone can explain the divergence in reform performance among TEs.

Next, I test the impact of reform as well as geography on growth and convergence. Generally, I test for convergence in the two senses mentioned earlier: does reform raise growth above European levels; is growth inversely related to starting income after controlling for reform?

Regarding the growth data, I first measure at the maximum time period possible for each country, that is, I calculate growth rates starting with the first year in the 1990s when their dominant economic policy was implemented (taken from Table 4.9). I estimate the impact of reform on this full sample of countries over the longest time span for which data are available.

This is the right sample for estimating the impact of reform on growth since countries with negative growth rates are legitimately part of the evidence. But it is not obviously the right sample for answering questions about convergence, since it is clear that the negative growth countries are not now converging to European income levels. We do not need regression evidence to prove that.

A better question is whether the countries that have achieved a sufficient level of reform that output has started to grow – whether those countries are now on a path to convergence. Are the growth rates of these countries sufficient for convergence? Is there evidence that growth is inversely related to income within this group?

To answer these kinds of questions I first look at recent growth rates for those countries that have achieved positive growth for at least three years and, alternatively, look at their growth rates during the latest three years in our sample (1996–98). My list of these positive-growth countries is shown in Table 4.13, where countries are classified into three groups: positive-growth countries; countries that continue to decline; and three ambiguous cases – Albania, Bulgaria and Romania. The positive-growth countries are countries for which real GDP follows a U-shaped pattern: an initial decline, some reforms, followed by at least three years of positive growth that is not interrupted by a further, significant output decline. No-growth countries are countries that have seen no significant positive growth. Two of the ambiguous countries, Bulgaria and Romania, have seen a few years of modest positive growth followed by a further output decline, and therefore do not fall easily into the first two categories. Albania experienced fast growth for four years followed by a short sharp crisis in 1997 and then complications due to the Kosovo situation. I decided to use Albania's growth from the middle period as an indicator of growth it could attain without these complications. Table 4.14 shows the year in which the positive-growth countries achieved a turnaround and the growth rates since the turnaround.

Table 4.13   Broad growth patterns for transition countries

Positive-growth countries	No-growth countries	Ambiguous countries
Armenia	Kazakhstan	Albania
Azerbaijan	Moldova	Bulgaria
Belarus	Russia	Romania
Croatia	Tajikistan	
Czech Republic	Turkmenistan	
Estonia	Ukraine	
Georgia		
Hungary		
Kyrgyz Republic		
Latvia		
Lithuania		
Macedonia		
Poland		
Slovak Republic		
Uzbekistan		

Definitions
Positive-growth countries   GDP follows a U-shaped pattern: an initial decline, some reforms, followed by at least three years of positive growth that is not interrupted by a further, significant output decline.
No-growth countries   No positive growth, insufficient reforms.
Ambiguous countries   A few years of positive growth are followed by a further output decline.

REGRESSION RESULTS

The regression in Table 4.15 tests for the effects of geography, culture, income of the country and market memory as explanations for how intensively countries pursued reforms. The result is that only market memory has any explanatory power. Statistically, the combination of the Baltic and FSU dummies in

Table 4.14   Growth rates of positive-growth countries and year of turnaround

	Year output started growing	Average growth since then
Kazakhstan	1995	0.21
Uzbekistan	1995	1.01
Czech Republic	1992	1.93
Macedonia	1996	3.06
Hungary	1993	3.32
Slovenia	1992	3.93
Azerbaijan	1995	4.76
Latvia	1993	4.87
Poland	1991	5.01
Croatia	1993	5.56
Slovak Republic	1993	5.61
Lithuania	1994	5.65
Armenia	1993	5.92
Kyrgyz Republic	1995	6.34
Estonia	1994	7.05
Belarus	1995	7.45
Georgia	1994	7.91

Source: Author.

regression 2 are essentially the same variable as market memory (measured as years under socialism). Note that the regression explains as much as 64 per cent of the variance in reform policy in the early 1990s. Alternative regressions using the reform index in the same year for all countries (1992) are similar. There is no evidence of an income effect here according to which richer countries were more prone to pursue reforms. Hence there is no evidence here for convergence or divergence effects working through income–reform–growth.

The regressions in Table 4.16 are designed to explain growth performance over the maximum time period currently available for all TEs. The time period for computing growth starts in the first year in which political conditions permitted the country to adopt its own policies. I test for: (i) the effect of geography through the potential GDP variable (but alternative geography variables yielded similar results); (ii) convergence through the initial GDP variable; and (iii) the impact of reform effort through two measures of the reform stance, one in 1992 and one that is dated in the first year in which the country had its own policy. The main result is that the reform variable trumps the other measures (see Figure 4.1 for the graphical evidence). In this sample that includes both positive- and negative-growth countries, reform is a powerful explanation for relative performance. There is no evidence that growth has been inversely related with income within this group of countries over this extended time period (no beta convergence).

Table 4.15   Regressions explaining choice of reform

	(1) Reform index, 1st year	(2) Reform index, 1992
Distance from major ports	0	0
	(0.44)	(0.5)
Religion dummy	0.1	0.13
	(0.99)	(1.07)
Log of GDP at start of reforms	−0.04	−0.05
	(0.44)	(0.58)
Years under socialism	−0.01	
	(2.54)*	
Baltic dummy	−	0.15
		(0.93)
Former Soviet Union dummy	−	−0.25
		(2.32)*
Constant	1.37	1.06
	−1.98	−1.45
Observations	25	25
R-squared	0.64	0.64

Notes:
Absolute value of *t*-statistics in parentheses.
* significant at 5% level.
The dependent variable is the reform index reported in Table 4.9. Distance from major ports is the distance in kilometres from the country's capital to one of four major ports in the world (Tokyo, Rotterdam, New York, Los Angeles). Religion dummy takes the value one for countries that are not predominantly Orthodox or Muslim.

The conclusions about convergence change when we look at more recent growth of the countries that have achieved a certain amount of success – at least in the sense of stopping the overall output decline. In the regressions in Table 4.17, differing reform intensity does not explain the difference in growth rates of the countries that have turned the corner. Here we see longer-run forces such as geography and initial income beginning to play a role. Countries with favourable geographic endowments are starting to grow faster, and poorer countries are also starting to grow faster. Further, the regressions suggest that the simple gap between these two variables (the difference between where a

country is now and where it is projected to be in the long run based on its
geography) does just as well in the regression as each variable separately. See
Figure 4.2 for the graphical evidence behind this result.

*Table 4.16   Regressions explaining growth in transition countries since the
start of reform*

	(1) Growth	(2) Growth
Log of starting GDP	–2.06	–2.91
	(1.26)	(1.38)
Potential GDP	0.03	0.03
	(1.09)	(1.07)
Reform index, 1st year	18.35	–
	(4.55)**	
Reform index, 1992	–	14.59
		(2.92)**
Constant	4.41	13.16
	(–0.35)	(–0.81)
Observations	25	25
R-squared	0.63	0.47

Notes:
Absolute value of *t*-statistics in parentheses.
** significant at 1% level.
The dependent variable is annual growth in real GDP per person since the reforms started in each
country. Our dating of when reform started is given in Table 4.9. All transition countries are
included, even if the reforms were very limited. The variable labelled 'Reform index, 1st year' is
the reform index at the start of reforms, again from Table 4.9. Results using the reform index for
1992 are presented for comparison. Potential GDP is taken from Table 4.12. It is an inverse measure
of the extent of geographic disadvantage. 100 means that the country can achieve 100% of EU
income, 50 means 50% and so on.

*Table 4.17   Determinants of growth rates of transition countries that have
stopped the output decline*

	(1) *Growth1*	(2) *Growth1*	(3) *Growth2*	(4) *Growth2*
Reform index	–2.37	–2.93	–4.09	–4.17
	(0.77)	(1.37)	(1.1)	(1.61)
GDP – actual (measured as per	–0.06	–	–0.07	–
cent of EU average in 1995)	(1.55)		(1.33)	

Table 4.17   continued

	(1) *Growth1*	(2) *Growth1*	(3) *Growth2*	(4) *Growth2*
GDP – potential (measured	0.05	–	0.06	–
geography variables)	(2.98)*		(3.03)**	
GDP (actual minus potential)	–	–0.05		–0.06
		(3.24)**	–	(3.24)**
Constant	3.96	3.99	4.32	4.33
	(2.90)*	(3.03)**	(2.62)*	(2.73)*
Observations	17	17	17	17
R-squared	0.43	0.43	0.43	0.43

Notes:
Absolute value of *t*-statistics in parentheses.
* significant at 5% level; ** significant at 1% level.
Growth1: Average annual growth of all countries that have achieved positive growth, measured since positive growth first started for each country.
Growth2: Average annual growth of all countries that have achieved positive growth, measured over the period 1996–98.

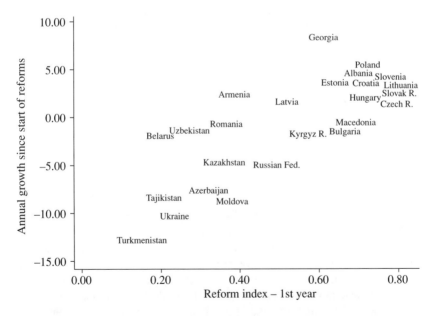

Note: The reform index is taken from Table 4.9 and growth is annual average growth in real GDP per person between the start of reforms and 1998 (starting date also in Table 4.9).

Figure 4.1   Positive relation between reform and growth in transition countries

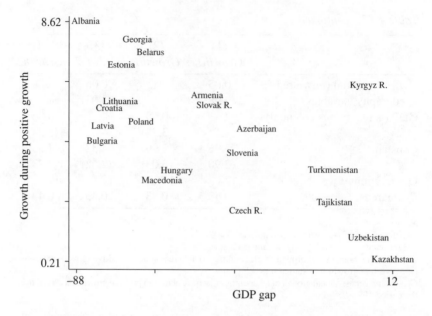

Note: Actual income is measured as a per cent of the EU average, and potential income is measured as a per cent of the geographically defined maximum. For example, Albania, Georgia and Estonia are a long way from their potential, but Turkmenistan, Tajikistan and Uzbekistan are close to their potential (because of their remote locations). The argument is that recent growth has been related to this gap rather than income alone. Note that the Kyrgyz Republic is an exception to the general tendency.

Figure 4.2   *Relation between growth in recent years of countries that have achieved some positive growth and the gap between actual and potential income*

CONCLUSION

Ten years after the fall of the Berlin Wall, the group of countries from the former Soviet bloc are not growing faster than Western Europe on a consistent basis. The evidence here suggests that the slow and desultory implementation of market-orientated reforms is the primary 'proximate' cause of this (Figure 4.1). The lack of reforms in some countries may have deeper explanations. Although the data do not show that the lack of reforms is particularly related to distance from Europe, they do show that 'market memory' or time spent under socialism accounts fairly well for the variance in reform across countries. It is also the case that three dummy variables (FSU, Baltics and Eastern Europe) are statistically equivalent explanations for the variation in reform. Essentially, the data do not permit me to draw any conclusions about the determinants of reform action on a more subtle level than this.

The extent of reform remains the best single explanation for the variation in growth that we have seen during the first ten years. However, the data do not permit finer conclusions about exactly which elements of reform are crucial, and so I have not included this in this chapter. The reason is that the elements of reform are highly correlated and we simply do not have sufficient data. But the inability to be precise about the effect of sub-components of reform should not be taken to undermine strong results about general indexes of reform.

Finally, I have also shown some evidence here that the group of countries that are not in continued free-fall have begun to grow in ways that show the influence of longer-run factors such as geography and starting income levels. This result is tentative, but nevertheless suggestive of patterns that we have observed in other parts of the world that have not been under central planning.

NOTES

1. I thank participants in the CASE conference on transition and growth in post-communist countries, Lucjan Orlowski and Jeffrey Sachs for helpful comments. This chapter draws from previous research that is part of a project on Economics and Geography at the Center for International Development at Harvard University.
2. Many observers rightly stress the large measurement problems in GDP figures from TEs (see, for example, Lajos Bokros, Chapter 2 in this volume). However, it has never been proved that measurement problems are so severe as to reverse some of the basic empirical results such as the positive connection between reform effort and subsequent growth (as illustrated in Figure 4.1). Since reforming countries are harder on the former state sector, there is some reason to believe that the measured numbers are biased against showing a positive effect of reform.
3. European TEs: Albania, Bulgaria, Croatia, the Czech Republic, Hungary, Macedonia, Poland, Romania, the Slovak Republic and Slovenia. Southern Europe: Greece, Italy and Spain. FSU: Armenia, Azerbaijan, Belarus, Estonia, Georgia, Kazakhstan, the Kyrgyz Republic, Latvia, Lithuania, Moldova, Republic of the Russian Federation, Tajikistan, Turkmenistan, Ukraine and Uzbekistan. EU-15: Austria, Belgium, Denmark, Finland, France, Germany, Greece, Ireland, Italy, Luxembourg, the Netherlands, Portugal, Spain, Sweden and the United Kingdom.
4. The EBRD indicators are published in November of each year and are based on mid-year data.
5. For example, Johnson and Sheehy (1996).
6. Published as a supplement to the *Wall Street Journal Europe*, detailed citations are in Johnson et al. (1997, footnote 35).
7. Available from Freedom House web site.
8. One example is Johnson et al. (1997, p. 180 and Appendix A), which describes the Shleifer in more detail.
9. Thanks are due to Ratna Sahay and Jeromin Zettelmeyer for personal communication on this issue.

REFERENCES

Berg, Andrew, Eduardo Borensztein, Ratna Sahay and Jeromin Zettelmeyer (1999), 'The evolution of output in transition countries', IMF Working Paper 99/73, Washington, DC: IMF.

de Melo, Martha, Cevdet Denizer and Alan Gelb (1996), 'Patterns of transition from plan to market', *World Bank Economic Review*, **10** (3), 397–424.

Freund, Caroline and Christine Wallich (1995), 'Raising household energy prices in Poland: Who gains? Who loses?', Policy Research Working Paper No. 1495, Washington, DC: World Bank, August.

Gomulka, Stanislaw (1970), 'Extensions of the golden rule of research of Phelps', *Review of Economic Studies*, **37** (1), 73–93.

Gomulka, Stanislaw (1990), *The Theory of Technological Change and Economic Growth*, London and New York: Routledge.

Gray, Dale (1995), 'Reforming the energy sector in transition economies: selected experience and lessons', World Bank Discussion Paper No. 296, Washington, DC: World Bank.

Havrylyshin, Oleh, Ivailo Izvorski and Ron van Rooden (1998), 'Recovery and growth in transition economies 1990–97: a stylized regression analysis, IMF Working Paper 98/141, September, Washington, DC: IMF.

Johnson, Bryan T. and Thomas Sheehy (1996), *Index of Economic Freedom 1996*, Washington, DC: The Heritage Foundation.

Johnson, Simon, Daniel Kaufmann and Andrei Shleifer (1997), 'The unofficial economy in transition, *Brookings Papers on Economic Activity*, No. 2, 159–221.

Kaufmann, Daniel and Aleksander Kaliberda (1996), 'Integrating the unofficial economy into the dynamics of post-socialist economies: a framework of analysis and evidence', in Bartlomiej Kaminski (ed.), *Economic Transition in Russia and the New States of Eurasia*, International Politics of Eurasia series, **8**, Armonk, NY and London: Sharpe, pp. 81–120.

Maddison, Angus (1996), *Monitoring the World Economy, 1820–1992*, Paris: OECD.

United Nations Development Programme (UNDP) (1999), *Transition 1999: Human Development Report for Europe and the CIS*, New York: UNDP.

Warner, Andrew M. (1999), *The Impact of Geography on Income Levels: Estimates from Regions of Large Countries*, unpublished manuscript, Harvard University, October.

Appendix Table 4A.1   Data used in regressions

	1	2	3	4	5	6	7	8	9	10	11
	growth0	growth1	growth2	reform1	reform92	airdist	pout1	gap	gdp1	timeus	religion
Albania	4.33	8.62	1.90	0.70	0.66	1640	100	−88	1,958	40	0
Armenia	2.23	5.92	5.70	0.39	0.39	3272	59	−47	2,105	65	0
Azerbaijan	−8.01	4.76	4.80	0.31	0.25	3620	41	−33	2,817	65	0
Belarus	−1.94	7.45	7.50	0.20	0.20	1550	90	−65	5,946	65	0
Bulgaria	−1.73	4.38	−4.40	0.66	0.86	1750	100	−80	4,557	40	0
Croatia	3.26	5.56	5.10	0.72	0.72	1110	100	−77	3,847	40	1
Czech Republic	1.16	1.93	0.70	0.79	0.86	690	86	−35	9,852	40	1
Estonia	3.41	7.05	7.50	0.64	0.64	1400	100	−73	4,484	45	1
Georgia	8.04	7.91	9.30	0.61	0.32	3070	79	−69	1,810	65	0
Hungary	1.86	3.32	3.90	0.74	0.78	1160	92	−56	6,536	40	1
Kazakhstan	−5.02	0.21	0.20	0.35	0.35	5300	4	12	4,395	65	0
Kyrgyz Republic	−1.79	6.34	6.30	0.60	0.33	5180	8	3	2,414	65	0
Latvia	1.33	4.87	6.20	0.51	0.51	1430	100	−80	3,846	45	1
Lithuania	2.46	5.65	6.20	0.78	0.55	1190	100	−76	4,428	45	1
Macedonia	−0.85	3.06	1.00	0.68	0.68	1710	77	−62	3,222	40	0
Moldova, Rep. of	−8.92	–	−5.10	0.38	0.38	1840	96	−90	2,336	65	0
Poland	5.01	5.01	5.90	0.72	0.82	1130	100	−67	4,770	40	1
Romania	−0.90	–	−3.30	0.36	0.45	1820	100	−81	4,236	40	0.5
Russian Federation	−5.18	–	−2.10	0.49	0.49	2220	39	−19	5,584	65	0
Slovak Republic	2.27	5.61	5.70	0.79	0.86	1010	86	−46	7,072	40	1
Slovenia	3.93	3.93	4.00	0.78	0.78	1000	100	−36	10,455	40	1
Tajikistan	−8.62	2.25	−0.40	0.20	0.20	5230	13	−8	1,616	65	0
Turkmenistan	−13.08	3.33	−11.90	0.13	0.13	4400	17	−10	3,509	65	0
Ukraine	−10.51	–	−4.40	0.23	0.23	1840	100	−90	4,192	65	0
Uzbekistan	−1.63	1.01	1.00	0.26	0.26	4925	10	2	2,785	65	0

Notes:

growth0   The first column gives annual growth in real GDP per person since the reforms started in each country. The dating of when reform started is given in Table 4.9.

growth1   Average annual growth of all countries that have achieved positive growth, measured since positive growth first started for each country.

growth2   Average annual growth of all countries that have achieved positive growth, measured over the period 1996–98.

reform1   The variable labelled *Reform1* is the reform index at the start of reforms, again from Table 4.9.

reform92 Reform index in 1992.

airdist   Distance from major ports is the distance in kilometres from the country's capital to one of four major ports in the world (Tokyo, Rotterdam, New York, Los Angeles).

pout1   Potential GDP is taken from Table 4.12. An inverse measure of the extent of geographic disadvantage. 100 means that the country's potential income due to geographic considerations is 100 per cent of the EU potential income.

gap   Actual gap with the EU (Table 4.2) minus potential gap (*pout1* above).

gdp1   GDP in US dollars pc at the start of reforms – dates in Table 4.9.

timeus   Years under socialism.

religion Religion indicator.

5.   Growth convergence: A comment on Warner[1]

Stanislaw Gomulka

The organizing idea of the chapter by Warner is that the ultimate factors important for growth fall into two categories: nature-given physical environments and man-made institutional reforms and economic policies. Hence his argument, rather unusually strong for economists, that geography matters a great deal: how close to the European Union or the USA, how far from the coast, how tropical, how mountainous? Reforms and policies are in turn related to the quality of civil society and the magnitude of international assistance, hence these matter too. Finally, the effects of reforms and policies are related to the size of the entrepreneurship capital, which accumulates slowly over time. In transition economies, it was an important part of country-specific initial conditions in 1989.

I do not find this approach wrong, nevertheless it has serious limitations. To begin with, international assistance might be important to initiate growth in some poor countries, but it cannot and does not play much of a role in sustaining rapid growth in those countries over a prolonged period. It did not play a major role in the success of the richest countries. Geographical factors may explain why some parts of the world's land mass (Siberia, parts of Africa) are significantly more hostile to development than others, and hence remain underpopulated and underdeveloped. However, those factors cannot explain why the two countries north of Rio Grande, USA and Canada, have become so much richer than the countries south of it, and why, in the Sea of Japan Basin, Japan has been much more successful than China or Korea during the last century. Or, in Europe, why some geographically well-placed countries (Spain, Portugal, Ireland, Greece, Central and Eastern Europe) lagged behind the European leaders for so much of the time during the past two centuries. Nor do they contribute significantly to explaining the persistently slow economic development of the Indian subcontinent during the same period. Following Adam Smith and Joseph Schumpeter, among others, the author, probably quite rightly, regards entrepreneurship capital and civil society as the principal, ultimate causes of growth. The problem is, however, that these two factors are also in part the effects of growth. For a full-blown theory, they would have to be endogenized and, for such a theory to be testable, they would also need to be observed and measured.

In my approach to growth (Gomulka, 1971 and 1990), I find it useful to begin by noting the large and increasing duality of the world economy during the past century. This duality is extremely strong not just in terms of the level of GDP per head, but also in terms of the extent of variation, among countries and, over time, of the GDP growth rate. Moreover, I argue that the key sources of growth are different in the developed part of the world (which I call the technology frontier area – TFA), and in less-developed countries. These differences are so distinct and large that two substantially different growth theories are required.

The TFA currently consists of the economies of the USA, Western Europe and Japan. Three stylized facts of this area stand out: an extreme concentration in it of the world's total research and development (R&D) activity, a remarkable stability of the trend growth rate of the US GDP per capita (or per man hour), and a low level of this rate. The once high growth rates in Japan and Western Europe have declined during the 1980s and the 1990s to the low and stable US trend growth rate, in agreement with the technological convergence hypothesis (Nelson and Phelps, 1966; Gomulka 1971 and 1990; Abramowitz, 1986; Barro and Sala-i-Martin, 1992). It is interesting that this convergence to a common growth rate and the (more-or-less) common GDP per capita has occurred despite significant differences in national savings rates. This independence of the TFA's trend growth from the investment rate is in agreement with the neoclassical growth model of the Swan–Solow type. But, as noted by Jones (1995b), the empirical evidence from developed countries is at variance with much of the so-called 'new growth theory' of Romer (1986, 1990), Lucas (1988), Grossman and Helpman (1991a and b), and Aghion and Howitt (1992, 1999). This evidence also strongly suggests that in the TFA it is the growth rate of inventive activity, linked to the growth rates of R&D inputs, which has been and is the most important single growth determinant. Other potential determinants (export shares, physical investment rates, inward orientation, the strength of property rights, government consumption, regulatory pressure) are apparently much less important. This evidence supports the R&D-based growth models proposed earlier (for example, Phelps, 1966; Shell, 1966 and 1967; Nordhaus, 1969; Gomulka, 1970 and 1971. See also Jones, 1995a).

However, the stylized facts of growth are much different for countries beyond the TFA. There, growth rates vary substantially, both between countries and over time. These rates can be high, much higher than in the TFA, despite very low own R&D capabilities. Clearly, it is the international technology transfer, which, for them, is the most important single growth determinant. Hence the great influence on the rate of growth of reforms and policies, and to some extent also geographical factors, which hinder or facilitate this transfer. The scope for such transfer is also greater when the technological gap is larger. This relationship underpins the Gerschenkron hypothesis of advantages of relative backwardness (Gomulka, 1988). These advantages are still enjoyed by fairly developed economies, such as most of those belonging to the OECD group. The growth convergence within this group in the post-Second World War period has occurred despite considerable stability in national capital–output ratios. This implies that this growth convergence has not been of the (neoclassical) Swan–Solow type, as sometimes suggested, but was driven by the technological convergence. However, highly backward countries tend to have underdeveloped physical, institutional and human capabilities to learn and take effective advantage of foreign innovations (Abramowitz, 1986). At levels of development below a certain threshold, the relationship between growth and backwardness is consequently negative (the anti-Gerschenkron relationship). Hence the full cross-country relationship between the GDP per capita growth rate and the development gap is hat-shaped, the growth rates tending to be highest for the medium-developed countries (Gomulka, 1971 and 1990).

Given the large variation of policies and institutions among countries, this hat-shaped relationship is only a broad tendency. Moreover, the policies and institutions which affect most international technology transfer may also change over time in individual countries, giving rise to sudden slowdowns, even reversals in the catching-up process during some periods and to sudden spurts during other periods.

The transition economies of Central and Eastern Europe belong to the medium-developed group. The institutional reforms of the 1990s have created, in most of these countries, a microeconomic and institutional environment conducive to the effective use of their entrepreneurship capital. In such countries, the magnitude of international technology transfer is related positively to both capital accumulation and the development gap. This transfer is also greater in countries that are successful in creating and maintaining a stable macroeconomic environment.

These arguments have been tested empirically. My own test used the post-Second World War data for 15 countries in Western Europe, Latin America and the Pacific Rim (Gomulka, 1997). Charles Dumas (1998) extended this group of countries to 20, taken from the same three regions. Using the same model, he obtained improved regression results:

$$g_Y = -2.22 + 0.195(I/Y) + 5.63 \log(y^{USA}/y) - 5.92 \log(1 + g_p) \qquad (5.1)$$
$$\quad (-3.6) \quad (7.9) \qquad (14.5) \qquad (-6.8)$$

where *t*-ratios are indicated in brackets, and where $R^2 = 0.80$. In this relationship, the time unit is a ten-year period, and g_Y is the percentage growth rate of GDP, I/Y is the investment/GDP ratio, y is the per capita GDP at purchasing power parities, and g_p is the percentage rate of inflation (of the GDP deflator), all being ten-year averages.

The actual and estimated growth rates are shown in Table 5.1 for the 20 countries in the sample.

In the regression equation, $\log(1 + g_p)$ equals approximately g_p (expressed as a fraction), so (5.1) implies that an increase in the trend rate of inflation by a percentage point reduces the trend growth rate of GDP by 0.06 per cent. The inflation rate is strongly correlated with the inflation variance, so the latter may also serve as an instrumental variable for instability factors.

For those transition economies which are EU candidates, the ratio y^{USA}/y equals about 4, and $\log 4 = 0.6$. Thus, according to this Gomulka–Dumas equation, the catching-up factor contributes now about 3.4 percentage points to their growth of GDP. For Poland during the last few years, the I/Y ratio has been in the range 20 to 25 per cent and the inflation rate some 10 to 15 per cent. Using our growth equation, these numbers translate into a GDP growth rate in the range from 4.7 per cent (for $I/Y = 20$ per cent and $g_p = 15$ per cent) to 5.8 per cent (for $I/Y = 25$ per cent and $g_p = 10$ per cent). A further increase of the I/Y ratio by 5 percentage points, to 30 per cent, would raise the growth rate to 6.8 per cent, and a reduction of the inflation rate by 7 percentage points, to 3 per cent, would raise it further to 6.9 per cent. However, after a decade of growth at between 6 and 7 per cent, the ratio y^{USA}/y would decline from the present level of 4 to about 3, reducing the contribution of the catching-up factor by 0.7 percentage points, and reducing the growth rate from 6.9 to 6.2 per cent, by the year 2010.

This exercise is not intended to provide precise estimates of the growth rate for specific time periods. The purpose is rather to estimate the trend growth rate which reflects broad and long-term experience of a group of countries thought to be representative for medium-developed and market-based economies.

The theory underlying the regression equation (5.1) is highly non-classical because technology is assumed to be country specific, not common worldwide. The catching-up factor is consequently related to international technology diffusion, hence also to the technological gap. The size of this diffusion is in turn related to investment in physical and human capital, so much so that the neoclassical law of diminishing marginal productivity of capital is partially suspended. This reactivates the importance of national savings (and capital accumulation) as the key growth determinant.

After the first decade of transition, domestic savings tend to be low in most transition countries. This stems from two reasons: the inherited policies of large social transfers and the negative effect on incomes of the transformational recession. Following the first wave of reforms (liberalization, stabilization and privatization), the transition countries turn to implementing reforms and policies

Table 5.1 *Key data and estimation results for 20 countries, second half of twentieth century*

	Period	I/Y (%)	$\log(y^{USA}/y)$	$\log(1 + g_p)$ (times 100)	g_Y (%) actual	estimated
Belgium	1956–65	19.7	0.159	1.07	3.94	3.12
	1966–75	23.0	0.124	2.62	4.15	3.35
	1976–85	19.7	0.070	2.33	1.93	2.20
	1986–95	17.7	0.070	1.27	2.16	1.87
France	1957–66	22.8	0.179	1.93	5.81	3.88
	1967–76	26.1	0.121	3.28	4.32	3.90
	1977–86	22.2	0.071	3.82	2.15	2.63
	1987–96	20.1	0.072	1.03	2.04	2.37
Netherlands	1957–66	26.4	0.164	1.61	4.68	4.48
	1967–76	25.8	0.138	3.18	5.07	4.01
	1977–86	20.1	0.077	1.66	1.72	2.39
	1987–96	20.9	0.090	0.69	2.59	2.74
UK	1957–66	17.7	0.120	1.38	2.89	2.35
	1967–76	19.9	0.118	4.11	2.42	2.60
	1977–86	17.8	0.103	3.98	2.07	2.04
	1987–96	17.3	0.097	1.95	2.02	2.01
West Germany	1950–60	24.1	0.482	1.31	8.63	7.08
	1960–70	26.5	0.234	1.55	4.55	5.16
	1970–80	23.6	0.189	2.21	2.74	4.12
	1980–90	22.7	0.150	1.21	2.25	3.63
Italy	1957–66	23.4	0.223	1.53	5.50	4.44
	1967–76	24.0	0.163	4.24	4.52	3.83
	1977–86	24.3	0.106	5.99	2.61	3.25
	1987–96	19.9	0.089	2.41	1.82	2.42
Turkey	1957–66	15.1	0.487	3.83	5.45	5.18
	1967–76	19.1	0.470	5.75	6.80	5.69
	1977–86	22.9	0.404	1.74	3.56	5.15
	1987–96	24.4	0.415	2.26	4.41	5.23
Japan	1957–66	33.3	0.394	1.71	10.19	8.03
	1967–76	36.1	0.228	3.41	7.15	6.90
	1977–86	30.4	0.124	1.29	4.12	4.89
	1987–96	30.0	0.082	0.44	3.03	4.47
Korea	1957–66	13.7	0.623	6.36	5.53	6.06
	1967–76	25.6	0.605	7.34	9.69	8.20
	1977–86	30.1	0.464	5.08	7.82	7.88
	1987–96	34.4	0.351	2.63	8.31	7.78

Table 5.1   continued

	Period	I/Y (%)	$\log(y^{USA}/y)$	$\log(1 + g_p)$ (times 100)	g_Y (%) actual	estimated
Malaysia	1976–85	30.2	0.412	2.54	6.82	7.54
	1986–95	30.6	0.362	1.16	7.74	7.22
Indonesia	1967–76	13.6	0.715	1.38	7.39	6.49
	1977–86	24.4	0.628	5.60	6.21	8.27
	1987–96	32.7	0.576	4.23	6.89	9.50
Thailand	1956–65	16.7	0.631	0.66	6.05	7.07
	1966–75	24.4	0.606	2.44	7.45	8.25
	1976–85	27.8	0.539	2.61	6.58	8.28
	1986–95	35.5	0.476	1.99	9.38	9.23
Taiwan	1957–66	18.5	0.646	2.13	8.41	7.49
	1967–76	27.2	0.580	3.41	9.87	8.50
	1977–86	27.1	0.442	2.55	8.44	7.20
	1987–96	23.1	0.320	1.13	7.27	5.34
Colombia	1956–66	18.9	0.409	5.47	4.37	5.10
	1967–76	19.5	0.433	6.19	5.63	5.40
	1977–86	19.1	0.402	9.40	3.9	4.84
	1987–96	20.0	0.400	9.43	4.17	5.00
Argentina	1976–85	23.8	0.218	55.7	0.07	1.29
	1986–95	17.3	0.301	46.0	2.86	1.35
Brazil	1966–75	26.2	0.484	10.5	8.20	6.96
	1976–85	21.7	0.391	29.4	4.26	4.06
	1986–95	21.2	0.393	90.2	2.34	0.41
Chile	1968–77	14.6	0.292	38.8	1.09	1.16
	1978–87	16.4	0.351	10.5	3.38	3.76
	1988–96	25.7	0.350	6.03	7.20	5.84
Mexico	1957–66	16.6	0.388	1.81	6.65	4.66
	1967–76	21.2	0.358	4.13	6.47	5.14
	1977–86	23.6	0.323	16.1	3.52	4.58
	1987–96	21.4	0.341	14.0	2.49	4.44
Peru	1967–76	16.4	0.393	6.35	2.63	4.39
	1977–86	22.9	0.397	25.7	2.45	4.59
	1987–96	20.2	0.449	55.4	1.90	2.78
Australia	1957–66	26.3	0.141	3.95	4.57	4.09
	1967–76	26.4	0.131	3.61	4.75	4.04
	1977–86	24.6	0.100	3.57	2.89	3.38
	1987–96	22.7	0.103	1.62	3.20	3.15

Source: Dumas (1998).

intended specifically to promote savings. These include pension reforms, whereby state pensions are reduced sharply and private pension schemes are established, and tax reforms intended to lower sharply both subsidies and direct taxes of individuals and companies.

The European Union candidates can also attract foreign direct investments in a volume that is significant in relation to GDP. The macroeconomic risks to investors could be reduced further, and substantially, once the new EU members become a part of the euroland. When this happens, and only then, domestic savings could no longer be a constraint on investment, and therefore no constraint on growth.

Public investments have a significant contribution to make in promoting growth in all those areas in which positive externalities are present. These areas include, typically, physical infrastructure, research and education. Public spending in these areas has been curtailed radically during the first decade of the transition. A reduction of social transfers is also needed for the purpose of reversing this past trend.

NOTE

1. This comment was written in response to the paper presented by Professor Warner at the Conference. His chapter in this volume contains additional material, which while consistent with the original presentation, remains outside the scope of this comment.

REFERENCES

Abramowitz, Moses (1986), 'Catching up, forging ahead, and falling behind', *Journal of Economic History*, **46** (2), 385–406.
Aghion, Philip and Peter Howitt (1992), 'A model of growth through creative destruction', *Econometrica*, **60** (2), 323–51.
Aghion, Philip and Peter Howitt (1999), *Endogenous Growth Theory*, Cambridge, MA: MIT Press.
Barro, Robert J. and Xavier Sala-i-Martin (1992), 'Convergence', *Journal of Political Economy*, **100** (2), 223–51.
Dumas, Charles (1998), 'Sources of long-term growth since the 1950s', London: London School of Economics, manuscript.
Gomulka, Stanislaw (1970), 'Extensions of the golden rule of research of Phelps', *Review of Economic Studies*, **37** (1), 73–93.
Gomulka, Stanislaw (1971), *Inventive Activity, Diffusion and the Stages of Economic Growth*, Monograph No. 24, Aarhus, Denmark: Aarhus University.
Gomulka, Stanislaw (1988), 'The Gerschenkron phenomenon and systemic factors in the post-1975 growth slowdown', *European Economic Review*, **32**, 451–8.
Gomulka, Stanislaw (1990), *The Theory of Technological Change and Economic Growth*, London and New York: Routledge.

Gomulka, Stanislaw (1997), 'Sources of long-term growth since the 1950s', London: London School of Economics, manuscript.

Grossman, Gene and Elhanan Helpman (1991a), *Innovation and Growth in the Global Economy*, Cambridge, MA: MIT Press.

Grossman, Gene and Elhanan Helpman (1991b), 'Quality ladders in the theory of growth', *Review of Economic Studies*, **58** (1), 43–61.

Jones, Charles I. (1995a), 'R&D-based models of economic growth', *Journal of Political Economy*, **103**, 759–84.

Jones, Charles I. (1995b), 'Time series tests of endogenous growth models', *Quarterly Journal of Economics*, **110** (May), 495–525.

Lucas, Robert E. Jr. (1988), 'On the mechanics of economic development', *Journal of Monetary Economics*, **22** (July), 3–42.

Nelson, Richard R. and Edmund S. Phelps (1966), 'Investment in humans, technological diffusion and economic growth', *American Economic Review*, **56** (2), 68–75.

Nordhaus, William D. (1969), *Invention, Growth and Welfare*, Cambridge, MA: MIT Press.

Phelps, Edmund S. (1966), 'Models of technical progress and the golden rule of research', *Review of Economic Studies*, **33** (April), 133–46.

Romer, Paul M. (1986), 'Increasing returns and long-run growth', *Journal of Political Economy*, **94** (October), 1002–37.

Romer, Paul M. (1990), 'Endogenous technological change', *Journal of Political Economy*, **98** (October, Part 2), S71–S103.

Shell, Karl (1966), 'Towards a theory of inventive activity and capital accumulation', *American Economic Review*, **56** (May), 62–8.

Shell, Karl (1967), 'A model of inventive activity and capital accumulation', in Karl Shell (ed.), *Essays on the Theory of Optimal Economic Growth*, Cambridge, MA: MIT Press, pp. 67–85.

6. Remarks on globalization, openness and macroeconomic stability in transition economies

David Lipton

Globalization brings benefits and imposes disciplines on all countries with open economies, not least the transition economies (TEs). Ten years after Poland's historic leap to a market economy, Poland is experiencing both the benefits and rigours of globalization.

I first visited Poland ten years ago, with my colleague Jeff Sachs, to talk about economic reform with Solidarity economists and strategists. Arriving the day after Solidarity's breathtaking electoral victory in June 1989, I recall two conflicting impressions. First, the sense of awesome possibility posed by a country galvanized to remake itself and join Europe. And second – something that at times is hard to recall in the light of what has since occurred – the vast distance Poland would have to travel to achieve its goals.

Another impression I recall from my first visit was the economic isolation of Poland. To telephone home required booking a call for eight hours later, or an hour later if you paid double. There were no foreign newspapers or magazines. The drab goods in the stores were not Western goods. I learned later that the Western businesses most interested in Poland were commercial banks, but they were interested in order to divine whether Poland was going to default on the syndicated loans that had been incurred to prop up the ailing communist economy.

What a difference a decade makes. Now, Poland is so much a part of the world economy that its policy makers must track recession and recovery in Germany and Japan and must also keep an eye on global investor sentiment. Both are so vitally important to maintaining a growth record that is the envy of Europe. I remember realizing vividly that Poland had progressed from depending on the International Monetary Fund (IMF) to depending on world markets when a Polish finance minister, visiting us at the Treasury, was more interested in Larry Summers's views about US monetary policy than IMF lending policy. In fact, policy makers must track events from Korea to Brazil. Moreover, the capital markets follow every twist and turn in Poland. Now, I can sit at my computer every morning and read the profusion of assessments of Poland made by Wall Street analysts every day. Before travelling to Poland, I read Citibank and ING Barings' latest weekly reviews of Poland. They contained twenty pages of analysis and forecasts. The analysts in international banks pore over every word of Monetary Policy Council members for clues to interest rate policy just as they do with Alan Greenspan. In just a decade, Poland has gone from debt-ridden, hyperinflating and stagnant to being referred to as the new convergence play in Europe.

Being part of the new global economy has its rewards, but it also has its risks. That is what I want to address. On balance, Poland gets high grades for managing globalization. It has reaped the rewards and managed the risks. Many other TEs have also done well, each with its own strengths and weaknesses. For TEs, globalization means foreign direct investment in industry, commerce and finance, which brings in capital, technology and managerial know-how that will sustain growth and a convergence of living standards towards levels in advanced countries. But globalization also means vulnerability, as the emerging market countries saw during the global financial crisis when private flows of external capital fell by 200 billion USD over a two-year period. Not only were the fast-growing countries in Asia devastated, but Russia suffered significantly from that sharp reversal of capital market sentiment. And in turn, Central Europe suffered from the collapse of Russia. Now that the international crisis has subsided, it is opportune to study the lessons from that episode to be able to guard against any adverse effects from a recurrence of crisis.

What the world learned in Asia is that extreme destabilization can occur even when the old IMF prescription – sound macroeconomic fundamentals – is satisfied and when the old World Bank prescription – high savings and strong public expenditures on education and health – is satisfied. A healthy and vigorous debate has ensued about whether the origins of the crisis are to be found in the inherent instability in international capital markets or in the management of policies in the crisis countries. Was the crisis a financial panic? Or was it the inevitable comeuppance for countries with weak laws, weak regulation and weak structural policies, in short with crony capitalism?

Whatever you conclude about this debate, a new consensus is emerging about one part of the agenda, how countries should protect themselves to weather the rigours of globalization. That new consensus goes beyond the old Washington consensus, and treats a broader range of subjects, not only macro policies, but also structural policies, competition policies, regulation, laws and institutions. That emerging consensus is being incorporated into the so-called 'new international financial architecture'. In that discussion, most of the radical new ideas for new supranational institutions (like a global central bank or a global credit insurance agency) have been set aside, because they were impractical and ran up against the prerogatives of sovereignty. So, perhaps we might do better to refer to the 'new international financial plumbing'. But, it would be wrong to conclude that the new plumbing is unimportant. That is because the formulation of the new consensus has prompted much thinking about the anatomy of capitalism, what makes markets work and what does not, what can be done to strengthen capital markets.

So, what is the new, emerging Washington consensus? And what are we to make of it?

I shall leave aside the important and complicated subject of getting investors and creditors to improve their assessments of risk in international capital markets through improved regulation and other measures. I want to focus solely on the subject of the lessons for the management of laws, institutions and policies in emerging market countries.

The first and obvious conclusion of the international community is that policy management needs to be better. As Leszek Balcerowicz has said before – a point he made to President Bill Clinton at the G22 meeting in autumn 1998 – there is little doubt that countries attacked by the capital markets were attacked because of weaknesses in policies, institutions and finances. Poland was not attacked. Other well-managed countries were not attacked. Particularly instructive is the experience of Taiwan, with its current account surplus, healthy budget, high reserves, low short-term debt, and more sound banking sector regulation. Taiwan executed a controlled devaluation and totally escaped crisis. That recitation of virtues mirrors the new policy prescription: avoid excessive foreign currency debt, avoid short-term debt, avoid low international reserves, avoid fixed exchange rates, avoid capital account liberalization until you have strengthened supervisory and prudential systems and so on. Given that the markets focus pressure on countries with problems, it is no longer practical to expect sustained capital market confidence without adherence to that prescription.

Beyond policies, a number of important conclusions are emerging about structural policies, institutions and laws. So the second conclusion, of course, is that private ownership matters, a subject treated by Stanley Fischer and Ratna Sahay (Chapter 1 in this volume) and by Andrew Warner (Chapter 4 in this volume). That conclusion is rooted in the experiences of TEs. Whether it was Poland or Russia, academics, policy makers, and the international financial institutions (IFIs) community had to ask itself the proverbial question: now that communism has turned an aquarium into fish stew, how do we turn fish stew into an aquarium? Answering that question required re-examining the building blocks of capitalism. One of the principal challenges in Central and Eastern Europe (CEE) was to restore private ownership. Privatization was debated: which should come first, privatization or restructuring? Should there be give-aways to citizens or initial public offerings (IPOs) to entrepreneurs? Should banks and other financial institutions be privatized and, if so, early or late in the process?

The verdict of recent history, with the recent commentary of the World Bank's Joe Stiglitz (1999) notwithstanding, in the transition as well as the emerging market economies is that private ownership matters, and that sooner is better than later. When privatization is delayed, corporate governance is weak, entrepreneurs focus on acquiring assets rather than managing them, banks and corporations are manipulated for political purposes to serve the interests of government; and public financial institutions generate quasi-fiscal deficits that undermine the macroeconomic stability. By contrast, private ownership makes possible improved corporate governance and more efficient resource utilization, but also importantly it creates a constituency for reform, especially for liberalization, tax reform and legal reform. The clear relationship between ownership and development shows up in the data. The World Bank's (1999) new database on financial development and structure shows, for example, that public bank assets constitute 70 per cent of total assets in low-income countries, 40 per cent in middle-income countries and about zero per cent in high-income countries.

Third, the structure and competitiveness of financial systems matters. The emerging market crisis has focused much attention on the distinction between bank and non-bank finance. Economists had long believed that banks fostered investment, by promoting relationship-based corporate governance, permitting borrowers a long-term focus, and giving security against illiquidity. But in the 1990s, the European and Asian experiences have been negative, while the US and TEs' experiences have shown the value of market-centred systems. The World Bank's data show that bond market capitalization is almost four times as high in high-income countries compared to middle-income countries and stock market capitalization twice as high. When Korea's banking system failed it was clear that the monopolization of finance by banks and the close relationships between government, banks and chaebols had evolved from an engine of development to an engine of overlending to chaebols. That is why the USA and the IMF put so much emphasis on improving competition in Korea's financial sector. The prescription – an end to government-directed lending, liberalization of capital markets to make possible greater bond and equity finance, and openness to foreign ownership – is applicable to many other countries, transition and emerging alike. Russia's battle between the central bank and the Securities and Exchange Commission (SEC) regarding the primacy of banks and capital markets is but another example.

Fourth, the global financial crisis should put legal reform squarely on the agenda. We all mention legal reform when we recite our list of desired reforms. But unfortunately it is not getting its due attention. Legal reform may prove to be the most important determinant of financial market health. When Russia first broached the subject of legal reform in 1993, the World Bank hesitated at first because it had never sponsored a legal reform programme, did not have knowledgeable staff, and was worried that it was not part of its mandate. Now, we can see that successful corporate governance depends on the protection of the legal rights of shareholders and creditors. This is more surprising to those of us in advanced countries who take these rights for granted than to investors in transition and emerging markets. I recall discussions with the Russians in the early 1990s regarding share registration, depository and clearing institutions and thinking that no Main Street American worries when he calls his broker to buy shares of stock whether he really owns it, whether someone could defraud him. Russia's untamed capital markets – with recent, prominent cases such as Yukos Oil – show vividly how expropriation undermines capital market development.

More generally, the Asian crisis cases show how shaky corporate governance can become without a sufficient legal foundation. Impressive new research argues that countries with strong legal protections for the rights of shareholders and creditors have better corporate governance and that this is reflected in deeper and stronger capital markets, lower costs of capital, and more effective and efficient savings mobilization (La Porta et al., 2000). This research finds superior performance in countries with a tradition of common law, with its emphasis on property rights and contracts, in comparison with those countries following the Napoleonic or German civil law traditions. Where the state has asserted its strength, corporate governance is weak and the ready substitute models, state enterprises and family-owned companies, have predominated. Under those two models, the first in transition economies and the second in Asia, firms have sought access to capital through connections, based on relationships or with the state. Neither has produced sustained efficiency, or the reputation needed to attract outside capital and deepen capitalization.

Turning to a few issues for TEs that are suggested by these lessons, I shall offer some comments specific to Poland, but I believe that these points have broad applicability in transition countries.

First, TEs must accept and take account of their external environment as never before. A key implication of CEE's successful transition is that it is now part of an interdependent global economy and will have to live with both good and bad consequences. I know that in Poland there is criticism of government, because of the growth slowdown in 1999. But when Germany has recession and Russia collapses, Poland can minimize losses but it cannot fully escape. In fact, a look at the region shows that the more advanced the transition (looking at the factors just discussed) and the better protected against contagion, the less severe the impact of external factors. The Czech Republic has fallen victim to recession, while Poland is seeing merely a slowdown in growth. Poland's currency remains strong, capital inflows continue, and the banks have not been imperilled. Clearly, Poland's strong policy base has inoculated it against the worst, and has limited the damage.

Second, there is a need to avoid complacency. Avoiding the worst of the crisis is not enough. To preserve macroeconomic stability in the future and to make steady progress on the road to membership in the European Union (EU) – key goals for countries in the region – requires steady progress on a number of fronts.

Let me briefly mention macroeconomic management, structural reform and public infrastructure.

Perhaps little needs to be said about the need to maintain sound finances as an anchor of a sound economy. In Poland, for example, there has been steady attention to limiting the scale of budget deficits, even as difficult and fiscally expensive structural reforms have been undertaken. And the central bank's tight rein on money and credit has brought inflation down to single digits and pointed in the direction of achieving Western European levels.

Perhaps less obvious, but equally important is exchange rate policy. Each of the CEE countries faces the long-run goal of participating in European Monetary Union (EMU), which will only be achieved if there are no serious disruptions from the external sector in the meanwhile. This has two implications. First, monetary policy needs to be conducted with exchange rate competitiveness in mind. In 1998, as Germany's slowdown led to an export slowdown for Poland, interest rates were lowered, which curbed exchange rate appreciation and stimulated domestic demand. At present, capital inflows seem ample to cover Poland's current account deficit. But, maintaining exchange rate flexibility and monetary policy flexibility is key to coping with whatever is to come.

Second, the trend towards widening the exchange rate band is another wise move. On the face of it, a widening of the band may seem an anomaly for a country aspiring to join the EU and adopt the euro. Hungary, by contrast, is maintaining a tight band and a decelerating crawl. But there is wisdom in the floating exchange rate approach. After all, it was the narrow snake of the European Monetary System (EMS) that collapsed in 1993. Western Europe then widened its band and let currencies float until locking in rates last year. Poland's approach is similar. Moreover, the Asian crisis shows vividly how capital markets can force central banks to defend and then abandon pegs and the immense cost of such a failure. As Poland progresses towards Europe, the worst outcome would be to be pushed into a defence of the band by some combination of mistakes, adverse shocks and capital market fears.

Also important is steady progress on structural reforms. Virtually in collapse in 1989, Poland has worked to build the infrastructure of capitalism. Poland has privatized many of its banks and has paid attention to banking supervision. The regulation of the equity market is credited with building a market-based capital market and strengthening corporate governance. Yet, looking forward, Poland's transition remains incomplete, and where it remains incomplete, weaknesses remain. Another potential weakness is corruption. Poland has avoided the morass of corruption that has befallen Ukraine and Russia. But for any country that aspires to joining the EU, not being as corrupt as Ukraine is not enough. What is needed is to set a high and comprehensive standard of transparency. There can be no casual political acceptance of corrupt or politically manipulated institutions. Completing the second generation of reforms, building the culture of law, and instilling transparency are easier to say than do. But those things are important, of course, because they advance the goal of raising living standards and joining Europe. But also because they reduce the risk that Poland will be derailed on the path to Europe by a debilitating crisis.

Third, there is a need to build a public infrastructure suitable for the twenty-first century. Poland's inadequate infrastructure is part of the lasting heritage of communism that has not been erased ten years after. Whenever foreign investors sing the praises of doing business in Poland, they inevitably add the complaint that poor infrastructure is a major constraint on a larger scale of operations, including using Poland as an export platform for Europe. I am sure that infrastructure is a serious issue for domestic investment as well. The government needs a clear accountability for developing a comprehensive and coordinated long-term infrastructure programme. That programme should provide public goods that the private sector will not provide, but it can include private construction and public/private financing arrangements that lessen the immediate budget impact. Also, the government needs to make room in the budget for the inevitable call on public resources. That means even greater urgency for completing second-generation reforms, completing the restructuring of the coal sector and moving on to other sectors, and more generally, limiting the size of the public sector's involvement in the current economy.

Finally, politicians need to take account of the fact that Poland lives in a globalized world. It is remarkable how successfully Poland has remained on the path to Europe through numerous changes of government. But the journey is not yet complete. And as that journey continues, the markets will be focused on Poland as never before. We saw that when Italy and Spain were viewed as convergence plays before their achievement of EMU. At present, the markets do not consider that investment in Poland contains significant political risk. It is incumbent upon Poland's political players to keep it that way.

In closing, as we look back over the last decade, we should all marvel at the progress that the transition economies have made, especially Poland. As we look forward to the next decade, what should we expect? Living standards rising rapidly towards EU levels? CEE countries comfortably ensconced in the EU, with their citizens using the euro? That is not too much to strive for. But to do so, countries in the region will need to keep an eye on the international economy to take account of an ever-changing global environment.

REFERENCES

La Porta, Rafael, Florencio Lopez-de-Silanes, Andrei Shleifer and Robert Vishny (2000), 'Investor protection and corporate governance', Journal of Financial Economics, forthcoming.
Stiglitz, Joseph E. (1999), 'Whither reform?', Paper prepared for the Annual Bank Conference on Development Economics, 28–30 April, Washington, DC: World Bank.
World Bank (1999), *World Development Indicators*, Washington, DC: World Bank.

PART II

Financial Openness and Approaches to
Monetary Integration

F32 621 113-24
P34 F33
P33 E52 (CEEC)
P24

7. Global integration of financial markets and its consequences for transition economies

Marek Dąbrowski

INTRODUCTION

Recent acceleration of global integration can be attributed to several factors, including a trend towards liberalization of economic policies in both developed and developing countries that has evolved over the last two decades. The economic transition from a command economy to a market system in Central and Eastern Europe (CEE) and the former Soviet Union (FSU) has additionally strengthened this tendency. Specifically, the following market-orientated measures applied by developing and transition economies (TEs) have contributed to global financial integration:

- advancing capital account liberalization;
- liberalization of financial markets and the banking system;
- transnational expansion of large banks and banking groups; and
- privatization of banks and other financial institutions.

Apart from policy and regulatory framework, the technological progress in transportation, telecommunication and information systems has played an enormous role in global integration. Technological progress along with education have brought all international economic players closer together, shortening distances, thus lowering the cost of trade and capital transactions.

As increasing integration of financial markets has become the most dynamic and controversial aspect of globalization processes in the last two decades, this chapter will concentrate on discussing its advantages and disadvantages as well as its consequences for monetary policies and exchange rate regimes in TEs.

ARGUMENTS FOR AND AGAINST CAPITAL ACCOUNT LIBERALIZATION

Increasing financial integration has both its advocates and opponents. This relates particularly to freedom of short-term capital movement and pace of capital account liberalization.

On the one hand, fast capital account liberalization can increase macroeconomic vulnerability of emerging market economies exposing them to unexpected external shocks, changing market sentiments, and, therefore, to contagion effects of external financial crisis. This increases the risk of global financial turbulence coming from numerous imperfections of international capital markets (Rodrik, 1998). The opponents of fast capital account liberalization argue that chain, panic reactions as those observed after the Asian and Russian crises can be very harmful for individual countries, and for the world economy as a whole; they may lead to a worldwide financial crisis and recession. These opponents also argue that economic benefits of fully free capital movement, particularly in the case of developing countries, are not apparent (Rodrik, 1998; Stiglitz, 1998).

Large capital flows can be particularly dangerous for countries with weak financial and corporate sectors lacking proper prudential regulations. These countries may have a limited capacity to absorb shocks related to large capital movements. All these arguments may call for rather slow and careful capital account liberalization.

On the other hand, there are arguments in favour of a free capital movement. First, a full capital account liberalization improves resource allocation and contributes to the development of financial markets. Both effects may stimulate economic growth, *ceteris paribus* (Klein and Olivei, 1999). Second, it supports the development of international trade and investment and, therefore, it contributes to growth prospects (Fischer, 1998). Third, it facilitates investment portfolio diversification, and assets and liabilities management in financial institutions in both capital exporting and importing countries.

Finally, unrestricted capital flows limit a country's economic sovereignty. Though it may sound provocative, capital liberalization is a good idea for many developing and transition economies, often suffering from political instability or from the lack of clear constituency in favour of stable macroeconomic policy and market reform. Exposed to day-to-day assessment by global financial markets, the governments in these economies are restrained in continuing bad policies or resorting to populist experiments. The danger of greater external vulnerability is usually the best argument in favour of pushing forward difficult reforms, cutting public expenditures, improving corporate governance and accounting standards, banking supervision and so on. According to Dornbusch (1998 p. 24), '[t]he capital market fulfils an important supervisory function over economic policy'. Countries that really follow good policies, as they are broadly understood, are less susceptible to the contagion effects of international financial crisis.

The above assertions lead to another, maybe also provocative hypothesis. Although economic, political and social costs of financial crisis are usually high, the crisis itself can play a useful role. In relation to government policy, its effect is similar to that of a bankruptcy on the micro level. It punishes unsustainable and inconsistent economic policies or an irresponsible political behaviour on the one hand, and too risky lending practices of financial investors on the other. As shown by the experience of the last decade, open populism or evident inconsistency in macroeconomic policies that are observed *ex post* by investors could trigger sudden capital outflow and currency collapse. In addition, speculators can play against *ex ante* policy inconsistencies or against a conflict between too many policy targets (as in the case of the sterling crisis in 1992). Thus, the danger of financial crisis can impose a necessary discipline on policy makers and mitigate moral hazard bias on the private lender side.

For these reasons, free capital movement may benefit many developing and transition economies.

TECHNICAL DIFFICULTIES WITH CAPITAL CONTROLS

Developing and transition economies that, for any reason, decide to limit free capital movement may face obstacles in finding effective instruments to do so. Increasing sophistication of financial products and transaction techniques makes exercising effective capital controls more difficult, particularly when a country has already crossed a certain liberalization threshold. Attempts to impose capital controls in today's financial environment usually lead to market distortions, which in turn result in inventing new financial instruments, which allow market players to bypass the imposed restrictions. In essence, most financial derivatives have been devised to deal with existing capital controls.

Ineffective capital controls may lead to undesired consequences, such as regulatory loopholes that undermine the reputation of governments and legal systems while opportunities of arbitrary decisions create a fertile ground for corruption.

Vast empirical experience shows that control of capital outflows can hardly be effective. As Edwards (1999 p. 24) states,

[T]hey are easily circumvented, encourage corruption and, in most historical episodes, have not helped the adjustment process. A major drawback of controls on outflows is that, in most cases, they are not used as a temporary device to face a crisis situation. Instead, they become a permanent feature of the country's incentive structure.

This assertion has been confirmed by the experience of financial crises in Bulgaria (1996–97), Russia, Ukraine and other CIS countries (1998–99). Capital outflows cannot be prevented if market players see arbitrage opportunities or if they simply try to protect their wealth. Such circumstances trigger utilization of a broad range of capital flight techniques, including standard current account transactions such as underinvoicing of export and overinvoicing of import. Moreover, reintroducing controls on capital outflows at the time of financial crisis is not only ineffective but also damaging to the country's reputation.

For the same technical reasons, quantitative (administrative) restrictions on capital inflows are equally ineffective, as confirmed by the recent Polish or Hungarian experience (Rybinski and Linne, 1999). In place of administrative restrictions, some economists advocate controlling capital inflows by taxation of foreign exchange transactions in the form of the so-called Tobin tax (1978), which in fact has never been practically implemented. Alternatively, they propose a Chilean system of mandatory deposits (Stiglitz, 1998; Eichengreen, 1999). However, despite subsequent attempts to tighten these deposits in 1991–98, capital inflows were not reduced in Chile (Edwards, 1999; Gallego et al., 1999). Although these measures contributed to extended maturity of foreign debt and reduced stock market instability, they failed to insulate the Chilean economy from the Asian shock of 1997–98, or to increase the degree of monetary policy independence. They also involved costs, namely, higher real interest rates for small and medium-sized enterprise borrowing.

Summing up, capital controls are highly ineffective from the point of view of both effective resource allocation and the political economy of the reform process. In a country that has already established a relative freedom of capital movements, a return to capital controls may damage its credibility, and it may inhibit the reform process. Capital controls cannot replace prudent economic policies and institutional development.

However, in economies which have only started the financial liberalization process, such as China, the issue of proper sequencing is very important. First, capital account liberalization should follow trade liberalization as trade restrictions decrease chances for effective capital allocation (Cooper, 1998). Second, capital accounts liberalization cannot be introduced without building a sound banking system with prudent corporate governance and financial supervision.

LIMITED ECONOMIC AND MONETARY SOVEREIGNTY

Globalization increases competition in international markets of goods and services, in capital markets and, to a smaller extent, in labour markets. Economic agents can diversify business activity by moving investments and assets between countries and currencies. They can take advantage of currency arbitrage, of differences in legal infrastructure and regulatory systems, including taxation, property rights protection, and the overall country risk. For these reasons, the national sovereignty becomes limited even if the country does not formally belong to any integrated bloc, such as the European Union. Limited sovereignty affects a country's social, economic and political life, and it raises the standards of economic and political responsibility. It serves as a disciplining mechanism against trade unions' wage and political demands, and for this reason, most trade unions do not favour globalization.

Effective currency arbitrage, regardless of whether it is conducted between countries or between currencies in one country, undermines the monopoly power of the monetary authority to issue the national currency and to collect seigniorage. This also relates to the countries that apply capital controls. In fact, currency substitution is no longer limited to the extreme situations, such as hyperinflation or war. It can take place in any country at any time, when economic agents decide that they can realize gains or reduce risk by moving their assets away from the national currency.

A currency arbitrage has a strong impact on macroeconomic conditions, particularly on monetary policy. For example, most of the concepts of the aggregate demand fine tuning, by using the tools of monetary and fiscal policies, assume (either explicitly or implicitly) that economic agents must use the national currency exclusively and that currency substitution is not an effective option. Hence, economic agents are willing to accept money illusion and to pay the resulting inflation tax. However, in today's highly integrated world economy, which allows for free capital movement and effective currency arbitrage, the aggregate demand management is more limited than it was two or three decades ago, particularly in countries with less credible macroeconomic policy and weak microeconomic foundations.

CHOOSING SOUND MONETARY POLICY AND EXCHANGE RATE REGIME

The principle of the 'impossible trinity' (Frankel, 1999) states that a country must give up one of the three goals: exchange rate stability, monetary independence or financial market integration (see Figure 7.1). It cannot have all three simultaneously. Assuming that increasing capital mobility is irreversible, more countries face the choice between monetary independence and exchange rate stability. In practice this means either retaining monetary independence under a free floating exchange rate or giving up monetary independence by adopting an extreme version of exchange rate fixing, such as a currency board, monetary union, or a unilateral adoption of a foreign currency.

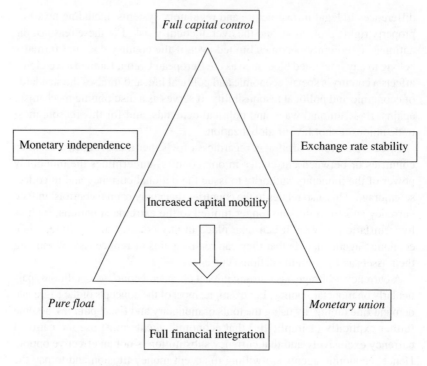

Source: Frankel (1999).

Figure 7.1 The impossible trinity

Such extreme solutions mean phasing out intermediary regimes, including adjustable peg, crawling peg, crawling band, targeted band and managed float, and thus eliminating the active role of exchange rate in stimulating export. This view has been gaining ground in recent economic literature (Mundell, 1999; Krugman, 1999; Eichengreen, 1999). Nevertheless, some economists, for instance Frankel (1999), defend the possibility of compromising between monetary independence and exchange rate stability on theoretical grounds. In practice, the compromise will be increasingly difficult for many reasons. The first and most fundamental reason is that compromised solutions are unlikely to provide the advantages of both extremes, that is, an exchange rate anchor and a sufficient discretion in managing domestic liquidity. On the contrary, they may bring both a substantial exchange rate variability (actual or expected when the peg is not viewed as credible) and make money supply exogenous (that is, being out of the control of the monetary authorities). Second, compromised regimes are technically very difficult because of fluctuating demand for money and changing market expectations. Moreover, the pressure from current economic and political conditions may bring temptation to go beyond the compromise. Third, transparency, and, therefore, credibility of intermediary regimes, is lower than that of the extreme solutions. The weaknesses of intermediary regimes, that is, insufficient transparency and credibility, have been manifested during the financial crises of the 1990s (Obstfeld and Rogoff, 1995; McCallum, 1999; Eichengreen and Hausmann, 1999; Institute for International Economics, 1999).

Developing and transition economies can draw lessons from the 1992 ERM crisis, which was particularly striking in this respect. At that time, macroeconomic fundamentals in the UK were relatively sound. Nevertheless, market players suspected that in the case of a speculative attack against the pound, the monetary authorities would rather give up exchange rate stability than increase interest rates rapidly and, therefore, sacrifice growth and employment objectives. This assumption became a self-fulfilling forecast when the market began testing the soundness of the sterling exchange rate. The experience of the 1992 ERM crisis inspired further advancement of the so-called 'second-generation model of currency crises' (with multiple equilibrium), in which the intermediary exchange rate regime, such as the adjustable peg, triggers speculative attack (Eichengreen et al., 1994; Obstfeld, 1994).

In other theoretical models, the so-called 'first- and third-generation models', intermediary regimes are not considered a primary cause of currency crisis. Instead, they contribute to developing the crisis spiral after the start. According to these models, a crisis originates from fiscal imbalances or soft budget constraints on the micro level. The intermediary currency regimes are not credible enough to stop speculation and they are not flexible enough to absorb market pressures (Obstfeld and Rogoff, 1995).

The choice between two extreme regimes ought to be discussed in the context of currency competition (for example, whether a specific currency has a chance to sustain competition from other currencies and at what price) and trade characteristics of a given economy. Hence, it seems that free floating is not the optimal solution for small open economies, not only because it brings exchange rate variability, which increases transaction costs. It is also a very difficult and costly option for countries that suffer from high or moderate chronic inflation, have recent inflationary memory, a low level of monetization, lack sufficient political and institutional credibility and so on. This implies that free float under independent monetary policy is a viable option only for large economies or economic blocs (for instance, the USA, Japan and the eurozone). It may also be viable for some other countries that have managed to establish an international reputation with respect to their currencies and their monetary authorities (for example, Canada, Australia, New Zealand, Switzerland and the UK, if it decides to stay out of the EMU). Other countries will be forced, sooner or later, to join one of the main currencies or currency blocs.

The above hypothesis is confirmed by the results of empirical research demonstrating the low credibility and high macroeconomic costs of floating and intermediary currency regimes in a number of Latin American countries, in contrast to the high credibility and good results of a free float in Australia (Eichengreen and Hausmann, 1999). By contrast, Panama, by adopting the US dollar as a national currency, in the 1990s recorded the lowest inflation rate, the lowest spreads on long-term bonds, the highest level of monetization, and one of the highest rates of GDP growth among Latin American countries.

CAN TRANSITION ECONOMIES SUSTAIN MONETARY INDEPENDENCE?

Post-communist countries face the same strategic choice between monetary independence (and free floating) and joining one of major currencies. Intermediary regimes, dominating so far in the region, have become increasingly fragile, as confirmed by the crisis episodes in Bulgaria (1993–94 and 1996–97), Russia (1994 and 1998), Kyrgyzstan (1996 and 1998), the Czech Republic (1997), Ukraine (1998) and most other CIS countries (1998–99). Although these crises stemmed primarily (with the exception of the Czech Republic) from deep fiscal imbalances financed, to a significant extent, by money emission (Markiewicz, 1999), intermediary exchange rate regimes did not help to contain the crisis spiral.

Table 7.1 shows a relatively low level of monetization in most TEs, which indirectly confirms the low level of credibility of monetary policies in these countries. In fact, the actual situation is even worse than that illustrated in the table, as monetization data relate to total money supply, including a foreign exchange component that is significant in a number of TEs.

The low monetization level is pervasive in FSU countries, where it has deteriorated further after a series of devaluation crises during 1998–99. Additionally, the general quality of transformation policies and government institutions in these countries as well as the political stability in the entire region are the lowest. In such a fragile environment, choosing a free floating exchange rate system does not offer a reasonable perspective. Thus, giving up monetary independence seems to be unavoidable sooner or later, if these countries want to build a sound and stable macroeconomic environment. Moreover, a possible currency board regime may be considered by economic agents as not credible enough (because of the danger of its abandonment or manipulation), and, therefore unilateral dollarization or euroization become the only acceptable option.

The same concerns apply to the Balkan region, where this process has already started. Recently, Bulgaria and Bosnia introduced currency board regimes (with currencies linked to the Deutsche mark), while Kosovo and Montenegro adopted the Deutsche mark as their national currency.

Table 7.1   Monetization (M2/GDP) in transition countries, 1997

Country	Monetization (%)
Georgia	6
Armenia	9
Kazakhstan	10
Ukraine	14
Kyrgyz Republic	14
Azerbaijan	14
Belarus	16
Russia	18
Lithuania	19
Moldova	22
Mongolia	23
Romania	25
Latvia	28
Bulgaria	34
Poland	40
Hungary	41
Estonia	42
Slovenia	42
Croatia	43
Slovak Republic	68
Czech Republic	71

Source: IMF, International Financial Statistics; Jarocinski (1999).

Estonia and Lithuania run currency board regimes, and Latvia has a monetary regime close to an informal currency board. Differences in monetization levels reflect a different level of political commitment and institutional strength of the adopted regime (stronger in Estonia than in the two other countries).

Only a few Central European countries seem potentially suitable for running their own independent monetary policies. This relates primarily to the Czech Republic and Slovakia, representing the highest level of monetization, the lowest level of dollarization, and a lack of high inflation or hyperinflation experience. Hungary, Poland and Slovenia, enjoying a relatively good international reputation, are other potential members of this group. However, it is an open question as to how high the macroeconomic costs of sustaining the competition from other currencies in the longer run will be. High interest rates in Poland can signal difficulties in building the necessary monetary reputation.

Prospects of the near EU accession create another dilemma for this group of countries. Although they are potentially able to continue their independent monetary policies, the EU membership will mean joining the eurozone at the end of this process. This raises the question of when to give up monetary independence. Some authors (Bratkowski and Rostowski, 1999a and 1999b; Mundell, 1999) propose to accelerate this moment and to do it even before the formal EU accession, through either an earlier unilateral euroization or the introduction of a currency board.

Optimal timing of giving up monetary independence by the EU candidate countries needs to be discussed in the context of many contradicting arguments. On the one hand, an earlier accession to the eurozone would allow the high current account deficits during the pre-accession period to be dealt with, thus avoiding a painful and risky period of ERM-II. It would give a chance for earlier inflation and interest rate convergence (Dąbrowski, 1999; Rostowski, 1999). On the other hand, a premature abandoning of an exchange rate shock absorber may exert pressure on a real sector and expose the economy to higher GDP volatility.

REFERENCES

Bratkowski, Andrzej S. and Jacek Rostowski (1999a), 'Zlikwidowac zlotego' (Abolish the zloty), *Zeszyty BRE Bank–CASE*, No. 44 (September), Warsaw: CASE and BRE Bank SA, 7–10.
Bratkowski, Andrzej S. and Jacek Rostowski (1999b), 'Wierzymy w euro' (We believe in the euro), *Zeszyty BRE Bank–CASE*, No. 44 (September), Warsaw: CASE and BRE Bank SA, 11–15.
Cooper, Richard N. (1998), 'Should capital-account convertibility be a world objective?', in Stanley Fischer, Richard N. Cooper, Rudiger Dornbusch, Peter M. Garber, Carlos Massad, Jacques J. Polak, Dani Rodrik and Savak S. Tarapore (eds), *Should the IMF Pursue Capital-account Convertibility?*, Princeton University, Department of Economics, International Finance Section Essays in International Finance No. 207, pp. 11–19.
Dąbrowski, Marek (1999), 'Macroeconomic and fiscal challenges facing Central European countries during the EU accession process', CASE Reports No. 26, Warsaw: CASE–Center for Social and Economic Research.
Dornbusch, Rudiger (1998), 'Capital controls: an idea whose time is past?', in Stanley Fischer, Richard N. Cooper, Rudiger Dornbusch, Peter M. Garber, Carlos Massad, Jacques J. Polak, Dani Rodrik and Savak S. Tarapore (eds), *Should the IMF Pursue Capital-account Convertibility?*, Princeton University, Department of Economics, International Finance Section Essays in International Finance No. 207, pp. 20–27.
Edwards, Sebastian (1999), 'How effective are capital controls?', NBER Working Paper No. 7413, November.

Eichengreen, Barry (1999), *Toward a New International Financial Architecture: A Practical Post-Asia Agenda*, Washington, DC: Institute for International Economics.

Eichengreen, Barry and Ricardo Hausmann (1999), 'Exchange Rates and Financial Fragility', NBER Working Paper No. 7418, November.

Eichengreen, Barry, Andrew Rose and Charles Wyplosz (1994), 'Speculative attacks on pegged exchange rate: an empirical exploration with special reference to the European Monetary System', CEPR Working Paper No. 1060, London.

Fischer, Stanley (1998), 'Capital-account convertibility and the role of the IMF', in Stanley Fischer, Richard N. Cooper, Rudiger Dornbusch, Peter M. Garber, Carlos Massad, Jacques J. Polak, Dani Rodrik and Savak S. Tarapore (eds), *Should the IMF Pursue Capital-account Convertibility?*, Princeton University, Department of Economics, International Finance Section Essays in International Finance No. 207, pp. 1–10.

Frankel, Jeffrey A. (1999), 'No single currency regime is right for all countries or at all times', NBER Working Paper No. 7338, September.

Gallego, Francisco, Leonardo Hernández and Klaus Schmidt-Hebbel (1999), 'Capital controls in Chile: Effective? Efficient?', presented at the IMF/World Bank Conference on Capital Flows, Financial Crises, and Policies, 15–16 April, Central Bank of Chile, Research Department.

Institute for International Economics (1999), *Safeguarding Prosperity in a Global Financial System. The Future International Financial Architecture*, A Council of Foreign Relations-Sponsored Report, Washington, DC: Institute for International Economics.

Jarocinski, Marek (1999), 'Monetization of the Moldovan economy', CASE, mimeo.

Klein, Michael and Giovanni Olivei (1999), 'Capital account liberalization, financial depth, and economic growth', NBER Working Paper No. 7384, October.

Krugman, Paul (1999), 'The return of depression economics', *Foreign Affairs*, **78** (1), pp. 56–74.

Markiewicz, Malgorzata (1999), 'Fiscal policy and disinflation in transition economies', *Studies and Analyses*, No. 127, Warsaw: CASE–Center for Social and Economic Research.

McCallum, Bennett T. (1999), 'Theoretical issues pertaining to monetary unions', NBER Working Paper No. 7393, October.

Mundell, Robert (1999), 'The priorities for completing the transition and the model for the future', Paper to the 5th Dubrovnik Conference on Transition Economies: 'Ten Years of Transition: What Have We Learned and What Lies Ahead', 23–25 June, Dubrovnik, Croatia.

Obstfeld, Maurice (1994), 'The logic of currency crises', NBER Working Paper No. 4640.

Obstfeld, Maurice and Kenneth Rogoff (1995), 'The mirage of fixed exchange rates', NBER Working Paper No. 5191.

Rodrik, Dani (1998), 'Who needs capital-account convertibility?', in Stanley Fischer, Richard N. Cooper, Rudiger Dornbusch, Peter M. Garber, Carlos Massad, Jacques J. Polak, Dani Rodrik and Savak S. Tarapore (eds), *Should the IMF Pursue Capital-account Convertibility?*, Princeton University, Department of Economics, International Finance Section Essays in International Finance No. 207, pp. 55–65.

Rostowski, Jacek (1999), 'The approach to EU membership: the implications for macroeconomic policy in applicant countries', CASE–CEU Working Papers Series No. 26, Warsaw: CASE–Center for Social and Economic Research.

Rybinski, Krzysztof and Thomas Linne (1999), 'The emerging financial system of Poland: institutional constraints and external links, *Studies and Analyses*, No. 154, Warsaw: CASE–Center for Social and Economic Research.

Stiglitz, Joseph (1998), 'Must financial crises be this frequent and this painful?', McKay Lecture, Pittsburgh, Pennsylvania, 23 September, http://www.worldbank.org/knowledge/chiefecon/index.htm

Tobin, James (1978), 'A proposal for international monetary reform', *Eastern Economic Journal*, **4** (3/4), pp. 153–9.

(EU, CEEC) P33 E52
P24 E62
F33

8. Unilateral adoption of the euro by EU applicant countries: the macroeconomic aspects

Andrzej Bratkowski and Jacek Rostowski

INTRODUCTION

Many commentators have noted the fact that the so-called 'Eastern enlargement' of the EU is unique, in the sense that never before have countries which are so much poorer than the EU been admitted. Furthermore, they are being admitted to an EU which is far more internally liberalized (the single market) and integrated (EMU) than previously. Finally, the applicant countries are far more liberalized internally and open internationally than was the case with the previous enlargement to relatively poor countries (the so-called 'Southern enlargement' of the 1980s). We believe that this unique combination of circumstances is likely to generate unanticipated problems for the applicant countries in their conduct of macroeconomic policy in the run-up to EU and later EMU accession,[1] and the best solution to these problems, for those countries whose reserves are adequate, is rapid unilateral adoption of the euro *before* EU entry.

The problems we predict stem from the combination at one time of the following factors: (i) expected rapid growth in the applicant countries (far faster than in the EU itself); (ii) real appreciation resulting from the well-known Harrod–Balassa–Samuelson effect; (iii) free capital movements; (iv) the need to satisfy the Maastricht criteria and join EMU within ten years. These factors are likely to lead to high current account deficits, which it will be difficult for the authorities to limit to prudent levels. At the core of our analysis lies an attempt to combine what we know about the macroeconomics of rapidly growing poorer countries with the standard prescriptions of the Mundell–Flemming model and the institutional requirements of the pre-EU and pre-EMU accession periods. We describe these underlying pressures in the next section, and discuss standard macroeconomic policy responses and their drawbacks in the third and fourth sections. In the fifth section we describe how unilateral adoption of the euro would work and the final section concludes.

MEDIUM AND LONG-RUN TRENDS IN THE APPLICANT COUNTRIES

There are three principal effects, which are likely to exert a 'demand' for current account deficits (and for the matching capital account surpluses to finance them).

First, expected income growth: people who expect to be richer in the future than they are at present will behave rationally if they smooth their consumption path by borrowing today in order to consume more now, and repaying their debt later. At the level of a whole country this leads to foreign borrowing (capital inflow) and a current account deficit. If a number of countries expect their economies to grow, the faster-growing ones should borrow from the slower. Applicant countries are expected to be fast growing for a number of reasons: (i) they have stopped pursuing the very bad economic policies which they had in the past under central planning (pervasive government control, extensive subsidies, massive foreign trade distortions and so on); (ii) considerable gains from learning by doing within the institutional infrastructure of the market economy which was initially non-existent (for example, the bankruptcy courts, customs services, financial institutions), can be expected to continue for some time to come; (iii) new structural reforms which are coming on-stream (for example, pensions' reform, privatization of utilities); (iv) expected benefits of EU and EMU membership.

Second, the well-known *Harrod–Balassa–Samuelson* (HBS) effect means that richer countries have higher price levels than poorer ones. Its corollary is that faster-growing economies will experience real appreciation of their currencies relative to countries with slower growth (either as a result of higher inflation, or of nominal appreciation). The importance of this phenomenon in transition economies (TEs) has been pointed out in the seminal paper by Halpern and Wyplosz (1997). The simplest way to understand the HBS effect is to assume that economies produce two kinds of goods: tradables (for example, manufactures, primary products and agricultural products) where productivity differs between countries and can grow at different rates across countries, and non-tradables (for examples, services and construction) where productivity is constant and uniform throughout the world.[2] Finally, one assumes that all goods, but in particular tradables, are sold on perfectly competitive markets, and also that labour is homogeneous and labour markets are perfectly competitive. In such a world, differences in income between any two countries are due exclusively to the productivity of their tradable goods sectors. In the faster-growing economy, productivity in the traded goods sector rises faster than in the slower-growing one, with the result that real wages must rise faster.[3] However, because of the homogeneity of labour and the competitiveness of labour markets, real wages must increase by the same amount in both the tradable and non-tradable sectors. Since productivity in non-tradables is constant, this means that prices have to increase in this sector. The faster the growth rate of productivity in the traded goods sector the faster the rate of price increase in the non-traded goods sector. As a result, if the share of the two sectors is similar in the two countries, average prices will rise faster in the faster-growing country even if the nominal exchange rate is constant, implying real appreciation. If the nominal exchange rate is not constant, then it is average prices adjusted for the change in the nominal exchange rate (that is, in the currency of the foreign country) which will rise faster in the faster-growing country, also implying real appreciation. Now, real appreciation means that national income measured in foreign currency rises faster than when it is measured in domestic currency. As a result the command of domestic residents over foreign goods and services increases faster than indicated by the growth of real GDP at domestic prices (in which the inflation in the non-tradables sector is discounted). This higher than conventionally measured real growth justifies more smoothing of consumption, and a higher current account deficit than otherwise.

Third, equally important, if a large part of the government's debt is denominated in foreign currency (as is the case in many TEs), then, real appreciation leads to a decline in the ratio of public debt to GDP, and, therefore, in the ratio of public debt to the potential tax base. Even if the Ricardian equivalence is only partial, residents can expect a lower share of taxes in national income that will be needed to service the existing public debt. This raises future disposable income and the desire to smooth consumption (and to raise the current account deficit) along with it.

To illustrate the above points we start with the equation for the current account (CA) obtained from Obstfeld and Rogoff (1996):

$$CA_t = B_t - B_{t-1} = Y_t - C_t - G_t - I_t \qquad (8.1)$$

where B is the net foreign assets owned by the residents of the country (including their government), Y is national income, C is consumption, G government expenditure and I investment. It is assumed, for the moment, that G is fully financed by taxation. In the long run, the CA should be in balance, the economy should have zero net foreign assets and therefore the net present value of consumption should equal the net present value of net income $Z = Y - G - I$. The representative consumer, faced with uncertainty, maximizes the expected value of the intertemporal utility function:

$$U_t = E_t[\sum_{s=t}^{\infty} \beta^{s-t} u(C_s)] \qquad (8.2)$$

where t is the present and s is the date of every future period, subject to the constraint:[4]

$$NPV(CA) = NPV(B) = NPV(Y - C - G - I) = 0 \qquad (8.3)$$

which implies:

$$NPV(C) = NPV(Y - G - I). \qquad (8.4)$$

The operator E_t [.] is 'a mathematical conditional expectation – a probability-weighted average of possible outcomes, in which probabilities are conditioned on all information available to the decision maker up to and including date t' (Obstfeld and Rogoff, 1996, p. 79). C_t^* is what we call the level of consumption generated by the above procedure at time t. The CA is then given by:

$$CA_t = Z_t - C_t^*. \qquad (8.5)$$

So that the CA shows a surplus if $Z_t > C_t^*$ and a deficit if $Z_t < C_t^*$. The first point above (rapid expected growth of the applicant countries) implies that, with consumption smoothing, it will be usually the case that $Z_t < C_t^*$, and CA_t < 0. Second, the HBS effect means that growth of national income in real foreign currency terms will be faster than in real domestic currency terms, justifying a higher time path of C_t^* and larger CA deficits than would otherwise be the case. Third, real appreciation reduces the absolute value of B_t/Y_t and since $B_t < 0$ is normal in fast-growing economies, this leaves scope for an increase in negative net foreign assets (net foreign liabilities or debt), which by equation (8.1) leads to a larger CA deficit. Perhaps most useful of all, equation (8.3) shows us that if the residents of an applicant country revise their expectations of the $NPV(Y)$ upwards, as it has been argued happens at various times during the transition process,[5] then they should also increase C_t^* for all t. If current Z_t does not increase by as much as C_t^*, and there is no reason why it should, then the CA deficit will also increase.

At the same time, there are a number of supply factors inducing capital inflows, which are likely to be present in the applicant countries:

1. Increased productivity in the tradable goods sector and increased relative prices in non-tradables lead to an increased return on capital in both sectors in the fast-growing country. Observation of these trends will make foreign lenders willing to provide increased loans to the private sector within applicant countries.
2. The 'Visegrad Three' (Poland, Hungary and the Czech Republic) all have full liberalization of inward foreign direct investment (FDI) flows, including

repatriation of profits and principal. Furthermore, OECD membership means that they are already committed to freedom of outward capital flows and short-term capital movements. Some countries believe that – in practice – the extent of these latter freedoms can still be limited at present.[6] Whether this is so is unclear. In any event, upon EU entry truly fully free capital accounts will be unavoidable. Thus, much of the period preceding EMU entry will be one of fully free capital accounts.

3. Increased maturity of the institutional infrastructure will strengthen creditors' property rights and exit possibilities for shareholders.[7] The prospect of imminent EU membership can be expected to raise foreign investors' awareness of the progress that has been made in this regard.

From the perspective of foreign investors, high expected growth rates and real appreciation in applicant countries means increasing asset values. This may induce a further inflow of capital, causing further real appreciation together with a desire for higher CA deficits and higher private sector foreign debt on the part of applicant country residents, so that a 'capital inflow–real appreciation' bubble may develop, with the real exchange rate rising ever more above its medium-term equilibrium level[8] until, finally, the bubble bursts. Thus, setting a ceiling on the CA deficit at some prudent level may be a justified aim of public policy in the applicant countries. The dilemma of conducting macroeconomic policy with such an aim and under the conditions which are likely to hold in the run-up to EU and EMU membership, is the subject of the next section.

FISCAL AND MONETARY POLICY IN THE APPROACH TO EU AND EMU MEMBERSHIP

What policies will allow applicant countries to keep their CA deficits at 'prudent levels'? We first look at an adaptation of the consumption-smoothing model discussed in the previous section to help us analyse the policy implications in the medium term, and then at short term the Mundell–Flemming model.

We adapt the model by adding tax revenue as a determinant of the current account, and by specifying the medium-term determinants of the right-hand side of the CA equation. Including tax revenue is justified by the weakness of the empirical evidence for Ricardian equivalence (for example, Wilcox, 1989). G and I can be spent on imports just like C and, therefore, subtract from any positive CA_t, while taxes subtract from disposable income which could be spent on imports. Since $Y - C = S$ (savings) we rewrite (8.1) as follows (including the behavioural determinants of the variables on the right-hand side):

$$CA_t = B_t - B_{t-1} = S_t(Y, \varepsilon) - (G_t - T_t) - I_t(r^*, \eta). \qquad (8.6)$$

We make the Keynesian assumption that savings depends on national income and the neoclassical assumption that investment depends on the world interest rate r^*, and add the shift variables ε and η which represent the effects of (upward) changes in expectations regarding growth. Increases in the variable ε cause S to decline, while increases in η cause I to increase.[9] Changes in both variables are assumed to be random, but are restricted to being non-negative (that is, if $\varepsilon_t < \varepsilon_{t-1}$ when random values of ε are drawn then we set $\varepsilon_t = \varepsilon_{t-1}$, and we do the same for η). Finally, consumers are assumed not to be able to anticipate future values of ε, or to calculate their expected value $E(\varepsilon_t) > 0$ (the same goes for η). We seek justification for these highly irrational expectations in the completely unprecedented nature of the transition from communism to capitalism.[10] Thus over time, but in a highly unpredictable way, the gap between I and S increases, increasing the CA deficit. The only way the authorities can offset this trend is to reduce the budget deficit $G - T$, possibly to the extent of turning it into a large surplus.

As in the earlier version of the consumption-smoothing model, an unanticipated reduction in the absolute value of B_t/Y_t (due to an increase in Y_t or to real appreciation) implies a reduction in net foreign liabilities (NFL) to GDP, since normally $B_t < 0$ in fast-growing economies, and therefore brings about a desire by consumers to increase the NFL/GDP ratio. As before, this implies a reduction in B_t below B_{t-1}, and therefore a CA deficit. However, we encounter an ambiguity regarding the policy implications of the model at this point: while the direct effects of a reduction in the budget deficit should reduce a CA deficit (the traditional two-gap model result), if a significant part of public debt is held abroad – as is the case in the applicant countries – an unexpected tightening in fiscal policy reduces government NFL and therefore induces the private sector to increase its own NFL. The result might be that total NFL remain unchanged. In such a case (which we can call the 'crowding in of private sector foreign debt') the CA deficit is unaffected by reductions in the fiscal deficit in the medium term.

This is the equivalent of so-called 'Ricardian equivalence' but regarding the impact of fiscal policy on the current account rather than on aggregate demand. Although empirical evidence for standard Ricardian equivalence is weak, we believe it may be stronger in the present context because of constraints originating from the international suppliers of credit. We know that these often look at the total indebtedness of a country's residents, both public and private, when assessing an individual resident's credit risk. Of course, the extent to which this actually happens depends on the proportion of the reduction in the fiscal deficit which goes to reducing foreign public debt below its previously expected level. The lower this proportion, the stronger the standard effect of public sector deficit reduction on the current account deficit will be. We shall see below that similar doubts as to the efficacy of fiscal policy for CA deficit reduction resurface even in the context of the Mundell–Flemming model and its application to policy making in the short term.

To analyse the implications of the effects we describe in the previous section for macroeconomic policy in the short term, we look at the Mundell–Flemming model with perfect capital mobility, risk-neutral investors and fully flexible exchange rates. We assume that in the short term the exchange rate is not expected to change, that is,

$$\rho_t + u_t = \rho^e_t = \rho_{t-1} \tag{8.7}$$

where the last period's expectations of the current period's exchange rate (ρ^e_t), which are simply the last period's actual exchange rate (ρ_{t-1}), efficiently predict the current period's actual exchange rate (ρt, where u_t is a normally distributed error term). In such a case, if there were a difference between the rate of return on domestic and foreign assets, investors would put all of their money into the asset with the higher return. Since both kinds of assets are held it follows that their returns must be equal. Since exchange rate expectations are static, it follows that rates of return (that is, interest rates) must be the same in the two countries:

$$i = i^* \tag{8.8}$$

where i is the domestic rate of interest, and i^* is the world rate (given exogenously). This means that the LM curve (representing equilibria in the 'money' market) becomes:

$$M/P = L(i^*,Y) \qquad L_1 < 0, L_2 > 0, \tag{8.9}$$

while the 'goods market equilibrium' IS curve becomes:

$$Y = C(Y - T) + I(i^* - \pi^e) + NX(Y, \rho P^*/P) + G \tag{8.10}$$
$$C_1 > 0, I_1 < 0, NX_1 < 0, NX_2 > 0,$$

where π^e is expected domestic inflation, P^* is the foreign price level, P is the domestic price level and NX is net exports (remaining variables are as conventionally or previously defined).[11]

The result in ρ,Y space is a vertical LM curve and an upward-sloping IS curve, as shown in Figure 8.1. Any tightening of monetary policy by the

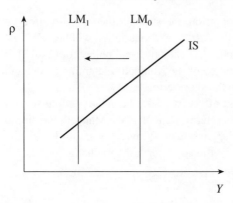

Figure 8.1   Monetary policy response to capital inflows in the IS–LM framework

authorities is immediately offset 'one for one' by capital inflows, because i cannot rise above i^*. This capital inflow must be offset by a deterioration of the current account, so that the policy is in fact counterproductive.[12] Intuitively we can understand this if we remember that, given that the domestic interest rate is fixed at the level of the world rate, a reduction in M can only affect the exchange rate, which appreciates, reducing NX.[13] If capital movements were not perfectly free in the very short term, so that the authorities could succeed in reducing M (in spite of their difficulty in raising i) this would have two offsetting effects. On the one hand, it would reduce Y, increasing NX and improving the CA balance. On the other hand, it would lead to a nominal appreciation of the domestic currency – a reduction in ρ – and if P (the domestic price level) is sticky downwards we would also have real appreciation, so that NX would decline and the CA balance would deteriorate (see Figure 8.1, where ρ is defined as units of domestic currency per unit of foreign currency, so that a decline indicates an appreciation). Which of the two effects will be stronger depends on the various elasticities, but in neither case is the policy likely to be very powerful. Returning to the case of perfect capital mobility in the short term, expanding rather than contracting M will lead to capital outflow (to obtain the infinitesimally higher interest rate abroad) and therefore to nominal deprecia-tion. In the short run there will also be real depreciation if prices are sticky, so that the CA deficit would be successfully reduced.[14] However, in the medium term increased M would lead to higher prices (not allowed for in the fixed price level Mundell–Flemming model), which would likely mean breaching the Maastricht criterion on inflation, and also to an erosion of the real depreciation and a reversal of the improvement in the current account. Thus, in the medium term, sustaining a 'prudent' level of the CA through expansionary monetary policy would require accelerating inflation which would clearly be inconsistent with the Maastricht inflation criterion.

If the exchange rate is credibly fixed, then the domestic authorities have no influence over M. They have to respond to sales (purchases) of foreign (domestic) currency with a supply of central bank domestic (international) reserves, so that M becomes entirely endogenous and cannot affect the current account in any way. Monetary policy is thus unlikely to be effective in reducing a current account deficit whichever of the two exchange rate regimes, floating or fixed, is in force. This result is confirmed by empirical studies, which find that in the Mundell–Flemming model and its Dornbusch (1976) extension, changes in monetary policy are unable to predict either nominal or real exchange rate changes (Obstfeld and Rogoff, 1996, pp. 622–6).

On the other hand, with fully free capital movements, the Mundell–Flemming model suggests that fiscal policy becomes highly effective in determining the CA balance, both under free and fixed exchange rate regimes. If the exchange rate floats and the fiscal deficit is reduced so that $G - T$ in equation (8.10) falls, then the IS curve in Figure 8.2 shifts to the left, leading to depreciation of the exchange rate without any effect on output: aggregate demand falls as a result of the direct effect of the fall in $G - T$ (together with any multiplier effects it may have) while the depreciation of the currency increases NX by an exactly offsetting amount. National income remains constant because it is determined by real money balances (M/P) in the money market equation (8.9), but the accompanying nominal depreciation leads to an improvement in the current account. The depreciation may have some inflationary effects over time, which

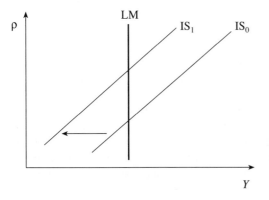

Figure 8.2   Fiscal contraction and the equilibrium exchange rate and output

may partially offset the CA improvement; however, with no increase in domestic M, such effects need not be very powerful. With a fixed exchange rate the model consists in (8.10) and:

$$\rho = \bar{\rho} \qquad (8.11)$$

In Y, ρ space this gives the equilibria as shown in Figure 8.3.

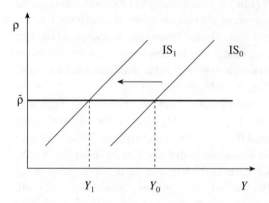

Figure 8.3   Output effects of fiscal contraction under fixed exchange rate

A reduction in the budget deficit causes a fall in Y and thus an increase in NX helping to achieve the aim of a 'prudent' level for the CA deficit. As previously stated, a reduction (increase) in M merely leads to an increase (reduction) in the international reserves of the central bank. The overall conclusion is that keeping the economy on course for EMU membership – in the face of the medium-term effects (described in the second section, above) which are pushing the applicant countries towards increasing CA deficits – implies ever-tightening fiscal positions for these countries. Since the Czech Republic and Poland already have fiscal deficits well within the Maastricht fiscal policy criterion, achieving a prudent CA position may require them to run significant budget surpluses in their last pre-EMU entry years.

This conclusion, though, is brought into question by the medium-term consumption-smoothing model we looked at earlier in this section. There we saw that also the effect of fiscal policy on the current account might be ambiguous. That result inspires one to ask whether there are other indirect effects of a tightening of fiscal policy which might cast doubt even in the short term on the conclusions we arrived at within the Mundell–Flemming framework. For instance, a tightening of fiscal policy could lead to a positive re-evaluation of the expected future worth of a country's currency, leading to its appreciation, rather than depreciation, and therefore to an increase in the CA deficit rather than a reduction. That this might not be mere theorizing is indicated by the view of some Hungarian economists that their currency's avoidance of rapid real appreciation over recent years has been due to the government's large fiscal deficit, something which cannot be explained in the Mundell–Flemming framework or even in the standard version of the medium-term consumption-smoothing model. Furthermore, evidence from OECD countries shows that, while sharp reversals of fiscal policy may affect the CA deficit in the expected direction, the link between fiscal and CA deficits is usually insignificant (Obstfeld and Rogoff, 1996 pp. 144–5). This is the kind of result which Knight and Scacciavillani (1998) have in mind when they draw the rather gloomy conclusion that exchange rate movements and current account changes may, in fact, be indeterminate.

INFLATION, INTEREST RATES AND EXCHANGE RATE REGIMES IN THE PRE-EMU ACCESSION PERIOD, AND THEIR IMPLICATIONS FOR CONFORMITY WITH THE MAASTRICHT CRITERIA

Because of their expected rapid growth rate, the HBS effect may be very strong in the applicant TEs. Thus, in the 1990s real appreciation has occurred at a rate of 2 per cent per annum in Portugal and only 0.4 per cent per annum in Spain (1990–97 for both countries), while in Poland it has averaged 7.5 per cent during 1993–97. This difference seems to be related to the difference in growth rates, with the Portuguese and Spanish economies growing at less than 2 per cent per annum, while Poland grew at about 6 per cent. As growth rates accelerate in the other applicant countries, we can expect rates of real appreciation to reach very high levels as well. The implications for the achievement of the Maastricht criteria for stage three of EMU by the applicant countries are profound.

First, it may be unwise for the applicant countries to achieve the inflation criterion, which at present requires that inflation not exceed the average of the three best performers within EMU +1.5 per cent. If the HBS effect required a real appreciation of 7.5 per cent per annum relative to the eurozone (as Polish experience suggests it might), then this criterion would imply an equal nominal appreciation of the same amount. Such a policy may entail two kinds of risks.

1. The current Maastricht inflation criterion is in fact unsuitable for countries in which a strong HBS effect operates, since it seeks to limit what is better thought of as a *relative price change* (between traded and non-traded goods) rather than as an increase in the overall price level. If, as we have assumed,

prices are constant in the traded goods sector of the rapidly growing country while productivity increases rapidly, then the nominal exchange rate can also remain constant without affecting that country's trade or current accounts. Increases in the prices of non-traded goods (resulting from the need to pay homogeneous labour higher wages in both sectors given the increase in its average productivity) have no effect on the CA or the equilibrium exchange rate. In fact, for prices to be constant in the rapidly growing country, its currency needs to appreciate nominally to such an extent that the ensuing fall in the domestic price of tradables compensates for inflation in non-tradables, so that:

$$- \alpha P_T (\partial \rho / \partial t) / \rho = (1 - \alpha) \pi_{NT} \qquad (8.12)$$

is required for $\pi = 0$ (where α is the share of tradables in national income, P_T is the price of tradables, ρ is the exchange rate defined as units of domestic currency per unit of foreign currency, π_{NT} is the rate of inflation on non-traded goods and π is the average inflation rate). But, assuming some downward price rigidity for domestically produced tradable goods, such a nominal appreciation implies deterioration in the trade and current accounts of the rapidly growing country. Furthermore, this would be a change, which the growth in the productivity of labour in its tradables sector by itself does not require, and which is therefore likely to be a move *away* from the equilibrium exchange rate.[15]

2. If nominal appreciation is sufficient for (8.12) to hold, then the interest parity condition:

$$- [(\partial \rho / \partial t) / \rho]^e + i = i^* \qquad (8.13)$$

may well imply negative short-term nominal interest rates in the applicant country.[16] For example, if we take the rate of nominal appreciation implicit in (i) meeting the Maastricht inflation criterion (of inflation not exceeding the average of the three best performing members of the eurozone +1.5 per cent) and (ii) having the same real appreciation *vis-à-vis* the eurozone as Poland did during 1993–97 (which together implies a nominal appreciation of 7 per cent per annum, if average eurozone inflation exceeds that of the best three performers by one per cent), then with $i^* = 4\%$, i needs to be minus 3 per cent! In the spirit of Dornbusch (1976), we suggest that this anomaly may be avoided through an initial upward jump in the value of the domestic currency, so that subsequent expected appreciation is low enough for $i > 0$. However, it is also possible that an 'appreciation bubble' may develop, with the exchange rate overshooting its sustainable level (and ultimately collapsing).[17] Alternatively, the expectation of nominal appreciation could put such downward pressure on the domestic interest rate that an explosion of domestic credit ensues.

Second, there are a number of difficulties in devising a suitable exchange rate regime for the CEE applicants for the period immediately prior to EMU entry. This matter has been discussed by Kopits (1999). However, we believe that Kopits has underestimated the difficulties which may arise. There are a number of possible exchange rate arrangements in the pre-EMU period, among them

1. *Fixed rate* (this is currently the mechanism applied in Estonia). Hungary has a variant of this, a pre-announced crawling devaluation of the currency with a very narrow band of permitted fluctuations around the central rate. As inflation decreases in Hungary, and the rate of crawl is consequently reduced to zero, the Hungarian system will converge on the Estonian one (unless the band for permitted fluctuations is considerably widened). As we have seen, such a system is very likely to be incompatible with the Maastricht inflation criterion, simply because of the operation of the HBS effect. Expected rapid growth will lead to high levels of capital inflows which may result in the need to choose between (a) dangerously high CA deficits, or (b) inflation well above that due solely to the HBS effect.[18]
2. *Wide fluctuation bands* (±15 per cent) around the central rate as in the current ERM-II. This was the case in Poland.[19] This is likely to lead to nominal appreciation and high CA deficits, but may give the possibility of fulfilling the inflation criterion. As Kopits points out, appreciation even beyond the fluctuation band does not infringe the Maaastricht exchange rate criterion. One danger is an 'appreciation bubble', which leads to a rate which is unsustainable. This could lead to a collapse of the exchange rate before accession to EMU (which *would* be against the Maastricht requirements), or to an overvalued exchange rate at the time of joining, which could mean a lengthy period of low growth within EMU.[20]

We can summarize the previous two sections as follows:

- The HBS effect means that there will be powerful pressures for real appreciation in the applicant countries in the medium term (Halpern and Wyplosz, 1997).
- Rapid expected growth, the HBS effect (via its effect on the ratio of foreign debt/GDP) and various factors increasing the supply of foreign capital, mean that applicant countries are likely to run large and growing CA deficits.
- Monetary policy will be either counterproductive, likely to risk the return of high inflation, or ineffective.

- Only fiscal policy *may* have the potential to effectively limit CA deficits to what the authorities are likely to consider prudent levels (and this is so under both fixed and flexible exchange rate regimes). As a result of their need to tighten fiscal policy in each successive year while they are EMU pre-ins, countries with relatively low fiscal deficits at present such as the Czech Republic or Poland, may therefore need to run substantial surpluses (possibly of the order of several percentage points of GDP) by the time they join EMU. We should consider the extent to which this is likely to be politically feasible.

- Tight fiscal policy may, however, prove ineffective in limiting CA deficits, as a result of its effect on the private sector's willingness to increase its foreign indebtedness. In that case there is a serious danger that a real appreciation boom–bust cycle may blow applicant countries off their course to EMU membership.

- The Maastricht Treaty inflation criterion for EMU membership should not be applied to the CEE applicant countries when the time comes for them to join the eurozone, although the exchange rate criterion should, of course, be maintained.

- A fixed exchange rate policy in the run-up to EMU membership will make the attainment of the Maastricht inflation criterion completely impossible (which will not matter if the latter has been dropped). However, a wide-band ERM-II type of arrangement carries its own risks of high exchange rate volatility.

UNILATERAL INTRODUCTION OF THE EURO

A number of CEE applicants have sufficient international reserves not only to exchange all existing domestic currency-denominated central bank monetary liabilities for euros (coins, notes and commercial bank reserves at the central bank), but also to create an emergency fund to provide lender of last resort liquidity to the banking system (since the central bank would no longer be able to create high-powered money – in euros – for this purpose).[21] In what follows we shall use the example of Poland, which we know best.

One way to implement unilateral euroization is simply to pass, as soon as is technically feasible,[22] the very law establishing the euro as legal tender, which would have to be passed in the CEE country concerned upon its entry into EMU by the traditional route. Only those parts of the law that relate to the role of the national central bank (NCB) would have to be different. Instead of providing for the NCB's membership of the European System of Central Banks (ESCB), they would provide for the NCB to run the lender of last resort facility for the banking system, using owned or borrowed international reserves. In the case of

Poland, whose international reserves are very high (about 26 billion USD) as a result of the sterilization policy pursued over the last five years in a vain attempt to avoid real appreciation of the domestic currency, about half of this sum would be used to exchange all the NCB's zloty-denominated monetary liabilities into euros. The remaining 13 billion USD would be paid into a 'banking sector liquidity fund' (BSLF) to be used in cases of runs on solvent but illiquid banks (Caprio et al., 1996). This amount is equivalent to some 90 per cent of sight deposits and 25 per cent of all deposits in the Polish banking system, and should therefore be quite enough. If there was reason to suppose that 13 billion USD might prove inadequate for this purpose, then the Polish government could obtain a euro-denominated credit line to supplement the funds of the BSLF, as the Argentine government has done.[23] In fact, a number of eurozone central banks do not have a lender of last resort facility *sensu stricto*. This includes the Bundesbank, which can only lend to banks for liquidity purposes against the security of government paper, and indeed also the ECB itself, which is similarly restricted.

The main advantages of rapid unilateral euroization are as follows:

1. A rapid reduction in interest rates due to the elimination of currency risk, to levels which exceed those in the eurozone only by the amount of pure country risk. Since Polish government paper currently trades at about 120 basis points above US Treasury paper of the same maturity, loan rates could be expected to fall to about 8 per cent compared to 15–20 per cent at present.
2. Lower interest rates on domestic currency-denominated government and central bank paper should save the public sector the equivalent of about 1.5 per cent of GDP per annum. This significantly outweighs the loss of central bank seigniorage revenue, which would amount to less than 0.2 per cent of GDP.[24] This would enable Poland to satisfy the Maastricht fiscal deficit criterion.[25]
3. Capital inflows would accelerate rapidly, boosting investment and economic growth.
4. Maybe most important, all these benefits could be reaped within two years (rather than the five we would expect Poland to need to enter EMU by the traditional route), and moreover, without the need to meet the Maastricht inflation criterion, with the ensuing need for nominal appreciation and its (possibly devastating) effects on the competitiveness of the traded goods sector.

The most frequently mentioned disadvantages of unilateral euroization have been:

1. Loss of seigniorage. We have already discussed and dismissed this.

2. The contractionary shock, which may result from unilateral euroization (Lutkowski, 1999). The benefits described above suggest that the effect is more likely to be expansionary than contractionary: falling interest rates will increase demand rather than reduce it, capital inflows will improve the supply side and the avoidance of nominal appreciation should help the traded goods sector in comparison to the traditional approach, while the improvement in the fiscal balance resulting from lower public debt service obligations will (at the least) not reduce demand.

3. Inertial inflation in the traded goods sector inherited from the zloty regime could continue after euroization, causing the traded goods sector to become uncompetitive (Buiter, 1995), which might require a long recession to cure. Our first response is that this problem can only be worse when a country follows the traditional approach to EMU, with its need for nominal appreciation to offset the HBS effect on the prices of non-traded goods, and when it is also exposed to the dangers of an 'appreciation bubble'. Second, under unilateral euroization any inertial inflation expected by the authorities can be allowed for by an up-front devaluation of the domestic currency at the moment of conversion. This is something which may not be allowed when countries follow the traditional route, as the exchange rate at which a country joins EMU has to be negotiated with existing members.

4. 'Real convergence' is required before the euro can be adopted safely (Orłowski and Rybinski, 1999; and Rosati, 1999). The argument takes two forms. In the first, it is argued that applicant countries need to develop industrial structures that are similar to the average of the existing eurozone members. Otherwise, ECB policy in response to an asymmetric supply or demand shock, which affects existing members differently from applicants, will be unsuitable for the needs of the latter. However, since a country like Poland accounts for about 2 per cent of eurozone GDP, its needs will hardly be taken into account when the ECB sets monetary policy, even when Poland becomes a fully-fledged EMU member. The argument is therefore one against *early* EMU entry in any form, and not against *unilateral* entry in particular. To what extent is it valid in this form? The first thing to note is that, while it is true that asymmetric shocks in the presence of heterogeneous industrial structures may make it impossible for the central bank of a monetary union to set monetary or exchange rate policy so that it would be suitable for all member countries, this need not mean that a country with an industrial structure which will make it respond differently to a shock than will the current members of a monetary union, should not therefore join. The reason is simply that, although central bank policy aims to offset the effects of shocks, it can usually do so only imperfectly. Thus, if the shock is expansionary for current EMU members (and therefore by assumption contractionary for applicants) central bank policy will only

partially offset the expansionary effect among current members. The expansion of economic activity among current members will thus help to offset the contraction among applicants. The question therefore becomes the following. Which will be stronger, the additional impact of expansion among current members on applicants *resulting from the greater integration of the applicants with the existing members of the EMU as a result of their accession* (via increased trade and capital flows over and above those which existed before their entry into the EMU), or the contractionary effect of the central bank's policy, which will now apply also to the new members? Second, we should note that the structures of the CEE applicant countries do not, in fact, differ much from those of existing EMU members. Thus, the structure of Poland's economy differs from the EU average more than does that of France or Germany, but less than those of Finland, Greece, Ireland or Sweden, two of which are not only members of the EU but also of EMU (Table 8.1). As regards the structure of industry, Poland's differs from the EU average less than do those of Ireland and Portugal, both of which are EMU members (Table 8.2). What is more, the share of intra-industry trade between CEE applicants and the EU (which is often taken as a measure of economic integration between countries) is lower than the share of such trade in the overall trade of the 'founding six' with the rest of the EU, but is approximately the same as the share of the countries of the so-called 'southern expansion' (Greece, Portugal and Spain) (Fidrmuc et al., 1999).

The second form the argument takes is the claim that CEE applicants need to make their economies more flexible before they can expose them to the discipline of the euro. If it were indeed true that the difference in economic structures between the applicants and current EMU members was such that the applicants would be subject to large shocks which were not offset significantly either by ECB policy or the effects of opposite shocks in the rest of the EMU, then it would be the case that more flexible markets would help to reduce the costs involved. One question would still remain: should we expect an improvement in the flexibility of European TEs in the five to seven years it would take them to join the EMU by the traditional route? While one can expect some further modest improvement in ownership structure, corporate governance, efficiency of government, and the elimination of some protectionist practices (for example, in banking, telecommunications and government procurement), one needs to set against this the new rigidities EU membership will introduce: the 'social chapter' of the Maastricht Treaty; new environmental, health and safety standards; the common agricultural policy and so on. On balance the CEE countries need not necessarily become more flexible over the coming half decade, and their recent performance in terms of such 'real' indicators as unemployment and growth suggests that they are certainly not outside the range of current EMU members.

Table 8.1   Structure of gross value added (%)

	Agriculture forestry and fisheries		Fuels and energy		Manufacturing		Construction		Market services		Non-market services		Distance from EU-15 average	
	1986	1995	1986	1995	1986	1995	1986	1995	1986	1995	1986	1995	1986	1995
Finland	7.5	3.1	3.0	2.7	24.6	26.6	7.8	5.7	38.1	40.3	18.9	20.7	9.7	13.9
France	3.9	2.5	4.8	4.0	21.4	18.9	5.4	4.7	47.1	51.9	17.4	18.0	4.1	4.1
Greece	16.2	14.2	4.2	3.7	18.9	13.8	6.9	6.2	38.3	47.3	15.5	14.7	15.8	14.7
Germany	1.8	1.0	4.7	4.0	30.7	24.1	5.5	5.4	43.3	52.1	14.0	13.4	7.0	3.6
Holland	4.4	3.3	8.7	6.3	18.1	16.9	5.1	5.2	51.7	57.6	12.0	10.7	10.1	8.7
Italy	4.3	2.9	4.9	5.9	24.1	21.1	6.1	5.1	47.7	52.2	12.9	13.0	3.4	2.4
Ireland	8.4	6.0	3.1	2.7	29.1	30.8	5.6	4.8	37.2	40.8	16.6	14.9	11.1	15.0
Portugal	7.2	3.7	5.3	4.2	27.5	23.7	5.1	5.3	41.6	46.2	13.2	16.9	6.6	6.4
Spain	5.6	3.1	5.9	5.8	23.1	19.8	6.5	8.7	46.8	48.0	12.1	14.6	4.3	5.2
Sweden	3.3	2.2	3.8	3.2	22.4	21.7	6.0	4.6	38.3	43.6	26.2	24.7	13.4	12.8
UK	1.6	1.6	8.2	6.0	23.7	20.9	5.8	5.0	45.2	53.7	15.5	12.7	3.5	3.4
EU-15	3.5	2.3	5.4	4.7	24.5	21.2	5.8	5.4	45.6	51.5	15.3	14.8	–	–
Poland	–	5.5	–	7.0	–	22.6	–	8.0	–	43.8	–	13.1	–	9.3

Source: Eurostat Yearbook 1997; Central Statistical Office (GUS) Poland.

Table 8.2 *Shares in gross value added in the manufacturing industry (%)*

	Textiles		Food processing		Transport equipment		Chemicals and petrochemicals		Electrical and optical equipt		Iron and steel		Distance from EU-10 average	
	1990	1995	1990	1995	1990	1995	1990	1995	1990	1995	1990	1995	1990	1995
Finland	3.5	2.3	12.2	11.0	4.7	4.2	6.5	6.5	9.2	15.5	4.4	6.5	7.05	7.65
France	4.4	3.6	8.3	8.4	9.8	7.9	8.7	9.1	10.6	10.5	5.1	4.5	0.99	1.98
Germany	3.4	2.3	6.3	6.3	12.4	10.8	9.5	9.5	14.0	11.7	7.4	6.7	5.31	4.66
Holland	2.5	1.7	15.8	13.1	4.9	3.4	14.2	12.5	10.5	9.4	3.6	3.7	10.69	8.12
Ireland	4.0	2.8	31.2	28.7	1.9	1.5	16.0	26.5	16.3	18.5	–	–	25.49	27.81
Italy	8.0	11.4	5.7	9.6	6.3	6.0	6.4	8.6	8.9	11.3	4.2	5.4	6.38	7.32
Portugal	19.4	13.8	9.3	10.7	4.8	3.4	4.8	3.6	5.0	5.5	2.9	1.4	16.98	14.00
Spain	8.1	7.0	14.4	15.5	9.6	11.4	8.4	10.0	8.3	8.7	4.5	4.4	7.10	7.53
Sweden	1.4	1.2	7.5	8.0	8.2	12.8	5.7	8.0	10.1	12.8	4.6	5.8	5.21	6.00
UK	4.8	4.5	11.5	11.4	11.4	9.3	9.1	10.0	10.7	11.1	4.3	3.8	3.50	2.58
EU-10	5.1	4.7	8.7	9.4	9.7	8.8	8.6	9.5	11.1	11.1	5.3	5.2	–	–
Poland 90/95	9.3	10.8	22.1	18.7	8.8	6.3	10.7	13.6	7.7	3.7	14.3	6.5	17.17	14.27
Poland 97		9.5		19.2		6.5		12.7		4.3		5.6		13.51

Source: Eurostat Yearbook 1997; Central Statistical Office (GUS) Poland.

One danger to which we have drawn attention ourselves (Bratkowski and Rostowski, 1999) is that the large influx of capital which we expect to follow upon euroization may lead to a credit boom, which could result in loose lending practices, the accumulation of bad debt, and ultimately a banking crisis. But European TEs must in any case expect very large capital inflows over the next decade (much of which will be mediated by their banking systems), so that they have to ensure a big improvement in the quality of their banking skills and bank supervision in any case. Unilateral euroization will merely increase the magnitude of the phenomenon.

Finally, we need to mention the differences between the unilateral euroization that we propose and the establishment of a currency board based on the euro as suggested by others (Dornbusch and Giavazzi, 1998). The precise differences will depend on the legal framework of the monetary system in each TE. As described above, and as applied to Poland, our proposal consists in unilaterally declaring the euro the only legal tender in the state. This makes the regime one likely to be more credible than a simple currency board. This is because under a currency board the domestic currency continues to exist, and the rules which bind it to the euro can be repealed. With euroization, exit is a harder process: a *new* domestic currency would have to be created and declared legal tender. But speculation against the continuation of the euro regime, that is, against the, as yet non-existent, new domestic currency would still be possible. It could be undertaken by borrowing in Poland and investing abroad – on the assumption that a 'new zloty', in which existing liabilities would be denominated would be created, and then devalued, by the authorities. To describe this 'exit path' should be sufficient to show how unlikely it would be, especially during the few years between unilateral euroization and full EMU membership. Furthermore, such an exit would also be possible after fully-fledged accession to EMU.

However, a stronger form of euroization is also possible. In the Polish context this would consist in abolishing legal tender altogether, and declaring the euro merely the currency in which government would collect taxes and pay its obligations, and having the central bank stand ready to convert all its zloty-denominated assets and liabilities into euro at the fixed conversion rate.[26] Because of the freedom of individuals in Poland to enter into contracts in any currency, and given the constitutional bar to retroactive legislation, this approach has the advantage of giving euro-denominated contracts full constitutional protection from conversion at a later date into 'new zloty' and subsequent devaluation.[27] Under such an arrangement speculation against euroization is indeed completely impossible, unless one wished to speculate on a change in one of the fundamental principles of the constitution!

CONCLUSIONS

The traditional route to EMU membership seems to be fraught with difficulties, the most important of which is the absence of macroeconomic policy instruments which would allow the CEE applicant countries to achieve the fiscal, exchange rate and inflation criteria of the Maastricht Treaty together with the maintenance of prudent levels of the CA deficit in the context of rapid economic growth and free capital movements.[28] Nor are the difficulties removed if the Maastricht inflation criterion were to be suspended for the CEE applicants as we have suggested. The problem of achieving the exchange rate criterion together with a prudent level of the CA deficit would remain. Unilateral euroization seems the best solution to this conundrum, and none of the objections which have been put forward against it are fully convincing when they are tested against the conditions obtaining in most of the first wave of applicant countries.

NOTES

1. We follow the common usage in referring to the 'third stage' of EMU as simply EMU.
2. In fact, it is sufficient to assume that productivity growth is lower in the non-traded goods sector, that its growth is uniform across countries and that returns to labour have a larger share in the non-traded goods sector. For a formal treatment of how differential productivity growth in the two sectors affects the real exchange rate between two countries, see Obstfeld and Rogoff (1996, pp. 204–12).
3. This need not lead to any increase in either the domestic or foreign prices of tradables produced by the fast-growing country, since unit labour costs denominated in foreign currency remain unchanged (the same number of domestic workers can produce more tradable goods and get paid proportionally more). For this reason the nominal exchange rate need not be affected in any way either.
4. Where $NPV(CA) = NPV(CA_t + CA_{t+1} + CA_{t+2} + \ldots + CA_{t+}\infty)$. The same holds for $NPV(B)$ and $NPV(Y - C - G - I)$ and so on.
5. This point has been made forcefully to us by Stanislaw Gomulka in personal communications.
6. This is the view of Kopits (1999). The present authors suspect that the current degree of capital account liberalization is so great in the 'Visegrad Three' countries, that remaining controls are not effectively binding (that is, they do not allow macroeconomic results, different from those which would occur in the absence of the controls, to be achieved).
7. In the presence of limited liability and asymmetric information in the provision of finance, there is increased risk to lenders as leverage increases, so that only part of the CA deficit can be financed through the accumulation of foreign debt by the private sector. The rest is financed by FDI.
8. And the CA deficit rising ever more above its sustainable level. The IMF has a very crude procedure for estimating the level of a country's sustainable CA deficit (Knight and Scacciavillani, 1998).
9. We are grateful to Stanislaw Gomulka for suggesting this approach.
10. A more acceptable way of putting this might be that $E(\varepsilon_t) = 0$, and the effects we are discussing will occur if the actual values of ε_t are positive and the same goes for η.

11. A more general formulation is:

$$Y = E(i^* - \pi^e, G - T, \rho P^*/P, Y) \qquad E_1 < 0, E_2 > 0, E_3 > 0, 0 < E_4 < 1.$$

12. If the international reserves of the central bank increase, then the exchange rate is not, in fact, fully floating.
13. This reduces Y. Hence in a small open economy with a floating exchange rate, contractionary monetary policy affects Y via ρ rather than via i.
14. Alternatively we can think of the expansionary monetary policy as causing a one-to-one offsetting capital outflow which by definition improves the CA. For the extent to which the final outcome necessarily involves a depreciation or not of the domestic currency, see Kouri (1978).
15. Much depends on the nature of what is produced by the non-traded goods sector. If it is exclusively non-storable services, then the result we described above indeed follows. If non-tradables include assets (for example, land or buildings, the returns to which are expected to increase with increased productivity in the tradables sector and real appreciation in the non-tradables sector), then the anticipation of these processes can be expected to induce a capital inflow, which will cause an appreciation of the equilibrium nominal exchange rate and will in fact help to stifle average inflation.
16. Because ρ is defined as units of domestic currency/unit of foreign currency, appreciation involves a reduction in it (that is, a negative growth rate of ρ), which therefore has to be subtracted from the domestic interest rate (giving a positive effect to the left-hand side of (8.13)) to arrive at the foreign interest rate.
17. The 15 per cent band of the current ERM-II mechanism could well be sufficient for such a bubble to develop. Once it had done so it would likely be allowed to break through the ceiling, since the alternative would be to acquiesce in higher inflation.
18. Due to the effect of capital inflow on the domestic money base. The ensuing inflation will ultimately lead to a high CA deficit as well.
19. In April 2000, Poland abolished the crawling devaluation and introduced free float.
20. The latter seems to be the current problem in Germany.
21. Estonia, the Czech Republic, Slovenia and Poland certainly qualify, with Slovakia and Hungary as possibles.
22. The British government has estimated that technical preparations – for example, in the banking system – would take less than two years in the case of the UK. Thus, if preparations began now, euroization would begin when euro notes already existed.
23. This possibility means that even countries which have international reserves which are only adequate to cover the euroization of coins and notes and other monetary liabilities of the NCB to the banking sector, can still establish a BSLF by setting up credit lines with eurozone commercial banks if their governments have a sufficiently good credit rating (for example, Hungary).
24. The National Bank of Poland earns seigniorage by emitting non-interest-bearing currency and depositing the international reserves it obtains in this way in interest-bearing foreign assets (US and German government bills and bonds, current accounts with OECD commercial banks and so on). This amounts to some 26 billion USD. About 4 billion of this, or one-sixth, would need to be converted into euro notes and coins for circulation within the country. The remainder, which would back the NBP's non-cash liabilities to the banking sector (obligatory and voluntary reserves and repos) as well as the institution's net worth (which would fund the 'banking sector liquidity fund' already described), could largely remain invested as at present. The gross loss of seigniorage would thus amount to about 240 million USD per annum (at an interest rate of 6 per cent) or merely some 0.18 per cent of GDP! To free the NBP's remaining international reserves to act as backing for its liabilities to domestic commercial banks and the contingent liabilities of the BSLF, repos, which were used to sterilize capital inflows, should be transformed into central government liabilities. The stock involved is about 7 billion USD. However, as a result of euroization, interest payments on this debt would fall from the present level of one billion USD to about 550 million USD annually.

25. For the last four years the consolidated general government deficit, measured according to EU statistical conventions, has remained stubbornly at about 3.3 per cent of GDP (0.3 per cent of GDP above the reference value).
26. Some commercial banks might want to convert first into euros and then into some other currency, but since they would be obliged to match their assets to their liabilities, and since depositors would usually want to convert into euros, most zloty instruments would be converted into euros. Some commercial banks' debtors might wish to convert their liabilities into non-euro currencies, which might cause a problem if it were unmatched by depositors' preferences.
27. We are grateful to Boguslaw Grabowski for this point.
28. The latter is an explicit requirement of EU accession, while the former is likely to be implicit.

REFERENCES

Bratkowski, Andrzej S. and Jacek Rostowski (1999), 'Wierzymy w euro' (We believe in the euro), *Zeszyty BRE Bank-CASE*, No. 44, Warsaw, 11–15.

Buiter, Willem (1995), 'Macroeconomic policy during transition to a monetary union', London School of Economics Centre for Economic Performance, Discussion Paper No. 261, September.

Caprio, Gerard, Michael Dooley, Danny Leipziger and Carl Walsh (1996), 'The lender of last resort function under a currency board: the case of Argentina', Policy Research Working Paper No. 1648, Washington, DC: World Bank.

Dornbusch, Rudiger (1976), 'Expectations and exchange rate dynamics', *Journal of Political Economy*, **84** (December), 1161–76.

Dornbusch, Rudiger and Francesco Giavazzi (1998), 'Hard currency and sound credit: a financial agenda for Central Europe', mimeo.

Fidrmuc, Jarko, Daniela Grozea-Helmenstein and Andreas Woergoetter (1999), 'Intra-industry trade dynamics in East–West relations', *Weltwirtschaftliches Archiv* **135** (2), 332–46.

Halpern, László and Charles Wyplosz (1997), 'Equilibrium exchange rates in transition economies', *IMF Staff Papers*, **44** (4), 430–61.

Knight, Malcolm and Fabio Scacciavillani (1998), 'Current accounts: what is their relevance for policymaking', in Olga Radzyner and Auriel Schubert (eds), *Current Account Imbalances in East and West: Do They Matter?*, Vienna: Oesterreichische Nationalbank, pp. 28–59.

Kopits, Gyorgi (1999), 'Implications of EMU for exchange rate policy in Central and Eastern Europe', IMF Working Paper No. WP/99/9, Washington, DC: IMF.

Kouri, Pentti (1978), 'International investment and interest rate linkages under flexible exchange rates', in Robert Aliber (ed.), *The Political Economy of Monetary Reform*, London: Macmillan, pp. 132–48.

Lutkowski, Karol (1999), 'Memorandum', mimeo, April, Warsaw.

Obstfeld, Maurice and Kenneth Rogoff (1996), *Foundations of International Macro-economics*, Cambridge, MA: MIT Press.

Orłowski, Witold and Krzysztof Rybinski (1999), 'Recepta na kryzys walutowy' (Prescription for a currency crisis), *Zeszyty BRE Bank–CASE*, No. 44, Warsaw, 17–19.

Rosati, Dariusz (1999), 'Jeszcze nie czas na likwidacje zlotego' (It's not time to eliminate the zloty), *Zeszyty BRE Bank–CASE*, No. 44, Warsaw, 21–4.

Wilcox, David (1989), 'Social security benefits, consumption expenditure, and the life-cycle hypothesis', *Journal of Political Economy*, **97** (April), pp. 288–304.

9. Central European economies in the aftermath of the Russian payments crisis

Lucjan T. Orlowski

INTRODUCTION

Economic reforms in Central European transition economies (TEs) have strengthened the institutional framework of their financial system and made them less vulnerable to contagion effects of world financial crises. They have been able to resist relatively well the negative pressures on their currencies and financial markets induced by the Russian crisis of August/September 1998. But they are still perceived as the emerging market economies since their economic transformation from a command to a free market system is hardly completed. A further institutional advancement of the financial system, improvements in corporate governance, and the pursuit of a more transparent, forward-looking stabilization policy are still among the key future tasks, completion of which will undeniably contribute to immunity of these countries to future world financial crises.

This chapter examines the consequences and the macroeconomic policy responses in Poland, Hungary and the Czech Republic to the Russian financial crisis. The analysis concentrates on contagion effects of the Russian payments moratorium and the subsequent wave of corrections in emerging financial markets, rather than on long-run spillover effects on Central European real gross domestic product (GDP). Various indicators that are believed to reflect the degree of vulnerability of TEs to financial contagion are reviewed. The chapter further argues that more transparent macroeconomic policies are helpful for generating signals of financial stability to world financial markets, thus strengthening resilience to financial contagion. It points to the inflation-forecast targeting monetary policy coupled with flexible exchange rates, such as currently applied in the Czech Republic and in Poland,[1] as an inherently transparent system.

The analysis begins from an overview of the underlying causes of the Russian payments crisis. It further elaborates on the efforts to 'decouple' the three examined central European economies from the Russian economic and financial problems and provides evidence of the magnitude of financial contagion. The chapter is concluded by suggestions for the development of appropriate policies that would shield the transforming economies from the transmission of shocks related to possible future financial contagion.

MAIN CAUSES UNDERLYING THE RUSSIAN PAYMENTS CRISIS

The August/September 1998 financial turmoil in Russia sent negative shockwaves throughout the integrated world financial markets. It contributed to severe downfalls of stock prices and to flight to treasuries not only in the emerging market economies, but also in industrialized countries.[2]

In the beginning of August 1998, the Central Bank of the Russian Federation (CBRF) issued a large tranche of the ruble-denominated credit in the amount equivalent to 3.3 billion USD aimed at recapitalization of small and medium-sized financial institutions. However, the banks quickly converted this injection of reserves into dollar-denominated assets driving up the dollar and causing an unsustainable slump of the ruble. The falling ruble sharply increased fiscal costs of servicing the Russian debt. Subsequently, on 25 August, the Russian government failed to make a 91.5 million USD payment on its debt, declared a 90-day moratorium on all public debt repayment, and announced a 32 billion USD Debt Swap Plan, restructuring the short-term ruble debt into long-term securities. These developments forced investors to incur large losses. At the same time, the CBRF declared trading of the Russian ruble on the Moscow Interbank Currency Exchange 'invalid' and subsequently suspended interventions to support the currency. The CBRF no longer had sufficient foreign currency reserves to intervene in foreign exchange markets. During the last week of August 1998 alone, the CBRF used 3 billion USD of its foreign currency (previously estimated at 10 billion USD) and 5 billion USD of monetary gold reserves to cushion the rapid depreciation of the ruble. During the one-year period ending on 26 August, the ruble lost 42 per cent of its value against the USD and the Russian stock market plunged 84 per cent in dollar terms. However, more than half of these losses was incurred during August 1998. The dramatic depreciation of the ruble-denominated assets contributed to severe runs on banks and to a widespread asset dollarization in Russia in the last quarter of 1998.

International financial institutions that prematurely engaged in large investments in Russia, particularly during the period 1996–98, were seriously harmed by the collapse of the country's financial system. Prior to the financial crisis, German banks, which in total invested more than 30.5 billion USD in Russia, incurred large losses from the ruble collapse; so did several Swiss banks. The total exposure of US banks to Russia before the crisis was estimated at 7 billion USD. To say the least, profits of international banks were seriously hurt regardless of whether their response to the crisis was to reduce their exposure by taking losses or to increase reserves against the questionable or non-performing Russian loans. In the end, investors who allocated large assets in the country with a poor state of public finance were severely punished.

In essence, the economic turmoil in Russia resulted mainly, if not exclusively, from the deep fiscal crisis. The country's nominal consolidated fiscal deficit reached 8.2 per cent of GDP in 1997, and the average budget deficit-to-GDP ratio in the period 1994–97 was 7.9 per cent (based on the Russian Ministry of Finance data). According to unofficial reports, the Russian Federation government collected only a minor fraction of planned tax revenues in the first half of 1998. The large, persistent deficit contributed to the enormous public debt and to extremely high and volatile interest rates. The primary reason for the fiscal deficit was the inability of the Russian federal government to collect taxes. Since the collapse of the former Soviet Union (FSU), changes in the taxation system went in many wrong directions (Orlowski, 1997). The system was gradually decentralized, resulting in a significant fiscal autonomy of local governments that reluctantly repatriated taxes to the central authority in Moscow. The 1993 Russian Constitution and the 1995 Act on the Federation Council granted considerable fiscal autonomy to independently elected local government officials. This resulted in their tendency to retain tax revenues and, at the same time, to present large spending bills to the central government. The country urgently needs to reform the taxation system, preferably in the direction of a tax-sharing system in which most of tax revenues are channelled to the federal authority and later redistributed to local governments.

To make things worse, prior to the crisis the Russian federal government failed to collect tax revenues from large enterprises dominating the country's economy. A vast majority of these monopolies, run by a relatively small group of wealthy industrial magnates (mostly former communist officials, who had made enormous fortunes on fraudulently conducted privatization), engaged in an egregious tax evasion. Among the most notorious debtors to the government were the largest energy companies, such as Gazprom, the world's largest natural gas company, and Unified Energy Systems. These companies, by permission of Prime Minister Victor Czernomyrdin (former Chairman of Gazprom and one of the perceived leaders of the 'military–industrial complex'), were allowed to pay their taxes not in cash, but in promissory notes trading in secondary markets at deep discounts. Based on CBRF estimates, the total notional value of these notes amounted to at least 50 per cent of the broad money supply M2 in 1997. Tax evasion by large monopolies shifted the tax burden to small enterprises and foreign companies that did not enjoy an adequate political support in Moscow, especially in the Russian parliament dominated by communists and nationalists. The efforts led by the ousted Prime Minister Sergei Kiriyenko to enforce payments of tax arrears by large enterprises, particularly those that customarily held cash in hard currency receivables in foreign bank accounts, did not succeed. Without the collection of tax arrears, the IMF assistance granted on 20 July 1998 could not be released.

Not only did Kiriyenko fail to receive necessary support from the parliament for his crusade against the industrial magnates, but his government seriously overestimated tax revenues by counting on more disciplined payments by large monopolies, on the one hand and, on the other, it built into the budget excessive expenditures that it could not finance. The most painful outcome of the gap between fiscal revenues and expenditures was the government's inability to pay wages of employees of state-owned enterprises. Prior to August 1998, Russian miners, transportation workers, teachers and other public sector employees could not receive any compensation for up to eight months of their work. The unpaid wages in the public sector amounted to 0.4 per cent of GDP at the end of June 1998.

The structure of budget revenues of the federal government was also erratic. The shares of corporate profit taxes, personal income taxes and (vastly evaded) value-added taxes in government revenues had been steadily declining. These taxes were replaced by duties on export and import transactions. Only at the beginning of August 1998, did President Boris Yeltsin eliminate exemptions of large state enterprises from paying a 20 per cent value-added tax. Various custom duties constituted an unprecedented, by international standards, 25 per cent of the Russian federal government budget revenues in 1997. Needless to say, various export and import taxes, quotas and licences levied by both federal and local governments created a fertile ground for corruption on the part of government officials. For instance, Russian exporters of crude oil customarily had to go through a complex system of quotas, licences and export taxes finding it necessary to pay bribes at each stage of the export approval process.

Before the crisis, Russian exporters notoriously deposited their foreign currency earnings in foreign banks, ignoring President Yeltsin's executive decrees aimed at forcing them to repatriate these earnings back to Russia and at reporting them to tax authorities. At the same time, some of the exporters extensively drained large government subsidies. Moreover, tax revenues from exports were negatively affected by two additional factors. First, the structure of Russian exports became eroded practically to crude oil and natural gas only. As the world prices of these commodities continued to decline until mid-1999, the country's export revenues deteriorated sharply. These exports could not be boosted by the depreciation of the ruble in foreign currency terms, because of the price-inelastic nature of the demand for these commodities. Second, the

1998 collapse of Russian financial markets had a damaging effect on the national savings rate. In 1997, Russia recorded a current account surplus of 4.0 billion USD, largely due to the advantage of gross national savings (equal to 20.2 per cent of GDP) over gross domestic investment (19.0 per cent of GDP). Further erosion of national savings contributed to the decline of a current account surplus to 1.5 billion USD in 1998.

The dramatic depreciation of the ruble in 1998 contributed further to the fiscal disarray. The deepening problems in the domain of public finance generated a public distrust in the Russian currency forcing the national economy to rely increasingly on non-monetary transactions. This process is examined by Gaddy and Ickes (1998) who view the Russian experience with the departure from a traditional, money-based economy as a 'virtual economy' system. Within this peculiar framework, the managers of large monopolies have increasingly relied on non-monetary transactions. Their financial obligations to tax authorities, to suppliers and to employees were satisfied predominantly through non-cash means. Gaddy and Ickes report that at least 40 per cent of all taxes to the Russian federal government in 1997 was paid in non-monetary terms. They quote the Karpov Commission report stating that the country's largest companies conducted 73 per cent of their business in barter and in other non-monetary means in that year. Although these large companies formally paid a decent 80 per cent of their tax obligations to the federal government, only 8 per cent of this payment was actually made in cash. The widespread application of barter transactions became an effective way of tax evasion by Russia's largest companies. Under the Czernomyrdin government, these enterprises were allowed to take advantage of far-reaching tax loopholes. In addition, they neglected to pay the wages of their employees. According to the Russian government estimate, the total value of unpaid wages in the public sector amounted to the equivalent of 2 billion USD at the end of September 1998. In an extreme case of fulfilling wage arrears, in October 1998 local governments in Siberia provided public school teachers with 15 bottles of vodka for each month of their unpaid wages. By all means, the 'virtual economy' has stalled the process of democratic reforms in Russia.

There are several key reasons for the failure of market-orientated economic reforms in Russia, including the corrupt privatization, in the course of which tens of billions of dollars of natural resources were given away to politically connected insiders. But more importantly, the country did not have a suitable institutional framework to carry out indubitable economic reforms. Foreign governments and institutions also share some responsibility for Russia's failure, particularly the International Monetary Fund, by exerting pressures on the Russian government in 1992 to defend the failing ruble zone by all means and to avoid an introduction of separate national currencies. Within the common currency system, the member countries of the Commonwealth of Independent

States (CIS) tried to compete for seigniorage revenues by injecting more money into the system in order to monetize large fiscal deficits. They consequently levied an 'inflation tax' on the entire ruble zone (Orlowski, 1994; Dąbrowski, 1997). This resulted in a huge absorption of near-hyperinflation primarily by Russia and contributed to a major distrust in the early economic reform of the Gaidar government.

The sweeping IMF lending to Russia in 1996 and 1997 totalling 22 billion USD also contributed to the crushing financial crisis. The Russian government borrowed heavily from foreign investors by issuing ruble-denominated Treasury bills. The international financial institutions fervently purchased these bills trusting that the IMF would always stand ready to bail out Russia.

In sum, a lack of a comprehensive institutional reform of the public finance domain was the common denominator of all underlying reasons for Russia's financial turmoil. If the present erratic system remains in place, future external funds are likely to be mismanaged and defrauded. Therefore, further injections of foreign public and private funds to Russia will not take place until a comprehensive reform of the fiscal system is enacted and implemented.

Russia's mounting macroeconomic instability and the financial crisis contributed to the contraction of its real GDP by 4.6 per cent in 1998 (which recovered in 1999 when the real output grew by 3.2 per cent). In contrast, the economic recession did not hit Central European TEs, which recorded a solid growth at that time.[3] The disparity in income growth and in the advancement of economic reforms between Russia and the well-performing Central European TEs was the main reason for decoupling the latter from the Russian problems. This in turn has helped to cushion negative effects of the Russian crisis in Central European TEs.

EFFECTS OF THE RUSSIAN CRISIS ON CENTRAL EUROPEAN ECONOMIES

The effects of external financial crisis on domestic markets are usually rather immediate. The economic literature refers to them as 'contagion effects' of external financial crisis, as opposed to 'spillover effects' that a crisis has on the real economy. Spillover effects certainly take more time to materialize.

Preliminary data and surveys of the three largest economies of the region – Poland, Hungary and the Czech Republic – prove that Central European financial markets were not severely affected by the Russian turmoil. In the wake of the crisis, the Moscow stock market experienced a significant correction of 86.7 per cent in USD terms by 20 October 1998, from the beginning of the year. At the same time, the Warsaw market fell by only 25.2 per cent, the

Budapest market by 31.0 per cent, and the Prague market by a mere 13.9 per cent in USD terms.

The Russian crisis had a considerably milder impact on the stability of exchange rates in Central Europe than did the Asian crisis. This point is proved in Table 9.1, which shows percentage deviations of residuals between actual and trend-fitted values of the USD in terms of the Polish zloty (PLN), the Hungarian forint (HUF), and the Czech koruna (CZK). The tested simple regression function is:

$$s_t = a + b\,t + \xi_t \qquad\qquad (9.1)$$

where s_t is the domestic currency value of the USD, t is the time trend, and ξ_t is the error term.

Table 9.1   *Percentage deviations of residuals between actual and fitted values of the USD in terms of Central European currencies, January 1996–October 1998 series*

Reported week	PLN/USD trend: residual/fitted %	HUF/USD trend: residual/fitted %	CZK/USD trend: residual/fitted %
11 July 1997	3.3	2.9	9.6
18 July 1997	8.2	3.8	10.9
25 July 1997	7.5	4.9	10.7
1 August 1997	8.0	6.0	11.7
8 August 1997	7.9	5.2	9.2
15 August 1997	7.8	4.4	9.1
22 August 1997	7.0	3.4	7.7
29 August 1997	7.1	3.4	8.0
5 September 1997	7.2	2.9	8.5
11 July–5 Sept. 1997 average	*7.1*	*4.1*	*9.5*
22 August 1998	–2.8	0.1	–4.2
29 August 1998	1.7	0.8	8.2
5 September 1998	–0.1	–0.5	–8.8

Sources: Own calculations based on OANDA, Inc. currency tables; Orlowski and Corrigan (1999).

For comparison, the period 11 July–5 September 1997 represents the aftermath of the Thai baht crisis, while the period 22 August–5 September 1998 coincides with the Russian moratorium on foreign debt repayments and the suspension of the ruble convertibility. Strong pressures on currencies of Central

Europe during the Thai baht crisis persisted for at least nine consecutive weeks in July and August of 1997. In contrast, a large and deep depreciation of Central European currencies at the time of the Russian crisis lasted merely one week, following the declaration of payments moratorium by Russia. The Asian crisis affected most severely the CZK, followed by the PLN. The HUF weathered the Asian contagion relatively well, very likely due to the narrower band of permitted fluctuations.[4] The monetary policy based on exchange rate stability coupled with the narrow band also helped the National Bank of Hungary (NBH) to cushion the impact of the Russian crisis on the HUF. Moreover, the NBH responded to the Russian crisis with monetary tightening, while the National Bank of Poland (NBP) cut interest rates at that time. The NBH decision to raise the rates was aimed at reaffirming its commitment to the exchange rate stability as the key monetary policy target. In contrast, the NBP lowered the rates to send a signal to the financial community that Poland is not vulnerable to contagion effects induced by the Russian crisis. NBP underpinned the message of decoupling the country's economy and its ongoing economic transformation from the fundamental problems of Russia.

The test results presented in Table 9.1, based on average weekly foreign exchange rates data, are comparable to those of Gelos and Sahay (2000) who use high-frequency data to examine foreign exchange and stock market fluctuations. They conclude that stock markets in the Czech Republic, Hungary and Poland showed stronger responses to the Russian crisis than to the Asian and the Czech koruna (May–July 1997) crises. With a relatively short time lag, the Russian stock performance had a well-defined negative impact on equity market returns in all three countries in the summer of 1998. There was no evidence of a positive contagion, that is, any positive shocks on Central European stock markets from the turbulence in Russia. Gelos and Sahay (2000) as well as Krzak (1998) demonstrate that the Budapest stock market was the most severely affected due to the high participation of foreigners.

Although there was a clear evidence of transmission of negative contagion effects from the Russian to the Central European stock markets, impulse responses in foreign exchange markets were less pronounced. Gelos and Sahay (2000) show only mild contagion from Russia to Poland and Hungary (and from Russia to Slovenia) primarily with regard to eurobonds. An intriguing finding in their study is a strong correlation between Russia and Hungary in exchange rate movements, but not between Russia and Poland. It is this author's opinion that these opposite reactions stem primarily from the difference between policy responses to the declaration of the Russian moratorium. As stated earlier, the NBH was forced to increase interest rates in compliance with the monetary policy focus on exchange rate targeting, while the NBP was able to cut interest rates in accordance with the system of more flexible exchange rates.

Similar results confirming a considerably stronger impact of the Asian crisis on the currencies of Central European TEs are obtained by Linne (1999). By applying cointegration analysis of exchange rate movements he finds that contagion effects of the Russian crisis on TEs' currencies were considerably milder than the Asian effects. Linne seems to suggest that systemic dissimilarities between Russia and Central Europe might have played a role in the weaker impact of the Russian crisis. He further argues that the mild effects of the Russian crisis might be related to the fact that this was the third in a row currency crisis affecting Central European TEs in the two years following the Asian and the CZK crises. Therefore, the investors' confidence in Central European financial markets was already eroded by the previous crisis episodes and, consequently, the contagion effects of the Russian crisis were relatively subdued. Another interesting result in Linne's study, yet somewhat puzzling and contradictory to Gelos and Sahay (2000), is a relatively strong correlation between fluctuations of the Russian and the Polish financial markets, while the correlations between Russian and Czech, and Russian and Hungarian markets appear to be considerably weaker.

Short-term spillover effects of the Russian crisis on real incomes of Central European countries were even less ubiquitous. A key reason for this mild impact was the relatively small export exposure of these countries to Russia and to other CIS countries on the eve of the crisis (7 to 8 per cent of the total export).[5] Nevertheless, intermediate, more dynamic effects of the Russian crisis on real incomes in Central European TEs are more complex. The reduction of exports to Russia has caused corrections of real GDP growth rates and a deterioration of current account positions. On the positive side, it induced downward pressures on inflation stemming from the slowdown of the economic growth and, in the case of Poland and Hungary, from a higher domestic supply of goods unsold to Russia. The effects of the Russian crisis on selected macroeconomic indicators in the three examined Central European countries are presented in Table 9.2.

As shown in Table 9.2, there was a mild deterioration of the actual GDP performance in the Czech Republic and, to a lesser extent, in Poland, while the Hungarian economy grew at a higher than expected rate. However, these results cannot be attributed solely to the Russian crisis. They are strongly affected by the lower than expected income performance in the European Union (EU) and, consequently, by disappointing Central European exports. Evidently, the current account positions of Poland and Hungary deteriorated sharply in the last quarter of 1998 and fell well below the levels forecasted prior to the Russian crisis by the WEFA Group. In contrast, inflation scores in all three countries were considerably better, showing further improvement in the fourth quarter of 1998 and even healthier in the first quarter of 1999. The currencies' performance and the growth of foreign exchange reserves were very good, demonstrating

Table 9.2 Corrections due to the Russian crisis: pre-crisis forecasts versus actual data for 1998

	Real GDP growth rates		Current account (%GDP)		CPI inflation*		Actual CPI inflation**		Currency per USD		Change in FX res. (%GDP)**
	Forecast	Actual	Forecast	Actual	Forecast	Actual	Dec.98–Dec.97	Mar.99–Mar.98	Forecast	Actual	Actual
Poland	+6.2	+4.8	−3.1	−4.4	10.7	9.9	8.6	5.6	3.50	3.59	+2.1
Hungary	+5.0	+5.1	−3.1	−4.8	13.5	12.3	10.3	9.3	222	218	+2.0
Czech Rep.	−0.3	−2.3	−3.3	−1.9	10.3	8.3	6.8	2.5	32.5	30.6	+5.3

Notes:
* monthly average data for the year.
** end-of-period data.
Forecasts are based on the WEFA Group: Eurasia Economic Outlook, formulated in the third quarter of 1998.

Source of actual data: National statistical offices of Poland, Hungary and the Czech Republic.

limited contagion effects of the Russian crisis. The HUF and the CZK actually outperformed the forecast and the PLN fell only slightly in spite of the series of interest rate cuts by the NBP in 1998. However, a further, sharper depreciation of the PLN was seen in the first quarter of 1999, induced by a sharp cut in interest rates by the NBP in January 1999 rather than by spillover effects of the Russian crisis.

During the Russian crisis in the third quarter of 1998, *Hungarian* total exports rose by a brisk 11.3 per cent comparing to the third quarter of 1997.[6] However, the dynamics of export slowed down from 17.3 per cent in the second quarter of 1998, very likely as a result of lower sales to Russia. The declining quarterly rate of export growth was more than compensated by the sharp increase in investment spending of 18.1 per cent in the third quarter, up from 12.7 per cent in the second quarter of 1998 comparing to the corresponding quarters of 1997. The growth rate of consumer spending was roughly the same during the Russian crisis as before it. Consumption rose by 4.1 per cent in the third quarter of 1998 (comparing to the third quarter of 1997), somewhat less than its second quarter growth of 4.3 per cent. Overall, the Hungarian real GDP growth rate actually accelerated to the annual rate of 5.6 per cent in the third quarter of 1998, up from the 5.1 per cent in the second quarter, primarily due to the sharp increase in large, infrastructural investment projects. The annualized real GDP growth rate slightly declined to 5.2 per cent in the fourth quarter of 1998 and to 3.4 per cent in the first quarter of 1999. However, this pattern may be attributable to seasonal fluctuations and to changes in the EU economy rather than to spillover effects of the Russian crisis.

The *Polish* economy continued a fast-pace growth at the time of the Russian crisis. According to Poland's Central Statistical Office, the country's real GDP grew at the annual rate of 5.0 per cent in the third quarter of 1998, down from the robust 5.3 per cent in the second quarter. But the real GDP growth slowed considerably to 2.9 per cent in the last quarter of 1998 and even more, to 1.5 per cent in the first quarter of 1999. Poland started a solid recovery in the second quarter, resulting in the overall growth of 4.1 per cent in 1999. The collapse of the economies of Poland's eastern neighbours and the decline in exports and cross-border sales were, at least partially, responsible for the Polish economic slowdown at the end of 1998 and in the beginning of 1999. The surplus on unregistered trade dropped from the peak of 6.2 billion USD in 1997, to 6.0 in 1998, and further to 3.6 in 1999. Moreover, between 1998 and 1999 Polish official exports to Russia declined by 53.5 per cent, while imports grew by 21.6 per cent. At the same time, the share of exports to Russia in total exports fell from 5.8 to 2.5 per cent while the share of imports from Russia rose from 5.1 to 5.7 per cent, primarily as a result of rising oil prices. In monetary terms, Poland's exports to Russia in 1999 fell by 1.1 billion USD compared to 1998. Despite a visible dent in the Polish economic growth, the Russian crisis did not significantly slow Poland's economic recovery; the country's real GDP regained the fast pace in the third quarter of 1999 and it is expected to accelerate to 5.3 per cent in 2000.

Overall, the Russian crisis did not damage severely either Hungary or Poland. On the contrary, they were among the world's fastest-growing economies in 1998, propelled primarily by an impressive boom in investment spending, including foreign direct investment.

The *Czech* economy experienced a real GDP contraction of 2.9 per cent in the third quarter of 1998, compared to 2.1 per cent correction in the second quarter. This income decline was rather independent of the financial problems of Russia and attributable to considerably lower investment spending. The country experienced internal economic problems, primarily in the banking sector, in the aftermath of the CZK crisis of May–July 1997. Both before and after the abandonment of the currency peg, inflation showed a high degree of persistence, exceeding that of its major trading partners by a wide margin. This persistence is viewed by Brada and Kutan (1999) as a key factor hampering the country's macroeconomic stability. The Czech Republic also experienced some political instability, namely the departure of the long-time government of Prime Minister Vaclav Klaus. This, in turn, reduced consumer expenditures considerably, curbed additionally by very high real interest rates.

Overall, the short-term spillover effects of the Russian crisis were almost non-existent in Hungary and the Czech Republic, and relatively mild in Poland. In the cases of Poland and Hungary, the weak downward pressure on income growth may have helped to prevent these economies from 'overheating'. In terms of the impact on stabilization policy, the crisis contributed to high unemployment, however, on a positive side, it simultaneously exerted downward pressures on Central European inflation resulting from a higher domestic supply of goods unsold to the FSU. By no means did the Russian crisis alone jeopardize the fiscal and monetary stability of these economies.

THE CASE FOR DECOUPLING

In response to the Russian crisis, the governments of Central European TEs vigorously emphasized that the state of their economic affairs was very different from that of Russia to reinforce 'decoupling' from FSU countries lacking reforms. To support this claim, they pointed to *the shift of export from the East to the West* throughout the 1990s, a move which in the face of the Russian crisis provided an effective defence mechanism against spillover effects.

Additional factors contributing to the immunity of Central European TEs to the Russian crisis were also emphasized. Among them, *systemic differences and the degree of advancement of economic reforms* played a critical role.

While Russia is still struggling to come up with a basic programme of transformation to a market system, these countries have entered the advanced stages of the economic transformation. They have all achieved a much higher level of fiscal discipline and monetary stability. Their tax collection is comparable to that of advanced industrialized nations and it remains in contrast to the rampant tax evasion in Russia. Their fiscal discipline resulted in considerably lower 1998 inflation than previously forecast, which continued a downward trend in 1999 as shown in Table 9.2. By comparison, Russia's 1998 CPI inflation increased to 56.4 per cent, mainly as a consequence of the central bank's massive credit injection to the country's enterprises and financial institutions struggling to survive. In addition, Central European countries have achieved a visible progress in corporate governance and institutional advancement of banks and other financial institutions and have established an effective system of prudential supervision and monitoring, in sharp contrast to the lack of progress in Russia. Monetary policy systems in Central Europe are also more advanced. Central banks of the Czech Republic and Poland have enacted complex systems of direct inflation targeting that allow them to expand exchange rate flexibility and, at the same time, to apply low inflation targets. This policy is aimed at reducing real appreciation of their currencies and, consequently, at lowering current account deficits and improving the risk structure of capital inflows (that is, encouraging more foreign long-term portfolio and direct investment over short-term capital inflows).

The second important factor disavowing the Central European TEs' association with Russia and other post-Soviet states is *their EU candidacy status* and the resulting comprehensive programmes of the EU accession. The ongoing preparations for accession provide them with specific tasks of structural adjustments and institutional development in compliance with the EU laws and requirements. Some of the structural changes in the agricultural and energy sectors would not be feasible outside of the EU accession strategy and the active EU financial support. Russia and other CIS countries do not enjoy the benefits of the EU resources stemming from the candidacy status.

DESIGNING DEFENCE MECHANISMS AGAINST FINANCIAL CONTAGION

Whatever the merits of empirical assessment of financial contagion effects are, the countries in transition need to construct a set of financial crisis indicators and to design policies preventing financial contagion.

In a study aimed at examining possible warning signals of financial crisis, Brüggemann and Linne (1999) attempt to identify the leading indicators of currency and banking crises for Central European economies. The authors apply the 'signals' approach to financial contagion advanced by Kaminsky and Reinhart (1999) and show that export earnings, real currency appreciation and large budget deficits are among the relevant indicators of currency and banking crisis in Central European TEs. In contrast, imports, capital flight and domestic real interest rates are of little value. These authors present empirical evidence of a close link between the balance of payments crisis and the banking crisis in Central Europe since financial liberalization has become more widespread.

Specifically, Brüggemann and Linne demonstrate that in the Czech Republic the signals of a forthcoming currency crisis could be traced back 18 months prior to its occurrence. The strongest signals were sent by the slowdown of exports, by sharp real appreciation of the CZK, and by the expanding budget deficit. Nevertheless, in the aftermath of the flexible exchange rate declared by the Czech Republic in July 1997, these variables showed considerable improvements. In Hungary (as well as in Romania), the currency crisis indicators were not explicit. Neither export, nor real exchange rates implied any forthcoming problems. Instead, the Hungarian banking crisis and the HUF exchange rate jitters were related rather to the undercapitalization of banks and to the poor quality of their loan portfolios.

The empirical research by Brüggemann and Linne (1999), as well as Gelos and Sahay (2000), Krzak (1998) and Orlowski (1999) implies that the next stage of the economic transformation in Central Europe will focus on establishing preventive measures and effective remedies against future financial contagion. Among the most essential tasks serving this purpose are more transparent and flexible monetary policies, a strong fiscal discipline, and a further advancement of the institutional development of the financial sector.

Without a doubt, Central European TEs will be susceptible to financial contagion as their capital markets are open to international financial investors and speculators and as there is no turning back from capital market liberalization. The three TEs have largely eliminated capital controls in compliance with the OECD codes of liberalization once they became OECD members. Under these circumstances, their financial markets and banking systems are exposed to foreign competition. Therefore, they are compelled to strengthen capacity building and institutional advancement of the financial sector (Fink et al., 1998). This process is far from being completed. Central Europe's banks are still burdened by corporate governance deficiencies, which make them particularly vulnerable to bank runs or massive withdrawals of deposits at the time of yet another world financial crisis.

In order to shield their economies from bank runs and currency attacks, the TEs need to accumulate foreign currency reserves in order to bring them to the level which is indispensable for defending banks in the case of the depository base drainage. Monitoring the relation between foreign currency reserves and

M2 money will be particularly useful for this purpose. The ratio of M2 to foreign exchange reserves will be relatively low in order to reduce the risk of banking system collapse related to bank runs. In my opinion, this ratio will not exceed a multiple of three since higher ratios would create an imminent danger of currency crisis as learned from the Asian experience during the 1997–98 crisis.

As I argue in Orlowski (1999), the effective protection of Central European countries against financial contagion can be accomplished through the creation of liquidity or the build-up of foreign exchange reserves as a secured, ready to use source of foreign currency loans. Large foreign currency reserves held by central banks are necessary to alleviate a devastating impact of speculative attacks and bank runs on banking systems in crisis-affected countries. When speculative attacks take place, the banking system is likely to incur large withdrawals of deposits and central banks are pressed to provide for the lost liquidity. The infusion of bank reserves, that is, the growth of central bank liabilities, needs to be matched by the corresponding increase in assets. This can be accomplished by a growth of domestic credit or by an increase in the domestic currency value of foreign exchange reserves. Consequently, it becomes essential that central banks in the economies affected by financial crisis have at their disposal large foreign currency reserves in relation to the broad money supply. The domestic currency value of these reserves will increase significantly as a result of devaluation or a steep depreciation of domestic currency that may follow a declaration of full exchange rate flexibility. This suggests that a crisis-infected economy will be well protected in the presence of a relatively low ratio of broad money (M2) to foreign exchange reserves, meaning that the reserves are sufficient to cushion a liquidity crisis in the banking system.

Table 9.3 shows ratios of M2 money to foreign exchange reserves for the crisis-affected economies of Asia and for the three Central European TEs. The Asian countries allowed for too much growth of domestic money balances, and thus they did not have sufficient foreign exchange reserves to defend their banking systems during the financial crisis. Large injections of the IMF lending into these economies were essential for preventing a possible collapse of their financial systems. In contrast, Central European economies appeared to be within the safety limits of foreign currency reserves, with the notable exception of the Czech Republic. However, since they are experiencing a continuous growth of monetization at levels comparable to those of the EU, they will need to achieve a proportional increase in foreign exchange reserves. All three TEs are considered to be attractive for both foreign direct and portfolio investment, thus their foreign exchange reserve positions are unlikely to be jeopardized in the foreseeable future. Yet, they need to monitor the relevant monetary ratios and to maintain high interest rates that will promote further accumulation of foreign exchange reserves.

Table 9.3   Ratios of M2 money to foreign exchange reserves (end-of-period data)

	1995	1996	1997	1998
Indonesia	6.90	6.39	4.51	3.12
South Korea	6.08	6.21	5.90	4.13
Malaysia	3.12	3.43	3.40	2.79
Philippines	5.75	4.49	5.14	4.49
Thailand	3.65	3.86	3.51	4.50
Czech Republic	2.71	3.25	3.60	3.34
Hungary	1.45	1.79	2.07	2.28
Poland	2.86	2.60	2.45	2.38

Source: Own calculations based on IMF, International Financial Statistics.

Moreover, in order to diminish the risk of financial contagion, these economies need to raise national savings. The 1997 savings rates of 19.7 per cent in Poland, 23.0 per cent in Hungary and 23.9 per cent in the Czech Republic were relatively low in relation to gross domestic investment (respectively, 22.9 per cent, 24.9 per cent, and 30.2 per cent). Nevertheless, the continuation of the negative net international investment position contributes to large current account deficits and it aggravates these countries' exposure to potential international financial contagion. Again, disinflation, domestic macroeconomic stability and high interest rates are necessary for facilitating a long-term growth of national savings.

A higher propensity to save is a direct function of a public confidence in the stability of a financial system that is likely to remain unscathed during a possible future financial crisis (Stiglitz, 1998). A high degree of financial stability in TEs depends on their ability to reduce inflation to a low, sustainable level. This can be accomplished by sound fiscal and monetary policies demonstrating a credible, forward-looking and transparent expression of government strategies, intentions and tactics in the area of macroeconomic stabilization. In essence, vulnerability to financial shocks can be reduced when monetary policy becomes predictable and transparent; when financial markets firmly believe in the temporary nature of such shocks and in an inevitable, quick return to financial stability. In my opinion, the governments of TEs will be well advised to generate financial stability *internally*, that is, by applying autonomous monetary policies, rather than *externally*, by rushing to a currency peg to the euro.[7] This can be accomplished effectively through a highly transparent, forward-looking and credible monetary policy system, such as *direct inflation targeting*. It is a policy framework based on a pre-announced future target of inflation along with a disclosure of appropriate policy tactics and means to reach this goal.[8] The system of direct inflation targeting accompanied by flexible exchange rates for transition economies is advocated in Orlowski (2000) where I examine its possible advantages and drawbacks consistent with the major tasks of transition. I further demonstrate the early empirical results of inflation targeting applied in the Czech Republic (as of January 1998) and in Poland (as of January 1999). The study views direct inflation targeting as a feasible policy approach for developing the necessary monetary convergence and financial stability in preparations for the EU/EMU accession.

On a final note, the EU candidacy status of the three TEs and their active preparations for accession to the Union are favourable for developing an effective cushion to international financial contagion. The EU integration process concentrates on the institutional advancement of these economies that is likely to result in better immunity of their financial markets and their banking systems to international financial crises.

NOTES

1. Flexible exchange rates have prevailed in the Czech Republic since July 1997. Poland allowed the zloty to float fully on 12 April 2000.
2. This section is a revised version of my analysis in Orlowski (1999).
3. The Czech Republic was an exception. It experienced a relatively mild recession attributable mainly to internal problems rather than to the Russian crisis.
4. The target band for the HUF was ± 2.5 per cent on either side of the parity, while the band for the PLN was ± 7.0 per cent at that time.
5. This reduced exposure constituted a major shift from these countries' previous 75–80 per cent export dependency on the FSU countries in the last years of the CMEA (Council for Mutual Economic Assistance) trading bloc existence.
6. The data reported in this section are taken from the National Bank of Hungary quarterly reports.
7. This represents a contrary view to that of Bratkowski and Rostowski (Chapter 8 in this volume), as well as Dąbrowski (Chapter 7 in this volume).
8. For a thorough examination of theoretical models and practical approaches to inflation targeting, see Bernanke et al., (1999). Mishkin (2000) proposes a set of conditions for an effective implementation of inflation targeting in emerging market economies.

REFERENCES

Bernanke, Ben S., Thomas Laubach, Frederick S. Mishkin and Adam S. Posen (1999), *Inflation Targeting: Lessons from the International Experiences*, Princeton, NJ: Princeton University Press.
Brada, Josef C. and Ali M. Kutan (1999), 'The persistence of moderate inflation in the Czech Republic and the koruna crisis of May 1997', *Post-Soviet Geography and Economics*, **40** (2), 121–34.

Brüggemann, Axel and Thomas Linne (1999), 'How good are leading indicators for currency and banking crisis in Central Europe? An empirical test', Halle Institute for Economic Research: Discussion Paper No. 95, Halle, Germany, April.

Dąbrowski, Marek (1997), 'The reasons for the collapse of the ruble zone', in Lucjan T. Orlowski and Dominick Salvatore (eds), *Trade and Payments in Central and Eastern Europe's Transition Economies*, Westport, CT: Greenwood Press, pp. 145–69.

Fink, Gerhard, Peter R. Haiss, Lucjan T. Orlowski and Dominick Salvatore (1998), 'Central European banks and stock exchanges: capacity building and institutional development', *European Management Journal*, **16** (4), 431–46.

Gaddy, Clifford and Barry Ickes (1998), 'Russia's virtual economy', *Foreign Affairs*, **77** (5), 53–67.

Gelos, R. Gaston and Ratna Sahay (2000), 'Financial market spillovers in transition economies', IMF Working Paper 00/71, Washington, DC: International Monetary Fund.

Kaminsky, Graciella L. and Carmen M. Reinhart (1999), 'The twin crises: the causes of banking and balance-of-payments problems', *American Economic Review*, **89** (3), 473–500.

Krzak, Maciej (1998), 'Contagion effects of the Russian financial crisis on Central and Eastern Europe: the case of Poland', Oesterreichische Nationalbank: *Focus on Transition*, No. 2, 22–37.

Linne, Thomas (1999), 'Contagion effects of Central and East European currency crises', Halle Institute for Economic Research: Discussion Paper No. 96 (April), Halle, Germany.

Mishkin, Frederic S. (2000), 'Inflation targeting in emerging market countries', *American Economic Review: AEA Papers and Proceedings*, **90** (2), May, 105–9.

Orlowski, Lucjan T. (1994), 'The disintegration of the ruble zone: driving forces and proposals for policy change', *Aussenwirtschaft*, **49** (1), 101–30.

Orlowski, Lucjan T. (1997), 'Russia's economic stability: recent evidence and policy implications', in Armand Clesse and Vitaly Zhurkin (eds), *The Future Role of Russia in Europe and in the World*, Luxembourg: Luxembourg Institute for European and International Studies, pp. 183–208.

Orlowski, Lucjan T. (1999), 'The Asian and the Russian financial crises: propagation effects and policy responses in Central Europe's transition economies', Halle Institute for Economic Research: Discussion Paper No. 104 (October), Halle, Germany.

Orlowski, Lucjan T. (2000), 'Direct inflation targeting in Central Europe', *Post-Soviet Geography and Economics*, **41** (2), March 134–54.

Orlowski, Lucjan T. and Thomas D. Corrigan (1999), 'Volatility of Central European exchange rates: reaction to financial contagion and policy recommendations for EU accession', *Russian and East European Finance and Trade*, **35** (6), 68–81.

Stiglitz, Joseph (1998), 'The role of international financial institutions and the current global economy', Address to the Chicago Council on Foreign Relations, Chicago, 27 February.

PART III

Reforming Social Safety Nets

10. Reforming welfare states in post-communist countries[1]

Nicholas Barr

This chapter argues that the communist welfare state was, for the most part, well-adapted to the old order and – precisely for that reason – is systematically and predictably ill-suited to a market economy.

Since the range of the welfare state – income transfers, health and health care, and education and training – is far too large for a single chapter, discussion is restricted in several ways. First, though reform involves both an economic transition, from central planning to a market economy, and a political transition, from totalitarian to more democratic forms of government, this chapter discusses only economic aspects. Second, the chapter focuses on what is distinctive about the transition from plan to market, as opposed to developmental issues, or more general discussion of the reform of the state sector. Thus the chapter concentrates on *systemic* issues and hence on the principles of reform rather than on country-specific detail. Third, there is no attempt to cover all the components of the welfare state. Most of the chapter is about income transfers and, within those, pensions; there is some discussion of education, but only aspects which are directly relevant to systemic change. Health, though vitally important for economic, political and social reasons, is not discussed, partly for reasons of space, and partly because the issues it raises are more managerial than systemic. Put another way, discussion of reforming outdated health sectors in transition economies (TEs) sounds very much like discussion of reforming outdated healthcare systems in other countries. Finally, the chapter concentrates mainly on the advanced reformers of Central and Eastern Europe (CEE), with some discussion also of Russia, but with only limited discussion of the other former Soviet Union (FSU) countries.

The chapter starts by setting out the simple analytics of transition. That discussion establishes a reform agenda which shapes the rest of the chapter: assisting labour market adjustment; relieving poverty; reforming pensions; and adjusting education. Each section has a similar structure, setting out in turn the problem and its location in the transition process, strategic policy directions, and assessment of progress to date. The final section concludes with a view ahead.

THE ANALYTICS OF TRANSITION

Was reform inevitable? The first part of the answer is that central planning failed, as manifested by low, and in some countries eventually negative, growth rates in the 1970s and 1980s throughout CEE and the FSU, at living standards well below those of Western countries. Thus a central objective of transition is to increase living standards. The second part of the answer, offered in a spirit of pragmatism not ideology, is that market forces, whether explicitly in the West or implicitly as in the fast-growing provinces of China, are the major allocative mechanism in all countries with sustained growth. For market forces to translate into such growth requires a large array of supporting institutions (Barr, 1998a), including effective government; but no modern, technologically advanced country has maintained satisfactory growth rates through central planning. The question facing reformers, therefore, is not whether to move towards market allocation, but what sort of balance between market and state they seek, for example, to use Wilensky and Lebeaux's (1965) terminology, whether to pursue a residual or an institutional welfare state.

To shape subsequent discussion, I want to explain the underlying architecture of the systemic change.

The Old Order

For the purposes of this chapter, the old order can be described in terms of five outrageously simplified stylized facts:

1. Every worker got the same, low wage.[2]
2. Wages were topped up by generous universal benefits such as family allowance, pensions, subsidized food, housing and heating, often provided by enterprises.
3. Work was guaranteed, and jobs were for life.[3]
4. Resources were allocated by central planning.
5. Government was totalitarian.

The last two aspects are acutely relevant to education and training and are taken up in the section on education below.

The first three stylized facts have a major bearing on the shape of income transfers. They imply that the communist system had no unemployment (because of stylized fact 3), and hence no (or virtually no) system of unemployment benefit. It had no poverty, at least officially (because of 1, 2 and 3), and hence no poverty relief except for groups like the frail elderly. It had no sophisticated targeting (because of 1). The flat income distribution had important implications: benefits were universal, since no selectivity by income level was needed; for similar reasons, there was generally no personal income tax (its absence being regarded as one of the victories of socialism); and the state's administrative capacity was weak, both because no sophisticated targeting was needed and because most benefits were delivered by the enterprise.

The Effects of Transition

This was the state of play in the late 1980s. Of the many effects of transition, for present purposes three stand out.

1. The distribution of income and earnings widened. This outcome represents progress to the extent that it results from competitive market forces, for example rising wages for skills, which are in demand. It is adverse to the extent that it results from criminal activity or the exploitation of a monopoly position. If we wave a magic wand to remove all the adverse reasons, the remaining increase in the dispersion of pre-transfer income is, in many ways, a sign of *success* – it shows that the market is generating incentives which are essential for economic growth – and as such is a permanent feature of transition and post-transition economies.
2. Output fell, leading to a disproportionate decline in tax revenues. Though growth has resumed in most of the reforming countries, output generally remains below its 1989 level, often considerably so. Output in the Commonwealth of Independent States[4] (CIS) as a whole (Table 10.1) is not much more than half of its 1989 level. In only four countries, Hungary, Slovakia, Slovenia and – pre-eminently – Poland, has output returned to or exceeded its 1989 level.[5] Thus this second transition effect remains true in all but a few countries.
3. Job security ended.

Several results follow directly.

Open unemployment As a direct consequence of (2) and (3), there was a sharp increase in unemployment which, as Table 10.2 shows, exceeds 10 per cent in most of the CEE and Baltic countries, as well as Russia. This outcome is bad because unemployment is costly in terms of forgone output and in personal terms. It is, however, up to a point necessary, in that at least a minimum level of unemployment is an inescapable price for the dynamic efficiency of market allocation. It is noteworthy that unemployment in countries such as Bulgaria and Romania whose reforms faltered is, broadly speaking, as high as in aggressive reformers like Poland.

Table 10.1　Real GDP in Eastern Europe, the Baltics and the CIS compared with 1989

	Projected real GDP in 1999 (1989 = 100)
Albania	91
Bulgaria	66
Croatia	79
Czech Republic	95
Estonia	79
Hungary	99
Latvia	60
Lithuania	65
FYR Macedonia	60
Poland	121
Romania	74
Slovakia	101
Slovenia	107
Eastern Europe and the Baltic states	101
Armenia	42
Azerbaijan	46
Belarus	75
Georgia	33
Kazakhstan	59
Kyrgyzstan	62
Moldova	30
Russia	53
Tajikistan	43
Turkmenistan	53
Ukraine	35
Uzbekistan	89
CIS	53
Eastern Europe, the Baltics and CIS	77

Note:　Countries in italics are those where output has returned to or exceeded its 1989 level.

Source:　EBRD (1999, Table 1.1).

Rising poverty is an inexorable consequence of (1) and (2). As a proposition in pure logic, falling output coupled with a widening income distribution leads to increased poverty. Notwithstanding the well-known problems of methodology and measurement facing attempts to quantify poverty (for a summary, see Barr, 1998a, Ch. 6), the logic is amply supported by empirical evidence. According to the World Bank estimates (World Bank, 1999, p. 6), the number of people living on less than 4 USD per day in CEE, the CIS and the Baltic countries rose from 14 million in 1989 to 147 million in 1996. Table 10.3, based on the same poverty line, gives a broad indication of the pattern across different countries. The richer countries, particularly the Czech Republic, Slovakia and Slovenia had few people with incomes below 4 USD per day in either the late-1980s or mid-1990s and, on that measure, thus experienced little increase in poverty.[6] The radical reformers, in contrast (Poland, Estonia, Latvia and Lithuania) experienced substantial increases in the poverty headcount, from 6 per cent of the population to 20 per cent in Poland, and from one per cent to 37 per cent in Estonia, though in all those countries strong growth should reduce these figures fairly rapidly. In less successful reformers, in contrast, the increase in poverty was greater (in Romania from 6 to 59 per cent, in Russia to 50 per cent and in Ukraine to 63 per cent) and with little likelihood of any short-run improvement.

Table 10.2   Unemployment rates, selected transition countries

	Unemployment rate, 1998 (estimated)
CEE and the Baltic countries	
Bulgaria	12.0
Czech Republic	7.5
Estonia	9.6
Hungary	7.8
Latvia	9.2
Lithuania	6.4
Poland	10.4
Romania	10.3
Slovakia	11.9
Slovenia	14.5
Newly Independent States (NIS)	
Belarus	2.3
Moldova	1.6[*]
Russia	12.4
Ukraine	3.7

Note: [*]1997.

Source: EBRD (1999).

*Table 10.3   Poverty rates (% of population) 1987–1988 and 1993–1995,
              selected TEs*[*]

	Poverty headcount	
	1987–88	1993–95
CEE and the Baltic countries		
Bulgaria	2	15
Czech Republic	0	<1
Estonia	1	37
Hungary	1	4
Latvia	1	22
Lithuania	1	30
Poland	6	20
Romania	6	59
Slovakia	0	<1
Slovenia	0	<1
NIS		
Belarus	1	22
Moldova	4	66
Russia	2	50
Ukraine	2	63
Average CEE and NIS without		
Central Asia	3	43

Note: [*]The poverty line is 120 international dollars per capita per month.

Source: Milanovic (1998, Table 5.1).

Ineffective targeting, a third strategic outcome of transition, follows from (1).
Because of the decline in tax revenues, the problem is critical. A system designed
for a flat earnings distribution, continuous employment and labour shortage,
predictably misallocates benefits in the face of a diversified distribution. In
Weisbrod's (1969) terminology, two problems of targeting arise. First, horizontal
efficiency aims to avoid gaps in coverage, that is, to hit *all* the poor. The inherited
inadequate systems for addressing unemployment and rising poverty are two
clear failures under this head. Second, vertical efficiency seeks to avoid leakages
of benefit, that is, the concern is to hit *only* (or mainly) the poor. However,
benefits designed for a flat distribution will, by definition, fail this test in the face
of a diversified distribution, pensions being a particularly egregious example.
It is therefore not surprising that high public pension spending has been a

particular concern and, for this and other reasons, pension reform has been a central – and politically highly salient – issue for policy makers.

Resulting Reform Directions

For these reasons, the inherited system was systematically dysfunctional relative to the needs of a market economy. Strategic reform directions thus follow directly from the nature of systemic change discussed in the next three sections.

ASSISTING LABOUR MARKET ADJUSTMENT

The Problem

Policy makers face a series of interrelated problems, all directly related to transition.

- *Rising open unemployment* afflicted all the successful reformers (Table 10.2). It was in part cyclical, caused by falling output, and hence by falling demand for labour. It was also structural, arising from labour with the wrong skills and/or in the wrong place. The burden of unemployment fell particularly on some groups. Women were laid off in larger numbers than men in the early transition, because their tasks were considered non-essential, because inherited social legislation like generous maternity leave made women more costly to employ, and sometimes because of outright discrimination. Long-term unemployment increased rapidly, as did youth unemployment; and geographical mismatches between jobs and workers produced large and persistent regional differences in unemployment.
- *An acute shortage of resources* for dealing with the problem was a major constraint, not least because of the collapse in tax revenues associated with falling output and restructuring.
- *An acute shortage of administrative capacity* in the face of intractable administrative problems was a further constraint. Part of the problem is that there was no pre-existing system on which to build. The old system had employment exchanges, but their function was entirely different: to find *workers* in an era of labour shortage, rather than to find *jobs* in the face of rising unemployment. There is a second set of difficulties. In the West, unemployment benefits are designed on the assumption (unrealistic, but tenable) that there is a binary divide between employment and unemployment. In the TEs the problem is complicated, particularly in less-advanced countries, by the size of the grey economy and the scope

for small-scale agriculture. As a result, the distinction between employment and unemployment becomes blurred, making it difficult to define unemployment and even more difficult to find measurable indicators which can be implemented cost-effectively to determine whether a particular applicant is, or is not, eligible for benefit.[7]

* *Major incentive problems* A helpful incentive structure arises where:

poverty line ≤ unemployment benefit < minimum wage < average wage,

the relation between unemployment benefit and the minimum wage being particularly important. Because of the inherited compressed wage distribution, however, the poverty line, unemployment benefit and the minimum wage in the early transition were hardly differentiated; and the difference between the minimum wage and the average wage was also smaller than is typical in the West. Though the wage distribution decompressed significantly in the advanced reformers,[8] acute problems of benefit design persist in countries where wage differentials remain relatively small.

* *Impediments to occupational and geographical labour mobility* included inadequate housing markets and the fact that many social benefits were organized by enterprises.
* *A skills mix not well-suited to a modern market economy* The resulting issues of education and training are taken up in the section on education, below.

Strategic Policy Directions[9]

Early transition policies

Open unemployment: problem or solution? The inherited distortions and sharp output decline made labour shedding from the state sector both necessary and desirable. A central question, however, is whether higher rates of unemployment speed reform. On one view, a rapid shake-out of labour creates a pool of unemployed workers on which the growing private sector can draw. The resulting policy strategy is to subsidize unemployment. An alternative view is that, though some unemployment is necessary, private firms prefer to recruit people currently employed in the state sector. High open unemployment, on this view, is not a prerequisite for restructuring. The resulting policy strategy is to subsidize employment.

In part, the argument depends on the nature of unemployment. As already discussed, employment in industrialized countries is largely a binary phenomenon (that is, a person is either employed or unemployed, either employed or retired), whereas in developing economies the problem tends to be that of underemployment. Thus unemployment, to an important degree, is a social construct rooted in the institutional structure of the labour market.[10]

Two patterns of labour market adjustment to some extent parallel these two different constructs. In most of CEE the brunt of adjustment fell on employment. Unemployment rose sharply. It later declined, at least in the advanced reformers, in part because of strong private sector growth in countries like Poland, Hungary, the Czech Republic and Slovenia and, perhaps more importantly, because people dropped out of the labour force through early retirement or because they stopped registering as unemployed once their entitlement to unemployment benefit (in most countries 6–12 months) had expired. The pool of long-term unemployed showed little turnover, reinforcing the point that higher unemployment does not necessarily speed up restructuring.

A very different pattern of adjustment was found in several of the CIS countries, where the brunt of adjustment fell on wages rather than employment. Workers often retained their attachment to their enterprises, even with little or no pay, and thus continued to enjoy some enterprise benefits. Thus market disequilibrium manifested itself through underemployment. With demand stagnant and labour immobile, again it is not clear that higher unemployment is a prerequisite for reform.

Income support　There is no controversy about the need for institutions offering income support to people who are unemployed. The agenda for policy makers involves the design of unemployment benefit in a way that addresses the problems discussed earlier – rising unemployment and an acute scarcity both of fiscal and administrative resources. In that context, flat-rate benefits have particular advantages in the early transition. They are cheap, since nobody receives unemployment benefit above the minimum. They are administratively easier than earnings-related benefits: it is still necessary to establish whether or not a person is eligible but, having established that, no calculation of benefit is necessary – a major advantage in the early transition when there were few calculators and even fewer computers. A third, more arguable, advantage is that flat-rate benefits, by offering most workers a lower replacement rate[11] than earnings-related benefits, create improved incentives to find work.

Thus the short-run strategy for unemployment benefit abandons insurance and consumption smoothing as objectives, concentrating solely on poverty relief. In World Bank parlance (Holzmann and Jorgensen, 1999), benefits are limited to risk coping.

Active labour market policies　Benefits have the critical palliative purpose of cushioning the impact of restructuring. Active labour market policies address a second aspect of reform by helping people to find earning opportunities through employment or self-employment. Such policies are of three sorts: job information, training measures and job creation.[12] In the short run the most that can be done is to introduce simple, cost-effective job-information and job-matching systems.

Addressing constraints on labour mobility   The lack of effective housing markets is a major impediment. Though the issue cannot be solved in the short term, starting reform *is* an early task. A second impediment is the fact that many social benefits are tied to the enterprise. This made sense in an era of full employment, jobs for life and soft budget constraints. Enterprises administered most short-term benefits; and they paid contributions *en bloc* on behalf of their workers.[13] As a result, the social insurance/pension authorities knew neither about individual contributors (unnecessary when everyone could be presumed to have a full contributions record) nor about individual recipients (unnecessary for universal benefits). Thus a system which was rational under the old economic order is dysfunctional in a world where not everyone has a job, where labour mobility is high, and where competitive pressures, especially international competitive pressures, make enterprises sensitive to the substantial compliance costs of benefit administration.

Thus a major reform direction is to move most benefits out of the enterprise, for example, transferring most administration of contributions and benefits to the social insurance/pension authorities. Strengthening administration – no less important for being identified here only briefly – assists labour mobility and also opens new policy options, for example, a capacity to raise the basic pension fully in line with inflation, but pensions above the minimum by a smaller amount.

Though the nature and direction of change is clear, its speed is not. If the strategy, as in the advanced reformers, is through open unemployment, reform should proceed expeditiously. If, as in Russia, many workers retain their formal attachment, the case for decoupling is to that extent perhaps less urgent.

Medium-term options

Income support   Though policy in the early transition may have to concentrate scarce resources on protecting the minimum benefit, there are several advantages to strengthening the relation between contributions and benefits once economic conditions permit. A clear relation between contributions and benefits reduces incentives to evading contributions. It is helpful if some of the impetus to enforce contributions comes from incentives rather than administrative activity, not least because enforcing contributions, particularly in the growing private sector, will be a continuing problem. Second, and more strategically, a closer relationship between contributions and benefits brings back the insurance and consumption-smoothing function of benefits, both of which imply a system of earnings-related benefits. This makes it possible to have a well-designed social insurance strategy, with poverty relief increasingly based on tax-funded benefits such as social assistance and family allowance. In World Bank parlance (Holzmann and Jorgensen, 1999), this brings risk-mitigation back into the picture.

Active labour market policies As fiscal and administrative constraints relax, more sophisticated policies become an option. However, though there is general agreement about the importance of information facilities to help match unemployed people with prospective employers, the cost-effectiveness of training and public employment schemes is a controversial area, discussed further below.

Addressing constraints on labour mobility Removing most benefits from the enterprise is undoubtedly necessary in the medium term, even if not in the short term.

Investing in human capital is discussed in the section on education, below.

Progress to Date

Designing unemployment benefit
Early systems of unemployment benefit in CEE tended to be generous by Western standards. In Poland in the early 1990s, for example, workers received benefit equal to 70 per cent of their previous wage for the first three months of unemployment.[14] Other countries similarly tended to have high replacement rates. However, budgetary crises, rapid inflation and incomplete indexation eroded benefits, which were pulled down to close to the minimum wage thus – by an administratively cumbersome mechanism – leading to a de facto flat-rate benefit. Some countries, including Albania and Poland, subsequently adopted a system of explicit flat-rate benefits. The advantages of this approach in the initial period of transition have already been discussed.

Eligibility criteria in some countries were at first excessively generous. Under the initial Polish law, for example, a person was eligible for benefit if he or she had no job, thus making it possible for groups such as students and housewives to claim. Such excessive generosity was subsequently withdrawn. In addition, the duration of benefit (unlimited in the first Polish law) is restricted in all countries to between 6 and 12 months, after which workers have to rely on social assistance.

By now, the issue in most countries is not primarily one of coverage, but of refining the incentive structure of benefits and, in the medium term, modernizing benefit administration.

Active labour market policies

The effectiveness of active labour market policies (ALMPs) are assessed by the OECD (1997), Godfrey and Richards (1997) and Boeri et al. (1998). There are two sets of reasons why they do not appear to have made much difference, even in the advanced reformers. First, expenditure on such programmes has been low, typically because the rapid growth of unemployment meant that benefit spending crowded out active labour market policies. Second, on limited evidence, programmes have not been particularly effective. Góra and Lehmann (1995), though optimistic about the beneficial effects of job information, conclude that training schemes in Poland appeared to do little to increase the likelihood of finding a job. Micklewright and Nagy (1994) find that places on training programmes in Hungary went disproportionately to people with favourable labour market characteristics – the most likely to have found work anyway. Limited evidence (Puhani and Steiner, 1996) suggests that public employment schemes can stigmatize participants, thus reducing their chances of subsequent employment. For such reasons, Jackman (1998, p. 148) concludes that 'ALMPs do not of themselves . . . offer a solution to the unemployment problems of the transition economies'.

Strategic assessment

A number of troubling issues remain. First, the measures described above have not prevented the emergence of long-term unemployment, particularly in CEE. When a person's eligibility for unemployment benefit expires after at most 12 months, he or she is forced into dependence on his or her family, reliance on income-tested poverty relief, and/or informal (and non-taxpaying) activity. Western evidence shows that the longer a person remains unemployed the lower the probability of escaping from unemployment.

A second, more radical, question hinted at in earlier discussion is whether the strategy of introducing Western-style unemployment benefits – that is, of subsidizing unemployment rather than employment – is the right one. Jackman's (1998, p. 152) assessment of labour market policy concludes:

> There would be some point to such a policy if unemployment played a productive role in economic restructuring, but we have seen that the opposite is the case. Unemployment is not the route by which workers move from the declining state sector to the private sector. Unemployed workers are less attractive recruits for private firms than workers in state firms, and a policy leading to higher unemployment may thus have restrained rather than encouraged the growth of the private sector.

RELIEVING POVERTY

The Problem

Policy makers face three sets of problems.

The first problem concerns the *rising numbers of poor people*. Table 10.3, above, shows how poverty has increased. Within those aggregates, single-person pensioner households and large families have been particularly afflicted. The problem is compounded where people suffer not only a loss of income, but also reduced access to healthcare and education. Alongside greater numbers, policy makers need also to cope with different types of poor people. Traditional recipients such as the frail elderly and people with major physical or emotional problems require residential or domiciliary care from skilled (and scarce) social workers. In contrast, the 'new' poor are generally able bodied and less in need of social care than of income support and help with finding a job. Policy design should distinguish the very different jobs of social care on the one hand and benefit calculation on the other, and should ensure that the former does not crowd out the latter.

Second, *acute shortage of resources*, as discussed earlier, is a consequence of falling output and the resulting fiscal crisis.

The third problem is an *acute shortage of administrative capacity* in the face of intractable administrative problems. Targeting, particularly via an income test, is administratively demanding at the best of times. Perhaps to an even greater extent than with unemployment, matters are complicated by the extent of own-production and activity in the grey economy. The resulting problem for policy design is that it is hard to measure income accurately or cost-effectively, correspondingly reducing the usefulness of income-testing as a mechanism for targeting.

Strategic Policy Directions[15]

Early transition policies

As the income distribution widens and the duration of unemployment increases, there is a clear and uncontentious need for a wide-ranging system of poverty relief capable of administering income support to large numbers of able-bodied people. Depending on fiscal capacity, countries have a choice between two strategies seeking respectively to eliminate poverty by bringing everyone up to poverty line, or to ameliorate poverty by concentrating on the poorest of the poor. The problem for policy makers is how to implement poverty relief with few resources and little administrative capacity, where income testing is difficult or impossible.

Indicator targeting[16]   One way forward is to use indicators of poverty, which can be measured more easily than income. The idea is best illustrated by example. Assume: only redheads are poor; all redheads are poor; there is no hair dyeing technology. In these circumstances it is theoretically possible, by paying a redhead benefit (that is, by using red hair as an indicator) to eliminate poverty completely, as defined by the poverty line. In addition, because benefits go *only* to the poor, expenditure is minimized; since having red hair is exogenous to the individual (the third assumption), adverse incentives are minimized; and because identification is easy, administrative demands are small.

Indicator targeting can have significant advantages over income testing. Where indicators are highly correlated with poverty, targeting is accurate. Where the indicator is beyond the control of the individual, disincentives for recipients are weaker.[17] Where the indicator is easily observable (for example, the number of children in a family) it is less demanding administratively.

This suggests a strategy in which targeting is based on such variables as age (for example, extra assistance to the very elderly), the number of children in the family, employment status and health. Notwithstanding its advantages, the approach is not flawless. None of the indicators is perfectly correlated with poverty and, as a result, there are gaps in coverage and leakages. Not the least of the reasons why such benefits might leak out to the non-poor is that none takes account of household circumstance; for example, a very elderly person living alone is much more at risk than one living in the same household as his or her children and grandchildren.

Local discretion plus block grants   A different approach – as a complement to or substitute for indicator targeting – is through local discretion plus block grants. Localities may be better informed than central government about who is genuinely poor, and thus better able to target on a discretionary basis. Benefits could be in cash, in kind, or both. However, if central government underwrites the costs of local poverty relief, localities have no incentive to contain costs. Thus local discretion should be combined with block grants from the centre to localities. The resulting package has the advantage (a) of containing costs, (b) of minimizing administrative demands, while (c) being reasonably well-targeted. Less optimistically, discretion can have an arbitrary element and thus opens the way to horizontal inequality (that is, identical poor families in different localities are treated differently) or, at worst, to corruption.[18] Thus the approach may be a feasible short-run stopgap, but is no panacea.

Medium-term options
As fiscal and institutional capacity advances, more ambitious anti-poverty targets become possible. In the early transition, it is fiscally impossible to seek to bring everybody up to a realistic poverty line (that is, to eliminate poverty),

so that concentrating on the poorest of the poor is probably the only option. Over time, it becomes possible to aim at closing an increasing fraction of the poverty gap.

Second, more effective enforcement activity becomes possible on both the tax and benefit sides. As a result, third, judicious use of income testing becomes more realistic. Finally, as the rule of law builds up and administrative capacity strengthens, a move from discretion towards a rule-based system of poverty relief becomes realistic.

Progress to Date

Institutional developments
An archetypal Western-style scheme of social assistance pays benefits designed to bring people up to a published poverty line on the basis of an income and/or wealth test. All the TEs have reformed or introduced systems of social assistance but, as analysed by Milanovic (1998, pp. 126 ff.), with important differences.

1. Having a low income is necessary to qualify for benefits, but in all countries, recipients must also fulfil other criteria, for example, the presence in the household of someone who is old or handicapped, or a determination that the family is 'dysfunctional'.
2. The strategy for poverty relief places heavy reliance on indicator targeting, for example, old age and disability pensions, family allowance, milk and food for school children, and additional assistance for regions with dispro-portionate numbers of poor people.
3. Assistance is often in kind.
4. Benefits are designed to alleviate poverty, not to eliminate it; thus benefits are not intended to make up the whole of the difference between a family's income and the poverty line.
5. Administration is often local; and benefits may be dependent on the local availability of resources, that is, there is a local budget constraint.

These deviations from Western-style benefit systems respect the constraints, discussed earlier, facing TEs. They minimize the requirement to measure income exactly (element (2), above), attempt to respect fiscal constraints (elements (1), (4), and to some extent (5)), and minimize administrative demands (elements (3) and (5)), and thus can be argued, at least strategically, to be moves in the right direction.

Impact on poverty
Table 10.4 draws on Milanovic's (1999) study of social assistance in five countries based on household surveys for various years between 1993 and 1995.

- *Concentrated* systems, in Milanovic's terminology, disburse relatively generous benefits to relatively few households. Thus coverage is narrow but deep. One example is Poland, which paid social assistance to only 3.7 per cent of households (line 1) but, partly for that reason, paid the most generous average benefit of 54 USD per month, making up 22 per cent of a recipient household's total spending. Estonia, similarly, gave relatively generous benefits (33 USD per month, that is, about 15 per cent of a recipient household's spending) to relatively few people (2.7 per cent of households).
- *Dispersed* systems paid relatively small benefits to relatively large numbers of households, that is, coverage was broad but thin. Hungary, with nearly one-quarter of households receiving benefit, had by far the greatest coverage, followed by Russia with 13 per cent. In both countries, however, benefit covered under 5 per cent of recipients' expenditure.
- *Irrelevant* systems pay small benefits to few people, and hence do little to relieve poverty. Bulgaria is a case in point.

Table 10.4   The effectiveness of poverty relief

	Poland 1993	Estonia 1995	Hungary 1993	Russia 1993	Bulgaria 1995
Per cent of households receiving social assistance	3.7	2.7	24.4	13.0	2.55
Average benefit per recipient household (USD/month)	54	33	17	5	10
Benefit as per cent of expenditure of recipient households	22.1	14.8	4.7	3.5	4.1
Targeting efficiency (per cent of social assistance expenditure going to the lowest decile)	20.5	34.7	27.2	8.2	22.3
Effectiveness in relieving poverty (spending on social assistance as per cent of the poverty gap of the lowest decile)	9.4	7.0	28.8	3.3	1.3

Source: Milanovic (1999, Tables 11 and 12).

How effective were these expenditures in relieving poverty? The fourth line of Table 10.4 gives a measure of vertical targeting efficiency, defined as the percentage of total social assistance expenditure going to the poorest 10 per cent of households. Targeting was far from perfect: even in Estonia, the country with the tightest targeting, only about one-third of social assistance spending went to the lowest decile of households; in Hungary the figure was closer to a quarter and in Bulgaria and Poland closer to one-fifth. Targeting in Russia was staggeringly bad – the poorest 10 per cent of the population received considerably *less* than 10 per cent of social assistance spending.

Targeting is a measure of *who* benefits; the last line of the table measures *how much* they benefit, showing the extent to which spending on social assistance reduced the poverty gap[19] for the lowest 10 per cent of households. In Hungary, with relatively generous benefits for a large fraction of households, benefits relieved nearly 30 per cent of the shortfall below the poverty line of the incomes of the poorest decile. Poland relieved close to 10 per cent. In Bulgaria in contrast, social assistance relieved barely more than one per cent of the poverty gap of the poorest 10 per cent of households.

REFORMING PENSIONS

The Problem[20]

With unemployment benefit and poverty relief, the central problem is of avoiding gaps in coverage (the horizontal efficiency issue). With pensions the issue is to improve vertical efficiency, that is, to avoid fiscally unaffordable leakage of benefit.

The old system of pensions, although perhaps well-adapted to the old economic order, is ill-adapted in several ways to the needs of a market economy.

The first concerns the *ease of access to benefit*. A low retirement age was seen as one of the victories of socialism. In addition, many workers received a pension below that age, for example the concessions to miners, military personnel and civil servants and, in some countries ballerinas, teachers and the like;[21] and access to disability pensions was also generous. The number of pensioners was increased further by generous early-retirement provisions in the early transition.

> As a result [of low pensionable age], the typical woman in the Czech Republic enjoys five more years of retirement than her American counterpart, and seven years more than her German counterpart. For men the difference is closer to one year. The comparison for Hungary, Poland and Russia is broadly similar. (World Bank, 1996, p. 78).[22]

The second concerns the *unsustainable cost*. The high cost of pensions is shown in Table 10.5. The cause of it was not primarily generous pensions, but the large number of pensioners resulting from the low retirement age. Table 10.6 illustrates the scale of the problem. Column (1) shows the age dependency ratio, that is, the fraction of the population of pensionable age, column (2) the system dependency ratio, that is, the fraction of the population receiving a pension. If nobody below pensionable age received a pension, the ratio of (2):(1) would be 100 per cent. In reality, there are always some recipients below pensionable age, for example disability pensioners, so that there will always be some 'leakage'. In Croatia, Latvia and Lithuania the leakage is about 20 per cent. In Poland, in contrast, the leakage is 75 per cent and in Slovenia 86 per cent. Thus in the last two countries, not far short of half of all pensioners are below the official pensionable age.

Table 10.5   Public pension spending in the CEE and the Baltic countries, 1989 and 1997 (% of GDP)

	1989	1997
Albania	5.7	4.0
Bulgaria	8.2	6.2
Croatia	na	11.9[*]
Czech Republic	8.3	8.9
Hungary	9.1	9.4
Latvia	na	10.7
Lithuania	na	7.0
FYR Macedonia	na	10.1
Poland	6.5	15.1
Slovakia	6.7	8.0

Note: [*]1996.

Source: World Bank Social Challenges of Transition Data Base.

Third, *pensions were generally low* – the result of a head-on collision between ease of access and fiscal constraints. The result is like trying to spread a small piece of butter over an enormous slice of bread – giving too little to too many at too high a fiscal cost.

Fourth, there were *generous pensions for privileged groups*. The various concessions to particular groups like miners have already been mentioned. While pensions always have a political dimension, such concessions were the outcome of non-transparent politics.

Table 10.6   Age dependency and system dependency ratios, 1996, selected countries

	Age dependency ratio (1)	System dependency ratio (2)	(2):(1) (%)
Croatia	32.3*	39	121
Estonia	35.0	46	131
Hungary	36.0	41	114
Latvia	35.0	42	120
Lithuania	32.0	39	122
Poland	28.0*	49*	175
Russia	30.5	46*	151
Slovenia	29.0*	54*	186

Note: *1995 data.

Source: EBRD data.

Strategic Policy Directions

Towards a solution

Methods of organizing pensions   In making pension contributions, an individual seeks to exchange current production for a claim on future production. There are two broad ways in which I might do this: by saving part of my wages each week I could build up a pile of *money* which I would exchange for goods produced by younger people after my retirement; or I could obtain a *promise* – from my children, or from government – that I would be given goods produced by others after my retirement. The two most common ways of organizing pensions broadly parallel these two sorts of claim on future production. *Funded* schemes are based on accumulations of financial assets; *pay-as-you-go* (PAYG) schemes, ultimately, are based on promises.[23]

Under either approach, what matters is *the level of output after I have retired.* The point is central: pensioners are not interested in money (that is, coloured bits of paper with portraits of national heroes on them), but in consumption – food, clothing, heating, medical services and so on. Money is irrelevant unless the production is there for pensioners to buy.

Given the centrality of output, the next questions are how it might be increased, and what role pensions might play. In principle, output can be increased in either or both of two ways:

- Increasing the productivity of each worker, by increasing the quantity of capital, improving its quality, and/or improving the quality of labour.
- Increasing the number of workers from each age cohort. This will involve reducing unemployment, increasing labour force participation, particularly by married women, raising the age of retirement, and/or importing labour.

Thus, the menu of policies to increase output, for example in the face of adverse demographics, is:

1. More and better capital equipment, for example, robots.
2. Improving labour through more education and training.
3. Policies to increase labour supply, for example by married women by offering better childcare facilities.
4. Raising the age of retirement.
5. Importing labour, either directly (more relaxed immigration rules) or indirectly (exporting capital to countries with a young labour force).

The effects of funding on growth are discussed below (see pp. 194–203). The key points to note at this stage are that the central variable is output, that funding pensions has no bearing on output-increasing policies (2)–(5), and hence that policy should consider the *entire* menu of policies, not focus exclusively on pension funds.

Strategic policy directions   What does this tell us about policy design? If policy makers think that pensions absorb too high a fraction of output (for example, because of population ageing), there are two and only two strategies:[24]

- Increase output via any or all of (1)–(5), above.
- Reduce pension costs, by reducing the average pension, that is, reducing living standards in retirement, and/or by reducing the number of pensioners, that is, keeping the annual pension constant but reducing the duration of retirement.

Note the potency of raising the retirement age, which reduces the number of pensioners and *simultaneously* increases the number of workers, and is thus a doubly powerful mechanism for reducing pension spending. It achieves this outcome not through reduced living standards in retirement, but via a shorter period of retirement.

Early transition policies

Increasing output above its pre-transition level (the first of the options just discussed)   This is not yet an option in most of the TEs, though it will increasingly become so, at least in CEE and the Baltic countries.

Reducing the number of pensioners   Raising the age of retirement has been discussed, and in Poland, Hungary, Croatia and the Czech Republic legislated. However, the average age of retirement has not yet risen. Indeed, the average age at which a pension was first paid *declined* in the early transition in most countries (World Bank, 1996, p. 78). Though the facts are clear, policy is a difficult balance between competing objectives. The argument for raising the pensionable age is the resulting saving in public expenditure. There are two arguments for caution. First, moving too precipitately risks the political sustainability of the reforms. Second, the demotivating and debilitating effects of long-run unemployment, especially for the young, are well known.

Another way of reducing the number of pensioners is by withdrawing the right to combine work and pension.[25] Again, there is a conflict of objectives. On the one hand, current policy is costly. This suggests that there should be a retirement test (for example, withdrawing pension, partly or wholly, from anyone who earns more than a fairly small amount). The counterargument is that early retirement makes it easier to make older workers redundant, and thus assists restructuring. This suggests that during the early transition, rather than impose a *retirement* test, it is worth considering a *change-of-job* test, whereby individuals who retire but find another job are allowed to keep at least part of their pension. The difficulty with this approach is its problematic implementation. Soviet enterprises were adept at organizing fictitious job changes.

Reducing the average pension   Up to a point, pensioners have been relatively protected in comparison with other groups in the population. Milanovic finds that 'poverty rates for people of retirement age . . . are only about one half of the country average in Hungary and Poland, and even less in the Czech Republic and Slovakia' (1998, pp. 102–3). This finding should not, however, be misinterpreted. The fact that pensioners have been *relatively* protected does not mean that they have been fully protected in *absolute* terms.[26] Real pensions declined: in many countries the pension was not indexed, so that over time people were pulled down to the minimum pension (which was indexed), thus approximating a system of flat-rate pensions.[27] In addition, evidence suggests that single-person pensioner households – disproportionately very old women – are prominent among the poor.

It may be that in the short run the ability to contain pension spending is very limited. Perhaps this is the right outcome, not only on grounds of practicability but also in terms of intergenerational equity. A case can be made for special treatment of the current older generation.

> In much of CEE and the [CIS] inflation destroyed the financial savings of the elderly. Unlike the young, they will not have the opportunity to recoup their losses in the market economy. A case can therefore be made on equity grounds for special treatment. (World Bank, 1996, p. 80)

Medium-term options
Medium-term policy is less constrained.

Output growth   This has resumed in many of the reforming countries, and the number of countries whose income exceeds that prior to transition will increase – correspondingly easing pension finance.

Increasing the age of retirement   The only politically feasible (and, arguably, the only fair) way to increase the age of retirement is to phase in the change over time.[28]

Strengthening the relation between contributions and pensions   There are at least three reasons for strengthening the relationship once economic conditions permit: on equity grounds (for example, the early retirement provisions for ballerinas discriminate against other groups in the workforce); to minimize distortions to individual retirement decisions; and because of the strong incentive to evade contributions if workers do not see a clear relationship between contributions and benefits.

Though there is a strong case for strengthening the relationship between contributions and benefits, the extent to which it is *strictly* actuarial is a policy option, that is, individual benefits do not have to be exactly related to contributions, but benefits should be related *at the margin* to individual contributions, and contributors and beneficiaries should perceive this to be so. The argument is important. It is open to policy makers to have a pension formula which is redistributive (as, for example, the US system) in the sense that worker A, who has twice the earnings of worker B over his or her working life, gets a pension which is higher than B's, but less than twice as high. However, if either A or B retires early, his or her pension should be actuarially reduced relative to the pension he or she would have received at age 65.

Phasing in private pensions   This topic is discussed extensively below.

Progress to Date: Reforming State Pensions

There has been a huge amount of discussion and considerable action on pension reform. From a welter of detail two strategic trends emerge: a move towards more actuarial state pensions (discussed in this section), and towards private, funded second- and third-tier pensions (discussed in the next). Both aspects are discussed in detail by Rutkowski (Chapter 13 in this volume).

Institutional developments

Pension reform in several TEs has been influenced by recent reforms in *Sweden*, which introduced what is known as a 'notional defined-contribution' state pension in legislation passed in June 1998 (for details, see Sweden: Federation of Social Insurance Offices, 1998).[29] The key features of the scheme are:

- The basic state pension remains PAYG, financed through a social insurance contribution.
- Though this year's contributions are paid out in this year's benefits, the social insurance authorities open a notional (or virtual) individual account which keeps track of contributions, just as for a 'real' fund. Specifically, each worker's cumulative account attracts a notional interest rate reflecting average income growth.
- At the time a person retires, he or she will have accumulated a notional lump sum. The resulting pension is calculated on the basis of (a) the size of the lump sum, combined with expectations about (b) the lifetime of the current cohort of retirees and (c) output growth over the estimated period of retirement.
- The basic arrangements are adjusted in that (a) there is a safety-net pension for people with low lifetime earnings, (b) periods spent caring for children carry pension rights, and (c) there is a ceiling on contributions.
- The individual can choose to retire earlier or later, the pension being actuarially adjusted.

In *Poland*,[30] the first tier of the new Polish pension, enacted in 1998, is very similar to the Swedish conception. It is a universal, mandatory, publicly-managed PAYG defined-contribution (DC) system. The social insurance authorities maintain an account for each contributor, who accumulates notional capital.[31] The resulting pension depends only on the notional capital accumulation, the person's age at retirement, and average life expectancy of the relevant cohort. The minimum retirement age is 65 for men and 60 for women; other than that, the retirement decision is a matter for individual choice. During a contributor's working life his or her notional fund is indexed in line with the growth of the real wage bill (and hence in line with trends in productivity and employment); in retirement, pensions are indexed to a pensioner price index.

Latvia, too, introduced notional DC pensions. Each contributor's social security account is credited with contributions (up to a ceiling) as though it were an explicit savings account, thus creating notional capital. On retirement, a person receives a pension based on his or her accumulation of notional capital, based on life expectancy at retirement. Retirement age is flexible, with pensions adjusted actuarially.

Hungary adopted less far-reaching reforms to its state pension arrangements.[32] Under reforms in 1998, the first-tier pension was amended by increasing retirement to 62 for men and women, strengthening the link between contributions and benefits, increasing the qualifying period for full pension, subjecting benefits to taxation, and shifting indexation from a net-wage basis to half of real earnings growth. As with all the other countries there is a minimum pension guarantee in the form of a social assistance pension.

In *Croatia*, with effect from January 1999, the retirement age was increased to 65 for men and to 60 for women, and the pension formula made less generous, by basing pensions on a person's full career rather than his or her best ten years, and by indexing pensions 50 per cent to changes in prices and 50 per cent to changes in wages. The combined effect of these and related changes is to reduce public pension spending by one per cent of GDP.

Pension reform in other CEE countries, for example the Czech Republic, has been more modest, mostly aimed at improving the sustainability of the PAYG scheme (see Rutkowski, Chapter 13 in this volume).

Towards an actuarial system

The idea of notional DC pensions is for social insurance pensions to mimic an annuity, in that the pension a person receives (a) bears an explicit relationship to contributions, (b) is based on lifetime contributions, and is adjusted for (c) life expectancy and (d) economic developments. Individuals can respond (e) by adjusting their age of retirement. The introduction of element (c) is an important innovation.

There are important arguments in favour of these arrangements. First, they simultaneously give people choice *and* face them with efficient incentives. For example, they assist choice about retirement by allowing people to choose their preferred trade-off between *duration* of retirement and *living standards* in retirement, but face them with the actuarial cost of those decisions. In addition, the closer the connection between contributions and benefits the greater the extent to which contributions are perceived as contributions rather than taxation; to that extent notional DC schemes reduce the tax wedge. In contrast, as Gruber and Wise (1998) show, badly designed state schemes contain incentives which can have strong adverse effects. These arguments point to something that is insufficiently understood in that there is much flexibility within PAYG schemes. Many of the problems of state social insurance systems are not inherent in the social insurance mechanism, but are soluble.

A second set of advantages is that notional DC schemes also address many of the problems of privately managed individual funded accounts. As discussed below (see pp. 194–203), all pension schemes, whether state or private, face systemic risks such as demographic change or macroeconomic shocks. Private pensions, in addition, face investment risk (that is, differential pension portfolio performance) while a fund is building up, plus the risk of unanticipated inflation once the pension is in payment.

There are some *potential problems*, and a number of questions need to be asked. First, will individuals respond to actuarial incentives? Suppose that people live longer, leading to a reduction in the state pension. People can respond by delaying retirement, in order to maintain their pension. Will they do so? They will only if $p > t$, where p = the percentage actuarial increase in pension from deferring retirement for a year and t = the individual's marginal rate of time preference. Thus, if people have a high marginal rate of time preference, making the retirement age endogenous will do little, if anything, to encourage later retirement.

Second, the arrangements reduce policy flexibility. The idea of notional DC embodies the implicit promise that a change in contributions will lead to a comparable change in benefits. This could cause problems if the contribution rate is too low.

Third, estimates of life expectancy become politically sensitive if a person's pension is adjusted to take account of the expected lifespan of the cohort. This can cause problems in countries with weak political capacity.

A final issue is that redistribution from richer to poorer takes place only because the state guarantees a minimum pension for all contributors. Beyond that, that a person's pension is strictly related to his or her previous contributions, so that a person who earns twice as much receives a pension which is twice as large. Not everyone would agree with the implied equity judgement.

It can be argued, in conclusion, that the reforms in Poland and Latvia represent considerable progress. Most particularly making the retirement age endogenous, albeit the obvious solution, is a major advance.

Containing state pension spending

A second core issue is the need for public spending in general, and pension spending in particular, to be compatible with economic growth. As discussed earlier, at a given level of output, the only way to reduce total pension spending is either to reduce the average pension or to reduce the number of pensions in payment.

Introducing private pensions, while potentially reducing state pension spending in the longer term, when the new funded schemes are mature, does nothing to reduce pension spending in the short term. Indeed, the need to finance the transition to a new pension regime generally *increases* public pension spending in the short to medium term. In the words of an IMF study: 'the fiscal costs of undertaking such a shift [to a fully funded scheme] may be very high, and ... meeting those costs may require, in many cases, an amount of fiscal adjustment that is substantially higher than what would be needed to fix the PAYG system' (Chand and Jaeger, 1996, pp. 32–3).

It follows that if the scale of public pension spending is thought to impede growth, the only solution is to reduce public pension spending. *Whatever* strategy for pension reform is adopted, moves to make the PAYG scheme sustainable are essential. As Table 10.5 (above) shows, however, there has been little progress on this latter policy agenda. This is not surprising in countries such as Croatia, Latvia or Macedonia, where output remains considerably below its 1989 level.[33] The extent to which Poland is an outlier is clear when one realizes that public pension spending remains at about 15 per cent of GDP despite Poland's high growth rate.

Where policy makers wish to reduce total pension spending, the way forward is to find ways of reducing the number of pensioners rather than by reducing pensions. Both political realities and the intergenerational equity arguments discussed earlier suggest that the process should be phased.

Progress to Date: Introducing Private Pensions

Institutional developments
Virtually all countries have discussed the introduction of private, funded pensions, and a significant number have started on legislation, including Estonia, Hungary, Latvia, Lithuania, Poland and Slovenia in the CEE and Baltic countries, and Russia, Ukraine and Kazakhstan among the CIS. In Poland, Hungary, Croatia and Latvia, the initial phase of reform has already been enacted.

In *Poland*, reforms take an integrated approach. Alongside the notional DC first tier discussed earlier is a mandatory, privately managed, DC second tier. The two tiers are closely linked: they use the same contribution base[34] and retirement age, and are both DCs. The minimum pension guarantee is based on both tiers; and both tiers are being phased in, being mandatory for people born after 1969.[35]

The second-tier pensions will be managed by competing pension funds. Regulation of those funds includes constraints on the composition of their investments,[36] and major requirements about disclosure of information. The freedom of individuals to change funds is heavily circumscribed. These arrangements are supplemented by a third tier of voluntary contributions, with incentives to encourage employees and employers to set up voluntary group pension schemes.

In *Hungary*, the second-tier pension is through individual funded accounts, paying DC pensions. Such funds may be established by employers, professional associations, the Pensions Insurance Administration, voluntary pension funds or by local governments. Such entities can choose whether to run the funds themselves, or to contract other organizations such as insurance companies to manage them. The legislation contains detailed regulation about the establishment, organization and financial management of these funds; and before opening for business each pension fund must be approved by the newly established Pension Fund Supervision office. Each fund must produce a guaranteed yield. Individuals are free to move between funds provided they pay the costs of such a move (for fuller details, see Gerencsér, 1997).

Croatia has also legislated to bring in second-tier pensions, which will be mandatory for people under 40 at the time the new scheme starts in July 2000. The scheme will be financed by diverting a fraction of pension contributions to individual accounts.

A number of other countries, notably *Estonia* and *Latvia*, are actively considering a mandatory, private, funded second-tier pension.

Kazakhstan is an outlier: in advocating a move to a Chilean-type system, in which mandatory, privately managed, competitive funded pensions replace the state scheme, it is contemplating reform which would be radical for any country, and *a fortiori* for a Central Asian country.

How should these developments be assessed? In an overview chapter like this, detailed, country-by-country assessment is neither possible nor desirable. Instead, I want to put forward four key messages, which provide the necessary background for assessing actual and proposed reforms:

- risk is unavoidable;
- private pensions have important prerequisites;
- the range of choice over pension design is large; and
- the links between funding and growth are complex and controversial.

Risk

The future is an uncertain business, and no pension scheme can give certainty. The first group of risks, broadly speaking, are systemic.

1. *Macroeconomic shocks* affect all pension schemes – with PAYG by shrinking the contributions base (or the rate of growth of the contributions base), and with funding by reducing the value of the financial assets on which funds are based (for fuller discussion, see Barr, 1998a, Ch. 9).
2. *Demographic shocks* affect PAYG schemes, again, via effects on the contributions base – other things being equal, the smaller the generation of workers the smaller the contributions base. With funding the mechanism is more subtle, but equally inescapable, operating through a mismatch between demand and supply in either the goods market or the assets market. The mechanism merits explanation. If there is a large accumulation of pension funds when the workforce is declining, the high level of spending by

pensioners out of their accumulated savings will reduce the rate of saving in the economy, and possibly lead to aggregate dissaving. Pensions face pressures through either or both of two mechanisms.

- Assume the price of pensioners' financial assets remains unchanged. In that case, net pensioner consumption is greater than saving by workers; and at full employment this causes demand inflation, which erodes the purchasing power of pensioners' accumulated funds, and hence their consumption.
- Alternatively, there could be deflation of pensioners' financial assets. If the desired sales of assets by the large pensioner generation exceeds desired asset purchases by the smaller succeeding workforce, asset prices will fall. In consequence, the lump sum received by the representative pensioner, and hence the resulting annuity, will decline.

In sum, the argument that funding insulates pensioners from demographic change should not be overstated. The policy implication is that demographic change is not *per se* a strong argument for shifting the balance of pension finance towards funding.

3. *Political risks* As discussed shortly, all pension systems depend critically on effective government.

All pension schemes face these systemic risks. Private pensions face additional risks.

1. *Management risk* Pension funds require substantial regulation to protect consumers in areas too complex for consumers to protect themselves. There is no need to belabour the point, exemplified by scandals in the USA and the UK (UK Pension Law Review Committee, 1993; UK Treasury Select Committee, 1998). Separately, management may be honest but incompetent.
2. *Investment risk* Even if managed with complete probity and high competence, pension funds face the risk of differential pension portfolio performance. Two people with identical earnings and contributions records may end up with very different pensions. Consider individuals A and B with identical lifetime contributions profiles: if A retires when the stock market index stands at 5000, and B retires six months later when the stock market has fallen to 4000, B's pension will be 20 per cent lower than A's. More generally, a stock market downturn could adversely affect the lump sums, and hence the annuities, of an entire cohort. A 20 per cent fall is far from fanciful: it could be triggered by sharp stock market falls in other countries or by broader financial crises elsewhere, with no need to invoke

more apocalyptic events (oil shock, AIDS pandemic, assassination of major world leader and so on).

Up to a point, these risks can be reduced. The average return to pension funds is boosted by keeping costs low, for example, by collecting contributions through payroll deductions and by limiting advertising expenditure. A second approach might be to require funds to be run on fairly simple lines, for example, as tracker funds, rather than actively managed, thus reducing or eliminating the lower tail of pension fund performers. Third, if people are obliged to convert on the day they retire, and if they are obliged to retire on their sixty-fifth birthday, the value of their pension is to a significant extent a lottery. To reduce the resulting inequity, it is therefore essential to allow flexibility over the timing of conversion of a person's lump sum into an annuity.[37] The remaining – significant – investment risk is inherent in the logic of individual funded accounts.

3. *Annuities market risk* The annuity a person can buy with his or her lump sum depends on (a) the expected duration of retirement, that is, the remaining life expectancy at the time he or she retires, and (b) the interest rate the insurance company expects to earn over the lifetime of the annuity, in particular the rate of interest on long-term gilts. There is an element of uncertainty about the first variable. More important, however, the return – even on long-term gilts – varies, so that a person who retires during a recession, with low interest rates, may receive a significantly lower annuity than someone who retires during a period of higher interest rates.

   A second, and separate, problem, is that the annuities market is thin: with competing insurance companies, each company has only a small share of the market, and hence only a few people in each age group. Thus the opportunity of economies of scale is lost and, consequently, transactions costs are high. This reduces the value of an annuity, quite independently of interest rate fluctuations.

Does a multi-tier system reduce risk? Given the range of risks just discussed, it is sometimes argued that a multi-tier system reduces risk because it 'reduces the exposure of workers to political, investment, and country-specific risks . . . [B]road diversification across differing financial and managerial sources is the best way to insure in an uncertain world' (World Bank, 1994, p. 239).

That proposition, however, is analytically true only if the risks of the two systems are negatively correlated or, at a minimum, are orthogonal to each other. Applying this criterion to the risks above, economic risk and demographic risk are common to both funding and PAYG. Funded schemes, in addition, face management risk, investment risk and annuities market risk. It *may* be that political risks (for example, unsustainable PAYG systems) and investment/management risks are independent. The last is, ultimately, an empirical question. Because of citizens' perceptions, funded schemes in some countries at some times in their history might have greater legitimacy. But the simple risk-spreading argument should not be accepted uncritically.

Though all these arguments are directly relevant to all the TEs, a number are particularly pertinent.

- Macroeconomic stability and regulatory capacity may be particularly at risk in all but the advanced reformers.
- TEs are particularly vulnerable to management risk and stock market risk.
- There is a question of whether, in the short run, pension funds are the most efficient use of scarce private sector skills.

Prerequisites
In discussing pension reform, it is useful to distinguish (a) prerequisites which apply to *all* reforms, over which policy makers have little choice (discussed in this section) and (b) those features over which policy makers have explicitly to make choices (discussed in the next).

The first prerequisite concerns *financial assets and financial markets*. A number of points, though obvious, should not be overlooked. First, the whole process requires that both government and citizens are reasonably well-informed about the operation of financial markets. In some less-advanced reforming countries there is still a belief, even at high levels in government, that if a fund is 'private' and the money 'invested', a high real rate of return is inevitable, with no understanding either of the nature of the risk, or of the connection between financial variables and real variables such as national output and employment levels.

Second, and equally obvious, funded schemes require financial assets for pension funds to hold and financial markets for channelling savings into their most productive use. Two apparent solutions are blind alleys. If pension funds hold only government bonds, this appears to address the lack of other financial assets. However, the resulting schemes are, in effect PAYG, since both the interest payments and subsequent redemption depend on future taxpayers. Thus there is no budgetary gain, no channelling of resources into productive investment, and considerable extra administrative cost.

Another option is to use the pension savings of a transition country to buy Western financial assets, thus getting round the absence of domestic financial markets. As discussed below, the problem with this approach is that it entirely forgoes the growth-inducing potential of private pensions. Thus the prerequisites of financial assets and financial markets really *are* prerequisites.

Private sector capacity is essential, given the heavy administrative demands of private pensions. A lack of capacity runs the risk that excessive administrative costs will erode the investment return to pensioners. Since there is a fixed cost to running an individual pension account, the issue is of particular concern for small pensions. At worst, deficient administrative capacity puts at risk the viability of private funds.

A third prerequisite concerns *effective government*. The 'Washington consensus' now increasingly recognizes the key role of government.

> I argue that the failures of the reforms in Russia and most of the former Soviet Union are not just due to sound policies being poorly implemented. I argue that the failures go deeper, to a misunderstanding of the foundations of a market economy . . . For instance, reform models based on conventional neoclassical economics are likely to under-estimate the importance of informational problems, including those arising from the problems of corporate governance; of social and organizational capital; and of the institutional and legal infrastructure required to make an effective market economy. (Stiglitz, 1999, Abstract)

> Capitalism is revealed to require much more than private property; it functions because of the widespread acceptance and enforcement in an economy of fundamental rules and safeguards that make the outcomes of exchange secure, predictable, and of reasonably widespread benefit. Where such rules and safeguards, such institutions, are absent, what suffers is not just fairness and equity, but firm performance as well . . . (Nellis, 1999, p. 16)

Effective government is essential *whichever* approach to pensions is adopted. The problem of government failure is most obvious in the case of PAYG schemes built on fiscally irresponsible promises, coupled with an inability to collect contributions. Results include inflationary pressures and political instability. However, private pensions are also vulnerable. Fiscal imprudence leads easily to inflation which can decapitalize private funds; and inability to regulate financial markets creates inequity, and may also squander the efficiency gains which private pensions are intended to engender. As Thompson (1998, p. 22) puts it,

> It is also too early to know how effectively the new systems based on the defined contribution model will be insulated from irresponsible behavior. Politicians are not the only people who are prone to promise more than they can deliver. The defined contribution model requires sophisticated oversight and regulation to ensure that one set of problems resulting from public sector political dynamics is not simply traded for a different set of problems derived from the dynamics of private sector operations.

Nor is this a problem only for countries with less well-developed governments, as the British pension mis-selling scandal amply illustrates.

In contrast, effective government assists both state and private schemes. Governments throughout the OECD are putting into place cost-containing measures in the face of demographic prospects (see UK Department of Social Security, 1993). Recent reform in Canada and Sweden and earlier reform in the UK are prime examples. Government capacity, similarly, assists private schemes. As Diamond (1995, p. 94) points out,

> One advantage of investment in private assets is the potential contribution to the development of capital markets. This was a major benefit from the Chilean reform. But the capital market development did not come automatically from the introduction of the privately managed mandatory savings scheme. Extensive development of capital market regulation was a critical part of the privatization.

Effective government is therefore critical:

- to ensure macroeconomic stability, to protect pension accumulations, which are sensitive to unanticipated inflation; and
- to ensure effective regulatory capacity in financial markets for reasons of consumer protection in areas too complex for consumers to protect themselves. What is needed are tightly drawn up regulatory procedures *and* the resources to enforce them.

The latter task is more difficult than it looks: precisely because private pensions are such complex instruments, regulators need to be highly skilled – the sort of skills with a high price in the private sector. There are at least three strategic problems: that the regulatory regime collapses (or is ineffective); where that problem is avoided, that the regulatory regime becomes de facto state control, with the pension provider acting, in effect, as an agent of the state; or, where that problem is avoided, that the management and regulation of pension funds 'crowds out' other demands for scarce human capital.

The key lesson from countries like Chile, which have adopted radical pension reform, is that successful reform rests on two legs – private sector capacity *and* government capacity. There is an essential role for the state in pensions even if one distrusts politicians.

Political sustainability is a fourth prerequisite. Pension reform, particularly large-scale reform such as the introduction of funded pensions, is not an event but a process. Pension reform does not end when the legislation is passed, but needs continuing commitment from government, both for technical reasons, to ensure necessary adjustments to reform proposals as events unfold, and for political reasons, to encourage continuing political support. Reform which is regarded as a single, once-and-for-all event runs the risk of neglect, discredit and eventual reversal. One implication is the need for domestic ownership of reform, an aspect in which, it can be argued, the Polish reforms are on firmer foundations than those in Hungary (see Nelson (1998) for discussion of the politics of reform in Hungary).

Transparency is important both for political reasons, to ensure the legitimacy and hence political sustainability of reform, and for economic reasons, as a necessary ingredient if pensions are to fulfil their efficiency function of steering savings into their most productive investment use.[38] Transparency is needed in state pensions about their cost to the taxpayer and about the relation between contributions and benefits. With private pensions, there should be transparency about the costs of tax relief, and through annual statements giving details of a person's pension accumulation, predicted pension and administrative charges. For this purpose it is essential that annual statements have a common format, and are based on common definitions of rates of return, inflation and so on. Such transparency is essential to ensure that the claims of competitors are directly and precisely comparable. Chile sets a good example to more advanced countries, by requiring information to pensioners to be issued in a standard way.[39]

Table 10.7 summarizes the essential prerequisites, and serves as a check-list for policy makers contemplating pension reform and a guide to commentators assessing actual or proposed reforms. In meeting these prerequisites, advanced reformers like Poland and Hungary have the capacity for the sort of sophisti-cated reforms they are proposing.[40] It was precisely because of the demonstrable failure to meet several of the prerequisites that in 1998 the World Bank – coura-geously but completely correctly – withdrew its support for proposals to bring in mandatory second-tier pensions in Russia. Reference to the same criteria calls seriously into question the strategic direction of reform in Kazakhstan.

Table 10.7 Prerequisites for pension reform

	Essential for state scheme	Essential for private schemes
Public sector prerequisites		
Budgetary sustainability of state scheme	✓	–
Political sustainability of pension reform package	✓	✓
Capacity to maintain macroeconomic stability	✓	✓
Effective regulatory capacity	–	✓
Private sector prerequisites		
Financial assets	–	✓
Financial markets	–	✓
Adequate private sector administrative capacity	–	✓

The range of choice

Pension design is controversial. Perhaps the central debate is whether there is a single, dominant strategy. My answer is that there is not – and that policy makers face a large range of choices (for fuller discussion, see World Bank, 1996, pp. 81–3). The following questions far from exhaust the list.

1. How large should the first-tier pension be – should it be a minimum guarantee or larger?
2. How redistributive should the first tier be (more redistributive/less redistributive)?
3. If there is a second-tier pension, should it be funded or PAYG?
4. Should the second tier be managed by the state (Canada) or privately (Australia, Latin America)?
5. Should membership of a second tier be voluntary (Czech Republic) or compulsory (Chile)?
6. Should opting out of state arrangements be allowed (UK) or not (USA)?
7. How broadly should risks be shared? Should there be individual accounts (Argentina, Chile), or should it be possible for employers to organize schemes, as in many European countries? Should the individual face all the risk (individual, DC schemes), or should risk be shared with employers (employer defined-benefit schemes), or shared with the taxpayer (where private schemes receive some sort of state guarantee)?
8. To what extent does the state assist with indexing pensions? Once a person has retired, pensions based on an annuity are vulnerable to unanticipated inflation. A major design question, therefore, is the extent to which government offers pensioners protection against inflation and through what mechanism. To the extent that government does participate, this introduces a PAYG element into funded schemes.

Even if each of these issues is taken as a simple yes/no choice, the eight questions yield 256 possible combinations, the answers to which will depend not only on economic variables but also on a country's culture and history. In the TEs, given the range of choice and the extent of misinformation, well-informed public debate is particularly critical to ensure that any reforms, once enacted, take root.

Pensions and growth

Why is so much emphasis placed on reducing *state pension* spending? The argument is *not* an attack on pensioners. Nor is it a statement that state pension spending in the long run should be minimized (as opposed to optimized). The root of the policy is that public spending has to be compatible with sustained economic growth, one of the core objectives of transition. In the context of transition this means not only an imperative to keep budget deficits small, but also an imperative to shrink the size of the public sector to create headroom for a growing private sector. The World Bank's (1996) *World Development Report* (Ch. 7) talks about 'rightsizing' government, and makes it clear that economies can function well with governments of different sizes. There is no dispute, however, that the size of the state sector prior to transition (98 per cent of output in Czechoslovakia) was far too high to be sustainable.

The need for sustainable state pensions is motivated entirely by the need to create an incentive structure conducive to growth. Public pensions can contribute to long-run growth only in a negative sense of not hindering growth deriving from other sources.

Private pensions, it is argued, can contribute to growth both directly and indirectly. To summarize a large, complex and controversial literature (for fuller discussion, see Barr, 1998a, Ch. 9; Thompson, 1998, Chs 4–6), three points stand out. First, the magnitude of the impact of funding on growth is controversial. Second, the issue, in any case, relates only to one of the sources of growth. Hence policies concerned with growth should consider the *entire* menu of policies discussed above (see pp. 187–190), and not focus exclusively on pension funds.

A third issue particularly concerns TEs: funding contributes to growth only if it increases domestic investment. In TEs, however, domestic investment may be low yield and high risk, the *exact* reverse of what pension fund managers look for. Thus pensions policy faces a horrible dilemma: domestic investment puts old-age security at risk; foreign investment puts growth at risk. It may be that pension fund managers in advanced reformers such as Poland, Hungary and Slovenia do not face this dilemma; but it remains acute for many of the TEs.

Does funding contribute indirectly to growth by widening and deepening capital markets? As Diamond (1995) points out, though not an argument which applies to the OECD countries, it is potentially relevant in TEs. Again, however, the broader context is important: though a larger capital market may be a *component* of growth, it is not *on its own* a solution. As discussed earlier, the key lesson from Chile (to which the capital-market-widening-and-deepening argument is often applied (Holzmann, 1997)) is the effectiveness of reform outside the financial sector, as exemplified by the earlier discussion of the prerequisites for reform.

The contribution of capital accumulation to growth needs to be complemented by appropriately skilled labour, bringing us back to the issue of education which emerged at several stages in earlier discussion.

EDUCATION

The Challenge of Transition

Education raises many issues fundamentally different from those raised by income transfers. The topic is, however, important, both in its own right and – in the context of this chapter – as a component of labour market adjustment. As with income transfers, I want to argue that communist education was relatively well adapted to the old order, but is systematically dysfunctional relative to the needs of a market economy.

Educational achievement under communism was impressive. There was almost universal primary and lower secondary enrolment, and high levels of literacy and basic numeracy, with relatively equitable access, for girls as well as boys. Given these successes, the prevailing view in the early transition was that many aspects of education reform could wait. To explain why that view is wrong, it is necessary, first, to discuss objectives.

Objectives

The primary objective of education policy is to improve educational outcomes. These, it is now well established, derive from many sources, of which formal education is only one: parenting is key; natural ability is also part of the story; and there is increasing evidence of the link between childhood poverty and poor educational outcomes. Thus educational outcomes are both cause and effect of successful transition.

What, however, do we mean by 'good educational outcomes'? The primary purpose of education is to transmit knowledge and skills *and*, as important, attitudes and values. The last two, though frequently overlooked, are critical. As examples, consider the following statements which applied to a greater or lesser extent under the communist system: students should not disagree with their teachers; answers get higher marks if they conform with the prevailing ideology. In the West there is strong disagreement with the values contained in such statements, the prevailing values being that what matters is the analytical *content* of the argument, not the gender, status or ideology of the person making it.

Another part of the objective is to allow diversity. Families will have different views about subject matter, the role of discipline and the place of religion. Thus, the education package (and hence the meaning of a 'good' education) will depend on the economic, political and social structure of the country concerned.

Achieving this primary objective involves a number of subsidiary ones. Allocative efficiency (sometimes called *external efficiency*) is concerned with producing the types of educational activities which equip individuals — economically, socially, politically and culturally — for the societies in which they live. External efficiency applies to the totality of resources devoted to education, and also to the division of resources between different types and levels of education, so as to produce the optimal quantity, quality and mix. Separately, productive efficiency, sometimes referred to as *internal* efficiency, is concerned with running schools and other institutions as efficiently as possible. Equitable access, a third objective, can be justified both on equity grounds and because wasted talent is inefficient.

Internal inefficiency

Reform is necessary, first, because of gross internal inefficiencies in the old education system. The allocation of resources took no account of student or employer demand. The system was poorly coordinated, with resources often wasted on duplication of facilities, as each enterprise and ministry developed its own. With no incentives to use resources efficiently, there was gross over-staffing. Analogous problems arose with healthcare. In both sectors, the problems had the same source as and similar outcomes to those of state-owned enterprises generally. The clear solution for most state-owned enterprises was to return the relevant activities to the private sector. That solution does not apply to anything like the same extent to education and healthcare, *not* for ideological reasons, but because those sectors (unlike most other sectors) suffer from major market failures (for extensive discussion, see Barr, 1992, 1998a).

External inefficiency[41]

The old order　The second, and central, reason for reform relates to external efficiency. Two of the stylized facts listed in the beginning (see p. 170) – central planning and totalitarian government – are particularly relevant. They imply an education system with two strategic characteristics. First, communist education emphasized specialist expertise, that is, a mastery of a fixed body of knowledge, to enable workers to fit their allotted place in the central plan. Second, it encouraged conformist attitudes, since initiative was undesirable in a totalitarian environment and unnecessary for the central plan. Thus, 'education . . . emphasized conformity for all and specialist expertise for each' (World Bank, 1996, p. 124).

The implications of transition　Transition brought in market forces. Market economies need workers capable of responding in a flexible way to the changing demands of a fluid, dynamic system. Workers therefore need broad, flexible skills and a capacity for independent thought, that is, problem-solving skills and the initiative to use them. Democracy – a second effect of transition – also needs independent thought for a flourishing civil society and an engaged citizenry.

These are precisely the skills which communist education did *not* give. As a result, communist education, while well adapted to the old order, was dysfunctional in at least three ways relative to the needs of reform. There were gaps in knowledge. Curricula in subjects such as economics, management science, law, sociology and psychology were missing, irrelevant or underemphasized. The problem is greater than it appears: missing subjects lead to missing concepts and, in consequence, to missing words. 'Efficiency', for example, means something very different to a manager seeking to fill his or her quota under a central plan than to one seeking to increase profit and market share in a competitive system.[42] Though language develops rapidly, missing concepts and missing words can create communication problems which impede speedy and effective transfer of knowledge and skills.

A second problem was a lack of broad, flexible skills. Though basic education was in many ways superior to that in many Western countries, subsequent training was too specialized (the old system in Poland, for example, taught about 300 occupational skills in secondary technical schools, compared with 16 broad occupational programmes in Germany). Furthermore, there was little adult education (essential for mobility in a market economy), because workers were expected to remain in the same occupation throughout their working lives.

A third problem, though harder to document, was a lack of questioning attitudes. It is possible to assess independent thinking, in ascending order of difficulty, by measuring the ability to solve a known class of problem, by the ability to apply a given technique to a new problem, and by the ability to choose which technique to use to solve a new problem. Under communism, the upper end of this taxonomy was regarded with suspicion, and in some countries as seditious.

Figure 10.1 offers some indicative evidence. It shows the results of an international test of skills in mathematics and science designed to give results as comparable as possible across countries.[43] Children in the CIS, Hungary and Slovenia have test scores considerably above the international average. These, clearly, are successful systems. However, children in those countries do better in tests of how much they know than of their ability to apply that knowledge in new and unforeseen circumstances. For children in Canada, France and the United Kingdom, the ranking is precisely the reverse.

One interpretation of these results is that the two education systems were effective in achieving their very different objectives. Communist education gave narrow, specific skills to the mass of its population, encouraging the highest international excellence and creativity in only a small elite of politically trustworthy people. Western education seeks to encourage initiative much more democratically.

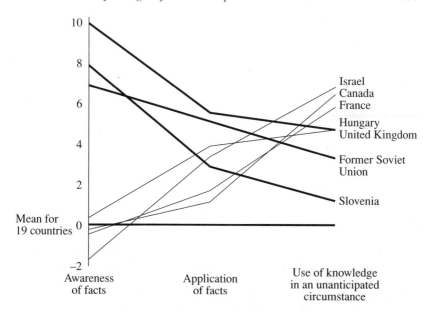

Note: Data are average scores of 9- and 13-year-olds on the second International Assessment of Educational Progress, conducted in 1991. The countries shown are those whose performance was above the mean of a sample of 19 countries.

Source: World Bank (1996, Figure 8.1). See also Kovalyova (1994); for technical details, see Education and Testing Service (1992a, b).

Figure 10.1 Science and mathematics test performance of children in selected transition and industrial economies

Policy Directions: Adapting Education to the Needs of a Market Economy

These results also point to directions for change, both to underpin democracy and to assist the conversion of human capital to that needed to support a market system. The challenge is threefold:

- pluralist textbooks covering revised curricula;
- examinations which place increased emphasis on the capacity to use knowledge, as well as to accumulate it; and
- training and more effective assessment of teachers to make sure that they work with the new curricula and develop new ways of teaching. This last – the need to rejig the human capital of teachers – is perhaps the greatest challenge.

In pursuit of these objectives, additional resources are needed, both for the tasks themselves and to increase teachers' pay; and there is a strong and continuing case for public funding and, for the most part, public organization of schools.

For tertiary education, in contrast, the strategic way forward involves a mixture of public and private funding and the use of market forces. This is an area of debate in the West, and a topic which is likely to become salient fairly soon in the advanced reformers (for discussion in an OECD context, see Barr, 1998a, Ch. 13; 1998b).

A VIEW AHEAD

Unfinished Business

The time scale of this section is intended to represent the lifetime of a parliament, that is, 4–5 years, and hence focuses more on the short term.

Unemployment
The core policy agenda for addressing unemployment includes:

- Robust, simple, well-administered benefit systems. In all but the most advanced reformers there are advantages in the short run of flat-rate benefits.
- Action to develop administrative capacity sufficient to calculate and distribute unemployment benefit.
- Cost-effective systems to help individuals find new jobs, including advice on job seeking and information about job opportunities.
- Training and retraining conducive to productive employment – though care is needed to avoid such activities becoming a budgetary black hole.

Poverty relief
A core programme would include:

- Simple, well-targeted systems of poverty relief, relying as much as possible on indicators other than income.
- Action to develop local targeting capacity.
- Provision of social care for the frail elderly and similar vulnerable groups.

Pensions

Ensuring sustainability of the state PAYG pension   Where options for cutting spending in the short run are limited, reform should ensure that public pensions are sustainable in the medium term.

Continuing work on prerequisites and other supporting institutions   Table 10.7 suggests a check list for policy makers of which several stand out. Is macro-economic stability a realistic assumption? Are financial institutions sufficiently wide, deep and robust? Specifically, is prudential regulation – both policy *and* implementation – adequate; and are there sufficient financial assets?

Informed democratic choices over pension reform   The wide range of choice was discussed above (see pp. 194–203). The major controversy (and not just in the TEs) is over the design of the second-tier pension. Should it be funded, as in Australia and some of the Latin American countries, or PAYG, as in Germany and Canada? Second, if funded, should it be mandatory, as in Australia, or voluntary, as in the Czech Republic? These are legitimate questions with no simple or automatic answer with universal application. The greater the extent of controversy, the greater the importance of informed and extensive public debate.

Education
In ascending order of difficulty and length of time required, what is needed are:

- Modern, pluralistic curricula and supporting textbooks.
- Action to improve the internal efficiency of the system.
- Teacher training, not just in new subjects but in *new attitudes towards teaching*.

Accession to the European Union

Several of the advanced reformers are pressing for early membership of the EU. The major links with the discussion of this chapter are labour market adjustment and the size of the public sector.

Labour market adjustment[44]
Economic adjustment in the face of a single European market will depend to a significant extent on the flexibility of labour markets, a central variable being the European Social Charter. Earlier British opposition to the Charter was based on the argument that it hindered labour market flexibility, indeed that it was an anti-competitive device. The relevance for the TEs is that strict adherence to the Social Charter would reduce their competitiveness, hence contributing to unemployment, fiscal pressures, and perhaps lower growth. The example of former East Germany is perhaps instructive in this respect. In contrast, the relatively large grey economy in many transition countries, whatever its disadvantages, represents a major source of flexibility, with highly competitive wages and little or no protection for workers.

Policy, again, is a delicate balance. Strict adherence to the Social Charter protects workers but, rather like the old economic order, may do so at the expense of growth. A looser adherence increases competitiveness, but at the expense of the security of at least part of the labour force. The extent to which the Social Charter is implemented is therefore potentially a central issue.

The size of the public sector

It is argued that within a single market, business will emigrate from high-tax jurisdictions, imposing downward pressure on public spending levels in the high-spending TEs. There are reasons, however, why this argument should not be overstated. First, public spending as a fraction of GDP, and hence tax rates, varies across existing members of the EU, with the UK at the lower end of the range. This has not caused a massive migration of industry to the UK, not least because tax levels are only one of the determinants of competitiveness. Second, downsizing the public sector in TEs is necessitated not by EU accession but because anything significantly larger would impede growth. Put another way, it is not EU accession which makes downsizing inevitable, but the needs of successful transition.

The Welfare State and Growth

The welfare state is one of the *fruits* of growth: as countries get richer they choose to spend more on it through more generous benefits and higher-quality health and education systems. It is also one of the *causes* of growth: it assists the development of human capital; it fosters redeployment of labour; and, perhaps more arguably, it can contribute to capital formation. The issue has cropped up repeatedly throughout the chapter; this section attempts to draw the strands together.

Spending and growth

It is not controversial to argue that beyond a certain point taxation harms growth. What *is* controversial is where that point is. In addition, as Atkinson's (1995, Ch. 6) survey makes clear, the connection between welfare state spending and growth is far from simple.

- For most of the postwar period, spending on the welfare state in Germany was higher than in Britain, yet German economic growth was faster.
- If it argued that the level of welfare state spending is too high then, as Atkinson points out, '[t]he Welfare State is no more than a co-defendant with other elements of the state budget' (1995, p. 123).
- Causation can be problematic. Do countries with higher spending reduce their growth rate, or do countries with lower growth and more poverty need to spend a larger fraction of GDP alleviating poverty?

- Looking at aggregates can obscure other key influences on growth, notably the detailed structure, and hence the incentive effects, of benefits. Benefits awarded without an income test, for example, may cost more but have less powerful adverse incentives.

Separately, the welfare state has benefits as well as costs. As I have written elsewhere (Barr, 1998a, p. 409),

> The welfare state is much more than a safety net; it is justified not simply by any redistributive aims one may (or may not) have, but because it does things which private markets for technical reasons either would not do at all, or would do ineffi- ciently. We need a welfare state of some sort for efficiency reasons, and would continue to do so even if all distributional problems had been solved.

Thus welfare state spending should be optimized not minimized. Even in the short run, even in poor countries, welfare-state institutions – albeit parsimo- nious ones – are essential. That does not mean that spending cannot be cut; but it probably cannot – and should not – be cut very much. Even in Western countries with the most powerful individualistic rhetoric during the early transition, public spending on the welfare state was substantial – about one- fifth of GDP in the USA and about one-quarter in the UK. While not benchmarks for the TEs, they illustrate the existence of an essential core, and hence the continuing fiscal salience of the welfare state.

Assisting effective labour markets
Unemployment benefits contribute to efficiency by assisting the movement of labour to more productive uses. Such movement is important in any economy; it is imperative in countries with inherited misallocation on the scale of the TEs. Separately, by easing the hardship of redeployment, such benefits are essential for the political sustainability of reform.

Effective labour markets require not only workers at the right wage in the right place, but also with the right skills. Here, too, there is a major misalloca- tion. Thus education and training are necessary to adjust inherited human capital. With capital and technology operating on a global scale, it can be argued that differences in human capital are today the major source of differential economic performance and, to that extent, human capital is even more important than in the past. Effective spending on education and training is thus an essential component of a strategy for growth. This is *not* an area for expenditure cuts; the emphasis, rather, should be on effectiveness.

Pensions and growth
A move to funded pensions may contribute to growth both directly, by increasing saving, and indirectly, by widening and deepening capital markets.

This, however, is a controversial and technically complex area. A key point made above (see p. 203) is that the funding debate focuses on only one source of growth; policies should consider the wide range of growth-inducing policies discussed above (see pp. 187–90).

Concluding Messages

In conclusion, here are a few broader messages.

There is no Holy Grail. Unemployment remains an unsolved problem even in the advanced industrial economies. Nor is there any simple answer to the poverty trap, whose ultimate source is the shape of the income distribution which, virtually throughout the world, is heavily skewed towards lower incomes. As a result, though we want to help people who are poor, we cannot afford to support the non-poor; thus we need to claw back benefit as people become less poor and, given fiscal constraints and the shape of the income distribution, have to do so quickly. To that extent a poverty trap in one form or another is inescapable.

In the case of pensions, there is no escape from risk. Since funding and PAYG are simply different financial mechanisms for organizing claims on future output, it should not be surprising that both are vulnerable to adverse pressures.

Improving the quality of and access to education remains a permanent part of the policy agenda throughout the advanced industrial countries.

Implementation is as important as policy. The welfare state both contributes to and depends on the success of the reforms. Effective government is critical for both aspects. It includes the capacity to devise policy, to carry policy forward politically, to implement laws in an environment untainted by excessive corruption, and to monitor the effects of policy. Within the welfare state, the importance of effective government – for administering state benefits such as unemployment compensation and poverty relief as well as for private pensions – has already been stressed. Private implementation, for example, the capacity to administer large numbers of individual pension accounts, is equally critical. It is a serious misunderstanding of reform, having designed the policy, to imagine that the task is largely over; without effective implementation – political and administrative – reform will fail.

Politics matter. Though not the subject of this chapter, reform depends critically on effective management of the politics of change. It was politics which made it impossible to reform pensions in Poland earlier, and effective political management, alongside technical expertise, which eventually made reform possible. In Hungary, it has been argued (Nelson, 1998), the politics of change were less effective, calling into question the robustness of political support for the funded second tier.

Looking at the transition countries more broadly, Dmitriev (Chapter 14 in this volume) points out that pension reform in Poland and Hungary was constrained by the existence of generous state pensions, creating large entrenched interests. Thus pension reform could only be marginal, for example, the phased introduction of a second-tier pension. In that sense, policy makers in less-advanced reformers, including many of the countries of the CIS, have a broader range of options, since state pensions, being small, have few defenders, and hence are in principle easier to restructure.

A final thought on politics. Fact 1: Poland adopted stringent reform policies in 1990. Fact 2: though there have been several changes of government, there has been consistent political support for the broad thrust of the reform policies. Fact 3: Polish GDP is the highest fraction of pre-reform GDP of all the TEs, and Polish growth the fastest. Similarly, in Slovenia – another highly effective reformer – political activity has maintained support for the reform policies. These outcomes are no accident. They are the result not only of the right policies (which, after all, were attempted by many countries), but also of effective political implementation.

NOTES

1. This chapter draws on two spells at the World Bank, where I learned a great deal from colleagues. An early draft was written while I was the 1999 Downing Fellow at Melbourne University. For comments and help I am grateful to Tamas Bauer, Michail Dmitriev, Zsuzsa Ferge, Stanisława Golinowska, Richard Jackman, Deborah Mabbett, Branko Milanovic, Edward Palmer, Tanya Proskurakova, Dena Ringold, Michal Rutkowski, Jan Rutkowski, Jeffrey Sachs, Winfried Schmähl, Judith Shapiro, Sándor Sipos, Igor Tomeš and Stanisław Wellisz. As always, Gill Barr listened patiently to my ruminations and productively kicked lumps out of earlier drafts.
2. 'Key features of the prereform labor market [included] . . . [a] structure of relative wages characterized by compressed differentials bearing little relationship to the market value of workers' skills' (Jackman, 1998, p. 123).
3. 'Very low or nonexistent unemployment' (ibid.).
4. That is, the FSU minus Estonia, Latvia and Lithuania.
5. This is made as a broad-brush assertion, abstracting from the difficulties of measuring changes in output during the early transition.
6. That does not mean that many people in those countries have not experienced a fall in income – merely that *relative to a benchmark of 4 USD per day* poverty has increased very little.
7. For discussion of these problems in Russia during the early transition, see Barr (1993); for more recent discussion, see Jackman (1998).
8. By 1998 in Poland, for example, unemployment benefit was about three-quarters of the minimum wage, which was about 40 per cent of the average wage.
9. For fuller discussion, see Jackman and Rutkowski (1994), Jackman (1998) and Boeri et al. (1998).
10. Atkinson (1995, Ch. 11) stresses the importance of labour market institutions. On retirement, see Hannah (1986).
11. The replacement rate is the ratio of income on benefit to net income when in work, that is, with a 40 per cent replacement, an unemployed person receives benefit equal to 40 per cent of his or her previous wage.

12. See Boeri et al., (1998, Ch. 4) for fuller discussion, including the economic rationale for these programmes.
13. Thus if the employer contribution was 40 per cent of the gross wage, an enterprise with a monthly wage bill of 1 million USD would each month remit 400,000 USD to the social insurance authorities on behalf of all its employees.
14. For details of the early Polish experience, see World Bank (1993).
15. For fuller discussion, see Sipos (1994) and Milanovic (1998).
16. For a summary of the analytics of targeting, see Barr (1998a, pp. 237–40). The classic article on indicator targeting is by Akerlof (1978).
17. Since, in contrast with income-tested benefits, only the income effect works against labour supply.
18. In some countries, the potential for discrimination against the Roma would be a particular problem.
19. The poverty gap is the total shortfall of people's income from the poverty line, as a fraction of either (a) the poverty line or (b) total income. Index (a) gives a measure of the average depth of poverty, (b) the relative cost of relieving it.
20. For fuller discussion, see Barr (1994b).
21. In Latvia, early retirement was extended, *inter alia*, to dwarfs, pilots and wind instrument players (I am indebted to Louise Fox of the World Bank for this information).
22. For further detail, see Barr (1999, Table 11.1).
23. Funded pensions are paid from an accumulated fund built up over a period of years out of the contributions of its members. In contrast, PAYG pensions are paid (usually by the state) out of current tax revenues. For fuller discussion of the economics of pensions, see Barr (1998a, Ch. 9).
24. The theoretical option of financing pension spending by borrowing is ruled out by the scale of the expenditure.
25. Declining life expectancy could also act to reduce the number of pensioners. Quite apart from the manifest undesirability of such an outcome, evidence, at least in Russia, suggests that it is not Russian pensioners who are dying earlier than before, but people of working age (World Bank, 1996, Box 8.1).
26. There is another – technical – reason for caution in asserting the extent to which pensioners have been protected. Milanovic's results are based on income per capita, implying that all household members, including children, receive an equal weight. If instead children were given a lower weight, the poverty line for a household of four, of whom two are children, might be (say) 2.5 times that for a single person. Investigation using income per capita will find more poor children and fewer poor old people than with a poverty line in which children receive a lower weight. Similarly, the choice of a household definition of income assumes that older people share the resources of younger family members and thus finds fewer poor old people.
27. As Michal Rutkowski's chapter makes clear, at least in the Euroasian transition economies, pensions are able to do little more than provide poverty relief, that is, paying de facto flat rate benefits.
28. The UK has introduced reform to bring women's pensionable age (60) up to that of men (65). The increase will be phased in from 2010, leading to a common pensionable age of 65 by 2020. Under the reforms, the key date is 6 April 1950. For women born before that, pensionable age will continue to be 60. Pensionable age for a woman born on 6 May 1950 (that is, one month after the key date) would be 60 years and one month, for a woman born on 6 June 1950, 60 years and two months, and so on. Thus for women born on or after 6 April 1955 pensionable age will be 65 (see Tolley, 1996, Appendix 20A).
29. Under a *defined contribution* scheme, a person's pension is an annuity whose size is determined *only* by the size of his or her lifetime pension accumulation. Thus the individual bears the risk of varying rates of return to pension assets. Under a *defined benefit* scheme, usually run at a firm or industry level, the firm pays an annuity based on the employee's wage in his or her final year (or final few years) of work and upon length of service (a typical formula is one-eighteenth of final salary per year of service). Thus the risk of varying rates of return to pension assets falls on the employer (and hence also on the taxpayer).

30. For more detailed discussion, see Góra and Rutkowski (1998).
31. The system also has a small Demographic Reserve Fund.
32. See Gerencsér (1997); International Social Security Association (1998, pp. 16–17).
33. The table shows the ratio of P/Y, where P = total pension spending and Y = GDP. If Y falls by 40 per cent (in Macedonia, for example), P/Y will increase even if real pension spending is cut by one-third.
34. Of the total contribution five-eighths goes to the first-tier and three-eighths to the second tier.
35. Interestingly, during reform discussions, Polish policy makers actively considered 'endowing' pension funds with residual state assets scheduled for privatization. The final law, more modestly, authorizes the government to issue a specific type of government bond a few months in advance of a privatization, which the holders can convert into shares when privatization takes place. The purpose of this instrument (which has not so far been used) is twofold. First, it accelerates the privatization proceeds if that is necessary to bridge a difference between pension contributions and pension spending (a possibility given the need to phase in contributions to the second-tier funded pension while still paying out full PAYG pensions). Second, it acts as a signal that the government is prepared to ensure that pension revenues are adequate. This latter aspect turned out to be important in building political support for the reforms.
36. Funds can invest no more than 40 per cent of their holdings in quoted stock, 5 per cent in foreign shares, 10 per cent in the secondary stock market, 10 per cent in National Investment Funds, 10 per cent in National Bank of Poland paper and 15 per cent in municipal bonds.
37. In the UK, personal pensions can be converted into an annuity at any age between 50 and 75.
38. For fuller discussion of the importance of fiscal transparency, see IMF (1998).
39. Hidden charges for private pensions is a besetting problem in the UK, and one on which policy action is urgently needed. As a simple example of what is needed, credit card companies in Western countries are all required to use the same definition of the interest rate they charge customers in their promotional literature, thus making it easy for people to see which company is offering the best rate. In contrast, the price structures of airlines and telephone companies are not comparable.
40. On an early visit to Poland, in January 1990, I was faced with a radical pension privatization proposal at a time when the monthly inflation rate was 80 per cent and when – since there were no financial markets – there was no financial market regulation, thus violating two essential prerequisites of private pensions. Things are very different now.
41. This section draws heavily on Heyneman (1994), which underpins much of the analysis in World Bank (1996, Ch. 8).
42. As another example, during the early transition the term *income transfers* proved a consistent problem for interpreters and translators because there was little understanding of the distinction between wages (mainly related to individual productivity for reasons of economic efficiency) and transfers (mostly paid out of the state budget for distributional reasons).
43. For fuller detail, see Kovalyova (1994), Education and Testing Service (1992a, b).
44. This section draws on Boeri et al. (1998, pp. 92–4).

REFERENCES

Akerlof, George A. (1978), 'The economics of "tagging" as applied to the optimal income tax, welfare programs and manpower planning', *American Economic Review*, **68** (1), 8–19.

Atkinson, Anthony B. (1995), *Incomes and the Welfare State: Essays on Britain and Europe*, Cambridge: Cambridge University Press.

Barr, Nicholas (1992), 'Economic theory and the welfare state: a survey and interpretation', *Journal of Economic Literature*, **30** (2), 741–803.

Barr, Nicholas (1993), 'Income transfers in Russia: problems and some policy directions', *Economics of Transition*, **1** (3), 317–44.

Barr, Nicholas (ed.) (1994a), *Labor Markets and Social Policy in Central and Eastern Europe: The Transition and Beyond*, New York and Oxford: Oxford University Press for the World Bank (also available in Hungarian, Romanian and Russian).

Barr, Nicholas (1994b), 'Income transfers: social insurance', in Barr (1994a), pp. 192–225.

Barr, Nicholas (1998a), *The Economics of the Welfare State*, 3rd edn, Oxford: Oxford University Press, and Stanford, CA: Stanford University Press.

Barr, Nicholas (1998b), 'Higher education in Australia and Britain: what lessons?', *Australian Economic Review*, **31** (2), 179–88.

Barr, Nicholas (1999), 'Pension reform in Central and Eastern Europe: the good, the bad and the unsustainable', in Sami Daniel, Philip Arestis and John Grahl (eds), *Regulation Strategies and Economic Policies, Essays in Honour of Bernard Corry and Maurice Peston*, Vol. Three, Cheltenham, UK and Brookfield, USA: Edward Elgar, pp. 174–91.

Boeri, Tito, Michael Burda and János Köll (1998), *Mediating the Transition: Labour Markets in Central and Eastern Europe*, London: Centre for Economic Policy Research and New York: Institute for EastWest Studies.

Boone, Peter, Stanislaw Gomulka and Richard Layard (1998), *Emerging from Communism: Lessons from Russia, China, and Eastern Europe*, London and Cambridge, MA: MIT Press.

Chand, Sheetal K. and Albert Jaeger (1996), *Aging Populations and Public Pension Schemes*, Occasional Paper 147, Washington, DC: International Monetary Fund.

Diamond, Peter (1995), 'Government provision and regulation of economic support in old age', in Michael Bruno and Boris Pleskovic (eds), *Annual Bank Conference on Development Economics 1995*, Washington, DC: World Bank.

Education and Testing Service (1992a), *Learning Mathematics*, Princeton, NJ.

Education and Testing Service (1992b), *Learning Science*, Princeton, NJ.

European Bank for Reconstruction and Development (EBRD) (1999), *Transition Report Update*, London: EBRD.

Gerencsér, L. (1997), *Information on the Pension Reform in Hungary*, Budapest: Central Administration of the National Pension Insurance Fund.

Godfrey, Martin and Peter Richards (eds) (1997), *Employment Policies and Programmes in Central and Eastern Europe*, Geneva: International Labour Organization.

Góra, Marek and Harmut Lehmann (1995), 'Labour market policies in Poland: an assessment', Paper presented to OECD technical workshop 'What Can We Learn from the Experience of Transition Countries with Labour Market Policies', Vienna, 30 November–2 December.

Góra, Marek and Michal Rutkowski (1998), 'The quest for pension reform: Poland's security through diversity', Social Protection Discussion Paper 9815, Washington, DC: World Bank.

Gruber, Jonathan and David Wise (1998), 'Social security and declining labor-force participation', *American Economic Review: Papers and Proceedings*, **88** (2), 158–63.

Hannah, Leslie (1986), *Inventing Retirement*, Cambridge: Cambridge University Press.

Heyneman, Stephen P. (1994), 'Education in the Europe and Central Asia region: policies of adjustment and excellence', Europe and Central Asia Region, Report No. IDP-145, Washington, DC: World Bank (also in Russian).

Holzmann, Robert (1997), 'Pension reform, financial market development, and economic growth: preliminary evidence from Chile', *IMF Staff Papers* 44/2, 149–78.

Holzmann, Robert and Steen Jorgensen (1999), 'Social protection as social risk management – conceptual underpinnings for the social protection sector strategy paper', *Social Protection Discussion Paper* No. 9904, Washington, DC: World Bank.

International Monetary Fund (IMF) (1998), 'Code of good practices on fiscal trans-parency – declaration on principles', Washington, DC: International Monetary Fund.

International Social Security Association (1998), *Trends in Social Security*, (2), Geneva, Switzerland: General Secretariat of the ISSA.

Jackman, Richard (1998), 'Unemployment and restructuring', in Boone et al. (1998), pp. 123–52.

Jackman, Richard and Michal Rutkowski (1994), 'Labour markets: wages and employment', in Barr (1994a), pp. 121–59.

Kovalyova, Galina (1994), 'Comparative assessments of students in science and math', in Stephen P. Heynemann (ed.), *Education in the Europe and Central Asia Region: Policies of Adjustment and Excellence*, Europe and Central Asia Region, Report No. IDP-145, Washington, DC: World Bank.

Micklewright, John, and G. Nagy (1994), 'Flows to and from insured unemployment in Hungary', EUI Working Papers in Economics No. 41, Florence: European University Institute.

Milanovic, Branko (1998), *Income, Inequality and Poverty during the Transition from Planned to Market Economy*, Washington, DC: World Bank.

Milanovic, Branko (1999), 'The role of social assistance in addressing poverty', Third draft, Washington, DC: World Bank.

Nellis, John (1999), 'Time to rethink privatization in transition economies?', Discussion Paper No. 38, Washington, DC: International Finance Corporation.

Nelson, Joan (1998), 'The politics of pensions and health care delivery reforms in Hungary and Poland', Paper to Focus Group on Fiscal Reforms, Collegium Budapest, 27–28 March, Budapest.

Organization for Economic Cooperation and Development (OECD) (1997), *Lessons from Labour Market Policies in the Transition Economies*, Paris: OECD.

Puhani, Patrick and Victor Steiner (1996), 'Public works in Poland? Active labour market policies during transition', ZEW Discussion Paper No. 96–01.

Sipos, Sándor (1994), 'Income transfers: family support and poverty relief', in Barr (1994a), pp. 226–59.

Stiglitz, Joseph E. (1999), 'Whither reform? Ten years of the transition', Keynote Address, Annual Bank Conference on Development Economics, Washington, DC: World Bank.

Sweden: Federation of Social Insurance Offices (1998), 'Sweden', *The Future of Social Security*, Stockholm: Federation of Social Insurance Offices, pp. 192–203; for updates see also http://www.pension.gov.se.

Thompson, Lawrence (1998), *Older and Wiser: The Economics of Public Pensions*, Washington, DC: Urban Institute.

Tolley (1996), *Social Security and State Benefits Handbook, 1996–97*, by Jim Matthewman et al., Croydon, Surrey: Tolley Publishing Company.

UK Department of Social Security (1993), *Containing the Costs of Social Security – the International Context*, London: HMSO.

UK Pension Law Review Committee (1993), *Pension Law Reform*, Report of the Pension Law Review Committee, Vol. I *Report*, and Vol. II *Research*, London: HMSO.

UK Treasury Select Committee (1998), *The Mis-selling of Personal Pensions*, Ninth Report, Vol. 1, Report and Proceedings of the Committee, HC712–1, London: HMSO.

Weisbrod, Burton A. (1969), 'Collective action and the distribution of income: a conceptual approach', in Joint Economic Committee, *The Analysis and Evaluation of Public Expenditures*, Washington, DC: US Government Printing Office, pp. 177–97.

Wilensky, Harold L. and Charles N. Lebeaux (1965), *Industrial Society and Social Welfare*, New York and London: Free Press and Collier-Macmillan.

World Bank (1993), *Poland: Income Support and the Social Safety Net during the Transition*, Washington, DC: World Bank.

World Bank (1994), *Averting the Old Age Crisis*, New York: Oxford University Press.

World Bank (1996), *World Development Report 1996: From Plan to Market*, New York and Oxford: Oxford University Press.

World Bank (1999), *World Development Indicators*, Washington, DC: World Bank.

11. Welfare state reforms in post-communist countries: A comment on Barr

Stanisława Golinowska

My comment is an attempt to supplement assumptions and explanations presented by Barr, and rarely to verify them. I look at these issues from the Polish perspective, which probably resembles the views of colleagues from other Central European countries, and possibly the Baltic states. It is possible that colleagues from other former Soviet Union (FSU) states would have different comments on Barr, as the transformation of the welfare state in these countries comes hand in hand with a decline in economic growth.

WHY DID THE EASTERN BLOC SOCIETIES REJECT CENTRAL PLANNING?

From the economic point of view, the answer to this question is straightforward. It was an inefficient system, and the consequences of its inefficiency became transparent, taking a heavy toll on the everyday life of the society. From the social standpoint, the answer is much more complicated. The socialist welfare state gave everybody a sense of security and peaceful existence within the community of an enterprise, which despite low wages managed to satisfy the emotional needs of individual workers. Competition among employees was basically non-existent and the enterprise demonstrated a great deal of under-standing for human weaknesses and failures (Narojek, 1991). However, a low appeal of manufactured consumer goods coupled with shortages and long queues contributed to the rejection of this perceived peace. In addition, the lack of a proper motivation system that rewards responsibility, effectiveness and creativity resulted in either acquired helplessness or group selfishness and a 'swim with the tide' attitude (Marody, 1988). Eventually, a co-existence of different perceptions and assessments of the socialist welfare state led Poland as well as other countries of the region to a conviction that it is possible to combine market economy with a modified model of the socialist welfare state. Testimony to such a conviction are the Round Table Agreements (1989), the debates held during the drafting of the Constitution (1995–97), and one of its resulting provisions, which declares that the Polish state is a state of social market economy. However, the understanding of the social market economy was not consistent with the concept of the German social market economy, also known as 'ordoliberalism'. As interpreted by many Polish politicians, it was a combination of a modern and improved 'real socialism' with the market economy.

WHY IS THE REFORM OF THE WELFARE STATE ESSENTIAL?

While explaining the necessity of the reform of the socialist welfare state, Barr points to the shortcomings of the old order. As stated above, not all the features of the old system were perceived by the society as shortcomings.

I dare to claim that the development of the new system in Poland over the past decade has been characterized by the lack of coherence between economic and social reforms. While economic reforms were very much market orientated and introduced in a rather dramatic way, the social area has not been sufficiently defined. Major political circles and most eminent experts of the region believe that the socialist welfare state should be improved, updated, but not eradicated or even excessively constrained. A small group of policy makers and experts, usually with an economic background holds the view that social functions of the state should be narrowed and that social policy should undergo complex reforms. This is synonymous with transposing the old slogan coined by the trade unions in the early 1980s, 'yes to socialism, no to distortions ' into 'yes to the market, but no to the market distribution'.

Nevertheless, several major market-based institutional solutions were introduced in the social security area at the turn of the decade. The initial transition is sometimes referred to as 'the stage of reactive social reforms' (Horstmann and Schmähl 1999), a term indicating a reaction to consequences of the departure from the doctrine of total employment and labour market efficiency, as well as a reaction to the anticipated increase in poverty. As a direct response to new social problems, an institutional infrastructure for labour and social assistance was developed.

In the reactive stage, there were also spontaneous reactions, which moved the socialist welfare state in the direction of privatization and commercialization. On the one hand, a crisis in production and public expenditure reduced funds available for social services, and on the other, the bias towards microeconomic efficiency compelled businesses to limit social activities.

However, policy makers and experts have never openly and seriously discussed the new social policy model adjusted to the evolving economy.

SOCIAL CONSEQUENCES OF TRANSITION

While discussing the social consequences of transition, Barr points to three major problems: increased income inequality (both earnings and benefits); a decrease in public expenditure resulting from a slump in production and tax reforms; and unemployment and poverty as new social phenomena that have not been addressed by an adequate policy approach.

Income inequality is growing rapidly. Polish opinion polls point out that social acceptance of increased wage disparity resulting from hard work (intense, responsible and also performed under difficult working conditions) and high qualifications, has prevailed since the mid-1990s. Nevertheless, this acceptance does not imply the approval of inequality in wealth distribution by the society that continues to endorse egalitarianism. The view of the majority, with regard to progress, is that equality is more important than disparity (Marody, 1999). Currently, the acceptance of inequality is declining, also with respect to wages, because socially unacceptable sources of inequality have become more apparent. The rising inequality stems from a variety of factors. First, wages are boosted by the market, which rewards highly sought-after skills, responsibility and risk-taking and this has been perceived as fair. In response, private schools have mushroomed and the number of university students has doubled over the past several years. Second, the wage disparity in Poland also stems from the rising compensation of public officials, politically-dependent positions or business-linked functions, which reflects rent-seeking behaviour. There is also an increase in income by the so-called 'independent' economic entities within the public sector – they are not restricted by state efficiency requirements and are thus free to offer market-based compensation. Other public sector employees, including, recently, the doctors, are also demanding higher wages. Third, the growing inequality is also attributable to the development of various private services, rarely accepted by society, such as private security as a response to the poorly-functioning police or quasi-legal forms of entertainment. Even if the acceptable inequality factors prevail, the presence of the remaining ones is frustrating, leading to mounting social conflicts and negative opinions about the directions of social development (CBOS, 1998).

Transfer payments and taxes cannot alleviate the difficult situation in primary income distribution. The level of inequality remains high as redistribution measures are moderate, that is, personal income tax is not a great burden, whereas social security benefits tend to be low (Topińska and Styczeń, 1999). Consequently, the Gini coefficient for Polish wages does not differ from that for income. In contrast, in the West the difference is very significant. For instance, in the extreme case of Sweden the difference is more than double (48.7 for wages and other market income, and 23.0 for household income), in

Germany it is 15 points (43.6 against 28.2), and in the USA 10 points (45.5 against 34.4) (OECD, 1997).

Inequality of income and wealth distribution may pose a major threat to social stability in Poland. I do not promote social equality for all, but I am convinced that a rational approach can be developed, taking into consideration the destructive impact of wage extremes on the labour market and on social stability. In 1999, ten years after the beginning of transition, the Gini coefficient for wages exceeded 0.34 (own estimates) placing Poland among the states with the most diverse income, such as Italy or the USA. A higher disparity is observed only in several FSU countries (UNICEF ICDC, 1999).

Wage disparity in lower-income brackets is rather small due to frequent adjustments of the minimum wage. Overall, the wage disparity observed in Poland bears a negative influence on the labour market by limiting the employment opportunities of low-skilled workers and young people. It impairs wage expectations by encouraging wage demands independent of work quality and efficiency, based rather on comparisons with the most affluent groups (See Table 11.1.)

Table 11.1   Income distribution: Gini coefficient

Countries	1989		1997
Czech Republic	} 0.198	0.215 (1992)	0.239
Slovakia		–	0.249
Poland	0.275		0.334
Hungary	0.225		0.254
Bulgaria	0.331 (1992)		0.336
Romania	0.237		0.305
Estonia	0.280		0.361
Latvia	0.260		0.336 (earnings)
Lithuania	0.262		0.309
Belarus	0.229		0.249
Moldova	0.250		0.390 (1995 earnings)
Russia	0.265		0.385 (1995)
			0.483 (earnings)
Ukraine	0.229		0.413 (1995 earnings)

Source: UNICEF ICDC (1999).

Generally speaking, having overcome the crisis in manufacturing only in 1993, the problem relating to public expenditure in Poland comes down to setting priorities, and then to coordinating the pursued social policy by various state institutions and local governments. The inexperience of the young democratic system and the weakness of state institutions impede rational decision making, monitoring and supervision of social expenditures. Consequently, on one hand, there are numerous examples of abuse of benefits (particularly health benefits) and a free-rider behaviour, and, on the other, inefficient management, and item omissions and removals from the budget. Lack of proper coordination is particularly visible now, when four reforms, including the decentralization of state administration, have been launched.

According to Barr, targeting of public expenditures aimed at preventing unemployment and poverty is inefficient in transition economies (TEs) – both with respect to horizontal efficiency (coverage of all groups affected by the problem) and vertical efficiency (effective benefit distribution). In TEs, this issue is difficult not only because of technical factors but also because of psychological constraints.

The socialist welfare state provided more than just universal benefits. The socialist 'economy of shortages' applied additional benefits allocation criteria, such as awarding contributions to socialism and difficult living conditions. However, the society favoured universal solutions, since there was little trust in the fairness of allocation based on individualized criteria. A support for universal solutions has long prevailed in TEs despite policy makers' endorsement of the concept of benefits targeting. An example of a delay in targeting in Poland is the treatment of the family allowance, which used to be a universal, but largely symbolic benefit because of its low level. It was not until 1995 that the allowance was granted only to poorer families and the amount was increased slightly.

Barr is well aware that precise targeting of benefits based on the income criterion is difficult to implement and expensive to administer. Therefore, he recommends a pragmatic approach – targeting benefits on the basis of an easily identifiable non-income criterion, which, however, would be strongly correlated with income. He warns against decisions based on stereotypes and unverifiable opinions.

The income criterion has been dominant in the Polish system of social assistance. The distribution of limited funds among claimants who meet the overall requirements for benefit assistance is carried out by the local social administration centres, which make independent award decisions. Local social administration workers do seek guidelines from the central office, as they try to avoid sole decision-making responsibility in case of conflicts, but to no avail. The government insists on delegating the decision making to the local level in spite of frequent warnings from Western publications against excessive empowering of social administration employees. In other European TEs haunted by a larger scale of poverty than Poland, social security administration faces an even greater challenge. Theoretical assumptions are of little use for them.

SOCIAL PROTECTION OF THE UNEMPLOYED

Under central planning, the term 'full employment' often meant hidden unemployment. Jobs were created in the course of central planning. Reforms of the 1980s implemented in line with the 'three S' motto (self-reliance, self-financing and self-governance) granted enterprises a certain amount of discretion in setting wages and prices, but not in determining employment. Labour standards were low, and trade unions guarded their sustainability.

During transition, the concept of full employment underlying the socialist welfare state was rejected. Open unemployment became an essential means of achieving microeconomic efficiency. The explosion of unemployment occurred as a consequence of economic transition, and of a related crisis in production. Frightened policy makers and reformers responded to it by providing generous and easy to obtain benefits for the unemployed and their families (benefits were basically available on a declaration of unemployment). This also provided early retirement incentives to older employees. Eligibility criteria for unemployment benefits and their levels were modified 12 months after the initial introduction, however the retirement benefits were granted permanently. As a result, during the period 1989–92, the number of pension recipients increased by 20 per cent, whereas the retirement-age population grew by approximately one per cent. Thus the gap between the *demographic dependency ratio* (the number of retirement-age persons to the working-age population) and the *system dependency ratio* (the number of pensioners to the number of employed persons) widened.

The system of unemployment benefits was introduced in 1991 and has often been modified with respect to various unemployed groups. It provided a modest, *flat-rate* benefit, equal to 33 per cent of the average wage initially and then to 36 and 30 per cent. Eligibility criteria and the entitlement period vary. The extension of the benefit period by six months is subject to local labour market conditions and to the family situation (both parents must be unemployed). The level of benefits has been declining since the introduction of price indexation in 1996. This has been accompanied by a decrease in the number of benefit recipients in relation to all registered unemployed (currently slightly more than 20 per cent). This is a consequence of imposing certain restrictions on eligibility criteria, such as a ban on other forms of employment during the benefit period and the unemployment term limits.

Another question is whether the Polish unemployment benefits system is efficient with respect to its two basic goals: prevention of poverty and stimulating individuals to overcome unemployment by returning to work. In order to analyse this issue, we have to tackle two facts addressed by Barr. The first fact relates to the definition of unemployment. In Poland and in other TEs, unemployment does not necessarily mean a lack of work or a lack of income.

In any case, the unemployment status obtained as a result of a lack of an officially declared source of income is necessary to qualify for public healthcare. The second fact relates to growing structural unemployment, which occurs in regions that lack jobs. It also relates to the lack of appropriate skills among workers or to the lack of geographical mobility that often subjects the unemployed to the culture of poverty (they constitute the *underclass*). It seems that the solution currently applied in Poland (flat-rate benefits) is suitable to the situation in the Polish labour market. It is often simply a form of social assistance; however, the fact that unemployment benefits are provided by a labour centre, and not by a social assistance centre, may be of advantage. Labour centres provide information about job offers, thus they may reinforce the willingness of the unemployed to take up a job. As shown in Table 11.2, different unemployment benefit systems have been introduced in other countries of the region.

Other ways of overcoming unemployment include the so-called 'active labour market policies' (ALMPs). However, the public works which are applied in Poland as one such measure would not be efficient in regions that lack job offers (Puhani, 1998). Nevertheless, the unemployed performing useful public work for pay find themselves in a less demoralizing situation than those who receive unemployment benefits. In addition, public works can create an essential infrastructure that may attract private investors to the region.

OLD-AGE SECURITY SYSTEM REFORM

While it was necessary to develop a brand-new system of welfare state institutions to help the unemployed, old-age pension institutions were already in place. Their structure resembled that of similar institutions in Europe, especially in Central Europe, whose social insurance institutions were in the Bismarckian tradition. The problem of old-age pensions was considered to be a primary area of social security reform because of the high costs and vertical inefficiency of the old system, as pointed out by Barr. These high costs stem from the old problem, that is, the large number of old-age benefits, as well as from a new one, that is, the designation of old-age benefits as social protection for the unemployed.

The major problem, however, was related to the so-called 'old wallet' phenomenon, that is, pensions and social security benefits granted under the old system that were not subject to indexation. There was a need to support a large population of pensioners and social security recipients, whose financial situation continued to deteriorate due to the lack of benefit indexation inherited from the socialism era. This phenomenon was particularly acute in Poland and Hungary. Both states launched economic reforms more quickly than other post-

Table 11.2 Unemployment benefits in CEE countries

Country	Benefit type and level	Eligibility criteria in months	Duration in months	Minimum and maximum levels
Albania	Fixed; plus 5% for each child under 15 (max. 20%), less 50% if one parent works or draws a pension	12 (insured)	12	Min: min living standard Max: max wage
Bulgaria	Earnings based; 60% of gross wage	15 (employed)	4–12, based on employment length	Min: 80% of min wage Max: 140% of min wage
Czech Republic	Earnings based; 50% of net wage (first 3 months) 40% (subsequent 3 months)	12 (insured) 36 (employed)	6	Max: 150% of subsistence level
Estonia	Flat rate; fixed (7% of average wage in 1997; 21% of average pension)	6 (insured) 12 (employed)	6 (+3)	na
FYR Macedonia	Earnings based; 50% of net wage, 40% after 12 months for eligible persons	12	12	Max: average wage in public sector
Hungary	Earnings based; 65% of gross wage	12 (insured) 48 (employed)	6–12, based on employment length	Min: 90% of min pension Max: 180% of min pension
Latvia	Earnings based; linked to insurance and unemployment length; 50% of gross wage (under 5 years employment), 65% (over 25 years); 80% of the benefit level after 3 months, 60% after 6 months	9 (insured) 48 (employed)	9	na

Lithuania	Insurance length based; minimum benefit multiplied by years of employment (max 25 years)	24 (insured) 36 (employed)	6	Min: subsistence level; equivalent to about 30% of min wage Max: twice min subsistence level
Poland	Flat rate, fixed at 36% of national average gross wage (differs by employment length; 80% if employed under 5 years, 120% if over 20 years	12 (insured) 18 (employed)	12 (6–18) depends on the region	na
Romania	Earnings based; linked to employment length; 50% of net wage (under 5 years); 55% (5–15 years); 60% (over 15 years)	6 (insured) 12 (employed)	9	Min: 75–85% min wage Max: 200% of national average net wage
Slovakia	Earnings based; 60% of gross wage (for 3 months), 50% (after 3 months)	12 (insured) 36 (employed)	6, 9 or 12 age based	Max: 180% of min wage
Slovenia	Earnings based; 70% of gross wage (for 3 months), 60% (after 3 months)	12 (insured) 18 (employed)	3–12 (24), age and employment length based	Min: min income Max: 300% of min income

Sources: Clasen (2000) and own supplements.

communist countries. The discourse of this process in Hungary was described very accurately by Simonovits (1997).

There were strong social pressures in Poland, particularly those exerted by the Solidarity trade union, to solve the problem of benefit indexation and to eliminate the old wallet. Moreover, the government announced the introduction of a comprehensive benefit indexation in 1986 (heralded by the act of 1982), but failed to implement it, triggering increased criticism from the political opposition.

The failure to implement the indexation could have led to the excessive erosion of benefits in terms of their real value, and consequently, to widespread poverty among the elderly in the hyperinflationary environment that prevailed in Poland at the time (in 1989 the inflation rate reached 351 per cent and soared to 686 per cent in 1990). The implementation of indexation of the benefits base and the benefits themselves as well as the guarantee of indexation enacted by parliament was a favourable solution to this social problem. At the same time, the government increased the level of benefits for the oldest recipients (80 years and over). These decisions of 1990–91 led to an increase in average old-age benefit by 14.5 per cent in real terms, whereas average real wages remained almost unchanged (they declined by 0.3 per cent). Consequently, the ratio of the average old-age benefit to the average wage improved from 56 per cent in 1990 to 64 per cent in 1994.

The introduction of a defined contribution system with a flexible retirement age entails many practical problems, thus the implementation of the new solutions in Poland has not been fully successful. The statutory retirement age inherited from the old system has not changed (65 for men and 60 for women). The preservation of a different retirement age for males and females requires further explanation. Until recently, females were able to retire earlier, after having completed 30 years of work. They chose early retirement because of the underdevelopment of institutional care for the elderly and of childcare (Poland has set a negative example among countries of the region by having only about 30 per cent of pre-school-age children attending kindergarten). Women could thus fulfil the roles of grandmother, and of nurse for their elderly parents.[1] The current system deprives them of this dubious 'privilege'. However, a further increase in their retirement age would be a more radical solution and it would very likely face opposition from labour unions.

Another reform problem refers to the elimination of old-age privileges related to a specific industry or profession. This elimination is difficult to implement, particularly in the context of industry restructuring. While launching a new system, the government was forced to preserve the old-age benefits of employee groups who formerly enjoyed a preferential treatment, such as miners, steel and railway workers. As a result of their protest, the so-called 'bridge pensions' were developed, justified by particularly difficult working conditions. From a reform perspective, this constitutes an additional cost, but it is also a source of savings over the former system as the scope of bridge benefits is limited when compared to the benefits based on industrial and professional privileges.

Other countries will also face the problem of entitlements when launching a radical transformation of their own safety nets, unless a crisis in public expenditure forces them to narrow the publicly managed pillar. A possible solution to this issue would probably be the development of non-diversified flat-rate benefits (the Beveridge concept).

The development of the privately managed segment of the old-age security system was a very important aspect of the reform to economists and to financial markets. Having participated in a debate focusing on the old-age security system in the countries of the region, I would dare to say that the reform of the system has been fundamentally driven not by excessive costs of the system, but by the possibility of allocating public expenditure to internal capital generation (Golinowska, 1999; Ferge, 1999). To achieve this goal, it was necessary to limit the scope and the costs of the state-managed pension system, and thus, to make room for the privately managed segment. The idea of 'system improvement' had no appeal on its own, but combined with the capital segment development concept it met with support from the financial, especially the insurance, sector.

The second, expensive pillar of the pension system was introduced in Poland and Hungary as mandatory, privately managed, but supervised by the state. It was based on individual participation and private accounts. Funds for the second pillar were drained from the first pillar at the expense of continuous fund shortages at the state Social Security Office.

The expensive development of the privately managed segment is additionally burdened by the trade-off in allocation of scarce funds between alternative social goals, namely healthcare and education.

The quality of new financial institutions (pension funds) and their regulations are a source of optimism. In Poland, they are able to attract participants from the group of optional contributors (30 to 50 years old). In Hungary, the number of people joining pension funds surpassed all expectations, causing budgetary problems. It does not mean that pension funds bear no risk related to bad investment decisions or poor management, as noted by Barr. However, the biggest risk seems to be currently related to insufficient development of capital markets in the region.

EDUCATION REFORM

As Barr maintains, socialist education was ill-adjusted to the market economy, especially in regard to new economic and technological processes. In his opinion, the main drawback of the education system is the failure to teach skills and the excessive training in outdated fields at vocational schools. He also points to certain deficiencies in pedagogical methods, namely teaching obedience, conformity and opportunism, which inhibit initiative and creativity. Indeed, the dominant shortcoming of the current education system is the failure to teach skills, as proved by OECD research on functional illiteracy in which the members of post-communist societies, including Poles, did not score well (Białecki, 1996).

In Poland, this problem is mainly linked to its development level, specifically the late industrialization and a high percentage of the population working in agriculture. The majority of farm workers have completed only primary education. Moreover, the second half of the twentieth century was characterized by mass education at primary and vocational schools for the purpose of providing workers for large socialist enterprises. Since its inception, socialist industrialization had invested excessively in the declining industries. This led to a subsequent widening of the technological gap with the West, especially during the economic development of the 1970s (Kochanowicz, 1999).

Mass education was plagued by the low quality of teachers, stemming from low job requirements and poor remuneration. (See Table 11.3.) The economic crisis during the initial period of transition brought about a sharp reduction in expenditure on education, including social functions of schools and financial aid. There is evidence suggesting that there were inequalities in education spending in the 1990s, especially in the FSU and poorer parts of Southeast Europe, implying that the incidence of state spending on education may have shifted regressively (Flemming and Micklewright, 1999).

In Poland, highly skilled people began to be rewarded, resulting in a rising demand for education, which was met by the emergence of private schools. At the same time, the limited access to education for children from poorer and rural families became a major issue. As a consequence of government decentralization, which mainly affected education, schools started operating in very diversified environments. Positive outcomes of the reform were initiatives of parents and teachers aimed at enhancing the quality of education. These joint efforts led to the establishment of the so-called 'social schools' (which are private). Unfortunately, because of the commercialization of education, the issue of quality became secondary. (See Table 11.4.)

The Polish education reform was launched in September 1999, after ten years of vigorous effort, and it focused on changes in the organizational structure and in the curricula of primary and secondary schools. The main goal of the reform was to improve school management as well as to provide better educational equipment.

In spite of many efforts, the changes initiated in the education system are insufficient and they do not address shortcomings such as pre-school education,

Table 11.3 Assessment of socialistic education

Drawbacks	Advantages
Domination of the Marxist ideology in school curricula	Reduction of illiteracy; primary schools accessible to every child
Limited individual choices and grassroots initiatives among teachers and students	Social promotion of young people from working class and rural backgrounds, particularly at the primary and secondary levels
Domination of vocational schools in secondary education, resulting in limited range of specialization and avoidance of humanistic issues	Equal right to education for both sexes
Low job requirements and poor salaries, leading to poor selection of teachers at primary school	Lack of financial constraints to education thanks to scholarships, grants, inexpensive (subsidized) books and school supplies
Failure to adjust curricula to contemporary needs: gap between knowledge and skills	

Source: UNDP/CASE (1998).

Table 11.4   Public expenditure on education in CEE countries as a share of GDP (%)

	1990	1991	1992	1993	1994	1995	1996	1997
Czech Republic	4.1	4.1	4.5	5.2	5.4	5.3	5.3	4.7
Slovakia	5.1	5.6	6.0	5.2	4.4	5.1	5.0	–
Hungary	5.8	6.3	6.6	6.5	6.4	5.5	4.9	4.3
Poland	5.6	5.2	5.3	5.3	5.6	5.2	5.5	5.7
Slovenia	–	4.8	5.5	5.8	5.5	5.8	5.8	–
FYR Macedonia	5.9	6.8	5.4	6.0	5.7	5.7	5.9	5.4
Albania	4.2	5.0	4.2	3.3	3.2	3.8	3.2	–
Bulgaria	5.0	5.1	6.1	5.7	4.8	4.0	3.2	4.0
Romania	2.8	3.6	3.6	3.3	3.1	3.4	3.5	–
Estonia	–	–	6.1	7.1	6.7	7.1	7.3	–
Latvia	4.8	4.2	4.6	6.1	6.1	6.9	5.8	5.8
Lithuania	4.5	–	–	4.6	5.6	5.6	6.9	–
Belarus	–	4.6	5.3	6.0	5.8	5.5	6.1	6.6
Moldova[*]	–	–	7.8	6.0	7.4	7.7	9.4	8.9
Russia	3.7	3.6	3.6	4.0	4.5	3.6	3.8	4.2

Note: [*] in Moldova GDP has fallen dramatically and the ratio of spending on education has increased; spending on education in real terms has also fallen dramatically but less than GDP.

Sources: ICDC Unicef (1999) and own estimates for Poland.

reform of vocational education and the quality of higher education. Widespread and spontaneous commercialization of higher education, personnel shortages, limited classroom space and the lack of proper equipment may soon impair the quality of education.

Improving the education system for teachers and introducing a system of adequate remuneration are essential prerequisites to the achievement of any progress in education. The Polish education reform has failed to prioritize these issues.

ACCESSION TO THE EUROPEAN UNION

Plans to integrate with the European Union (EU) may help Poland to close the development gap typical for the outliers of the Western culture.

There are many conflicting expectations and a great anxiety concerning convergence of Polish social policy and labour market policy to respective policies of the EU. On one hand, people are convinced that a common social policy would create opportunities for raising social standards and extending the scope and quality of social functions exercised by the state. On the other hand, experts fear that the imposition of higher social standards will lead to an increase in the cost of labour. This, in turn, may be detrimental to small private companies. At the same time, the EU fears that the eastern enlargement may bring excessive immigration and increase income transfers to new members.

Barr warns the EU candidates against accelerated adjustment of social standards consistent with provisions of the EU Social Charter, referring to the UK's long-term opposition to these provisions (from 1989 until 1997). Provisions of the Charter may impair labour market flexibility and limit competition. The Polish labour code does not differ significantly from provisions of the Charter. It leaves little room for flexibility, which is a direct consequence of Poland's political history related to trade unions that were also a force fighting for political freedom.

However, the EU directives, which require enterprises to improve work safety and hygiene, may pose problems for Poland. Large companies may be able to afford investment in such improvements that may ultimately lead to technological progress. However, rapid adjustment to these standards will definitely take a hard toll on small and medium-sized companies (Golinowska et al., 1999).

The EU is concerned about economic emigration from the former Eastern bloc, which may stem from the income inequality, but these anxieties may be exaggerated. Looking from the perspective of the Spanish and Portuguese experience during their ten-year integration with the EU, both countries witnessed strong foreign capital inflows (both private capital and structural funds transfers). At the same time, labour emigration was exceptionally weak, to the surprise of EU policy makers and economists (Orłowski, 1998). Capital inflows reached about 140 billion USD (inclusive of direct investments and transfers only) which made it possible for both countries to create between 4 and 6 million new jobs. Outward labour migration reached no more than one-fiftieth of this amount, that is, 80 thousand permanent emigrants from both countries.

In the case of Poland, it has been estimated that even in the face of full and immediate liberalization of border traffic, the range of emigration should not reach 400 thousand persons during the initial five to seven years, given that the high GDP growth rate will be sustained (Orłowski and Zienkowski, 1998). The number of immigrants should decrease in the course of the transition period. Nevertheless, precise estimates of the size of labour migration are not feasible. It should be noted, however, that income-driven emigration from Poland has been going on for many years on the basis of bilateral employment agreements, and the number of emigrants stands at slightly over 300 thousand per annum (mainly to Germany). Research indicates that emigration is mainly stimulated by the demand of Western employers (mainly German) from selected segments of the labour market (Rajkiewicz, 2000).

FINAL REMARKS

The second stage of social reforms has begun in Poland. These reforms are less reactive and more focused on systemic transformation that would align the social sphere with the market economy and decrease the role of the state. An important conclusion to be drawn from problems at the launch of reforms is that the management of the reform implementation is a highly complex process burdened by a number of different conflicts. It is a highly responsible task that should be carried on by experts, rather than by politicians.

In the final part of his chapter, Barr makes an assumption that is related to the economy, rather than to social policy, but it may provide a new perspective on the welfare state. Success in reforming the economy and stimulating growth is a necessary prerequisite for the welfare state to exist, even though it is not a guarantee of its efficiency. This success depends on the determination of policy makers and on skilful reform management.

NOTE

1. The care for elderly people is measured by the nursing potential. It is the ratio of the number of females 45–69 years old to the total number of persons aged 70 and over (Schulte, 1996, p. 85).

REFERENCES

Białecki, Ireneusz (1996), 'Analfabetyzm funkcjonalny' (Functional illiteracy), *Res Publica Nowa*, **6** (93), June.

Center for Public Opinion Research (CBOS) (1998), 'Stosunek Polaków do nierówności dochodów i opieki socjalnej państwa' (Attitude of Poles to the income inequality and social protection of the state), Komunikat z badań No. 81, Warsaw.

Clasen, Jochen (2000), 'Change and choice in social protection. The experience of central and eastern Europe', Phare, Consensus Programme, University of York, pp. 113–52.

Ferge, Zsuzsa (1999), 'The politics of the Hungarian pension reform', in Katharina Mueller, Andreas Ryll and Hans-Juergen Wagener (eds), *Transformation of Social Security: Pensions in Central–Eastern Europe*, Heidelberg and New York: Physica-Verlag, pp. 231–46.

Flemming, John and John Micklewright (1999), 'Income distribution, economic systems and transition', Innocenti Occasional Papers, Economic and Social Policy Series EPS 70, Florence, Italy: UNICEF ICDC.

Golinowska, Stanisława (1999), 'Political actors and reform paradigms in old-age security in Poland', in Katharina Mueller, Andreas Ryll and Hans-Juergen Wagener (eds), *Transformation of Social Security: Pensions in Central–Eastern Europe*, Heidelberg and New York: Physica-Verlag, pp. 173–99.

Golinowska, Stanisława, Ludwik Florek, Witold Orłowski, Gertruda Uścińska and Jerzy Wratny (1999), 'Polityka społeczna Unii Europejskiej i jej konsekwencje dla Polski' (Social policy of European Union and its consequences for Poland), *Opracowania PBZ* No. 9, Warsaw: IpiSS.

Horstmann, Sabine and Winfried Schmähl (1999), *Transformation of Old-age Security in Central and Eastern Europe*, unpublished manuscript, University of Bremen.

Kochanowicz, Jacek (1999), 'Ekonomia polityczna konsolidacji reform' (Political economy of reform consolidation), in Jacek Kochanowicz (ed.), *Ekonomia polityczna konsolidacji reform* (Political economy of reform consolidation), CASE Reports No. 29, Warsaw, pp. 9–30.

Marody, Mira (1988), 'Antinomies of collective subconscious', *Social Research*, **55** (1–2), 97–110.

Marody, Mirosława (1999), 'Społeczne warunki konsolidacji reform ekonomicznych w Polsce' (Social conditions for consolidation of economic reform in Poland), in Jacek Kochanowicz (ed.), *Ekonomia polityczna konsolidacji reform* (Political economy of reform consolidation), CASE Reports No. 29, Warsaw, pp. 37–50.

Narojek, Winicjusz (1991), *Socjalistyczne 'welfare state'* (Socialist 'welfare state'), Warsaw: PWN.

Organization for Economic Cooperation and Development (OECD) (1997), 'Income distribution and poverty in 13 OECD countries', OECD Economic Studies No. 29, Paris.

Orłowski, Witold M. (1998), *Droga do Europy. Makroekonomia wstępowania do Unii Europejskiej* (A road to Europe. Macroeconomics of accession to the European Union), Łódź: Instytut Europejski.

Orłowski Witold M. and Leszek Zienkowski (1998), 'Potential size of the emigration from Poland after joining the European Union: an attempt of a forecast', *Research Bulletin RECESS/ZBSE*, No. 2, Warsaw.

Puhani, Patrick A. (1998), 'What works? An evaluation of active labour market policies during transition', PhD thesis, University of Munich.

Rajkiewicz, Antoni (ed.) (2000), 'Zewnętrzne migracje zarobkowe we współczesnej Polsce' (External economic migration in contemporary Poland), Włocławek, Poland: College of Liberal Arts, IPiSS.

Schulte, B. (1996), *Altenhilfe in Europa. Rechtliche, institutionele und infrastrukturelle Bedingungen*, BMfFSFJ, Stuttgart, Berlin, Cologne: Kohlhammer Verlag.

Simonovits, Andras (1997), 'Węgierski system emerytalny' (Pension system in Hungary), in *Systemy i reformy emerytalne. Wielka Brytania, Szwecja, Węgry i Polska*, Raport końcowy Phare ACE Programm 1995, Warsaw: IPiSS, pp. 77–104.

Topińska, Irena and Marek Styczeń (1999), 'Podatki i wydatki socjalne jako narzędzia redystrybucji dochodów gospodarstw domowych' (Taxes and social transfers as instruments of households income redistribution), *Opracowania PBZ*, No. 4, Warsaw: IpiSS.

UNDP/CASE (1998), *Human Development Report. Poland 1998. Access to education*, Warsaw.

UNICEF International Child Development Center (ICDC) (1999), 'Women in transition', MONEE Project CEE/CIS/Baltics, Regional Monitoring Report No. 6, Florence.

12. Comment on Barr

Stanisław Wellisz

What should a commentator do when asked to discuss a masterly study? First of all, he should praise it. Professor Barr gives an eloquent exposition of the thesis that 'the communist welfare state was, for the most part, well adapted to the old order and – precisely for that reason – is systematically and predictably ill-suited to a market economy'. He appraises the reforms of the social security, welfare and educational systems that have been instituted in various countries in transition. But by far the most important part of the chapter is devoted to the discussion of policy changes that are yet to be made.

In contrast to the economic witch-doctors, Barr does not offer cure-alls for social and economic ills. Instead, he gives a balanced exposition of the strengths and weaknesses of alternate institutional arrangements, and suggests which of them are likely to succeed, given the limited administrative capability of countries in transition. In short, his study can and should be read by anyone who has the welfare of society at heart.

Any commentator worth his salt must also find something to criticize. According to Barr, the funding of retirement pensions 'contributes to growth only if it increases domestic investment. In TEs, however, domestic investment may be low yield and high risk, the *exact* reverse of what pension fund managers look for. Thus pensions policy faces a horrible dilemma: domestic investment puts old-age security at risk; foreign investment puts growth at risk'. It is true that investing abroad does not raise GDP, but it *does* raise GNP – which is what really matters. I doubt, however, whether pension fund managers would be short of domestic investment opportunities. Foreign investment flows into the countries in transition show that, in the opinion of Western investors, the expected rate of return on investment in countries in transition *exceeds* the expected rate of return in the economically leading countries.[1] The fund managers will, doubtless, have many worries, but Barr's dilemma is not one of them.

But, to return to the heart of the matter, Barr's presentation raises a fundamental issue of how much 'welfare state' there should be in transition. 'Real socialism' was a welfare system *par excellence*. The state educated the citizens, gave them employment, provided for medical services, for their vacations, and made provision for their retirement. The system, for all its faults, virtually eliminated economic risk and uncertainty – but it did so at the cost of individual economic freedom. The market economy, by contrast, is driven by initiative, hence the success of transition depends on people becoming more self-reliant. The continued coddling of the population by the state is thus contrary to the spirit of transition. Purely economic arguments also speak in favour of a cutback of welfarism: the greater the welfare expenditures, the less there is for private and public investment and consumption. Yet, instead of decreasing, transition increased the demand for state aid. The change of the system made many victims. Unemployment rose sharply, especially among the elderly, the less educated and those with highly specialized skills for which there is no longer any demand.

The unemployment problem is exacerbated by labour market segmentation. Workers, discharged by declining industries, such as coal mining, basic steel, or defence establishments, are stranded because of low geographic and/or professional mobility. Unemployment payments help ward off abject poverty, but they weaken the workers' incentive to find work. Indeed, involuntary unemployment especially if it is long lasting is so demoralizing that many long-term unemployed cease to be fit for work. Such considerations – and also the raw economic fact that it is costly to compensate economic actors for *not* working – cause Barr to ask whether, for countries in transition 'the strategy of introducing Western-style unemployment benefits – that is, of subsidizing unemployment rather than employment – is the right one'.

To cure segmented market unemployment it is necessary to remove barriers to labour mobility. There is need to sweep away 'job protection' regulation which favours job-holders at the expense of job-seekers and which as OECD experience shows, worsens unemployment (Audenrode, 1994). It must be recognized that such liberalization measures are bound to encounter trade union opposition. Measures to foster spatial mobility are also likely to be politically controversial. Unemployment is heavily concentrated in rural areas and in small towns, but migration to large urban centres where, typically, unemployment is relatively low, is hampered by the 'housing shortage' prevailing in the latter. The remedy lies in the reinstatement of urban property rights, in the removal of barriers to trade in urban real estate, and in the elimination of rent controls, which discriminate against the newcomers.

Educational reform, as Barr points out, is another long-term remedy. Unemployment is the most severe among those who lack the education needed for work in a modern economy, especially among those who have only a primary education or less, and also among graduates of secondary technical schools. Former Soviet-bloc style secondary technical schools gave training aimed at the performance of specific, planned tasks. The narrowly trained technicians find it difficult to adapt to changes in tasks and in methods brought about by the transition. The future technicians should be given more general, more flexible training. But educational reform will help the future cohorts of workers, and not the workers who now are unemployed.

The ill effects of geographic labour market segmentation could also be mitigated by fostering capital mobility. Instead of bringing people where the jobs are, unemployment could be cured by bringing jobs to the people. At present, the capital market is geographically segmented. Enterprises now gravitate to the major business centres, because the surplus labour areas lack the necessary infrastructure. Improvements in transport and in communications would doubtless increase the attractiveness of rural or small-town locations. But given the limited means, there is reason – for now – to give priority to infra-structure in areas where there are significant economies of agglomeration.

Since none of the cures of labour market segmentation is quick acting, it is important to consider temporary alternatives to unemployment compensation. One such alternative is to undertake public works. In so far as workers who obtain public employment would otherwise be idle, the social cost of labour on public works is nil. In that sense, society gets something for nothing – and people have jobs. When, however, as often happens, there is a mismatch between the skills of the jobless, and the skills needed to execute the public works, unemployment persists.

Another alternative – now very popular – is to turn areas of heavy unem-ployment into 'special economic zones'. Enterprises locating in the designated areas qualify for tax reductions and other easements. But such concessions mean subsidies to capital, hence they encourage capital-intensive investment, rather than job creation, and subsidization of capital is a roundabout, costly, and ineffectual way to fight unemployment.

A third line of attack is through worker retraining. A major reason for unem-ployment in transition is the downsizing of Soviet-era industries unadapted to market conditions. The workers could, in principle, be retrained for other kinds of work. Experience shows, however, that retraining programmes are, for the most part, cost-ineffective.

The most direct way to foster employment is by granting wage subsidies to the target groups. This sounds like a radical proposal, yet wage subsidies are already used to fight unemployment caused by market segmentation. In Poland, for instance, wage subsidies are used to encourage the employment of handicapped workers. The system could readily be extended to encourage the employment of able-bodied workers of designated categories, such as discharged coal miners or inhabitants of a high unemployment area. Subsidies make it cheaper, hence more profitable, to engage workers. Subsidies are likely, therefore, to reduce local unemployment of the subsidized labourers.

What would be the global effect of wage subsidies? Would subsidies merely foster employment of the targeted workers at the cost of others? Not if subsidies were given only for the hiring of workers who, for reason of location or lack of appropriate skills, could not find jobs at full pay. Where unemployment is caused by market segmentation, the marginal product of the involuntarily unemployed is lower than the ruling wage inclusive of wage taxes. A 'targeted' worker is thus less productive than one who is employed at the ruling wage. It follows that more than one 'targeted' worker would have to be hired to replace one regular worker. Thus even if *some* displacement occurs, the number of job-gainers would be larger than the number of job-losers. Moreover, subsidies lower labour costs, and since demand for labour is not completely inelastic, total employment is bound to rise.

The dangers of displacement of fully paid workers by subsidized workers (and also the dangers of fraudulent collusion between job-givers and job-seekers) are lessened if the benefit levels are differentiated, with higher payments attached to the workers employed at lower wages and declining to zero at a ceiling wage. As unemployment in a given 'segment' of the market is reduced, the labour market tightens and wages rise, leading to a decline in the amount of subsidy and to an eventual subsidy elimination.[2]

When a worker who is eligible for a subsidy finds employment, he or she is taken off the unemployment roll. Thus, as long as the amount of wage subsidy is less than unemployment pay wage subsidization, wage subsidies lighten the fiscal burden falling on the government. It is likely, of course, that with the rise in employment, labour force participation will also rise, but, by the same token, the additional employment will contribute to the growth of output.

Let me now add a gloss on higher education to Barr's excellent discussion of educational reform.[3] The Polish constitution guarantees, presumably for equity reasons, tertiary-level free education. But even tuition-free universities remain beyond the reach of the poor, and in particular the rural poor, unable to meet the living expenses and the cost of educational aids. In the absence of means-related scholarships, tuition-free university education discriminates against the poor. Children of the well-to-do are over-represented (and children of the poor are under-represented) in the student body. Moreover, since universities prepare graduates for relatively high-paying jobs, the system perpetuates social stratification. The cost of 'free' universities is borne by the taxpayers, many of whom are far from rich, hence the system is regressive.

Social justice would be better served if those who benefit from education were required to pay for it. Equal access could be guaranteed by making tuition loans available to all and giving scholarships to those in need. An alternative way of making the beneficiaries pay for tertiary education is to charge no tuition, but to impose a surtax on the graduates' income. Either way, students would pay for the 'human capital' they gained through education. University research activities should, however, continue to be financed from public funds, because fundamental research, to paraphrase Adam Smith, 'can never be for the interest of an individual, or a small group of individuals, though it may frequently do much more than repay it to a great society'. Or, to put it in economic jargon, university research has strong externalities in the form of public knowledge, and therefore it requires public support (Romer, 1990). It must be recognized, of course, that teaching at the university level is closely related to research activities, hence the decision on the degree of state support is bound to create controversy.

At the very end of his chapter, Barr asks the question, which I pose at the beginning of my comments, namely, how much welfare state spending can countries in transition afford? In the absence of an objective social welfare function or of a social consensus on what is a 'good society' this question must remain unanswered.[4] Perhaps it is more meaningful to consider a narrower issue of growth versus equity.[5] Barr wants to allay our fears that more welfare expenditure means slower growth by pointing out that 'for most of the postwar period, spending on the welfare state in Germany was higher than in Britain, yet German economic growth was faster'. But the lack of simple correlation is no proof of an absence of causal relation. The fact that during the same period Germans smoked more heavily, yet lived longer than, say, Bangladeshis is no proof that smoking is harmless. Moreover, Barr's statement comes just at the time when Germany faces the need to scale down its welfare expenditure.

To be sure, the effect of income redistribution on growth is very complex (Alesina and Rodrik, 1994). *Ex ante* equity, by which I mean equality of opportunity, fosters growth, because equality of opportunity opens the possibility of advancement to the most able and the most ambitious. Preferential systems, be they called 'nomenklatura' or by any other name, close the door of advancement to the many, and favour the few. Such systems are not only socially unfair, but they are inimical to economic development. Once-and-for-all lump-sum redistribution – of which land reform is a prime example – does not affect the agents' economic behaviour, and it reduces social conflicts. As a consequence, as has been shown, the growth effects of land reform are positive (Persson and Tabellini, 1994).

In the case of countries in transition, however, income taxes are the only redistributive tool that is available to policy makers. High marginal taxes are known to reduce human effort and capital accumulation (Feldstein, 1995; Feldstein et al., 1995). The countries in transition thus face a dilemma: if they are to 'catch up' with Western Europe, they should avoid measures that discourage entrepreneurship, yet for ethical as well as for political reasons they cannot tolerate extreme income inequality.

Barr's central message is that 'there is no Holy Grail', that is, no single, best-of-all policy. His second key message is that 'implementation is as important as policy'. I would go even further: the ability to implement policies should be looked upon as a key element in policy design. All too often policy makers in countries in transition follow Mickiewicz's (a renowned Polish poet) advice and are guided by intentions rather than by the means. The result are pseudo-welfare states in which taxes, rules and regulations cripple the functioning of markets, and yet social justice is not served. Policy making, as Barr reminds us, should not aim at a theoretical optimum, but at best a feasible alternative.

NOTES

1. It is theoretically possible that, because of 'coordination failure' an economy may find itself in a 'low-level equilibrium trap' (see, for instance, Murphy et al., 1989, and Ciccone and Matsuyama, 1996). In such countries – it is said – it does not pay to invest in any single activity, and development can only occur if coordinated large-scale investment is simultaneously undertaken on a broad front. But such situations may only arise in economies which are virtually closed and which are characterized by increasing returns to scale in the 'modern' sector. In reality it is difficult to point to any country which is 'trapped' in this fashion, and the 'low-level equilibrium trap' model surely does not fit any of the European countries in transition.
2. The problem of graduation of wage subsidy is briefly discussed in Phelps (1997, pp. 112–16) and, in more technical detail, in Hoon and Phelps (1996).
3. As Professor Barr informed me, he omitted a discussion of university reform for want of time and space. He subsequently brought to my attention the expression of his views on higher education (Barr, 1998).
4. A discussion of the philosophical issues involved will be found in Vickrey (1953, 1973).
5. For a general discussion, see Baldassari et al. (1996).

REFERENCES

Alesina, Alberto and Dani Rodrik (1994) 'Distributive policies and economic growth', *Quarterly Journal of Economics*, **109** (2), 465–90.
Audenrode, Marc A. (1994) 'Short time compensation, job security and employment contracts: evidence from selected OECD countries', *Journal of Political Economy*, **102** (1), 76–102.
Baldassari, Mario, Luigi Pagnetto and Edmund S. Phelps (eds) (1996), *Equity, Efficiency and Growth: The Future of the Welfare State*, New York: St. Martin's Press.
Barr, Nicholas (1998), 'Higher education in Australia and Britain: what lessons?', *Australian Economic Review*, **31** (2), 179–88.
Ciccone, Antonio and Kiminori Matsuyama (1996), 'Start-up costs and pecuniary externalities as barriers to economic development', *Journal of Development Economics*, **49** (1), 33–59.
Feldstein, Martin (1995), 'The effects of marginal tax rates on taxable income: a panel study of the 1986 Tax Reform Act', *Journal of Political Economy*, **103** (3), 551–72.
Feldstein, Martin, James R. Hines, Jr and R. Glenn Hubbard (eds) (1995), *The Effects of Taxation on Multinational Corporations*, Chicago and London: University of Chicago Press.
Hoon, Hian Teck and Edmund S. Phelps (1996), 'Low-wage employment subsidies in a labor turnover model of the natural rate', Columbia University, Department of Economics, September, mimeo.

Murphy, Kevin M., Andrei Shleifer and Robert W. Vishny (1989), 'Industrialization and the Big Push', *Journal of Political Economy*, **97** (4), (October), 1003–26.
Persson, Thorsten and Guido Tabellini (1994), 'Is inequality harmful for growth?' *American Economic Review*, **84** (3), 600–621.
Phelps, Edmund S. (1997), *Rewarding Work*, Cambridge, MA and London: Harvard University Press.
Romer, Paul (1990), 'Endogenous technological change', *Journal of Political Economy*, **98** (5), S71–S101.
Vickrey, William S. (1953), 'The goals of economic life', in Andrew D. Ward (ed.), *Goals of Economic Life*, New York: Harper, 35–62, reprinted (1973) under the title 'An exchange between economics and philosophy', in Edmund S. Phelps (ed.), *Economic Justice*, Harmondsworth and Baltimore, MD: Penguin Books, 148–77.

13. Restoring hope, rewarding work: pension reforms in post-communist economies

Michal Rutkowski[1]

INTRODUCTION

This chapter focuses on changes that are taking place in the retirement pension systems of post-communist economies. These changes are not replicas of earlier models. They entail serious and often unprecedented reforms in managing the allocation of people's income during their lifetime. The common denominator of these reforms is the replacement of a vicious circle of low expected future pensions and declining contributions by a virtuous cycle of higher expectations and improved compliance that leads to higher savings, growth and, therefore, the actual value of future pensions. A key element of the change is an introduction of a close linkage between lifetime pension contributions and retirement benefits in a multipillar framework that comprises, *inter alia*, a mandatory funded pillar managed by the private sector. For current workers, pension reforms lead to an increase in the net present value (NPV) of future pensions ('restoring hope'), and an increase in the pension levels of those who earn more and work longer ('rewarding work'), while the minimum pension is preserved.

ENTERING THE 1990s AND THE IMPACT OF TRANSITION

Even though government intervention in the area of pensions in Europe has a 100-year history, the current systems were decisively shaped by changes introduced after the Second World War. The generation coming to retirement age in the next few decades had suffered during the war and was retiring in the midst of an economic and demographic boom. Many belonged to schemes that had become unfunded in the aftermath of the war. In addition, many lost savings during the conflict. It was not socially or politically palatable to allow these individuals to suffer a severe fall in income upon retirement. In some countries, the intergenerational transfer was accomplished by the introduction of a new pension scheme (for example, the Netherlands in 1957) while in others, it took the form of a huge increase in the benefit levels of existing schemes, as in the case of Germany in the late 1950s.

The former Soviet Union (FSU) had already moved in this direction in the 1920s. After the war, Central and Eastern European (CEE) countries adopted the model that essentially combined features of the Soviet and German systems. The systems in the East and West evolved in similar ways. Low ratios of pensioners to contributors were aided by increased labour force participation of females. Average replacement rates[2] increased due to strong economic growth. Despite rising life expectancy, retirement ages were kept relatively low (55/60 for women and men in the FSU, 60/65 in CEE, albeit with widespread sector privileges). Consequently, unfunded liabilities were allowed to increase sharply.

In 1990, the East and the West appeared to be quite similar in the area of pensions. Coverage – the ratio of contributors to labour force – was very high; populations were ageing (in some cases more so in the East); spending and contribution rates were rising. The low average actual retirement age in the FSU, 58.5 years for men and 54.6 years for women, was not much different from that in some Western European countries, such as Belgium, the Netherlands or Austria.

The underlying economic structure hid important differences. Coverage was artificially high in the formerly socialist countries, especially with respect to the rural population, and the institutions, which collected contributions from workers, were not well developed (only former Yugoslavia seemed to have achieved a significant degree of computerization in its pension system prior to 1990). In many cases, the administrative systems were decentralized to the local government level or even to the level of enterprises. Much of the recordkeeping was done at the enterprise itself and benefits were usually netted out of contributions to central agencies. In general, the system was not as decentralized as the enterprise-based schemes in China.

Another difference was the extent to which the East and West relied on private savings vehicles. While private pension provision was marginal in most of continental Europe, several rich countries (Switzerland, the USA, the UK and the Netherlands) had well-developed private pension institutions or at least significant occupational coverage (Japan, Germany). In many ways, however, the pension systems of countries like Italy and Germany were more similar to those in Slovenia and the Czech Republic than to those in the UK or Canada.

When the socialist system began to unravel, so, too, did the basic premises of the pension schemes in the region. Benefit formulas and eligibility conditions were tied to compressed wage structures and full-employment policies. Any redistribution was achieved within the scheme itself. Universal coverage and full employment meant that the only safety net needed was a minimum pension within the scheme and/or a progressive benefit formula. Under the socialist system poverty was considered as non-existent, hence the basic income support programmes were underdeveloped at the start of transition.[3]

The employment structure prior to the transition was also an important premise for the pension system. Large state-owned industries and collective farms ensured universal coverage and compliance. Finally, indexation mechanisms were less significant since prices were generally controlled.[4] After 1989, these assumptions were no longer valid as unemployment and inflation both reached double digits and enterprises were restructured or privatized.

It is important to note that the pay-as-you-go (PAYG) pension schemes of the centrally planned economies were not financially sound even before the traumatic events of the early 1990s. Low effective retirement ages combined with population ageing would have generated higher deficits and/or payroll tax rates when the large postwar cohorts began to retire around 2010. In many ways, the issues of a long-run sustainability crisis should have mirrored those being discussed in the OECD in the years leading up to the transition.

While population ageing would have forced a reassessment of medium-term prospects, demography played no role in the deterioration of pension finances in the early 1990s. Instead, a confluence of structural changes related to the transition led to an increase in the ratio of pensioners to contributors and this was the principal determinant of pension imbalances in the region. This implies that high system dependency ratios are likely to persist in most transition economies (TEs) in the foreseeable future and, eventually, to worsen for demographic reasons unless reform measures are implemented.[5]

The initial deterioration of pension finances was caused by political reactions to economic changes. In the first years of the transition, privatization and enterprise restructuring led to open unemployment. One reaction to this development was to ease early retirement conditions either through explicit programmes designed to absorb redundant labour via the pension system or through an informal policy of loosening eligibility requirements, often through the disability pension programme. The result of such policies was an increase in the number of pensioners as shown in Figure 13.1. This phenomenon was least evident in the Czech Republic where unemployment has remained at very low rates during the transition. Some of the larger increases came in the former Yugoslavia but Romania's massive early retirement programme in 1990–91 led to the largest increase in the region.

Early retirement also affected the denominator of the system dependency ratio by reducing the number of workers contributing to the pension scheme. Unemployment itself further reduced contribution revenues. In some countries, notably Albania, Bulgaria and Bosnia, significant out-migration of younger workers reduced the domestic labour force. Finally, the number of contributors and the amount of the income that they reported fell because of evasion. This last element was partly due to changes in the structure of employment

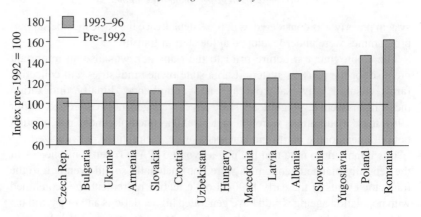

Source: Palacios and Pallares-Miralles (1999).

Figure 13.1   Growth in the number of pensioners for selected TEs

from large state enterprises to small, private firms and self-employed individuals. In the new environment, it was much more difficult to collect taxes using the old tax collection apparatus.

The result was a sharp decline in the number of contributors to the system as shown in Figure 13.2. Notably, the reduction in coverage rates in the TEs is greater in the lower-income countries, a pattern that corresponds to the international experience in market economies. While some improvement can be expected as tax collection agencies adapt to the new economic structure, inter-

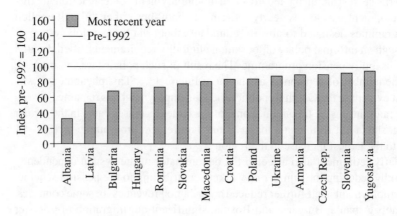

Source: Palacios and Pallares-Miralles (1999).

Figure 13.2   Decline in the number of contributors for selected TEs

national patterns suggest that coverage rates will remain at low levels in the poorer TEs for many years to come.

The combination of an increasing pensioner stock and a decline in the number of contributors led to large increases in the system dependency ratio as shown in Figure 13.3. The largest change took place in countries where all of the factors listed above were important. For example, in Albania, a massive early retirement programme was used to absorb unemployment in the 1990–92 period, an estimated 10 per cent of younger workers left to find work in Italy and Greece and the privatization of agricultural plots effectively ended contribution collection from farmers. By 1996 there were as many pensioners as contributors in Albania. Around the region, and to varying degrees, the increase in this key ratio led to (i) lower replacement rates; (ii) higher payroll taxes; (iii) higher deficits; or (iv) some combination of all three.

The decline in the number of contributors shown in Figure 13.2 captures only part of the revenue losses experienced during the 1990s. In some countries, the

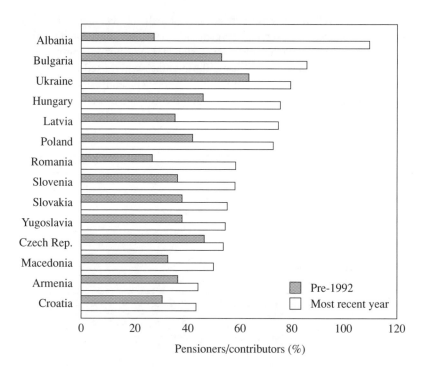

Source: Palacios and Pallares-Miralles (1999).

Figure 13.3   Change of the system dependency ratios for selected TEs

data on formal employment seriously overstates the actual number of workers for whom payroll tax obligations had been met in a timely fashion. Also, the change in the number of contributors shown in Figure 13.2 does not reflect the lost revenue from under-reporting of earnings, an important factor in economies such as Hungary where the number of self-employed has grown significantly.

A better indication of the deterioration of the revenue base is shown in Figure 13.4, which illustrates the relationship between the tax base (shown here as the covered wage bill to GDP ratio) and income per capita for more than 70 countries around the world. The TEs in the sample are highlighted.[6] In the worst cases, such as Armenia and Georgia, this ratio has fallen to below 5 per cent of GDP. At the other extreme, countries such as Slovenia have thus far experienced relatively little erosion of the contribution base. Almost without exception, those countries with the lowest covered wage bill ratios were forced to flatten the distribution of pensions and reduce average replacement rates. In the most severe cases, contribution revenues were not sufficient to cover even this minimum pension and a significant share of financing had to be provided by the central budget.

Pension levels fell in real terms across the region after 1989 along with every other type of income. However, it is not clear how pensioners have fared relative to working-age persons and their children. A standard indicator of benefit levels, that is, the replacement rate, has some deficiencies when used to compare pensioners' incomes with the rest of the population. The confusion lies in the denominator of this ratio, which may be either the average formal sector wage in the economy (first definition) or the income per capita (second definition).

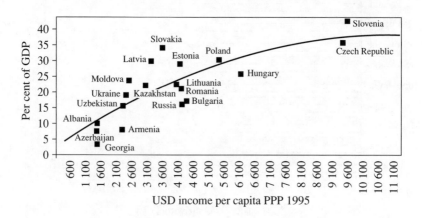

Source: Palacios and Pallares-Miralles (1999).

Figure 13.4   Ratio of covered wage bill to GDP in selected TEs, mid-1990s

The first definition may be used to derive the required contribution rate for a PAYG scheme, however, it may be misleading if used to measure the relative living standards of pensioners in the presence of a wide divergence between the formal sector average wage and the income per capita. For example, in poor countries, with low coverage, the second definition may yield a ratio two or three times higher than the first definition.

In a large sample of countries worldwide, the replacement rate based on the income per capita is about 10 per cent higher than the one measured by the average wage, although there is a significant variation.[7] This relationship is reversed in TEs, where the replacement rate based on the income per capita is 7 per cent lower than the one measured by the average wage.

There are several reasons behind the focus on the second replacement rate definition. First, the size of the formal sector in the region varies widely making the average wage a less reliable basis for cross-country comparisons of well-being. Other sources of income may form a large part of national income. Second, the household size and composition varies across countries, hence per capita measures are more appropriate. Finally, the first definition becomes problematic when wages rather than income per capita are compared across countries. For example, in some countries workers who do not receive wages but are not considered unemployed may or may not be included in calculating the average wage. Another problem lies in the different samples used in labour force surveys across countries. Applying income per capita figures could eliminate this dilemma. However, the reliability of national income data may vary inversely with the income level. To the extent that poor countries have a higher degree of unmeasured GDP, the replacement rates discussed below will overstate the relative position of pensioners.

Figure 13.5 shows some regional replacement rates defined as average pensions as a share of income per capita. The data represent the period 1994–96. While it must be noted that year-on-year changes in replacement rates were often significant, a pattern does emerge. The group with higher replacement rates includes the countries with higher incomes, stronger tax bases and higher pension spending to GDP ratios.

Poland and Slovenia have the highest spending ratios in the region, the result of generous benefits and the growth of the pensioner population (see Figure 13.1). The wage bill to GDP ratios in these two countries are covered at more than 30 and 40 per cent, respectively. On the other end of the spectrum are the poor countries of the FSU with their devastated tax base and low spending ratios. The demographic structure of these young countries is only part of the reason for low spending. Without revenues to sustain the schemes, pensions often go unpaid or are allowed to erode in real terms. In the case of Georgia, the next step was taken and a flat pension has been paid since 1996.

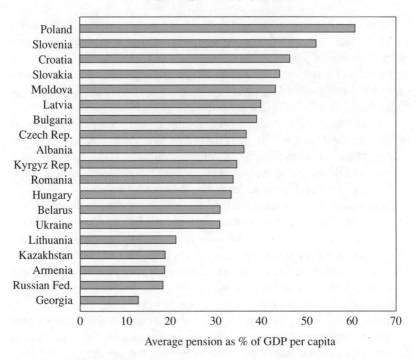

Average pension as % of GDP per capita

Source: Palacios and Pallares-Miralles (1999).

Figure 13.5   Replacement rates in selected TEs, mid-1990s

An important consequence of the deterioration of public pension finances during the early transition years was the impetus it gave the pension reform debate. Since many of the possible reforms would be phased in gradually, there was a desired development of long-run actuarial projections. These projections revealed a train rather than a light at the end of the tunnel for all but a few countries, due to predictable increase in the old-age dependency ratio associated with retirement of the TEs' baby boomers. The combination of the financial deterioration and increased awareness of the long-run demographic problem reduced confidence in the public pension promise. In some countries, where pensions were eroded by inflation or went unpaid for months at a time, the pension promise lost all credibility.

For those already retired, whose ability to save outside the public pension system had been severely limited under socialism, there were few options. For the most part, they were forced to concentrate on finding other sources of income ranging from farming small plots of land to remittances from children working abroad. It was not much different for older workers except in a few countries, like Hungary and the Czech Republic, where they began to supplement their public pensions through voluntary, private pensions made more attractive by fiscal incentives and flexible withdrawal conditions. The schemes and their incentives have been used disproportionately by higher-income workers above age 40. In countries where a legal framework for private pension savings did not yet exist, life insurance companies offered alternative annuity instruments to the same types of workers (for example, Poland and Slovenia). Finally, proposals for partial or full privatization of discredited public pension schemes emerged in almost every country. In some cases these proposals were accepted.

THE CHALLENGES AND DILEMMAS: HOW TO REFORM THE PENSION SYSTEMS?

The main objective of a retirement pension system, which is to ensure adequate income during old age, does not differ across economies. This objective can be achieved in a variety of ways. The old European tradition distinguishes two approaches. The first one, the Bismarckian approach, is based on earnings-related contributions giving entitlements to earnings-related benefits.[8] The second, the Beveridge approach, involves a state scheme that concentrates mainly on poverty relief rather than on aims like income smoothing, with private arrangements expected to take care of those aims. The current pension systems worldwide, including those in Europe, display enormous differentiation with respect to the ways of achieving their main objective. This adds to challenges facing transition economies (Holzmann, 1997).

A peculiarity of post-communist economies, which makes them particularly inclined to emphasize certain ways of achieving the objective of the pension system, is related to an enormous mistrust of the workers in the ability of the inherited pension systems to provide them with a decent pension for retirement. In other words, in the world of huge fiscal constraints and demographic pressures, the NPV of future pensions becomes very low, in particular for young workers (Milanovic, 1998). The evidence from TEs shows that when young workers realized that fiscal pressures and worsening demographics may deprive them of a promised pension, their compliance went down and they started shifting to the informal sector. This subsequently reduced the tax base for social security contributions and led to a combination of reduced pensions and increased social security tax rate. This, in turn, encouraged even more evasion. As a result, a vicious circle began making everybody suffer.

Not surprisingly, under these circumstances, the main theme of broader social discussions in TEs is the *need to make pension benefits closely linked to con-*

tributions. Many policy makers and trade union leaders believe that establishing such a linkage, especially the one that is based on a lifetime income, can break the bad equilibrium. This is because the NPV of future payments for young workers increases with the credible commitment of the government. Young workers are then likely to increase compliance. This compliance would increase even more, if at least a part of the system were privately managed with future pension linked to the investment return.

In addition, the drive towards contribution–benefit linkage in TEs is also motivated by the societal demand for a more transparent pension system, which is less vulnerable to political pressures and emphasizes personal responsibility.[9] In a nutshell, the societies in TEs want their pension systems to restore workers' hope that they will receive decent pensions, and reward workers' work by making pension levels dependent upon lifetime income-related contributions. An increase in the NPV of future pensions means *restoring hope*, and an increase in the levels of pension for those who earn more and work longer means *rewarding work*. Everybody agrees that a minimum pension should be preserved to avoid old-age poverty.

In the light of the values and expectations described above, the key long-term objective of the pension system in post-communist economies can be assessed by sustainability of the system based on (i) adequate minimum pensions; (ii) transparent and direct link between lifetime contributions and benefits; and (iii) diversifying sources of financing between current social security contributions and accumulated savings. This is why the desired reformed pension system is often described as a partially privatized system, which ensures an adequate minimum amount and links benefits to lifetime contributions. In this system, a part of the future pension of an individual depends on wage growth risks, and the other part on capital market risks.

Although objectives of the pension reform can be similar across the board in TEs, the constraints that result from both the initial conditions and the transition shock differ considerably. Two groups of countries could be distinguished by their abilities to move towards the objective of pension reform. This grouping is useful in assessing constraints.

The first group experienced modest declines in the covered wage bill and managed to maintain benefit levels relative to wages through a combination of budget transfers and high contribution rates. This was achieved even as the ratio of pensioners to contributors increased. These are mostly CEE countries, including Slovenia, the Czech Republic, Poland, Hungary, Croatia, the Baltic states, and, perhaps, Bulgaria, Romania and FYR Macedonia. Their pension bills have commonly ranged from 10 to 15 per cent of GDP. The perceived failure of the state monopoly in pension provision in these countries is based on a more subtle evaluation. First, although replacement rates have not always fallen dramatically, pensioners' incomes have been reduced relative to their lifetime incomes. Second, the current system is increasingly and correctly perceived to be unsustainable in the face of demographic trends in the coming decade. The group will be called European in the remainder of the chapter.

The second group consists of low-income countries where tax bases had all but collapsed during the transition. Even with high contribution rates, these countries were forced to cover benefits from central budget transfers. Given a general inability to collect other taxes, however, this source of financing was limited. As a result, benefits were either not paid or were allowed to fall significantly in real terms. This group includes Central Asian and Caucasian countries, as well as Moldova and Albania, and, perhaps, Russia, Ukraine and Belarus. Examples of incomplete indexation and/or accumulation of arrears to pensioners can be found in Armenia and Georgia, among others. In these countries, the failure of the public pension scheme is tangible in the form of a series of government defaults on past pension promises. The failure is also evident when comparing the negative rate of return implied by high contribution rates and low benefits being offered to current workers. This group will be called Eurasian in the remainder of the chapter.

An increasing number of policy makers in both groups of countries have realized that the PAYG pension systems monopolies are hardly sustainable, without profound reforms. On the one hand, the large unfunded liabilities placed a long-run burden on public finances and savings. On the other hand, the opportunity for developing the contractual savings sector that might play an important role in the capital markets was lost. Finally, high contribution rates raised labour costs and increased incentives to move to the informal sector.

The perceived failure of the public pension monopolies to protect pensioners and current workers as well as the growing consensus regarding the negative effects of the inherited system on growth led to calls for reform in many countries. It also induced a reassessment of the appropriate role of government in the area of pensions. The approaches of the two groups of countries in addressing pension-related risks would have to be different, at least in the short run. At the same time, a common long-run strategy for the region may also be emerging.

The state has a unique role in creating the legal environment in which institutions that allow workers to manage their risk can thrive. Prior to the transition, the institutions that offered risk management tools such as insurance companies were monopolized by the state. Private pensions did not exist. This obviated the need for a separate supervisory framework but produced poor results for different reasons. Most of the region have now passed new insurance legislation and more than half have passed private pensions laws. Nevertheless, most governments have failed to provide a legal and supervisory framework that allows individuals to save or insure with private sector actors and protect themselves against a host of contingencies. The best-known case of this failure is that of the pyramid schemes of Albania, but the lack of confidence in contracts and weak enforcement of existing laws is a regional phenomenon. A major challenge in the region is for governments to shift from direct pension and insurance provision to supervision.

Despite the fact that these schemes continue to function in European TEs, their foundations have been shaken and awareness of long-run unsustainability has grown. The effectiveness of a state monopoly as a viable venue to save and insure has been severely tested and, in some cases, rejected (see section below on 'The choices ahead'). This has led most of these countries to reform their existing schemes in two ways. First, there has been a clear tendency to reduce the redistributive elements of the various benefit formulas inherited from the socialist period. For example, the reform in Poland reduced the minimum pension significantly and the Hungarian reform phased out the progressive benefit formula. In Latvia, the old benefit formula was replaced by individual notional accounts intended to minimize intergenerational redistribution, although a minimum pension still applies. As discussed in the next section, the introduction of private pensions in the context of a multipillar scheme is also premised partly on creating a closer link between contributions and benefits.

An attempt to address the question of long-run sustainability has been the second common feature of the reforms in the European TEs. The events of the early 1990s made it clear that the public pension promise was not a riskless one. The partial defaults experienced during these years also increased awareness about the projected demographic pressures on the schemes. These were scheduled to worsen considerably as the baby boomers retired and as the systems fully matured.[10] Projections have now been made in practically every European transition economy and public discussions have raised general levels of awareness in some cases.[11]

Some concrete steps have already been taken. Hungary, Poland and the Czech Republic have raised retirement ages while Latvia anticipates doing it by way of the notional accounts framework. Indexation rules – set in place during the early years of the transition – have been shifted from wage to a combination of wage and price indexation in Hungary, Poland and the Czech Republic, or to price indexation in Croatia. Slovenia has recently introduced legislation that would reduce future expenditures by raising effective retirement ages and changing the benefit formula. The idea behind each reform is that it will put the scheme on a sounder long-run financial footing. While this may entail a reduction in the rate of return inherent in each of the pension schemes, it also reduces the riskiness of this particular part of a workers' retirement portfolio. Furthermore, the expansion of voluntary private pension alternatives (typically with favourable tax treatment) allows individuals to diversify into other types of investment and possibly to smooth out consumption more than can now be provided within the public pension schemes.

At present, many countries in the region do not have sufficient resources to provide earnings-related pensions. This is the case for most of the Eurasian economies whose resources are stretched and for whom a minimal consumption rather than consumption smoothing is the main issue. While reforms are still needed and long-term objectives still apply, the short-term objective has to be a better allocation of resources aimed at protecting the poor. More than anything else, the constraint is on collecting contributions. If coverage patterns around the world are any guide, it will be impossible to induce most workers to save until their incomes increase (see Figure 13.4).

Poverty has increased in most of the region since the early 1990s although there is evidence indicating that pensioners were much better protected than wage earners (Milanovic, 1998, pp. 102–4). In general, pension schemes in the region were intended to function as income-smoothing devices with redistribution built in and/or reinforcing redistributive wage policies. As mentioned above, many of the European TEs have sought to reduce redistribution and increase the insurance-like qualities of the inherited pension schemes. In its place, the minimum pension and social assistance programmes are supposed to help disabled and elderly individuals cope with poverty.[12]

In Eurasian TEs, the remnants of the pension scheme can provide little more than poverty protection. In most cases, the ratio of maximum to minimum pensions is already close to one (for example, Albania, Ukraine) while in others the distinction between social assistance and the contributory pension scheme are almost completely blurred, as in the case of Georgia. This is also true for particular schemes in some countries, such as the ones covering farmers in Poland or Albania. The majority of pension schemes covering the rural sector are de facto social assistance programmes, financed primarily by transfers from the central budget. Some countries, like Hungary, have recognized this explicitly by shifting the programme from the pension system to the central budget.

In many of the poorer and younger countries such as Albania or Turkmenistan, the informal risk-sharing mechanisms are likely to have played a significant role during the transition period. In Georgia, for example, pensioners report that 15 per cent of their income comes from private transfers. For some of the upper deciles, this is more than the income from public pensions. Little is known, however, about the role of informal intergenerational transfers in these countries.

The countries with the lowest replacement rates (based on income per capita) are generally the poorest in absolute terms in the region. Under these circumstances, policy makers face a stark choice between continuing policies of consumption smoothing albeit with more modest targets or temporarily focusing their resources on coping with the effects of the crisis. It would seem appropriate for the government of these countries to focus its role on providing coping mechanisms until the conditions, namely the ability to collect contributions, and the reliable state and private pension institutions, can be put in place.[13]

SHIFTING TO MULTIPILLAR SYSTEMS

In the European TEs, the government's role in consumption smoothing is not only continuing but it is also becoming more focused. A conscious attempt was made to link contributions more closely with benefits and to avoid internal redistribution to lower-income workers. It is hoped that such changes would provide better labour market incentives. At the same time, changes are proposed to set the schemes on a sounder long-run footing in order to reduce future deficits.

An extension of these arguments led to movements towards multipillar schemes in most of the European TEs.[14] These reforms shift a portion of the mandatory contribution to the pension system to private institutions that would establish an individual defined contribution account for each worker. The eventual pension is made up of a downsized public pension scheme plus a benefit purchased with accumulated funds from the so-called 'second pillar'.

The second pillar has been introduced in two of the European post-communist economies. In Hungary, the legislation was passed in 1997 and it was implemented in 1998. As a result, 1.2 million workers, mostly under age 40, have diverted part of their pension contributions to private pension providers. All new labour market entrants are required to join. In Poland, the new private pension funds were licensed. In 1999, Polish workers between ages 30 and 50 were given the choice to divert one-fifth of their overall pension contribution to these new funds. Workers under 30 were automatically included in the new scheme. In total more than 10 million people were covered by the new multipillar pension system in Poland.

This type of reform had the short-term effect of increasing the public pension deficit. Reformers pointed out, however, that it only made the growing pension debt more explicit. When combined with other reforms (for example, reduced benefits and higher retirement ages), the long-run fiscal effects could be quite positive. In fact, the reductions in the public scheme's benefits could be somewhat greater assuming that the contribution to the private scheme would yield a higher return than the growth of the wage bill. This seemed very likely for younger workers.

The opponents of the reforms claimed that while the return may have been higher, it was associated with a higher risk. A related argument favouring the multipillar alternative called for diversification of a worker's risk. Having experienced first hand the political or policy risks inherent in the public pension schemes, workers were receptive to the idea of spreading their risk between public and private sector institutions.[15] This argument has more than intuitive appeal and extends beyond diversifying between public and private sectors.

Moving to a multipillar system creates a funded component, which is invested in capital markets. This allows workers to achieve returns that are based on different kinds of assets. In the case of the public schemes, either the defined benefit (DB) or the defined contribution (DC) plans, the return depends on the growth of wages. In the case of the new private scheme, it depends on returns on capital. As long as these two are not correlated, some diversification gain is possible. Evidence from OECD countries shows that the correlation between the two is negative, supporting the diversification argument (Boldrin et al, 1999, pp. 310–12).

Funded schemes may benefit further from international diversification. To the extent that aggregate shocks affect a certain country or even region, diversifying internationally can reduce risk while providing the same or greater return. While the correlation between returns in rich countries' capital markets has been increasing, significant gains are still possible, especially in developing countries.[16]

In several countries reforms are still under way and the second pillar has yet to be introduced. In Croatia, a new multipillar system is set to begin on 1 July 2000. In Romania, a working group has proposed that 10 per cent of the overall contribution should be diverted to private pensions. This proposal is still being debated. In Latvia, Estonia, Bulgaria and FYR Macedonia, the second pillar has been accepted in principle and the governments are planning to introduce the new schemes in the near future. In contrast, a proposal spelled out in the 1998 White Paper to privatize a quarter of the system has been rejected in Slovenia.

Table 13.1 compares some of the key parameters of the reforms. Only one Eurasian TE, Kazakhstan, has introduced a multipillar system. In addition to being an outlier in this sense, it is also distinct in that it has moved fully towards funding, leaving the solidarity pillar role as one of coping with the risks of poverty in old age or disability.[17] The introduction of a multipillar pension system requires that the initial conditions in terms of financial market development and administrative capacities be met. It also requires a feasible financing plan of the transition costs, even though those costs are not real costs since the implicit debt to future generations is paid. Some countries in Group 1 and almost all in Group 2 do not meet these conditions. However, these countries are keen on pursuing the consumption-smoothing objectives of the pension system by introducing a close and transparent link between lifetime contributions and pension benefits.

The way to pursue these objectives in the absence of a possibility to introduce a fully funded (FF) pillar is to convert the PAYG pillar into the one based on the notional defined contributions (NDC) principle. The prototype of such reforms in TEs was Latvia who followed the reform designed in Sweden. Beginning with 1998 the Latvian pension system was converted into a new system based on individual accounts where pension contributions are notionally accumulated (that is, indexed) and the pension depends on the accumulated amount divided by the average life expectancy at the retirement age. The system has therefore automatic stabilisers enabling the pension level to be adjusted to changes in life expectancy. Also, the system encourages working longer, since the increases in the amount of pensions are actuarial rather than linear. In practice, this means that at the age of 62 or 63 an additional year of work yields an approximately 8–9 per cent increase in the amount of pension, not 2–3 per cent.

NDC was introduced in Poland on 1 January 1999 for the PAYG pillar of the pension system (accompanied by an FF pillar). Recently the NDC approach became very popular in some Eurasian TEs which, as discussed earlier, are not in a position to introduce a multipillar system yet. The Kyrgyz Republic has already introduced NDC while Moldova has adopted legislation linking benefits to lifetime contributions in the defined-benefit framework, but with an objective to move towards NDC soon. NDC-type proposals are being deliberated in Russia, while others, such as Azerbaijan and Uzbekistan have expressed interest in examining this option.

The introduction of NDC-type systems in Eurasian TEs poses a challenge for anti-poverty policies because the poverty rates in those countries are already high and future distribution of pensions will resemble the distribution of wages. Nevertheless, the permanent pension system is not the right instrument to deal with poverty, unlike the introduction of temporary flat-level pensions as an emergency measure. For this reason, these countries are advised to set the minimum pension at the adequate level prior to moving forward with the intro-duction of NDC once wages are already growing.

THE CHOICES AHEAD

Pension policies should begin with long-run targets because of their nature. In TEs as in the rest of the ageing world, a pension policy which allows individuals to smooth consumption between working life and retirement is a reasonable starting point. It prevents destitution and it is benign if not friendly to economic growth. For all of the usual reasons discussed above, this will require taxes and forced savings on the one hand and government enforcement and provision on the other. It does not, however, preclude a significant role for private provision, especially in the consumption-smoothing and insurance functions of the system.[18]

In recent years two trends have emerged globally. The first is towards greater pre-funding of pensions. This is due to concerns over fiscal sustainability in

Table 13.1 Features of multipillar proposals in selected TEs

	Starting date	First pillar	Projected pension fund assets in 2020 (% GDP)	Workforce in funded pillar (2000) (%)	Switching strategy
Hungary	January 1998	PAYG–DB	31	45	Mandatory new entrants Voluntary others
Poland	January 1999	NDC	33	70	Mandatory < 30, Voluntary 30–50
Kazakhstan	January 1998	Guaranteed minimum	30	100	Mandatory for all workers
Latvia	July 2001 (NDC January 1996)	NDC	20	72	Mandatory < 30, Voluntary 30–50
Croatia	January 2002	PAYG–DB	25–30	60–70	Mandatory < 40, Voluntary 40–50

Note: Forthcoming multipillar reforms: Romania, Bulgaria, FYR Macedonia, Estonia and, possibly, the Slovak Republic, the Russian Federation and Ukraine.

Source: Lindeman et al. (2000).

ageing countries and a desire for intergenerational fairness. The second is towards greater competition and private sector provision of pension services. As in other areas of economic activity, competitive actors are found to be more efficient at investing pension funds and less susceptible to political interference. While these trends are evident in the expansion of voluntary private pension provision, they are most clearly manifested in the multipillar reforms around the world.[19] Although each country has chosen different variants of this theme, the general policy objectives are the same. They include diversifying risks between PAYG and funding; reducing the distortions caused by the PAYG scheme where possible and taking advantage of the positive externalities of funded schemes; and reducing the pension debt as part of the package. This is a reasonable long-run policy for TEs as a whole, recognizing that the general principles will be customized to fit the specific characteristics of each country.

The present and the future multipillar reformers face a plethora of challenges. These challenges include (i) managing the transition; (ii) redefining the governments' supervisory role; (iii) designing the institutions in the second pillar; (iv) carrying parallel reforms to ensure the success of the multipillar scheme; and (v) recognizing own constraints. They can be elaborated as follows.

Transition strategies   The shift from a PAYG scheme to a funded scheme requires the government to make explicit what is currently an implicit pension debt. Having forfeited its ability to force workers to 'lend' money to the government in exchange for future pension promises, the government must find resources to pay existing obligations to current pensioners during the transition. The fiscal issues raised by such a shift may reduce the speed of the reform and are likely to affect the choice of the size of the second pillar.

Aside from the size of the new second pillar, the government also faces an important choice of cohorts that will be allowed, encouraged or forced to participate in it. This switching strategy must take into account several factors, including the fact that a DC scheme is likely to pay high benefits only to younger workers who can take advantage of the compound returns it offers. Another important factor is the legal protection of acquired rights under the old PAYG scheme.

Once the speed and scope of the shift from PAYG to FF is determined, the remaining issue is how to pay off existing obligations given the loss in revenues. The options are limited. New debt can be issued, expenditures can be cut, taxes can be raised and state assets can be sold. Tax financing will improve the savings and growth effects of the reform package, but it may be difficult to implement in the short run. Demand for debt (including long-term bonds) from new pension funds will increase, but diversification rules imply that much of the portfolio will be invested elsewhere. While exact proportions are difficult to ascertain, current reforms to date both in and outside the region appear to have combined debt and tax financing.

Redefining the role of government   An issue related to the design of the second pillar is the role of the government as guarantor. Limited and explicit guarantees have been extended in all the countries that introduce second pillars. The contingent liabilities implied are generally not quantified however. Moral hazard may also be significant. Government guarantees should be considered carefully and may be targeted at the most vulnerable, such as low-income workers.

Imposing guarantees on the private sector in terms of portfolio return limits may also create problems. Relative rate of return guarantees can restrict competition among funds and limit their ability to achieve the best risk–return combination. At its extreme, a high minimum return requirement on government securities may negate the diversification rationale of moving to a funded scheme.

The government's mandate as regulator and supervisor of the new scheme is more apparent.[20] In a system wherein workers are forced to join a private pension fund, the supervisory authorities should typically take a proactive stance towards participants. A strong supervision is a key factor in reducing the risk of fraud or theft in the new system.

In addition, some reforms envisage a more direct role for governments in the second pillar. For example, there may be an option for workers to stay in a government-sponsored pension fund that competes with the private fund. Another potential role would be as a provider of annuities (as has been accepted in Sweden). Finally, the government could act as clearinghouse for records and flows of contributions for the system.

Designing the second pillar   The role of mandatory private pension provision is limited to the savings and insurance objectives. The government is the only actor who can redistribute to the lifetime poor. Given the advantages in terms of reducing systemic risks and diversifying individual risk, the question is what is the appropriate size of the second pillar in this system? With the exception of Kazakhstan, the experience thus far has been that the multipillar schemes introduced in the region have retained the majority of the contribution in the residual public scheme (Hungary, Poland, proposals in Croatia, Latvia).

At least four issues arise with regard to the institutional arrangements in the second pillar. First is the question of what type of institutions will operate as pension funds? Should these be employer based or open funds chosen by individuals or some hybrid? Should the funds operate as profit-making firms or non-profit mutual societies? Should they be specialized institutions or should existing financial players be allowed to offer pension products as part of their business? What kind of minimum capital, membership size and other require-ments should be placed upon them? Should government institutions be allowed to participate, for example as a competing fund manager? Finally, who should be allowed to provide benefits (annuities, scheduled withdrawals) in the new system? All those issues have an impact on administrative costs of the system, and the more competition the higher both the costs and the benefits. Group mandates bring down the costs, but they limit the efficiency benefits of competition as well.

Parallel reforms[21]   Many countries in the region have not achieved a banking sector or capital market infrastructure which is conducive to the success of private contractual savings institutions such as mutual funds, insurance companies or pension funds. While some reforms can take place simultaneously and interim solutions may be designed, the relevance of these institutions in such countries is dubious. Among other things, a private pension fund system needs professional asset managers, liquid investment opportunities and a reliable banking system.

The link between the pension reform and insurance markets occurs both within the annuity portion of the old-age scheme and, potentially, in the area of survivors' and disability benefits. The ability of the insurance sector to provide annuity coverage effectively in these instances could eventually prove crucial in determining the success of the pension reform. The clear implication is that the reform of the insurance sector must be viewed as part of a multipillar reform and it must be taken into consideration in the design of the scheme.

Finally, the tax authorities may play an important role in collecting contributions for a new second pillar and in ensuring compliance.[22] Most TEs' tax administrations are undergoing major overhauls while others (for example, the former Yugoslav payments systems, ZPP) will have to do so in the coming years. The reforms in Poland and Hungary have suffered from poor planning as pertains to this parallel reform.

A legal framework for voluntary private pension provision has been or is being developed in several other countries. Most envisage DC pension schemes offered by employers or by 'open funds', which cater to individuals.[23] There are several advantages to restricting emerging pension sectors to DC plans versus DB plans. One advantage is that supervision issues during the accumulation stage are far less complicated. The nature of DB schemes requires that actuarial analyses be regularly generated using a host of assumptions in order to ensure adequate funding levels. However, these calculations become difficult to make and to monitor given the scarcity of individuals trained in modern actuarial methods as well as the lack of historical data on rates of returns and administrative costs, which could guide these assumptions. These extra difficulties contribute to higher costs and greater chances of errors and even fraud. They also introduce complications that can impede labour mobility.

The existence of regulations is not sufficient to protect private pension fund members, especially in countries where they have little or no experience. In Albania, a private pension law was passed in 1996 but only one private pension fund has been formed and the supervisory agency was never created. Given the general inadequacy of financial sector regulation, which led to the collapse of various pyramid schemes in 1997, it may be fortunate that private pension schemes did not proliferate after passage of the law. The Albanian situation may provide lessons for some of the poorer FSU countries in the process of developing private pension legislation. Legislation and regulations cannot be effective unless accounting, reporting, investment and other rules are enforced.

Recognizing different constraints Some countries will be able to face these challenges and simultaneously cushion the shocks that have affected certain vulnerable groups with improved coping mechanisms. Other countries begin from a more precarious starting point. Figure 13.6 illustrates these differences by plotting replacement rates from Figure 13.5 against average monthly pensions in US purchasing power adjusted dollars. While this not surprisingly shows a positive correlation, the vast range of absolute pension levels in the region and the varying capacities of these countries to go beyond income support programmes for the poor are striking. The disparity is evident when comparing Georgia (at the bottom left-hand corner), with its 12 per cent replacement rate on local income per capita and a monthly pension of 10 USD, with Slovenia, with replacement rates of about 50 per cent and absolute average pension levels of almost 500 USD.

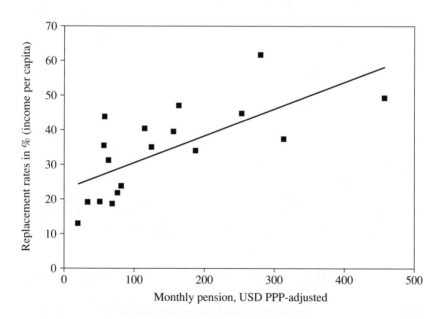

Source: Palacios and Pallares-Miralles (1999).

Figure 13.6 A wide range of absolute pension levels in the Eastern Europe and Central Asia (ECA) region

The low pension and wage levels found in the countries in the bottom left-hand corner of the figure make it difficult to enforce consumption-smoothing programmes, such as FF pillars of the pension system, in addition to the need to focus on poverty in the short run. Individuals would prefer low savings rates and will actively avoid compliance with forced savings schemes (as well as other taxes). This fact is reflected in the inverse relationship between informality and incomes in the region. From the point of view of the multipillar concept, it would also be problematic (but not impossible) to start a system with such low income levels given the fixed cost element in administrative charges for individual workers who could render a flexible and competitive scheme infeasible.[24] Finally, most of the challenges for multipillar reformers listed above will be more difficult for poor countries to overcome. Therefore, in poorer Eurasian countries, a short-term focus on paying pensions on time and on maintaining flat distribution of pensions seems appropriate. When wages start growing, these countries should consider a step-by-step movement towards a multipillar system, starting with an NDC-type system. NDC has the micro-economic advantages of the funded pillar, including incentives to work longer, actuarial adjustment of pensions and higher compliance, although it lacks macroeconomic advantages, such as increased saving rates and financial market development that ultimately contribute to higher growth.

While any approach is arbitrary, we could begin by separating those countries where an absolute pension level of say, 100 USD has been achieved. This approach could be considered as the threshold for Eurasian countries mentioned earlier. Based on Figure 13.6, this group includes Armenia, Belarus, Georgia, Kazakhstan, the Kyrgyz Republic, Moldova, Ukraine, Russia and Lithuania. European TEs would include those with more than 100 USD monthly pensions, namely Bulgaria, Croatia, Latvia, Slovakia, Poland, Hungary, the Czech Republic, Romania and Slovenia. This division is close to an earlier proposed qualitative distinction.

As discussed earlier, second pillars are being instituted primarily in European TEs, while Eurasian countries focus on first pillar reforms. Table 13.2 presents the overall progress of pension reforms in 25 TEs. The situation is changing fast as an increasing number of countries join the group of reformers.

CONCLUSIONS: CRITICAL ISSUES IN PENSION REFORMS

It has been widely concluded from the Chilean and some other Latin American experiences that a comprehensive pension reform – as opposed to a mere ratio-nalization of an existing system – had to be based on replacing a monopoly of the PAYG–DB pension system by a mandatory FF–DC system. From the perspective of post-communist economies, especially those in CEE, this reform

Table 13.2   Progress of pension reform in 25 economies

Country	Fundamental reforms	Second pillar	First pillar	Third pillar
Hungary	***	***	***	***
Poland	***	***	***	***
Kazakhstan	***	***	***	–
Latvia	***	***	***	**
Croatia	**	**	**	**
Estonia	**	**	***	***
Romania	**	*	***	*
FYR Macedonia	**	***	***	*
Russia	**	**	**	**
Slovenia	*	–	***	***
Bulgaria	**	**	**	**
Czech Rep.	*	–	***	***
Slovakia	*	*	**	***
Ukraine	**	**	**	**
Armenia	*	–	***	*
Georgia	*	–	***	***
Lithuania	*	–	***	**
Albania	–	–	***	***
Kyrgyz Rep.	*	–	***	–
Uzbekistan	*	–	*	–
Azerbaijan	*	–	*	–
Moldova	*	*	**	**
Belarus	–	–	*	–
Bosnia & Herc.	–	–	*	–
Tajikistan	–	–	*	–

Notes: * in preparation; ** approved; *** legislated.

Source: The author.

option, despite numerous advantages, has two essential flaws. First, it does not really diversify risks because a PAYG monopoly (within a mandatory system) is replaced by a funded system monopoly. Second, it is hardly implementable in the countries with a sizeable PAYG system due to transition costs. Most CEE countries fall into this category.

Hungary, Poland, Croatia, as well as Romania, FYR Macedonia, Latvia, Estonia, and, perhaps, Bulgaria follow a different path. The key concept of their reforms is to replace the PAYG monopoly with a genuinely multipillar system.

Sources of future pensions financing are to be diversified. Both the labour and the capital markets are to play their roles through the PAYG and funded part of the system, respectively. A part of the mandatory retirement system will operate within a PAYG framework, while the other part will be funded. As each of the pillars is exposed to different types of risks, the system's overall risk will be better diversified. The PAYG pillar is highly exposed to risks of population ageing, increasing unemployment, and political pressures. By these criteria, funded pillars are superior to PAYG. However, funded pillars cannot operate effectively in an environment characterized by prolonged inflation or financial market crises. From this standpoint, PAYG tend to be more effective.

At the same time PAYG pillars are increasingly reformed towards reflecting lifetime contributions, either in the DB framework (Moldova), or in the DC framework (Latvia, Poland, Kyrgyzstan). This direction of reform reflects a desire to increase the transparency and predictability of the system significantly and to improve incentives to contribute to the system. The motivating factor is the need to 'restore hope and reward work', by linking contributions and benefits closely in a lifetime horizon in a robust fashion.

Different countries emphasize different aspects of the systemic pension reform in different proportions depending on the constraints they face. While a movement towards multipillar arrangements and linking contributions to benefits is the right long-term strategy, the short- to medium-term choices will have to be different in European and Eurasian TEs because the constraints those groups face are different.

The common denominator to both types of reforms is a desire to bring the NPV of future pensions to the level of paid contributions, so that workers have an incentive to contribute to the system and to increase the base for paying current pensions. The net present vale of future pensions is a function of the *trust* in the system. Although in most reforms the future replacement rate may not increase, the trust in the system should improve hence the NPV of future pension may increase as well.

There are at least eight critical issues that have emerged from the wave of movements towards multipillar pension systems in TEs:

1. *Size and structure of the second pillar* The mandatory funded pillar should not be too small, otherwise administrative costs – largely fixed – could pose a problem. Before instituting a second pillar, it seems important to assess whether minimum financial market conditions have been met, and to keep to a few basic rules, such as complete separation of pension funds' assets from the assets of companies managing those funds. This separation, both legal and physical, ought to go along with the requirement that an independent depository holds the fund assets.

2. *Supervision capacity* Building supervision capacity takes time, unless there are already well-functioning institutions supervising investment funds, banks, or insurance companies, whose experience could be tapped easily.

3. *Administration and management* Significant administrative changes will have to take place in the contribution collection process, especially if a centralized collection of both first- and second-pillar contributions is chosen (a preferred option to lower administrative costs). It takes time and a great deal of technical assistance to introduce modern management information and computer systems. Decisions need to be made with respect to the allowed funds fee structure and investment regulations.

4. *Political will and transition costs* Although preparation of a reasonable strategy to finance transition costs (involving a combination of expenditure adjustment, debt, and, if possible, privatization revenue) is a *sine qua non*, political will is ultimately the deciding factor. As part of its strategy, the government will have to renege on some PAYG commitments. For instance, Slovenia has worked out the best and most professional financing strategy but the reform process – for lack of sufficient political commitment – has not moved forward as expected.

5. *Public support* In most cases the public has supported pension reform if it believed that (a) benefits and contributions were linked closely, so that benefits would reflect lifetime contributions; and (b) the role of the private sector in pension provision was to be increased at the expense of the formerly omnipotent social insurance institutions. The public should be provided with a wide range of information. Raising public awareness of the implications of demographic scenarios also facilitates the reform process. (Social support can be identified through opinion polls, conducted prior to completing the reform package.)

6. *Leadership* It is advisable that the government sets up pension reform offices that can focus on professional tasks by shielding them from political influence and from daily operations of pension management.

7. *Working with trade unions* Major trade union groups, if involved in the reform process from the start, could become its supporters, as the example of the Solidarity Union in Poland shows.

8. *Timing and speed* Work on reform should be completed fast. Opportunities for pension reform come and go. Political support varies with the circumstances that may have nothing to do with pension reforms. It is critical that the reform team seizes the opportunity and moves ahead quickly and decisively.

The way these issues are being resolved is a key determinant of a success or failure of the pension reform movement in post-communist economies.

NOTES

1. This chapter is an expanded version of the presentation for the conference 'Ten Years After: Transition and Growth in Post-Communist Countries', Warsaw, Poland, 15–16 October 1999. It draws upon the author's joint work with Robert Palacios and Xiaoqing Yu on the pension reform strategy for transition economies, and on Palacios's background paper. Comments of Nicholas Barr, Mikhail Dimitrev, Edward Palmer and Igor Tomes are gratefully acknowledged.
2. Replacement rate is determined by a ratio of pension to wage.
3. As Sipos (1994, p. 227) describes it, 'Since poverty did not officially exist, it is not surprising that the system of poverty relief was rudimentary'.
4. This simplification ignores differences between parts of the former Soviet bloc. It also does not apply as clearly in the former Yugoslavia, where for example, earnings-related pensions were supplemented with income-tested supplements and open unemployment was countenanced.
5. The ratio of pensioners to contributors in a PAYG pension scheme determines the level of benefits that can be paid for a given earmarked payroll tax. For example, when there is one beneficiary for every two contributors and the payroll tax earmarked for pensions is 25 per cent of gross wage, the average pension which can be financed is about 50 per cent of average gross wage. This assumes that benefits are paid only from contribution revenues earmarked for this purpose.
6. The fitted quadratic line is the result of a regression in which slope dummies for TEs are found to be significant and with an adjusted R^2 of 0.76. The results suggest that TEs in the mid-1990s had significantly higher covered wage bills than market economies at similar income levels did, while income per capita and the factors for which it is a proxy, explain most of the variation across countries.
7. For international comparisons of replacement rates, see Palacios and Pallares-Miralles (1999, p. 24).
8. At least this is what the Bismarck proposal looked like when it left the Reichstag and then became the antecedent of future contribution-based schemes around the world. Originally, Bismarck proposed a flat-rate poverty benefit.
9. In the Polish pension reform, the contribution–benefit link was the most desired feature of the new system in all the opinion polls. Also, early trade unions reform proposal (for example, the 'Solidarity' proposal of 1995) postulated this link (see Chlon et al., 1999), as an expression of personalistic values, as opposed to collectivist ones.
10. Full maturation was delayed in some countries by the expansion of coverage in the 1960s and 1970s as female labour force participation rates peaked.
11. See, for example, Palacios and Rocha (1998); Chlon et al. (1999); Government of Slovenia (1997).
12. This is why poverty-alleviating functions of the pension system are not treated in great detail in the descriptions of the Polish and Hungarian reforms. See Góra and Rutkowski (1998) and Palacios and Rocha (1998).
13. For example, see Palacios and Posarac (2000).
14. See Rutkowski (1998) for an overview of this movement in both European and Eurasian TEs.
15. This argument was used effectively in the Polish reform effort under the label 'Security through diversity'. See Government of Poland (1997), Góra and Rutkowski (1998), and Chlon et al. (1999).
16. See Holzmann (1998) for simulated risk-reduction effects.
17. In this regard, the Kazakh reform resembles the Chilean, El Salvadoran and Peruvian reforms in which no residual, unfunded contributory scheme remained after the reform.
18. For the detailed analysis of options and constraints regarding private pensions see Lindeman et al. (2000).
19. In addition to Hungary, Poland and Kazakhstan, multipillar schemes exist today in the following countries: Argentina, Australia, Colombia, Chile, Denmark, El Salvador, Mexico, Peru, the Netherlands, Sweden, Switzerland, the United Kingdom and Uruguay.
20. See Demarco and Rofman (1998) for a discussion of supervision practices in multipillar systems.

21. Tax treatment of funded pensions cannot be separated from the pension reform itself so it is not considered a parallel reform. Nevertheless, it is a crucial parameter of the new system.
22. See Demarco and Rofman (1999) for a detailed discussion.
23. A notable exception is Slovakia where the law allows employer-sponsored DB schemes. By the end of 1997, two private pension funds had been licensed.
24. One example of the need to impose strict limits on competition to minimize costs was the use of international bidding in Bolivia. Two pension administrators were chosen and the country was divided geographically into two memberships. The lessons are limited, however, given the fact that privatization assets worth 20–30 per cent of GDP were also used to build up the asset base of the administering firms, greatly reducing per cent charges.

REFERENCES

Boldrin, Michele, Juan J. Dolado, Juan F. Jimeno and Franco Peracchi (1999), 'The future of pensions in Europe', *Economic Policy*, No. 29, 289–320.

Chlon, Agnieszka, Marek Góra and Michal Rutkowski (1999), 'Shaping pension reform in Poland: security through diversity', Social Protection Discussion Paper No. 9923, August, World Bank.

Demarco, Gustavo and Rafael Rofman (1998), 'Supervising mandatory funded pension systems: issues and challenges', Social Protection Discussion Paper No. 9817, December, World Bank.

Demarco, Gustavo and Rafael Rofman (1999), 'Collecting and transferring pension contributions', Social Protection Discussion Paper No. 9907, February, World Bank.

Góra, Marek and Michal Rutkowski (1998), 'The quest for pension reform: Poland's security through diversity', Social Protection Discussion Paper No. 9815, October, World Bank.

Government of Poland (1997), *Security Through Diversity: Reform of the Pension System in Poland*, June, Warsaw: Office of the Government Plenipotentiary for Social Security Reform.

Government of Slovenia (1997), *White Paper on Pension Reform*, October, Ljubljana.

Holzmann, Robert (1997), 'Starting over in pensions: the challenges facing Central and Eastern Europe', *Journal of Public Policy*, **17** (3), 195–222.

Holzmann, Robert (1998), 'A World Bank view of pension reform', Social Protection Discussion Paper No. 9807, December, World Bank.

Lindeman, David, Michal Rutkowski and Oleksiy Sludnynskyy (2000), 'The evolution of pension systems in Eastern Europe and Central Asia: opportunites, constraints, dilemmas, and emerging best practices', Washington, DC: World Bank.

Milanovic, Branko (1998), *Income, Inequality, and Poverty during the Transition from Planned to Market Economy*, Washington, DC: World Bank.

Palacios, Robert and Montserrat Pallares-Miralles (1999), 'International patterns of pension provision', November, mimeo, Washington, DC: World Bank.

Palacios, Robert and Aleksandra Posarac (2000), *Options for Pension Reform in Georgia*, Washington, DC: World Bank, mimeo.

Palacios, Robert and Roberto Rocha (1998), 'The Hungarian pension system in transition', Social Protection Discussion Paper, No. 9805, March, World Bank.

Rutkowski, Michal (1998), 'A new generation of pension reforms conquers the East – a taxonomy in transition economies', *Transition*, **9** (4), 19–21.

Sipos, Sandor (1994), 'Income transfers: family support and poverty relief', in Nicholas Barr (ed.), *Labor Market and Social Policy in Central and Eastern Europe. The Transition and Beyond*, London and New York: Oxford University Press, pp. 226–59.

14. Do 'winners take all'? A comment on Rutkowski

Mikhail Dmitriev

WHY ARE WINNERS AND LOSERS OF TRANSITION SO DIFFERENT?

Lessons from the recent experience of transition, which are so clearly exposed by Michal Rutkowski in his chapter, could provide a valuable framework for the reassessment of a longer-term perspective of pension reforms. The cornerstone of his argument is a deep divide between the winners and losers of transition, which became so visible in the area of pension reforms.

The winners or Group 1 in the author's terminology include a vast majority of the countries of Central and Eastern Europe (CEE) and the Baltic states. They were the most successful at the initial stage of transition and remain relatively unaffected by the recent global financial crisis. According to the EBRD (1999, p. 73), 1998 real GDP in these countries was on average at 95 per cent of the 1989 level. The losers of transition or Group 2, which includes all the CIS members and Albania, are the least successful transition economies. On average, real GDP in the CIS countries in 1998 was at 53 per cent of the 1989 level. Replacement rates and pension expenditures as per cent of GDP are much lower in Group 2 as compared with Group 1.

In terms of pension reform, winners display a striking example of 'herd behaviour'. As we could see from Michal Rutkowski's chapter, almost every CEE country has already developed and/or approved proposals for a multipillar pension system, heralded by the now famous motto of Polish pension reform: 'Security through diversity'. The reform package includes the introduction of a funded pillar and a comprehensive restructuring of the existing pay-as-you-go (PAYG) pillar. The latter intends to link more closely contributions and future benefits for individual contributors via defined benefit (DB) or notional defined contributions (NDC) formulas. Basically, these reforms go along the lines of the standard multipillar reform package, promoted by the World Bank as a 'mainstream solution' worldwide since the mid-1990s.

270

However, looking at the losers of transition, we shall discover that with almost no exceptions pension reforms in this group are different from those in Group 1. The variety and even polarization of pension policies in this group seems to be much greater. The policies vary from almost zero reforms in Belarus to a radical flattening of pensions in combination with instant increase in retirement age in Georgia, and to transition to a fully funded system with minimal state guarantees in Kazakhstan. The 'Security through diversity' approach is also present in this group, at least in theory. The Russian government officially adopted it shortly before the crisis of August 1998.

Russia's programme of pension reform, adopted by the government in May 1998 was designed according to the guidelines of the World Bank. It emerged in late 1997 as a kind of strategic compromise, brokered by the World Bank at the moment when the Russian government was split over the issue of pension reform. The adoption of pension reform, fully backed by the World Bank, was then considered by many in Russia as a midway between radical and traditional approaches to the pension problem. However, this major exception in Group 2 did not survive the financial turmoil of 1998. Very recently the Russian Government was forced to reconsider the already approved reform programme. The emergency anti-crisis measures in Russia go in the opposite direction to the original plan. They are mainly focused on achieving the current balance of the pension fund via deindexation and compression of pensions in the existing PAYG system. The plans for both the decompression of a pension scale via NDC accounts and the introduction of a mandatory funded pillar are postponed indefinitely.

In his chapter, Michal Rutkowski implicitly regards the multipillar scheme as the model strategy for any transition country. The author considers the high income substitution rate at retirement, provided by such schemes as fundamental advantage. The high replacement rate could be sustainable in the long run due to better risk diversification and better resilience to the pressures of ageing, which are achieved by modification of the PAYG formula and introduction of partial funding in the second pillar. In fiscal terms, this model is expensive and therefore only the winners of transition can afford it unreservedly. Thus, adoption of this model by the winners could be regarded as a direct result of successful market reforms in these countries, which allow them to be more ambitious in social policy.

From such a perspective, pension reforms in Group 2 are considered mainly as a result of a general failure of market reforms in these countries. They are dictated by insufficiency of public resources and in the longer run are suboptimal both socially and economically. The urgent need for fiscal austerity requires emergency anti-crisis management and inhibits an immediate intro-duction of a socially and economically optimal 'Security through diversity' scheme among the losers. But such pension reforms are no more than just temporary deviations from the mainstream model, adopted by the majority of CEE countries. With the resumption of steady economic growth, fiscal impediments could be gradually overcome, thus allowing the pension policies of Group 2 to converge with the mainstream model adopted by Group 1.

Such an explanation of the deep divide between winners and losers can be regarded as winner-centred. This does not seem surprising given that the author's personal policy-making experience relates mostly to CEE countries. However, an answer to the question of whether or not the pension systems of Group 2 would evolve in the longer run towards the 'basic' model, favoured by Group 1, does not seem to be as simple as indicated by the author, particularly if the political economy dimension is considered more thoroughly.

With respect to the CIS, I would like to suggest an alternative, looser-centred explanation of the divide between the losers and winners of transition.

In a looser-centred interpretation the 'herd behaviour' of the winners of transition could be considered suboptimal in the long run and dictated mainly by political constraints. Due to an early success of market reforms, these countries never experienced any significant decline of pension benefits in real terms. Income substitution at retirement could be as high as 60 to 70 per cent. Such systems were too costly and actuarially unsustainable. But given the sheer size of entitlements, any attempts to downsize them radically or to tighten the eligibility criteria would have faced formidable political resistance and in most cases would be deemed to fail.

Under such circumstances, the 'Security through diversity' scheme was perhaps the only available compromise which could be politically acceptable and more or less actuarially sustainable. From a political economy viewpoint the major advantage of such a system is that it gives top priority to sustaining high replacement rates, while at the same time it allows a gradual easing of the fiscal burden by shifting part of the costs to a funded pillar. This policy compromise could be suboptimal in a broader context of economic transformation as will be demonstrated below.

On the contrary, the deep crisis experienced by the losers of transition could be regarded not only as a temporary distraction from the main route, but also as an opportunity to explore alternative solutions in reforming distortionary and actuarially unsound post-communist pension systems. The pension systems inherited by these countries from the communist past were dismantled or drastically downsized by 'the invisible hand' of the crisis prior to the adoption of pension reforms. In many cases the benefits became too small to be of any significance to beneficiaries. Therefore, from a political standpoint, it would have been much easier to tighten eligibility criteria or to abolish certain benefits.

For example, the average pension in Georgia was the equivalent of about 5 USD. Thus it was relatively easy for the government of Georgia to introduce a five-year increase in the retirement age, which was phased in over five years.

It meant that there were virtually no new retirees during the five-year period. For the same reason, the Kazakh government was able to implement a radical phasing out of early retirement schemes, which allowed room for the rapid introduction of a mandatory funded pillar.

The winner's preferred reform option, which is focused on achieving high income substitution at retirement, is off the agenda for the majority of losers due to the severity of fiscal constraints. This is true, at least in the medium term. But it is also true that, because of political constraints, numerous other reform solutions, which are readily available to losers, are completely beyond the reach of winners. Different reform options, available to losers, may be less generous in terms of replacement rates but remain far more growth friendly. They may also allow for effective poverty reduction among the elderly.

REFORM PRIORITIES FOR THE LOSERS

For poor countries, like the countries of Group 2, poverty alleviation among the elderly and high sustainable GDP growth for at least one working generation will remain a much more urgent priority than maintaining high replacement rates. Two alternatives – the flattened PAYG scheme and, under somewhat more favourable institutional circumstances, a fully funded scheme with minimal pension guarantees – may prove to be helpful in achieving high economic growth and poverty reduction among the elderly.

In contrast, an immediate decompression of the pension scale in the PAYG scheme that would allow for higher income substitution at retirement for the middle-class income earners in Group 2 could have undesirable consequences. Not only would it be too costly and, therefore, impede economic growth, but it could also hamper poverty alleviation among pensioners. This is demonstrated by the actuarial simulations on the Russian pension system, which were recently carried out by the author of these comments. Under more or less realistic longer-term growth scenarios for Russia, the PAYG formula, which guarantees minimal pension at 80 per cent of the subsistence minimum of a pensioner and expands differentials between minimal and maximal pension by 2.5 times, could be financially unsustainable for at least two decades (Dmitriev, 1999). This means that in the foreseeable future any significant decompression of pension scale in the PAYG scheme in countries like Russia could only be achieved via reduction of a minimal pension far below the subsistence minimum, that is, at a cost of impoverishment of pensioners receiving minimal pensions.

Achieving high sustainable economic growth should be considered as an ultimate longer-term priority for Group 2. The ability of these countries to maintain high growth rates will determine their chances of solving other economic and social problems.

A universal PAYG system, which is typical for continental Europe, barely exists among the very fast-growing economies that maintained the highest per capita GDP growth rates in the period between the mid-1980s and the 1990s. This system has high replacement rates and significant pension differentials according to the number of years of service, earnings or contributions. Two major types of pension systems could be identified among the very fast-growing economies: (i) the flat, inexpensive and sometimes rudimentary PAYG scheme; and (ii) a fully funded mandatory system with minimal pension guarantees. Among the very fast-growing countries, perhaps only Ireland maintained a relatively advanced PAYG scheme. However, there seems to be little coincidence in the fact that Ireland has the cheapest and simplest PAYG system in the EU. Unlike in most other EU member countries, pensions in Ireland are independent of wages or contributions but vary slightly depending on the number of years of service. In the mid-1990s, pension spending in Ireland was less than 4 per cent of GDP compared to the 9 per cent average for the EU (Hargreaves, 1999).

From this perspective, the pension reforms and adjustments carried out so far in some of the CIS countries could be considered as comparatively growth friendly. Both Georgian and Kazakh pension systems seem to resemble closely the pension systems of the fast-growing economies. Under the pressure of the crisis a number of other CIS countries including Russia are moving towards a more compressed benefit structure.

'SECURITY THROUGH SIMPLICITY AND ECONOMIC GROWTH'

The political aspects of population ageing are often neglected in the heated debate over pension reforms. But the importance of this dimension for the longer-term assessment of comparative advantages of various pension schemes is implied by the empirical evidence. Some of the relevant general points can be found in Alesina and Perrotti (1995).

As Michal Rutkowski mentions, the dependency ratios in many transition economies are relatively high by international standards. This may have important implications for electoral preferences. In countries with an ageing population, where pensioners and individuals at pre-retirement age are gaining influence as voters, the design of the pension system and the electoral choices may be closely interconnected.

In a European-style PAYG system with relatively high pension differentials and high replacement rates, the elderly voters will be interested in supporting higher pension benefits. They will do so even at a cost of imbalanced budgets, extended implicit and explicit public debt (partly equivalent to the tax on future generations) and excessive payroll taxes. These preferences could hardly be considered as growth friendly. The pension lobby in the overextended PAYG system is likely to be more pro-inflationary and less pro-business orientated. The political challenges faced by an overstretched PAYG system under such circumstances can be illustrated by the Italian pension system, which is heavily overburdened by early retirement schemes.

In a funded system, pensioners are more likely to be interested in fiscal stability, reasonably small public debt and low inflation, because the real value of their retirement accounts and annuities depends strongly on these factors. They will also be more concerned with the efficiency of financial sector and non-financial businesses, which affects the returns on funded accounts and annuities. This could make the electoral behaviour of the elderly more business friendly, more counterinflationary and more growth orientated.

The multipillar model combining fully funded and highly decompressed PAYG schemes of the NDC type, represents a compromise. In such a system, the elderly voters are normally driven by conflicting economic aspirations. At least in theory, pro-inflationary and countergrowth motivations of such voters inspired by a PAYG component could be essentially counterbalanced or perhaps even annihilated by pro-growth motivation related to the fully funded mandatory component. But this hybrid pension system is relatively novel and, therefore, it remains untested in terms of its growth friendliness and resilience to political abuse. The PAYG component in the emerging mixed systems of many CEE countries still remains relatively large. This makes any actuarially unsound manipulations with the pension formula in the PAYG component potentially damaging to macroeconomic stability and sustainable growth.

The recent Bulgarian example indicates that the long-term macroeconomic stability could be severely challenged at the very outset of the new multipillar pension system. The newly approved reform plan aims at nearly doubling the replacement rate from the current 33.3 per cent to over 60 per cent (Hristoskov, 1999). Even according to official estimates, the new Bulgarian system has been considered as actuarially imbalanced.

The NDC formula advocated by the World Bank is designed as a build-in mechanism, which allows benefits to be adjusted automatically, on a par with growth of life expectancy. But no matter how actuarially sound the NDC formula might seem to be, it cannot be insulated from political pressures. The recent experience of such diverse countries as Hungary or Russia demonstrates how politically easy it may be under certain circumstances to introduce significant adjustments in the PAYG formula in either direction: towards actuarial soundness or vice versa. In the countries with immature democratic institutions and irresponsible political parties in the legislature, any complex formula in the PAYG system is even more likely to become subject to populist and actuarially unsafe manipulations. In this respect, the system based on NDC accounts is likely to be more vulnerable than a funded system, in which returns are less sensitive to political manipulations.

The arguments presented here suggest that it might be rather difficult for the World Bank social planners to position their favourite multipillar model of pension reform as an optimal long-term solution for all transition economies, including the current losers of transition. I cannot fully share the recently expressed views by Orszag and Stiglitz (1999), who combine an attack on a funded pension system with a somewhat subtle excuse for already discredited PAYG schemes of continental euro-type. However, I would support their key message that the World Bank should abandon an inflexible multipillar approach to pension reforms and be prepared for a much broader range of solutions.

The 'mainstream' scheme of the World Bank may be a relevant solution for the relatively better-off countries of Group 1. However, political limitations aside, the trade-off between high income substitution at retirement and high sustainable economic growth may exist even for the wealthiest countries in Group 1. It can be illustrated by the case of Hong Kong. By the mid-1990s, this very fast-growing economy already belonged to the top ten richest countries of the world in terms of per capita GDP. In 1995 Chris Patten, the British Governor of Hong Kong, suggested the introduction of a universal PAYG scheme in place of the existing rudimentary system based on flat minimal benefit to the elderly of this former British colony. However, the proposal was strongly criticized by Zhou Nan, the main representative of Communist China in Hong Kong, as an unwelcome attempt to bring 'costly euro-socialist ideas' to Hong Kong (*The Economist*, 11 February 1995).

Unfortunately there is still too much of costly euro-socialism in the 'Security through diversity' model adopted by most of the CEE countries. This model entails high distortionary taxes on labour and replacement rates, which may not be actuarially affordable in the long run. These features of the model may take a toll on long-term economic growth in CEE.

The losers of transition, for whom fast economic growth remains an ultimate priority, could particularly benefit from more simple solutions. Either the flattened PAYG scheme, the fully funded system with minimal pension guarantees, or a combination of the two, could be among the acceptable solutions for the losers of transition depending upon the specific economic and political situation in a given country. From the losers' perspective, the motto of the Polish pension reform could be paraphrased as 'Security through simplicity and economic growth'.

REFERENCES

Alesina, Alberto and Roberto Perrotti (1995), 'The political economy of budget deficits', *IMF Staff Papers*, **42** (1), 1–31.

Dmitriev, Mikhail (1999), 'Financial crisis and the new challenges to pension reform in Russia', Moscow, Carnegie Moscow Center: unpublished report.

Economist, The (1995), 'Is Welfare unAsian?', 11 February.

European Bank for Reconstruction and Development (EBRD) (1999), *Transition Report*, London: EBRD.

Hargreaves, Deborah (1999), 'Pensions will squeeze European budgets', *Financial Times*, 23 November.

Hristoskov, Jordan (1999), 'The pension reform in Bulgaria: a new beginning', Sofia: unpublished report.

Orszag, Peter R. and Josef E. Stiglitz (1999), 'Rethinking pension reform: ten myths about social security systems', presented at the conference on 'New Ideas about Old Age Security', World Bank, Washington, DC, 14–15 September.

15. Pension reforms in transition economies – remarks and open questions: A comment on Rutkowski

Winfried Schmähl

A NEED FOR A COHERENT REFORM CONCEPT

'Ten years after', pension policies in some of the former socialist economies are undergoing a remarkable reform process. Following a period of crisis management, during which pension schemes were often transformed, more fundamental tasks of redesigning pension policies were taken up in the political arena, and in some of the countries they have been completed. This sequence is quite similar to the experience of Germany where major structural reforms did not take place until about one decade following the collapse of its economy and the political order in 1945.

However, in the former East Germany (GDR) the development of the pension reform was quite different. In principle, the West German pension schemes were implemented in the still existing GDR[1] in the process of German unification after 1989, together with the introduction of the German mark as a common currency on 1 July 1990. In this case, the basic long-term objectives of the pension schemes were clear from the early beginning and they were essential for designing different interim steps for transforming the pension arrangements. Transformation and transition is a process. The sequence of policy decisions concerning different reform steps and instruments should therefore be based on coherent guidelines and objectives. This is an important precondition for the development and implementation of a consistent policy, and it is particularly important in the case of pension policy because of its long-term character.[2]

The debate on pension policy after the collapse of communism and central planning took up the fundamental issues in designing pension schemes that had already been discussed at the end of the nineteenth and the beginning of the twentieth centuries when the bases for public pensions were laid in many countries.

As expected, after the overwhelming dominance of pay-as-you-go (PAYG) public pension schemes, a trend towards funded schemes, private arrangements and a multi-tier structure has emerged. An important aspect of this trend is the changing role of the state in the pension policy; the state becomes less of a provider and more of a regulator.

In the meantime, more radical reforms in Latvia, Poland and Hungary are receiving considerable attention from other, not only former socialist, countries because pension reform debates and a new public–private mix are major topics on the political agenda around the globe.

OPTIONS FOR PENSION REFORM

The key task of pension reform is not only to introduce a funded element, but also to redesign PAYG schemes. The academic debate on pension reform is often focused primarily on the shift from PAYG to funding and, therefore, it neglects other important tasks. In publications of the World Bank as well as in Rutkowski's chapter the expression 'reform' is reserved only for the measures that shift pension schemes (in part or in total) to funding. In my view, this approach is much too narrow because fundamental reforms are feasible, and they have already been determined, not only with respect to the volume, but also to the design and the structure of the first tier, which is a mandatory public PAYG scheme in most countries. The structure and scope of the first tier has an important impact on the second tier.

There are a number of alternatives in redesigning pension arrangements,[3] subject to country-specific conditions. Basic alternatives for different tiers are outlined in Table 15.1. For example, a central issue for the mandatory public first tier is the choice between the interpersonal redistribution (*ex ante*), or the intertemporal redistribution (that is, a close contribution–benefit link).

A tendency towards strengthening the contribution–benefit link in many countries is manifested not only by shifting towards private (funded) pensions but also by redesigning the mandatory public PAYG first tier. The introduction of defined contribution schemes, such as in Latvia and in Poland, is a straightforward approach. However, the strengthening of the contribution–benefit link can also be realized within defined benefit schemes.

A close contribution–benefit link may improve the willingness to contribute, reduce the under-reporting of earnings and therefore improve revenue collection. Aside from the fiscal aspects, it also implies that there are not only rights, but also obligations. Both have to be balanced, especially if the dominance of firms' contributions is shifted towards employees' direct contribution.

If a strengthening of the contribution and benefit link is aimed at in the mandatory public first tier, the pension level needs to be considered. In a mandatory scheme where people are required to contribute, the pension level must be higher than the level of a means-tested social assistance, particularly after a longer period of contributing. Otherwise, the credibility of a pension scheme will be undermined.

Table 15.1   Choices in designing different tiers of pension schemes

1st tier	Mandatory, PAYG	
	Public or private	volume,
	major goal:	pension level
	• avoiding poverty in old age	
	• income-related pension	
	defined benefit	
	defined contribution	
	Type of redistribution:	
	• interpersonal	
	• intertemporal (close contribution–benefit link)	
2nd tier	Mandatory or voluntary	
	Funded or PAYG	
	Public or privately managed	
	Linked to employment or company	
	Defined benefit or defined contribution	
3rd tier	Voluntary, privately managed, funded	
	Defined contribution	

Other factors also need to be considered in the determination of pension levels, including direct and indirect taxes, health insurance contributions of pensioners and medical co-payments.

If a close contribution–benefit link is aimed at, the adequate type of financing has to be considered. The redistribution of income over the life cycle should be financed by revenue from general public budgets.[4]

With respect to the instruments for collecting revenue for the general public budget there are some aspects in favour of indirect taxation. Indirect taxes can burden even the income from the underground economy if that income is consumed. In addition, the growing percentage of the older population will be financing general public tasks increasingly because of the relatively high consumption ratio of the elderly. However, to avoid undesired effects on real income distribution, VAT rates should differ for various types of goods according to their necessity.

Another important element of pension policy is the retirement age. The rules for claiming retirement, as well as disability pensions, result from the interaction between social and economic (especially labour market) policies. Today's pension-financing problems in transition countries stem from economic and not from demographic conditions. However, most of the European countries are affected by an ageing population and face an ageing workforce in the near future. Retirement ages have to respond to these developments. This implies that present and future tasks may differ widely, causing a conflict between the short- and medium-term objectives, and the long-term goals that are difficult to handle in the political process.

With respect to the ageing workforce, there is also a growing need for more retraining, especially of older workers, in preparation for a longer work life. An extension of the working life gives employees and employers incentives to invest in human capital because the time for amortization of investment becomes longer. Improvement of human capital and increasing productivity will decide about countries' ability to compete internationally.

The second tier of pension arrangement also has different possibilities. It can be linked to the employment and the firm or be independent. As shown in Table 15.1, supplementary pensions can be mandatory or voluntary. Taxation rules concerning saving, interest payments, assets and pensions can be applied either as an incentive, as in the case of voluntary pensions, or as a subsidy, for specific groups of the population in the case of mandatory additional saving.

In most countries income-related old-age security is more desired than benefits that only alleviate poverty. In general terms, countries with a low pension level in the first tier or with flat-rate benefits have introduced a second mandatory tier, while countries with an income-related first tier have mostly opted for voluntary supplementary pension arrangements. Contrary to a widely held belief, countries whose public pensions are focused on poverty relief are generally not as successful in realizing this objective compared to countries with income-related public schemes.[5]

PENSION FINANCING DILEMMA

Although the debate on PAYG versus funding is still biased, it is more balanced today than ten years ago. A balanced view needs to take into account country-specific conditions, that is, the prerequisites for introducing privately managed funded schemes.

The impact of funding on domestic saving is ambiguous. In contrast to results from theoretical models the empirical evidence is far from being conclusive. 'Capitalist economies do not behave like well-oiled equilibrium machines' (Solow, 1996, p. 301).

The ratio of pension assets to GDP for a given country does not give information on the level or development of a national saving rate. This is clearly demonstrated by the data for Germany and the Netherlands. As shown in Figure 15.1, the Dutch pension assets are about 75 per cent of GDP, whereas in Germany these assets constitute about 5 per cent of GDP (without occupational pension schemes based on book reserves). But the national saving rates in both countries are about the same.[6] Moreover, the growth of pension assets in the Netherlands is not reflected in higher saving rates. This example clearly demonstrates that one has to be very cautious in linking funding to macro-economic effects such as changes in national saving rates, investment and economic growth.

Funding may improve national financial markets, especially if they are not yet fully developed. However, a higher volume of funding can also increase the

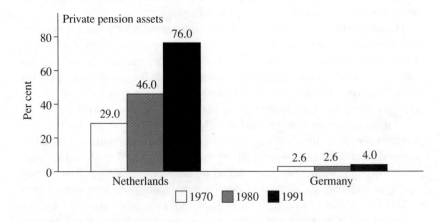

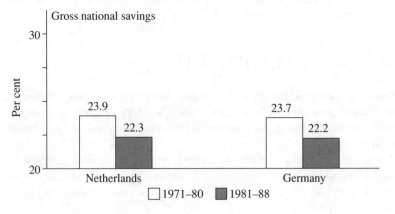

Source: Data taken from Thompson (1998).

Figure 15.1   Private pension assets and gross national savings (% of GDP)

volatility of financial markets. Both the volume and the volatility affect the income of pensioners, especially as funding becomes a universal financing instrument and as pension funds become dominant players in financial markets worldwide. As fund managers (pushed by shareholder value strategies) may apply rather similar investment strategies, their coordinated behaviour can induce large shocks to financial markets, particularly in smaller countries. These aspects should be taken into account when deciding on the methods of pension financing.

There are two different strategies for the introduction of a second mandatory element: (i) supplementing the first tier without scaling it down; and (ii) reduction of the first tier. The second approach is applied mainly because of the already existing, high contributions or the significant tax burden. In a transition period, this approach results in a deficit in the PAYG first tier, as in the case of Hungary, where a part of the contribution revenue has been shifted to the funded element, without increasing contribution rates.[7] There are several ways to finance this deficit in the absence of a state budget surplus. In Hungary, the deficit is presently financed from the state budget. In Poland, it is expected to be financed by revenues from the privatization of public firms.

Concerning the financing from privatization revenues, one must hope that Poland's experience with privatizing state firms will be different from the outcome of privatization in the former East Germany, where its effect on the public budget was really disappointing. Instead of expected additional revenue, the result was a big deficit.

If government finances the deficit by additional public debt, then an implicit public debt of PAYG system is replaced by an explicit public debt (with additional costs). If no deficit financing takes place, a further reduction in the PAYG is unavoidable.

INCOME SECURITY AND RISK

Concerning income distribution, attention should be paid to the effects for different cohorts. This is especially important if a reduction of the first tier takes place, which affects current pensioners and older workers who themselves have no chance to gain from the new supplementary scheme.

Cohorts are also affected differently if the indexation of public pension claims (or of accumulated pension capital in defined contribution schemes) during the working period differs from the indexation of pensioners' benefits. This happens if, for example, pension claims are linked to the development of earnings or contribution revenue, while pension benefits are linked to prices.

Different effects for men and women may also occur if there is a shift from public to private schemes due to, for example, the difference in life expectancies.

Pensioners' income may also be affected by the costs of managing funded schemes, including administrative and marketing costs, which can reduce the rate of return to a substantial degree. For this reason, a greater transparency regarding costs is necessary. In many countries the degree of transparency is very low.

In the new market economies a greater diversity of sources of income for the elderly is likely to develop. The public pension will lose some of its importance. However, this takes time, as can be seen in the former East Germany where social insurance pensions are still by far more important as the source of pensioners' income than in West Germany where a multi-tier structure in pension policy has been in place for a long time. Income from funded pension schemes can only be provided after a long period of saving, regardless of whether these schemes are mandatory or voluntary, linked to the firms or not. Therefore, the effects of new funded elements of pension policy on income protection of the elderly introduced in the new market economies may be detected only after a long transition period.[8]

PAYG schemes are more flexible in reacting to changing circumstances. This may have positive or negative implications. It becomes negative if decision makers do not take into account long-term effects by granting additional pension credits without taking into consideration their financing. This constitutes a political risk of PAYG schemes. But political risk also exists within funded pension schemes where changing rules for taxation may reduce the rate of return. Therefore, it is plausible to mix different types of pension schemes and financing methods in order to reduce the overall risk, especially if the risks of the different financing methods are not positively correlated. However, there are no general rules for this mix, because the level of risk also depends on the country-specific conditions, including political predisposition to establish and implement a regulatory framework and supervision. These are important aspects of risk management within privately managed funded schemes. Regulation and supervision are necessary, as demonstrated by the recent negative experience of countries with a long history of private pensions, such as the United Kingdom.

It is too early to draw firm and reliable conclusions concerning the outcome of major pension reforms, especially on income security of the elderly. The effects of funded schemes cannot be evaluated until they become an important component of the income package of future pensioners.

WHAT SHOULD NOT BE NEGLECTED . . .

A careful regular monitoring of the pension reform outcome is needed in order to prevent any negative developments. The international exchange of pension reform experience is also important. Although the experience of other countries cannot simply be copied, lessons from their accomplishments and failures can be helpful.

Public trust and support for pension policy is vital for its successful implementation. A mutual agreement on basic goals and objectives of the pension scheme among the public, the major political parties, trade unions and employers' organizations is essential for ensuring consistency of the pension policy even in times of changes in political power.

Public trust may be enhanced by well-informed and -educated mass media, capable of explaining very complex topics of pension policy. Therefore, investments in public relations, which provide important and reliable information for journalists will not be overlooked if they are to contribute to the success of pension reform.

NOTES

1. This is not the subject of this comment. For the analysis of structural changes in the process of integrating the pension schemes in the two parts of Germany that developed quite differently after the Second World War, see Schmähl (1992).
2. On the important economic and political role of social security in the process of transformation, see Schmähl (1994).
3. This is outlined in Barr (Chapter 10 in this volume); see also Schmähl (1999).
4. For a detailed discussion, see Schmähl (1998).
5. For details, see Korpi and Palme (1997).
6. For a further discussion, see Thompson (1998).
7. Projections of revenues and possible budget deficits become more difficult as more contribution options are available to pension scheme participants, for example, to stay with the 'old' scheme or to opt for the 'new' one.
8. Even the Chilean pension reform, enacted in 1980, cannot yet be evaluated concerning its effect on old-age provision, although often it is already labelled a 'success story'.

REFERENCES

Korpi, Walter and Joakim Palme (1997), 'The paradox of redistribution and strategies of equality: welfare state institutions, inequality and poverty in the Western countries', Institutet for Social Forskning Working Paper 3/1997, University of Stockholm.

Schmähl, Winfried (1992), 'Transformation and integration of public pension schemes – lessons from the process of German unification', in Pierre Pestieau (ed.), 'Public Finance in a World of Transition', *Public Finance*, Supplement 47, pp. 34–56.

Schmähl, Winfried (1994), 'On the economic significance of social security in the process of transformation from a socialist economy to a market economy', in European Institute of Social Security (ed.), *Problems of Transformation of Social Protection Systems in Central and Eastern Europe*, Yearbook 1993, Leuven, Amersfoort: Acco, pp. 25–50.

Schmähl, Winfried (1998), 'Financing social security in Germany: proposals for changing its structure and some possible effects', in Stanley W. Black (ed.), *Glob-*

alization, Technological Change, and Labor Markets, Boston, Dordrecht, London: Kluwer, pp. 179–207.

Schmähl, Winfried (1999), 'Fundamental decisions for the reform of pension systems', *International Social Security Review*, **52** (3), 45–55.

Solow, Robert (1996), 'The role of macroeconomic policy', in J.C. Fuhrer and J.S. Little (eds), *Technology and Growth*, Boston, MA: Federal Reserve Bank of Boston, pp. 298–301.

Thompson, Lawrence (1998), *Older and Wiser: The Economics of Public Pensions*, Washington, DC: Urban Institute.

PART IV

Political Challenges of Transition

16. Reflections of political and academic leaders of economic transformation[1]

JACQUES DE LAROSIERE (PANEL CHAIRMAN)

We have a very interesting and important session aimed at studying the politics of transition. Transition of course is not only a matter of economics. It is also, and perhaps principally, about building institutions, which are credible, impartial. The uniqueness of the transition process in the region is that it has been conducted hand in hand with democratization. It poses enormous challenges to the decision makers that neither countries like China, nor even the Western countries in their history, have ever encountered.

Now, the human pains, the social strains and the multiple shocks that are inherent to the process of liberalization put these new democratic parliamentary systems under stress. We have an enormous privilege to have on the panel four people who are economists in their own right. They are all economists by profession and they have not only participated, but they have led, in an active and forceful way, to bring about the transition and democratization process.

Many questions of course are on our minds. What are the policy dilemmas? Is it true that there is a dilemma between shock therapy and gradualism? What are the ways for nascent political parties to build their strategies? To build their own existence? To train themselves? How do the institutions work between parliaments and the executive branch? What is the interplay between labour unions and the government? All these are fundamental questions, which I am sure our speakers are going to talk about.

VACLAV KLAUS

It is a pleasure to have a chance to say a few words about political dimensions, the political aspects of transition. I am sure that there are very important political aspects of transition. We all know them. But I would say that there is no autonomy of the political side of transition, so I shall not be able to limit my comments to political issues in a narrow sense.

My point number one is that all transformation measures have been done by democratically formed political structures. At least in the Central and Eastern European region where political pluralism, parliamentary democracy, competition of political parties, unconstrained, which means absolute, freedom of the media, and so on, fully dominate. It is very important to say that I am not sure whether this is true in the same way if we move more to the east or to the south. But definitely, in the Central and Eastern European region it is the crucial assumption that we talk about transition. I enjoyed very much Yegor Gaidar's point when he said that he was only prime minister of Russia not the Tsar of Russia. This is an absolutely crucial point, which is very often misunderstood when we look at the process from outside. I would warn you to take it as a self-evident statement. It is not an irrelevant or empty statement. It suggests that the transition was not masterminded from above. It suggests that the transition was not dictated by one autocratic politician or another. It suggests that the transition was the product of a very complicated mixture – a very complicated mixture, as I always say, of intentions on the one hand and spontaneity on the other, of design and of action, of planned intended and unintended events. It is very important for evaluating or analysing the transition. It is easy to criticize the outcomes of such an evolutionary and uncontrolled process from outside when we are uninvolved, unengaged observers. It is very easy to criticize it from abstract theoretical positions, and it is very easy to criticize it from absolutist ideological principles. But a transition, and that is my second statement, is not an exercise in applied economics. It is not done in a laboratory. It is done in real life. I ask all the commentators to start with that assumption, because without that we do not understand anything. The task of politicians was definitely to get support for transition, for its basic building blocks. Some of us succeeded, some of us did not, and I think that our success or failure influenced the transformation costs dramatically. So Professor Barr ended his presentation with the last point here, saying that politics matters. I would stress that point again and again. The failure or success in this respect influenced the size of transformation costs dramatically. One of the many tasks the politicians had to tackle was to defend or rehabilitate the role of political parties. Those who are from this part of the world know that the word 'party' was totally discredited in the communist era and there were many attempts to start with, what I would call, the third way of thinking, that is, to base the political system on loose, fuzzy organizations and institutions like Civic Movements, 'civic' for us, National Fronts, national fronts for or against something or somebody, not to speak about Russia, United Russia, Choice, Jabloko and so on. So I consider the role of political parties absolutely crucial, and my experience tells me that there is a correlation between the presence of a standard political structure (by standard political structure, I mean a structure with well-defined political parties) and the success of transition. I believe that history will prove that I was right.

Another main task of politicians was to fight the romantic or pseudo-romantic point of view based on two dangerous, very dangerous, ideas. The first one was that it is possible, or even necessary when changing society, to look for new unknown untried solutions. I always stress that communism collapsed. It was not defeated, which is something that some of the heroes of our 'Velvet Revolution' do not like to hear. But I strongly argue that communism collapsed. It was too weak to be able to continue. So, to use the collapse of communism for creating another 'Utopia' was the first romantic, false, very dangerous idea we have to fight; and we spent days, weeks, months and years fighting those ideas in our part of the world. The second dangerous idea is that it is possible to get something for nothing, that there is such a thing (as in Milton Friedman's speech about a 'free lunch') as a free reformer, and that there are no transformation costs.

I believe the last ten years demonstrate that both ideas were and are wrong but we have to admit it has not been fully accepted in the post-communist world, until now, because of what I call the ER gap (the expectations–reality gap), which I consider an important indicator. The ER gap has been, in the last decade, steadily growing, not narrowing. There is no doubt that much has been accomplished in the past decade. We witness an enormous change in the basic substance of life in most of the transition countries, so the reality, the R, moved, in my opinion, visibly, evidently. But we can say that the expectations have been growing even faster, which means that the gap has been growing, which is a big complication for politicians in the countries in question. The road from communism to a free society and to a market economy is rocky but we have to accept it. Nevertheless some people do not want to take into consideration that there is no magic carpet that could avoid the necessity of our travelling. To my great regret, such a 'fairy tale' is still here. I have to say that this fairy tale was supported by the activity of some international consultants and advisors, investment bankers, powerful auditors and bureaucrats of various international organizations, who pretend that the only missing factors in the success of transition are insufficient listening to their advice and not following their advice. I must say that all of them represent a very powerful, very well-organized, rent-seeking pressure group and their interest is to prolong the transition as much as possible. So for them, to make the transition domestically without their advice is, of course, against their interest, and they try to block such successful transitions in our countries. Additional problems come from inside. I must say that for some people feeling bad feels so good that they 'invest' a lot in criticism, scepticism and in creating a bad mood. To fight such attitudes is a challenge, which the politicians do not win. At least, in my country.

Serious discussions of the political aspects of transition require dealing with several other important non-trivial issues. I shall name just some of them. Transition is a sequence of policy decisions, not one policy change. This is my answer to the question raised by our chairman, because the regional debate about gradualism versus shock therapy is completely missing the point. My first suggestion is to talk about transition as a sequence of policy decisions. Second, transition is based on human choices influenced by ideas, prejudices, dreams and interests. It is not based on scientific knowledge. To mention the famous Hayekian slogan 'human action or human design', I would repeat that the verities run on human action not by human design. Third, transition brings democracy, but more democracy typically enhances the power of interest groups in general and it is in their power to block the continuation of reforms in particular. Fourth, during transition from communism to capitalism, the first problem that we concentrated on was to solve the dichotomy oppression versus freedom, whereas the no less important dichotomy – anarchy versus order – was, especially in the first period, neglected or underestimated.

The final point I would like to make is that the critical factors affecting transformation costs are the interaction of formal versus informal rules and the gap between rules on the one hand, and policies and their implementation on the other. I would be able to discuss all of those issues with great pleasure but I shall stop now. Again I would repeat the same sentence 'politics matters'.

LESZEK BALCEROWICZ

I shall start with a truism. You would never get a complete and precise political theory, which would be able to foretell who wins elections, for example. Let me make several points, especially with respect to what I regard to be popular fallacies regarding political issues, at least with the mass media. The first fallacy is that political outcomes are fully determined by previous economic policy. There was a wave of such statements in the media in 1993–94, blaming 'shock therapy' or – more generally – economic reforms, for lost elections. This was a fallacy, as the same political outcome (lost elections) was preceded by quite different economic policies in different countries. Responding to the chairman's question whether there was a choice between 'shock therapy' and gradualism, let me say that there was a true choice but the choice was such – at least under Polish conditions – that the first option was very risky and the second was hopeless: it ruled out the prospect of economic success. Responding to Mr Klaus I would stress that one must have a strategy, but having a strategy does not eliminate the possibility of unintended consequences.

I would skip definitions of shock therapy or the radical approach versus gradualism. Is radical economic reform more risky than the gradualist one? Certainly not for the country as, under certain inherited conditions, being slow with stabilization and structural reforms is very risky if not hopeless. But also the political risk for the decision makers, at least in the longer run, is smaller under radical economic reform. Under certain initial conditions the choice, from the point of view of decision makers, is between the U curve and the L popularity curve. You start with high popularity in both cases and then you lose popularity, either permanently (under the gradualist approach) or not permanently (under radical reform); this is the choice.

Let me mention some other points. First, inherited economic conditions matter, but not so much how bad they are as whether they are likely to improve or get worse. I sometimes call such bad conditions that can improve, 'hidden treasures'; you might also have 'hidden burdens'. So one should analyse economic conditions from a political point of view, considering their possible dynamics.

Second, inherited political conditions matter, too. At the beginning of transition there was an old political structure and no democratic political parties, as they were banned under communism. In Poland there was 'Solidarity' – an opposition movement centred around a trade union. An interesting question is whether from the point of view of future economic policies it was better to have a vacuum or to have a large trade union movement as an opposition.

Third, obviously there are chance factors, which may be accidental, unintended but may have lasting consequences that are difficult to reverse. Let me illustrate this with one example that I shall now call an 'eccentric'. The fact that the Suchocka government in Poland was toppled in 1993 gave rise to lasting consequences. The post-communist opposition, which had won the elections, was given a great political gift – a dynamic economy – and it gained credibility thanks to this as many people linked them to good economic performance. The complete opposite happened in Bulgaria. The Bulgarian post-communists brought about an economic disaster, and the democratic coalition which succeeded them in power have had a much easier job to achieve strong political position than their counterparts in Poland.

This brings me to another point. In politics, like in sports, it matters what the relative political skills of one's partners and opponents are. One should always include these factors in the analysis.

Completing the list of points for further debate, I shall also mention the fact that money matters. Money matters in politics in developed democracies. Money also matters in politics in immature democracies. One of the great challenges is how to regulate this in such a way that politics is honest and that bad money does not drive good money. This is one of the topics that I think deserves more attention.

DANIEL DAIANU

293 – 96

The pressure of events, life, have forced me to think and try to deal with the intricate interplay between politics and economics. From the very start I should emphasize a perspective which I deem appropriate for judging this interplay. We are far away from the euphoria, the naiveties of the early 1990s, when 'the end of history' seemed to be the prevailing mood. Transformation has revealed itself as a very complex, time-consuming and frequently painful process, with its own achievements but also failures, with many unfulfilled expectations being rooted in the political process.

In a free society, all individuals are, arguably, free and the collapse of communism should have put a quick end to undemocratic politics, for people fought for political liberty as well. However, the real world of transition politics is quite different. One can see that through an increasing competition between democratic polity in function and political authoritarianism as a widely practised style in politics during transition. I would submit to your attention the question: why is authoritarianism so ubiquitous? Is it because of circumstances which one can easily detect in areas of the post-communist world, where there are wars, there are identity-seeking state entities, and there are economies in distress and poverty-stricken populations? One could claim that such severe circumstances impact on political dynamics, and that authoritarianism should not be surprising, at least temporarily. But will authoritarian politics fade away over time, as a result of economic progress and institutional change, or will it prove strikingly resilient following the logic of path-dependency? Or should one assume that authoritarian temptations fit human nature and the best one can hope for is the development of a proper mechanism of political checks and balances, which leaves the question, basically, unanswered. If a fundamental working assumption is that democratic polity means accountability, that politicians need to be responsive to the wishes of the people, then what are the dimensions for judging political challenges in a democracy in the making?

I would submit that there are several layers of judgement. One would be the respect for the very logic of checks and balances. Thus, politicians, public servants, can be highly conceited, arrogant, as individuals, but they are not assumed by democratic rules and procedures to be too arrogant as policy makers; they are expected to be responsive to the feedback which comes from citizens. A second layer of assessing *reform governance* is linked with remarks made years ago by Leszek Balcerowicz, that 'under extraordinary times, extraordinary politics and policy may be unavoidable'. Such a political *démarche* is not easy at all; it involves vision and good design. But again, it demands looking at the people, communicating, trying to be persuasive. Also, it asks for compassion. There is a lot for which policy makers should be compassionate. A third layer is the case of a major crisis. A major crisis may be temporary, with negligible consequences for the sense of direction of policy and its main components. But what happens if policy reversals are powerful and one could even envisage the emergence of many features of a *Kriegswirtschaft* (war economy) which may become quite entrenched. This brings us back to the phenomenon of authoritarianism. A friend of mine, who teaches at Berkeley, said that 'Latin America has been in transition for more than a hundred years'. I mention his astute remark for there is no iron law which predicates that all post-communist countries would become prosperous market-based economies and democratic polities, in the foreseeable future. Now if this proposition is accepted, implications should be drawn from it. Several speakers highlighted that only a small cluster of countries, in the close vicinity of the EU, show good results with transformation. Jeffrey Sachs pointed out the role of geography in this respect. There is much we should worry about by looking at the Balkans and in the Caucasian region. The 'Fujimori syndrome' is present in many transition countries.

Let me turn now to what determines good public governance. Without under-estimating policy itself, I would stress, as other speakers have done, initial conditions in a multi-connotational sense. I am not talking only about the legacy of resource misallocation and the lack of partial reforms, which, most of the time, cause very intense *anxiety*. I also have in mind what Elemer Hankiss, a Hungarian sociologist, called 'the second society'. Where partial reforms occurred before 1989 (such as in Hungary and Poland) society was more open, and to use Albert Hirschman's concept, citizens did have some *voice*. People found ways to voice their frustrations and their demands, and when the crucial moment came that society showed its superior transparency as compared to other post-communist countries. Leaders, who could run the engine of transition, emerged more quickly and visibly; also, they were more readily acknowledged *as leaders* by people at large. Conversely, there are national spaces where there is still an enormous lack of transparency. These spaces are very fuzzy. It is very hard to operate, to formulate and apply policy in such spaces; their vested interests are extremely powerful and there can be stiff opposition to change. In such a context I find quite inappropriate and self-serving the statement, which I frequently heard, that 'there is a lack of political will'. Janos Kornai once said that 'foreign advisors come and say: this is the blueprint, now you have to implement it. If you have stupid politicians that's your business'. He implied an almost total disregard for the political economy of reforms. Real life is not black or white, and there is no supreme upholder of truth. In addition, there is path-dependency at work, which does matter a lot.

This brings us to the issue of institutional change. On one hand, one can espouse the idea that there is an institutional vacuum; that energetic and visionary leaders can induce the build-up of institutions suitable for economic growth. On the other hand, I admit that I am pretty suspicious of the thinking which says that it takes only political will to build good institutions. Much more is involved. I place myself in-between; I believe that there is need for both firm leadership (constructivism) and organic evolution. I shall give an example. There is a debate between those who argue that the lack of law enforcement justifies why people try to enforce laws themselves, and those who are concerned about the lack of accountability, of rules and procedures, of a bad path dependency. Taking the law in one's hands poses great dangers; Colombia-type societies can be replicated in our part of the world. I think that institutional dynamics are not automatically driven by the logic that, at the end of the day, good institutions get the upper hand. Society can develop the bad sort of institutions and strong and evil-vested interests can capture the political process; façade democracy, or what Fareed Zacharia called 'illiberal democracy', would get entrenched – it could get even worse.

I would say a few words about the role of leaders. They can turn around the life of large organizations, turn a poor organization into a good one. The same can happen with society as a whole. But leaders need to enjoy an enabling environment in order to succeed. What does it take for someone to be successful, at the very top? Buttressed by my own experience as well I would argue that there is need for vision, cohesion and teamwork, empathy (much intellectual empathy), and the ability and power to deal with a stifling bureaucracy. Ministers need to speak 'the same language'. Technicians enrolled in a government can have a very hard time when they do not enjoy sufficient political support, particularly when a government is heavily politicized. In any case, they should resist the pressure of rent-seekers, of parties, which operate as rent-seeking organizations. Policymakers need to have a good grasp of the policy thrust and be able to deal with its technicalities; they should shun fundamentalism, be pragmatic in a good, intellectually healthy sense. There is need to have mastery of the programme to be implemented. Ownership is essential for building up genuine reputation. In several transition countries an increasing number of citizens believe that their countries are run from Washington, or Brussels. This is not necessarily good for domestic politics, especially when the economy fares poorly; this is a very serious issue. Last but not least, leaders need to be humble and compassionate, for there is much that they do not know and not a little of the misery surrounding them is due to their policies.

GRAMOZ PASHKO

The transition from communist societies into market democracies, particularly when one compares Southeast Europe with Central Europe, has features in common, but there are different 'transitions', different speeds, different changes and different areas. There are a myriad of factors that cause different divisions on the map of transition. The legacies of the past are one of these factors. The Balkans do not have the same legacy as Central and Eastern Europe. While democracy existed but was brutally repressed by Russian invasion in Central and Eastern Europe, the Balkans had never had such a system or the related institutions. If you look back in Balkan history, you see hardly anything that could be considered as a democratic tradition in the modern sense. After the Ottoman Empire, we had a period of autocratic regimes in the inter-war period almost everywhere, and then we immediately had communism. Most of the institutions of a proper state were created within this system. The revolution of the early 1990s had nothing to revive in our history, everything had to be created.

We tried to look back to find some points of reference to be followed, but it was impossible. We had nothing to conserve to become conservatives, we could not be liberal because we had nothing to liberalize, so we had to try to find a mixture. That is why, in that part of the world, numerous problems are still emerging and the transition seems never ending.

First, the societies in Southeast Europe have remained extremely paternalistic. In a certain sense this is the legacy of the tribal and Ottoman heritage, then the inter-war experience and finally extreme hard-line communism. Our hard-line communism consisted mainly of power, concentrated in the leader and not in the system itself. The system was identified with the person who was leading it, so the system became solely a matter of the personality of the leader. Then, during the revolution, the leader was thrown away together with all he symbolized, leaving a void in the system, but moreover requiring the need to replace him with somebody else, even if this would mean a new form of semi-authoritarianism. In the Balkans, with its absence of democratic culture and democratic tradition, semi-dictators take over and the whole reform process becomes a question of their will.

Professor Klaus spoke about the very sound pluralism in Central and Eastern Europe. Although I might say that we also have pluralism in our country, this does not mean democracy at all. Yugoslavia has pluralism as well. Slobodan Milosevic was elected in 'pluralist elections' but I doubt if there is anybody here who thinks that Yugoslavia is a democratic country. This brings us to another major issue in democracy, also problematic in the Balkans: the so-called rotation of power, acceptance of the results of the elections by the losing party, how to leave office when the elections are lost. This implies, of course, that the winning majority will respect the minority. However, this principle is not accepted in our weak democracies, and this is one of the biggest problems that our area is facing. We have leaders who agree to participate in the elections, in the competition, but they do not accept the result, and there is crisis after crisis; the entire reform machinery stops because of that. Somebody said here that in the last ten years Poland has had a 'soccer team' of prime ministers. Italy has had as many, and more, but that has not prevented it from becoming the sixth-largest industrial country in the world. Poland may have had many governments but it became a pioneer in the newly emerging democracies. We had only one in more than five years, but sometimes with the smallest crisis within the leadership the whole building collapses (Albania is a typical example of that).

Another important feature of the area is its geography, which in the case of Albania is of great significance. It was the poorest and the most isolated corner of Europe. This poverty and isolation created expectations among people that with the collapse of communism poverty would end immediately and the world would be opened wide to them. Disillusion quickly set in when they saw that capitalism did not change their lives overnight.

The backwardness was associated with communist egalitarianism, which had a direct impact on what I have called the 'ruralization of politics'. We have a politics that stems from the mentality of the farmers more than from an orientation towards new institutions and structures. This means that the content is too left wing, too socially orientated, more concerned with fighting poverty than pushing hard for growth; too much of an 'administratization' of the society, where the state is seen to need to regulate the society rather than that individuals be responsible for their community.

To conclude, let me insist again that geography matters, especially in those parts of the world. We have Yugoslavia as our neighbour, and this proximity distracts us and constrains all domestic and foreign policies, based on what will happen next door. That is something that is going to be with us for a long while.

JEFFREY D. SACHS

There are, as usual, a number of different aspects to the political question and I want to deal with one that I find very important as a lesson for all of us – what Leszek Balcerowicz has called 'the theory of extraordinary politics', or I would call 'the theory of the moment of opportunity'. There are times when everyday political life does not proceed as normal, but when the future is opened up in a very extraordinary way. These are times of financial crises that are very extreme, for example; times of war; times of the immediate aftermath of war; and times of the collapse of old regimes such as occurred here in 1989. These are times of de-colonization and the emergence of new countries, like in East Timor right now. These are times of the end of other kinds of abuses of regimes such as in Nigeria. We need a concept of what life is like at those moments, because it is very different from normal life. The main point I would stress about those moments is that outcomes are not predetermined, that it is quite possible to see vastly different social outcomes as the first aspect of these situations.

The second aspect is that expectations count fundamentally. When, in the middle of the Great Depression, Franklin Roosevelt said 'the only thing we have to fear is fear itself' he was not just coining a nice phrase. He was actually describing the core political crisis of the United States on 4 March 1933, which was the role of expectations as possibly having a decisive outcome.

The third point about these situations is that small changes can have huge effects. That is what high non-linearity or non-predeterminedness means. But this is the key point to understand. This is why tactics matter so much. This is why timing matters so much, why you cannot ever look back and just see the broad picture and think that you have really understood what has happened. Did there have to be war in Kosovo? Did there have to be the Bosnian conflict? If you take this misplaced historical determinism, you will fail to understand the nature of those moments.

Now I shall draw three implications of this. First, these are the moments when leadership truly counts. What is the fundamental role of the leader? The fundamental role of the leader is to mould expectations around a vision at these times. There are multiple possible visions. People can believe that we are always going to be at war, we are always going to be in chaos, or they may see a vision of a way out for their societies. Moulding expectations is the fundamental job whether it was Roosevelt in 1933 or Mazowiecki and Balcerowicz in 1990. Leadership truly counts. It does not always count. In normal politics it is very different, but in these moments it counts.

Second, and a point I stress whenever I get a chance because people do not believe it, and in my view they do not understand it adequately. A role of the outside world has huge consequences at these moments of opportunity and this is very poorly understood. This is not to say that the rest of the world runs a domestic society, or that domestic politics does not count. It is that, when small effects have huge consequences, a stabilization fund can make a big difference, or the lack of action can make a huge difference. Do not fail to understand this when you look at history.

The third implication is that failure at these moments is not just that you delay reform by a month, or six months, or a year. Failure can have lasting effects for decades, and this is another aspect of non-linearity in history when the situation is not predetermined. I shall give you a few examples.

I think we should take Lenin at his word, when he writes in his memoirs, 'If I didn't move that very hour, all was lost for the Bolsheviks'. Well damn it, he moved. But it is the most incredible thing to realize how close it came to not losing 75 years. I firmly believe that this was an accident of contingency not an accident of fate and I firmly believe that it was the neglect of the outside world caught in the same war that destroyed Russia. But the totally opportunistic way that Russia was dragged through 1918 contributed to the next 75 years of misery – and it was totally contingent, not socially determined, not historically determined, it was contingent. There is a wonderful new book that I would recommend to you, called *Hitler's Thirty Days to Power* by Henry Ashby Turner of Yale University. The book opens with the editorials on 1 January 1933 of all the major newspapers proclaiming that the fascist threat is over. Then in 160 pages the book goes hour by hour over the next 30 days and explains how the worst contingencies happened. It was a complete accident, because the Nazis had been losing power steadily in the elections of the autumn of 1932 and Hitler almost lost. The party almost broke up in the early days of January 1933 – a total contingency. Of course, there was the stupidity of the outside world that Keynes warned about, of having Heinrich Brüning go through the most extreme austerity to prove the point that the debt had to be reduced. Okay, they proved the point. Then there are the positive sides. Take a look at Ludwig Erhard in 1947; in a way he is the father of all the modern reforms. I know it, I have seen it. When I got to Bolivia in 1985, the person that I was advising said that Erhard was his model, and when I met Mr Mazowiecki on the first day of his government on 24 August 1989, he said 'I am looking for my Ludwig Erhard'. And he found him, of course. But when you look at the contingency of that weekend in Germany, fortunately the US authorities were 'out of town', so Erhard could do his reform. He grabbed the initiative and the timing of this was absolutely crucial. Do not believe that Germany was inevitably going to be a democratic society. Nobody believed that in 1947, which is why we had a Marshall Plan.

This was a close call. Take a look at the social democratic programme in 1948 in Germany. To believe that a democratic capitalist society was inevitable was a huge mistake and everybody who played an active role at that time knew that; Bolivia went the same way, and Poland. Certainly, there is no doubt in my mind that a moment of opportunity was decisively grasped, and you just have to look at the witnesses of January 1990 to know that.

Now, the point I want to make for the outside world is that while we love to celebrate the accomplishments of the inside world, which are of course the central element, there was a role for the outside world that really helped to shape expectations at a critical moment. This was, after all, the fundamental thing that needed to be done. Whether it was something as 'silly' (and I will put it in economic terms) as a stabilization fund of a billion dollars that gave Poland some confidence that it was not alone in the world, or the debt cancellation that came afterward, or the same debt cancellation that came to Bolivia, I have no doubt watching this that these were decisive events. Not because they were earth shaking, but because tactics and timing and small things made a big difference at the time.

Now let me give some other examples. I was with Ante Markovic in 1990 when he appealed to Western Europe to roll over the debts of Yugoslavia and he was told by the Europeans, 'We'll never do that', and his stabilization programme collapsed. I do not know whether it was a turning point in history, but it was an example of where a thumb on the balance might have made a profound historical difference for millions of people. In Russia, we do not know the end of the story yet. We can only pray that, as Yegor Gaidar told us, it is going to turn out right. But I remember when Gaidar met the G7 deputies on

23 November 1991 with David Mulford as chairman. I was waiting in the anteroom when Gaidar came out and I asked 'What did you talk about, the economic reform?'. He said, 'No, all they wanted to talk about for seven hours was paying the debt'. Don't believe that this does not matter in history. I could name many other examples. We hear a cry for help from the Balkans, where we are told, 'It is not just a matter of now or next month, it may be a matter of now or next generation'. Or we hear it from Nigeria right now. Or we will still possibly hear it from Russia – we do not know. Let's not be so foolish as to think that history is predetermined. Let's learn to seize these moments of opportunity and then think how we may be able to do something to affect them.

NOTE

1. This chapter includes the main presentations of prominent leaders of economic and political transformation. It is based on the transcript of the taped presentations that was provided by the organizers of the CASE conference. The transcript has been subsequently edited for the purpose of this volume and it was authorized by the speakers.

Index

Abramowitz, M. 95, 96
active labour market policies (ALMPs)
    177–8, 179, 180, 225, 237–9
actuarial pension systems *see* multipillar
    pension systems; notional defined
    contribution (NDC) pension
    systems; private pensions
adjustable peg exchange rates 118, 119
administrative capacity, shortage of in
    transition economies 175, 181, 267
age, of retirement 186, 188, 189, 190,
    224, 228, 244, 245, 249, 258,
    272–3, 280–81
    see also demography, in relation to
        pensions
Aghion, P. 26, 95
agriculture, share of in GDP in transition
    economies 21–3
aid, to transition economies 26–7, 40
Akerlof, G.A. 214
Albania
    economic performance 84, 85, 270
    economic reform programme in 4, 9,
        14, 297–8
    pension system 245, 247, 253, 254,
        255, 262–3
    unemployment benefit design in 179
Alesina, A. 240, 274
allocative (external) efficiency,
    education 204–7
annuities market risk, in relation to
    pensions 197
'appreciation bubble' 129, 136, 137, 140
Armenia 9, 63, 74, 248, 253, 264
ASEAN countries, GNP 53–9
Asian financial crisis 103, 106, 107, 114,
    115, 116, 154–5, 156
Åslund, A. 27, 36
Atkinson, A.B. 210
Audenrode, M.A. 237

authoritarianism, ubiquitous nature of
    294–5
Azerbaijan 21, 70, 75, 258

Balcerowicz, L. 24, 26, 104, 294, 298,
    299
    comment by 292–3
Baldassari, M. 241
Balkans 120, 295, 296–8, 301
Baltic countries
    economic performance 4–13, 21–37,
        67, 85–6, 90
    inflation and stabilization in 14–20
    welfare system in 171, 173, 194, 252,
        270
'banking sector liquidity fund' (BSLF)
    139
banking system 62, 78, 105, 107, 113,
    155, 160, 161–2
    see also capital; financial crises;
        financial markets, transition
        economies
Barberis, N. 44
Barbone, L. 51
Barr, N. 170, 173, 195, 203, 205, 208,
    211
    comments on 219–34, 236–41, 285,
        290
Barro, R.J. 95
Belarus 14, 19, 38, 48, 65, 67, 253, 264,
    271
benefits
    pensions 245, 249, 251, 258, 272, 281
    unemployment 177, 179–80, 224, 225,
        229
    see also contributions–benefit linkage
Berg, A. 35–7, 38, 78
Bernanke, B.S. 164
Beveridge approach, welfare benefits *see*
    flat-rate benefits
Bialecki, I. 230